Flight Training Manual

For Students and Instructors

NOEL STEPHENS

> John Williams
>
> You may not think I always appreciate the work you do. This is a thank you for the Night Owls Party.
>
> Love
>
> Nigel
>
> 1/2/90

ROBERT HALE · LONDON

First published in Great Britain 1989

Robert Hale Limited
Clerkenwell House
Clerkenwell Green
London EC1R 0HT

British Library Cataloguing in Publication Data

Stephens, Noel
Flight training manual for
students and instructors.
1. Aeroplanes. Flying, Manuals.
For private pilots
I. Title
629.132′5217

ISBN 0-7090-3712-0

For my family

Photoset in North Wales by
Derek Doyle & Associates, Mold, Clwyd.
Printed in Great Britain by
St Edmundsbury Press Ltd, Bury St Edmunds, Suffolk.
Bound by WBC Bookbinders Limited.

Contents

Foreword

The crowded environment of the present day airspace demands a high degree of skill and proficiency on the part of all users and particularly pilots, whether they are professional or amateur. Good basic instruction is an essential element in the achievement and maintenance of proficiency. The lessons learned by the pupil as he or she endeavours to gain a Private Pilot's Licence must be correct in substance and detail with high quality instruction backed up with appropriate reading material to register the lessons learned in the minds of student pilots which will stand them in good stead for all of their flying hours to come.

This book sets out, in time-honoured sequence, flight briefing material and subsequent flight exercises, a thorough presentation of the PPL course in simple and very clear text and diagrams. It is a valuable guide to instructors and students alike and will prove to be an essential reference during instruction and a useful aid to revision at all times.

Further reading is to be encouraged, but the value of this one volume will be appreciated by the many students and instructors who acknowledge that no one item is particularly difficult to understand in learning to fly, but there is a very large number of items to remember.

Fred S. Stringer BSc FRIN CEng FRAeS
Master of the Guild of Air Pilots and Air Navigators

Acknowledgements

Thanks to Eddie Ford, Monique Agazarian, Harold Bailey and Colin Beckwith for the encouragement I received during my time as a student pilot and student instructor. Your professionalism and dedication to the field of flying instruction was a vital inspiration towards the writing of this manual. My thanks to Veena Stephenson for her fine work on the technical drawings. Special thanks to Caroline Woodman, a kindred spirit, whose help and patience were invaluable during the final stages of publication, and also to Anna Smith, Rani, Fred Stringer and of course Robert Pooley.

Introduction

This manual is based on approved private pilot training syllabuses for use by both student pilots and flying instructors. Its purpose is to supplement the practical aspects of flight training given in flying schools and clubs by explaining the background information on each flight exercise in clear and concise terms. Each chapter begins with the knowledge required to understand a particular aspect of aircraft operation, followed by a description of the flight exercise itself and an instructor's guide where appropriate.

An elementary understanding of physics and mechanics would be an obvious advantage when studying the more technical information in this book; however, references to formulae have been kept to a minimum to keep things simple. To obtain maximum benefit from a training session, students are advised to study each chapter thoroughly before taking the air lesson. It must be emphasized here that since complete standardization of flight training is not possible due to the variety of training aircraft in use, nothing in this manual should be taken to supersede the published information contained in Pilot/Owners Operating Handbooks.

Flying Instruction

FLIGHT BRIEFINGS

A pre-flight briefing is simply a short lecture given by your instructor just before getting airborne for a flight lesson. During this the contents and objectives of the exercise will be covered in some detail, followed by an explanation of how the air lesson will be carried out. Relevant airmanship points, which can be described as good operating practices, will also be introduced during a pre-flight briefing.

Students will be expected to be already familiar with whatever background information is relevant to the particular exercise. Therefore, for maximum progress during training you are advised to study each chapter prior to taking the air lesson, and use the pre-flight briefing as an opportunity to ask any questions you may have.

Principles of Flight

THE AEROPLANE

Basic Aerodynamic Structure
An aeroplane is basically made up of a collection of structures called aerofoils. These are constructed of wood and fibre, glass fibre or aluminium and contain an internal framework which makes them very strong but light in weight. Figure 1 illustrates the plan view of a typical modern single-engined aeroplane.

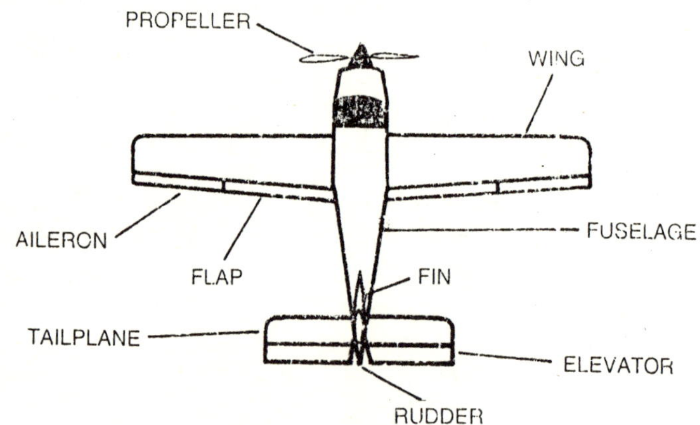

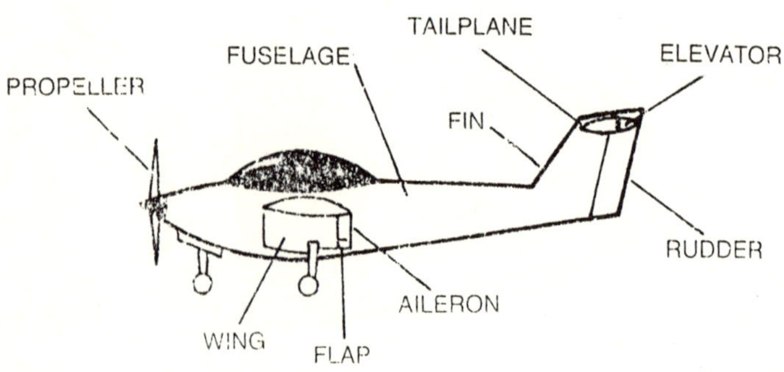

Fig. 1

Connected to the fuselage are the wings which provide the main lifting force that enables the aircraft to fly. Figure 2 shows the two different wing positions used on modern training aeroplanes.

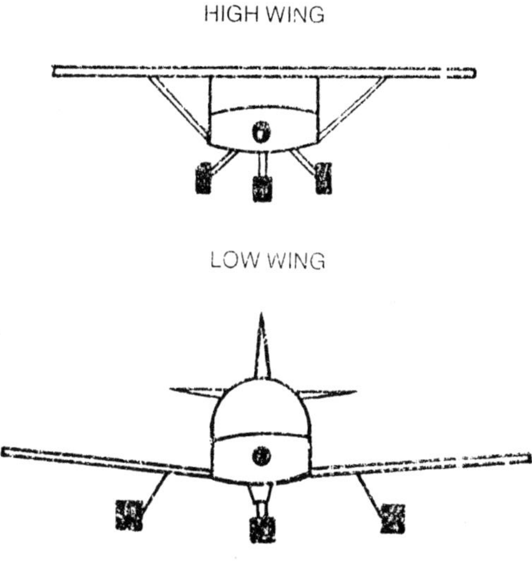

Fig. 2

Situated at the rear end of the aeroplane are the tailplane and fin. These are fixed aerofoils that help give the aeroplane stability in flight.

The ailerons, flaps, elevators and rudder are all movable aerofoils that are controlled from the cockpit and which the pilot uses to manoeuvre the aeroplane in the air.

The propeller, which is also an aerofoil, will transform the power generated by the engine into a propulsive force.

In order to understand how and why an aeroplane is able to fly it will be necessary to become acquainted with the subject of aerodynamics.

AERODYNAMICS

The science of aerodynamics involves a study of the forces that act on a body when in motion through the air.

An aeroplane in flight is acted upon by four forces – **lift, drag, thrust** and **weight**.

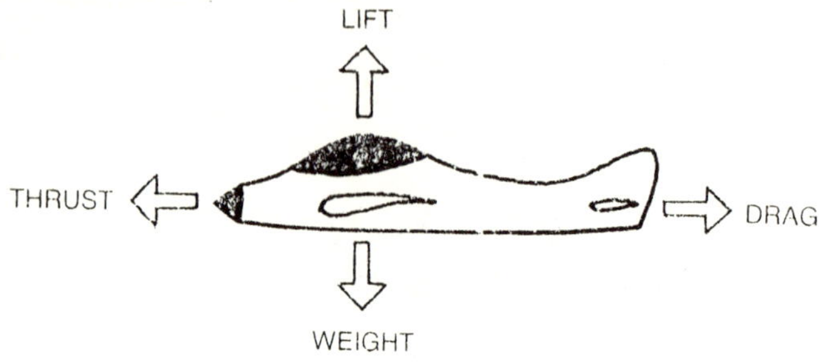

Fig. 3

Lift is created to overcome the weight of the aeroplane, thus enabling it to fly; thrust is created to overcome drag, which is the resisting force produced when the aircraft is moved through the air. The safe and efficient operation of an aeroplane depends on the pilot's understanding of how lift is created and sustained in flight.

Lift

In order to understand fully what lift is and how it is created it is necessary to remember Newton's Third Law of Motion – 'To every action there is an equal and opposite reaction'.

A bird is able to fly because its wings beat down sufficient air (an action) to lift and support itself (a reaction) in the air. This principle is similar to what happens when a gun is fired. The bullet is pushed out of the barrel, which is an action, causing the gun to recoil, which is an equal and opposite reaction. An aeroplane's wing does much the same thing. It forces down great quantities of air, causing the reaction called lift. This is accomplished by designing the wing to produce an effect called Bernouilli's Principle or Venturi Effect when it is moved through the air. A venturi is a tube that has a constriction in its centre, as in Figure 4.

Bernouilli's Principle

As air is a fluid, it can be made to flow and change its shape when a pressure is applied to it. Since free-flowing subsonic air is

A = #0
B = #1
C = #2
D = #3

AB = #4.

ABACABA

0

A

N = 8

(2 ** N-1) => 128 ?

(2 ** N+) =>

Clear Code = 2 ** N (2 ** N)

= ~~64~~ ~~128~~

= 256

considered incompressible, when flowing through a constriction such as a venturi it must accelerate. This increase in the speed of the air results in a decrease of air pressure inside the venturi. The reasons why this occurs are as follows:

1. The air entering the venturi contains two forms of energy – (a) kinetic energy (air in motion), and (b) static pressure (energy), which is the pressure exerted by the Earth's atmosphere. Therefore, the total amount of energy entering the venturi equals kinetic energy plus static pressure.
2. As the airflow approaches the venturi constriction its velocity increases, i.e. an increase in kinetic energy. But since energy cannot be created or destroyed, what actually happens is that some of the static pressure is converted into kinetic energy, which explains the decrease of air pressure in the venturi and the total energy content remains unchanged.
   Figure 4 clarifies this principle.

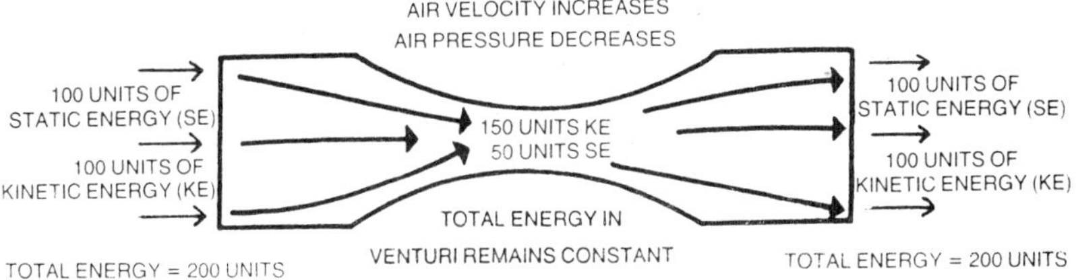

Fig. 4

Aerofoils, wings and lift

An aerofoil is a structure, such as an aircraft wing, whose shape produces a venturi-type effect when moved through the air, thereby creating an effective lifting force. Figure 5 introduces the terminology associated with aerofoils.

The **camber** of an aerofoil is the curvature of its upper and lower surfaces. Normally, the upper surface of an aircraft wing has a greater camber than the lower surface.

The **chord line** is an imaginary line connecting the leading and trailing edges of the aerofoil. The chord of an aerofoil is the length of this line.

The thickness of an aerofoil at any given point along its profile is known as its **depth of section**.

The **relative airflow** is the motion of an aerofoil relative to the surrounding air, and in undisturbed air it represents the forward

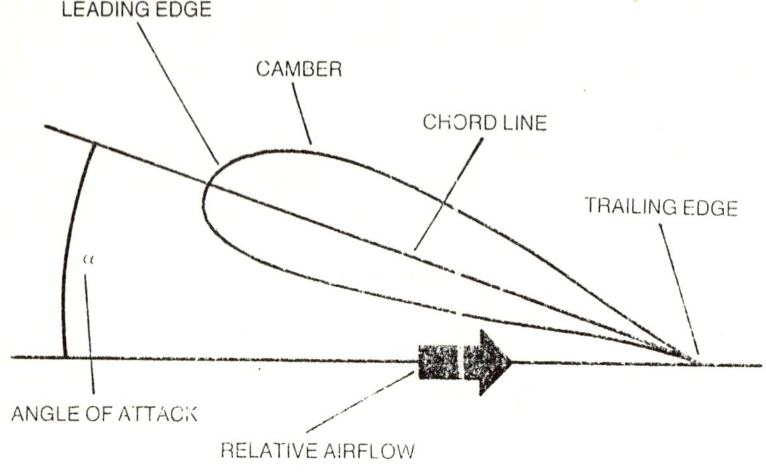

Fig. 5

velocity of an aeroplane and is parallel but opposite to the flight path.

The **angle of attack** is the angle between the chord line and the direction of the relative airflow.

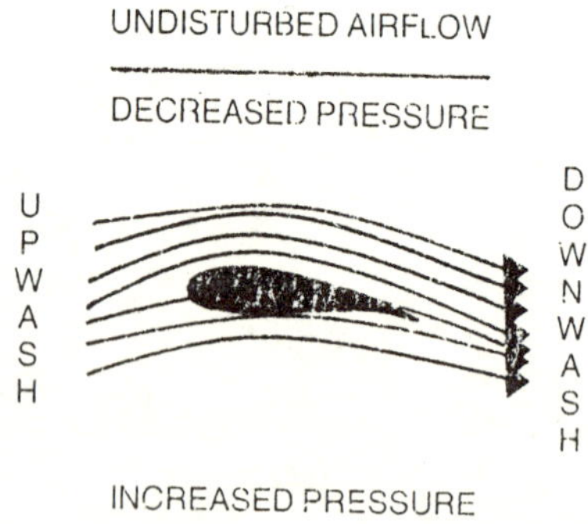

Fig. 6

Figure 6 illustrates the profile of an aeroplane wing and the pattern of airflow around it as it moves through the air. Note that the camber of the upper surface is shaped much like the bottom half of a venturi tube. The undisturbed airflow which is at some distance above the wing acts as the top half of the imaginary venturi tube.

As the air enters the constriction formed by the wings camber it accelerates and results in a corresponding decrease of air pressure along the upper surface of the wing. Now since air always moves from a high-pressure region to a low-pressure region, the relatively high-pressure air below the wing attempts to flow into the low-pressure region above the wing. However, this is not completely possible since the wing sufficiently separates the two regions of pressure and as a result it is forced to rise into the low-pressure region above it.

The low-pressure area above the wing will also influence the air approaching the leading edge. The air is attracted to this region and as can be seen from the diagram, it flows not only from ahead of the wing but also from below it. This is called **upwash** and results in an increase of the mass airflow above the wing. Notice also that this air above the wing flows downward as well as rearward. This action of the air is called **downwash**. The reaction to downwash is **lift**.

It follows therefore that additional lift can only be created by increasing the downwash, i.e. the greater the action, the greater will be the reaction.

When the wing is moved through the air at a larger angle (angle of attack) as in Figure 7 a more restricted venturi effect is created and correspondingly the effects of increased airflow and reduced pressure are increased. Larger quantities of air are attracted over the wing, more downwash is created and lift increases.

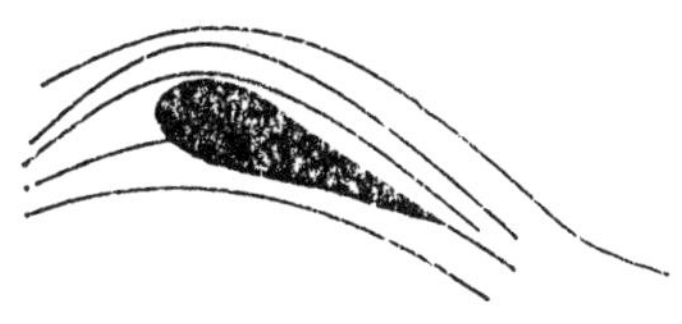

Fig. 7

Additional lift can also be created in a similar manner by simply increasing the speed at which the wing is moved through the air. Notice that the upper surface of the wing in Figure 7 has a greater camber than the lower surface. This type of wing shape, known as a cambered wing, is used on most modern training aircraft and causes the air above the wing to move faster than the air below it, so increasing the pressure differential and consequently the lift. As a result of this, cambered wings are able to produce lift even at negative angles of attack, but are attached to the aircraft fuselage at positive angles (angle of incidence) of between 2 and 3 degrees. Symmetrical aerofoils, such as the fin and tailplane of the aeroplane, require a positive angle of attack to produce lift.

Distribution of lift

Lift is generated from most parts of a wing, and since the speed of airflow will vary about a wing, the amount of lift will also vary from the leading edge to the trailing edge (see Fig. 8).

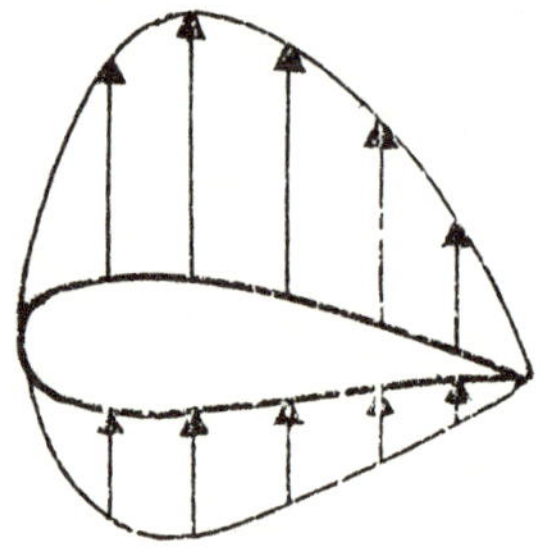

Fig. 8

An aeroplane wing that has a greater depth of section will produce more lift than a thinner one, if they are both flown at the same angle of attack and airspeed. This is because the displacement of air (downwash) will be greater over the thicker wing.

Centre of pressure

This is a point along the chord of a wing where the distributed lift is considered to be concentrated (see Fig. 9).

As the angle of attack is increased, the centre of pressure will tend to move forward. This movement is important when considering the stability of an aeroplane, which is discussed later.

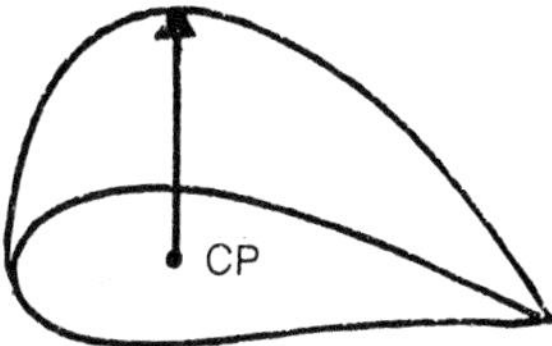

Fig. 9

Lift and drag

It was mentioned earlier that a resisting force called drag is produced whenever an aerofoil is moved through the air. This means that the total reaction (resultant force) produced by an aerofoil can be divided into two force components – **lift** and **drag**. This total reaction (TR) acts at approximately 90 degrees to the wing chord line. The lift force component acts at 90 degrees to the relative airflow, and the drag force parallel but in the opposite direction to the relative airflow (see Fig. 10).

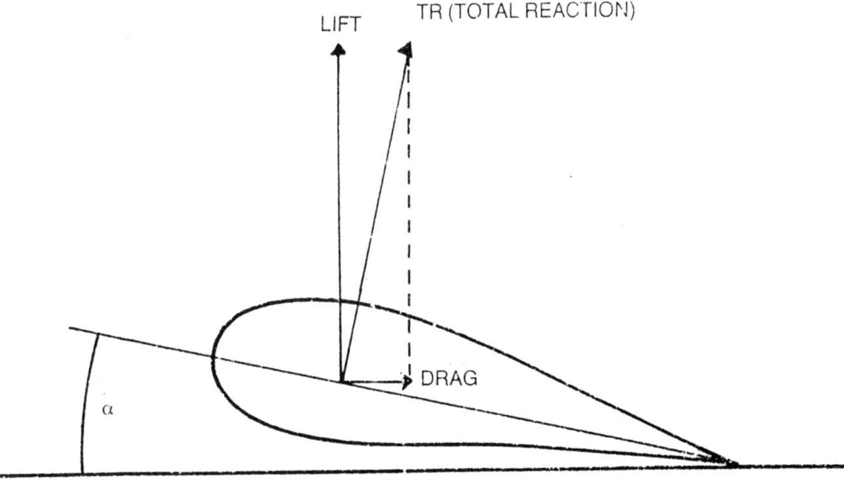

Fig. 10

As angle of attack or airspeed increases, the total reaction will become greater, so increasing the forces of both lift and drag (see Fig. 11).

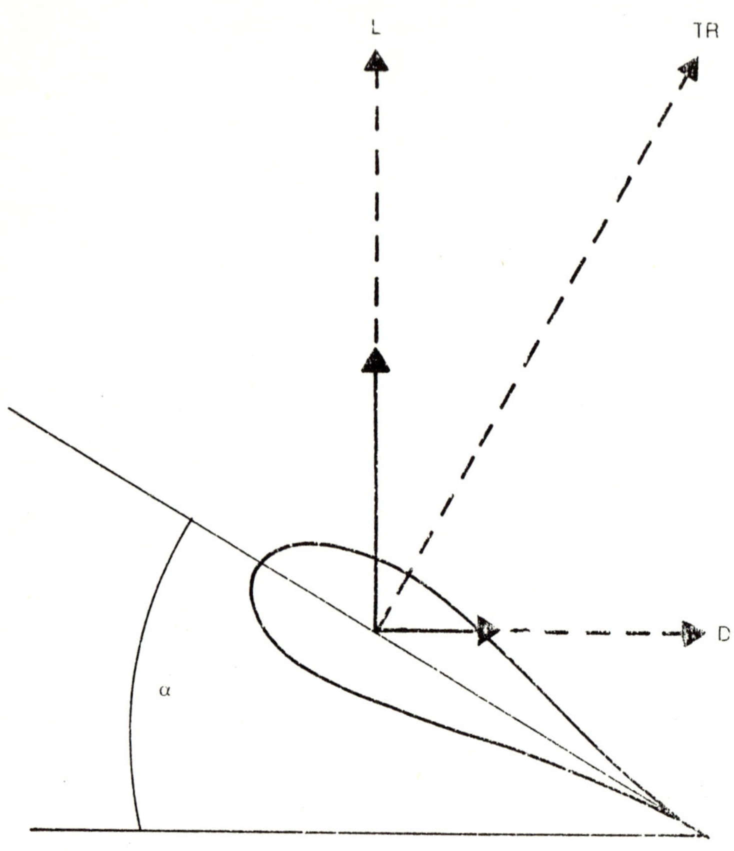

Fig. 11

Air density

It is important to realize that the amount of lift produced by an aerofoil will also depend on the density of the air through which it moves. Briefly, the density of a mass of air is determined by its temperature, pressure and humidity. Both temperature and pressure will decrease with an increase in height, but since air pressure reduces more rapidly than temperature, air density will decrease with height. Water vapour contained in a mass of air will also reduce its density. As its content increases the air density will decrease. It follows from this that the less dense the air is, the less lift will be produced by an aerofoil. All pilots must appreciate these factors when considering the performance of their aircraft while operating out of high-altitude airfields, or under hot and humid conditions.

Lift co-efficient

The co-efficient of lift (C_L) is the effective lift generated by an aerofoil and its values are a function of its design and angle of attack. A wing designed to produce lift at low airspeeds has a high co-efficient of lift. The opposite is true for a wing designed for high-speed aircraft.

Fig. 12

Changes in airspeed, angle of attack or the usage of devices such as flaps, which generate extra lift from a wing, will result in a

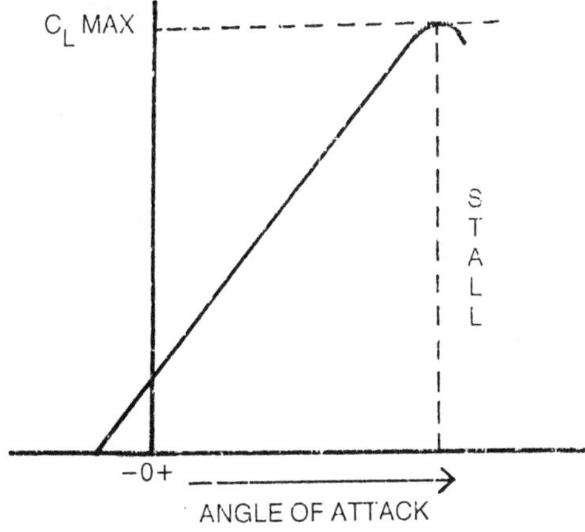

Fig. 13

change in the total lift produced. If airspeed is decreased, angle of attack must be increased in order to maintain the original amount of lift.

The co-efficient of lift values represent the efficiency of a particular wing in producing lift at different angles of attack. Figure 13 shows that increases in angle of attack cause increases in the co-efficient of lift. Note however that angle of attack cannot be increased indefinitely. At some set angle, which will depend on the design, a wing will produce its maximum co-efficient of lift. Any further increase in angle of attack will result in rapid losses of lift known as stalling. This is because the air will no longer be able to flow smoothly over the aerofoil.

An aircraft wing will stall at a specific angle of attack regardless of airspeed, aircraft weight, or attitude. This is a very important topic and it is covered in detail under 'Stalling' (see p. 140).

Drag

Drag is the force that acts against the forward movement of an aircraft through the air. This resistance will vary according to the aircraft's size, shape, speed of movement and density of the air.

Figure 14 shows that the total amount of drag that acts on an aircraft can be divided into two groups.

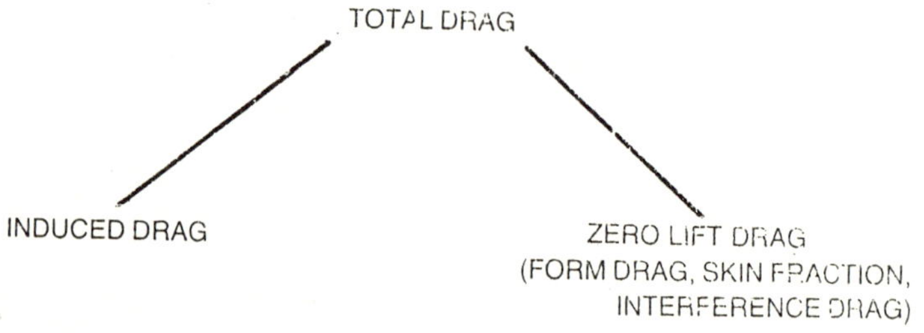

Fig. 14

Induced drag

This is the portion of total drag created as a consequence of the production of lift.

As mentioned earlier, a wing attempts to separate the high- and low-pressure regions of air which surround it. But since this is not completely possible, some of the high-pressure air curls around the wingtip into the low-pressure region above it, as shown in Figure 15. This action of the air is also responsible for the creation of wingtip vortices, which will be covered in another section.

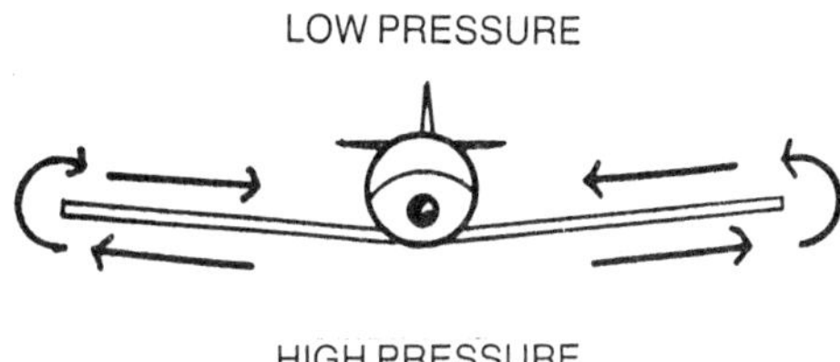

Fig. 15

This movement of the air will induce a slight change in the actual relative airflow and as a result the wing will have an angle of attack that is less than the undisturbed flow angle (see Fig. 16).

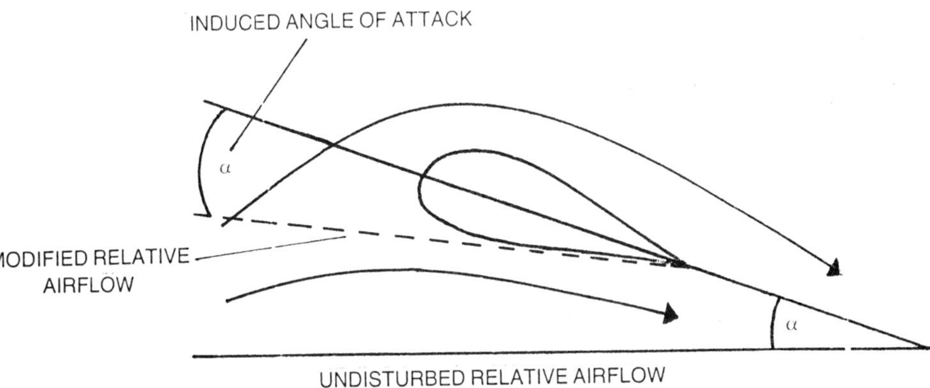

Fig. 16

Because total lift will now act at 90 degrees to the modified relative airflow, it will be tilted backwards at an angle to the direction of flight, as shown in Figure 17.

The vertical component of lift will directly oppose the weight, and the rearward component of total lift will cause the retarding force of induced drag. As angle of attack increases, the pattern of

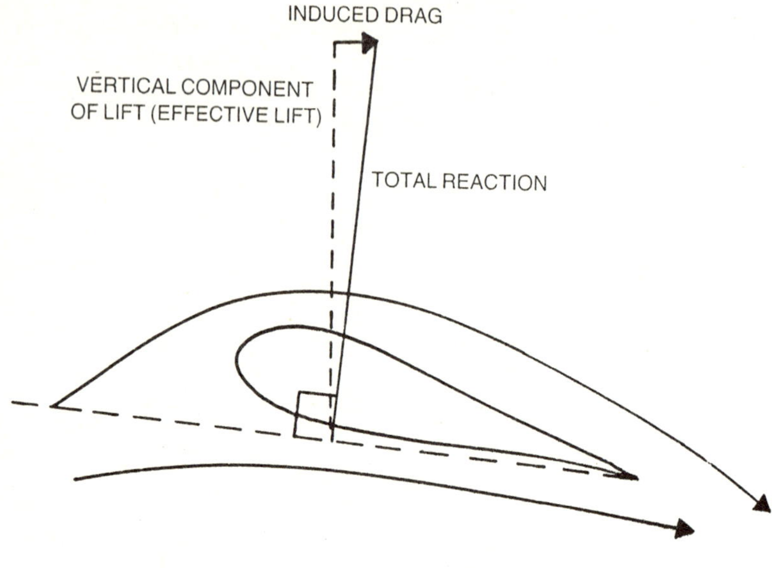

Fig. 17

airflow modifies further and induced drag will increase. Similarly, if the angle of attack is decreased, the amount of induced drag created will be reduced.

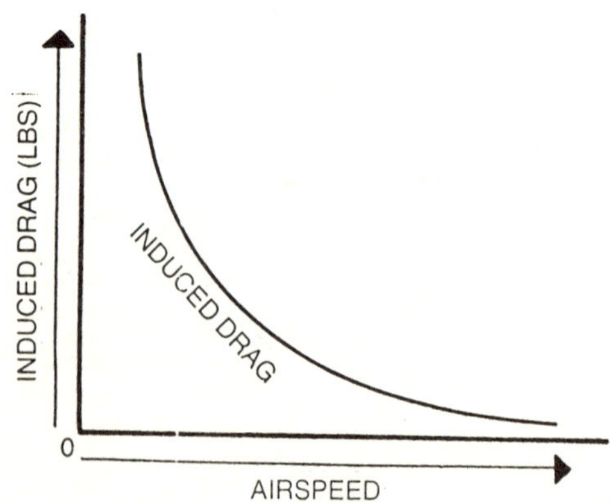

Fig. 18

Since induced drag is a by-product of lift, it will also be affected considerably by changes in airspeed. The graph in Figure 18 shows that induced drag varies inversely with the square of the speed.

This means that as airspeed reduces, induced drag increases, but at a much faster rate. For example, if speed is reduced by one-half, induced drag will increase four times.

Aspect ratio

This is the relationship between the span of a wing and its chord. For a given wing area, a wing that has a high-aspect ratio will produce less induced drag than a low-aspect ratio wing at the same airspeed and angle of attack. This is because the smaller wingtips of a high-aspect ratio wing reduces the spillage of air from the high-pressure to low-pressure regions. Figure 19 illustrates an example of two wings of equal area, but different aspect ratios.

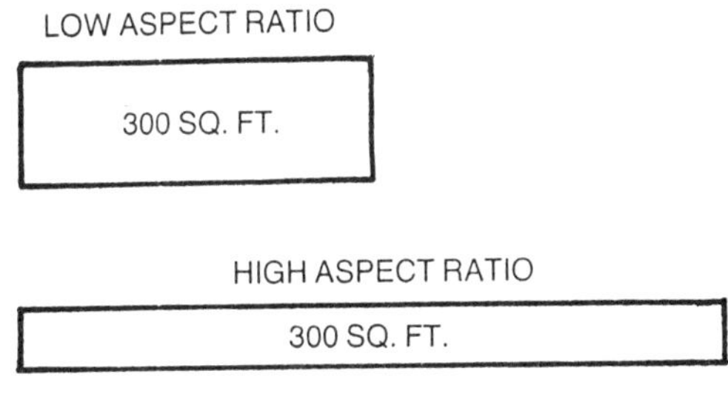

Fig. 19

Parasite drag (or zero lift drag)

Parasite drag is any drag that is not a consequence of the production of lift. It is created by the displacement of air when the aeroplane is in motion, its surfaces generating turbulence and retarding smooth airflow.

Parasite drag that is created by the actual shape of the aeroplane is called form drag. This type of drag can be minimized by streamlining any surface that is exposed to the air. A streamlined shape is one that results in a smoother passage through the air. Figure 20 shows that a teardrop-type shape is very effective in achieving this, and so reduces form drag.

When an aircraft is in motion, there will be friction between its surfaces and the air. The drag created as a result of this is called **skin friction**. The rougher a surface is, the greater the skin-friction drag produced. This is why aeroplane surfaces are made as smooth as possible and must also be kept as clean as possible.

A UNSTREAMLINED

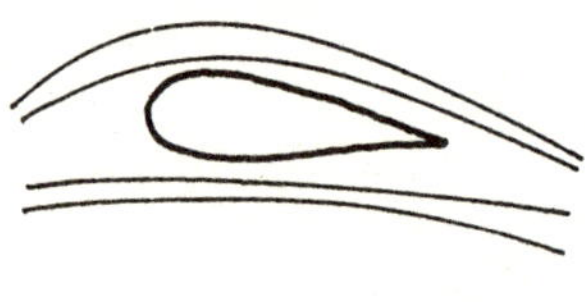

B STREAMLINED

Fig. 20

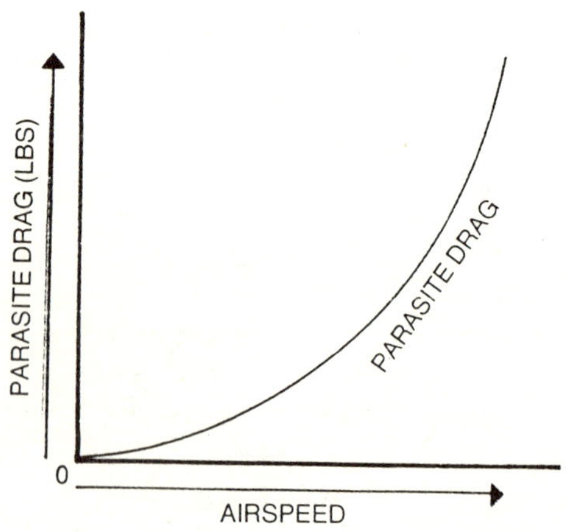

Fig. 21

Parasite drag is also created when the various airflows over an aeroplane join together and form turbulent currents, such as at points where the wings are attached to the fuselage. This is known as **interference drag** and can be reduced by the use of fairings and fillets, which are shaped to result in a smoother joining of the airflow and a reduction of turbulence.

Unlike induced drag, parasite drag increases when airspeed is increased, as shown by the curve in Figure 21.

Total drag

Total drag is the sum of induced drag and parasite drag.

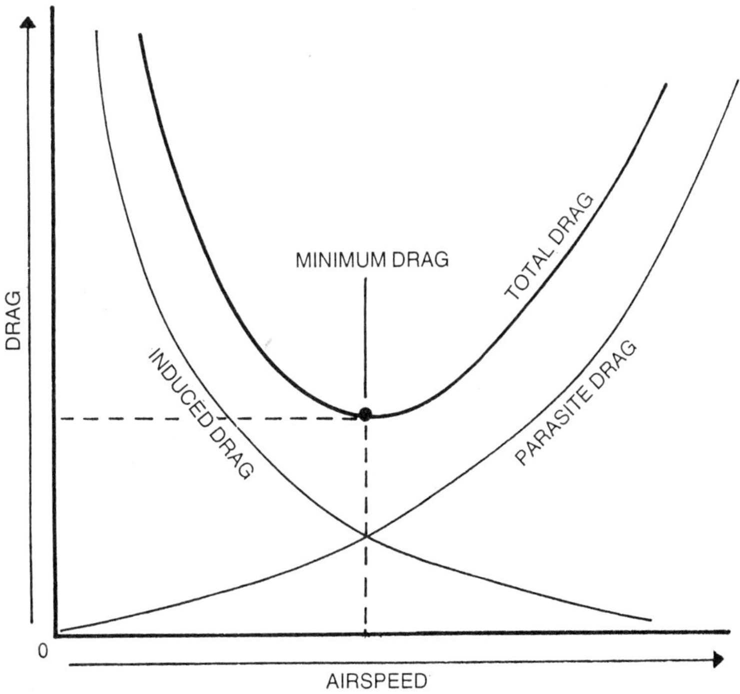

Fig. 22

Figure 22 illustrates the variation of total drag with airspeed for a given aeroplane. The drag curves show that parasite drag increases with velocity and induced drag decreases with velocity. It can be seen that the minimum total drag occurs at the speed where both curves intersect. An aeroplane flying at its minimum drag speed will operate with the best lift to drag ratio. In other words, the aeroplane will be flying at its optimum angle of attack and creating the least amount of drag for the lift required to support itself.

A practical application of the best lift-to-drag ratio is during a power-off glide, when, by using the minimum drag speed, the maximum horizontal distance can be travelled. Maximum range can also be achieved by flying at this speed since it results in the most efficient use of fuel. This airspeed can be found in the flight manual of the aeroplane you are using.

Thrust

Thrust is the force that must be produced to overcome drag. In a steady flight condition, when a constant airspeed and altitude is maintained, thrust equals total drag. If thrust exceeds drag, the aeroplane will accelerate until both forces reach an equilibrium.

A propeller converts the power of an engine into thrust. The efficiency of this conversion is important to an aeroplane's performance. Since a propeller is actually an aerofoil, its efficiency will be subject to all those factors that affect aerofoil efficiency, such as angle of attack, and also its speed of rotation.

Fig. 23

Weight

The force of weight is simply the actual weight of the aeroplane and is termed 'one G'. Weight always acts downwards towards the Earth's centre. The centre of gravity (CG) is a point where the total weight of the aeroplane is concentrated. The symbol for the centre of gravity is shown in Figure 24.

The effective weight, or load factor, can be increased above the normal one G by flight manoeuvres and turbulence. This is why aeroplane structures are built to withstand load factors that are greater than the aeroplane's weight. The subject of stresses due to

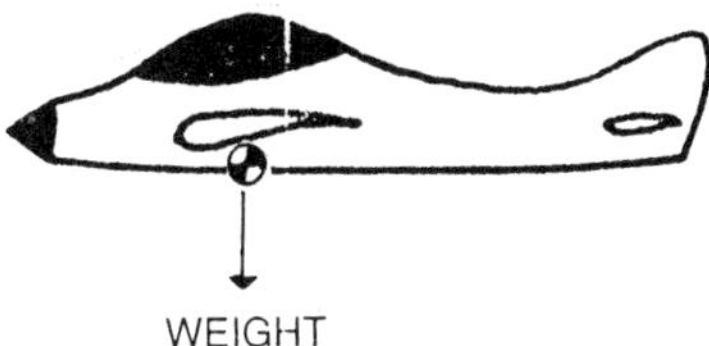

Fig. 24

flight manoeuvres is covered in more detail under 'Advanced Turning' (see p. 254).

STABILITY

Planes of movement (see Fig. 25)
An aeroplane has three planes of movement:

1. the **pitching plane** about its lateral axis
2. the **rolling plane** about its longitudinal axis
3. the **yawing plane** about its vertical axis.

Aeroplanes are designed to remain controllable, manoeuvrable and stable throughout their complete range of intended operations. They must respond positively to control inputs by the pilot, be manoeuvred along given flight paths and at the same time possess adequate inherent stability to return to a steady flight path without any action by the pilot when disturbances such as gusts are encountered. The stability characteristics of an aeroplane are described as its **positive static** and **positive dynamic stability** about each axis.

Positive static stability is the tendency for an aeroplane to return to its original state of equilibrium following a disturbance. However, due to inertia, an aeroplane will not immediately do this – a series of oscillations will occur. Aeroplanes are designed so that these oscillations are small and decreasing until eventually the original state is resumed in the shortest possible time, as illustrated in Figure 26.

This characteristic is described as an aeroplane's positive dynamic stability and can be defined as the time required for the aeroplane's response to its static stability.

YAW
LONGITUDINAL AXIS
LATERAL AXIS
PITCH
ROLL
VERTICAL AXIS
YAW
VERTICAL
AXIS
PITCH
LATERAL AXIS
ROLL
LONGITUDINAL
AXIS

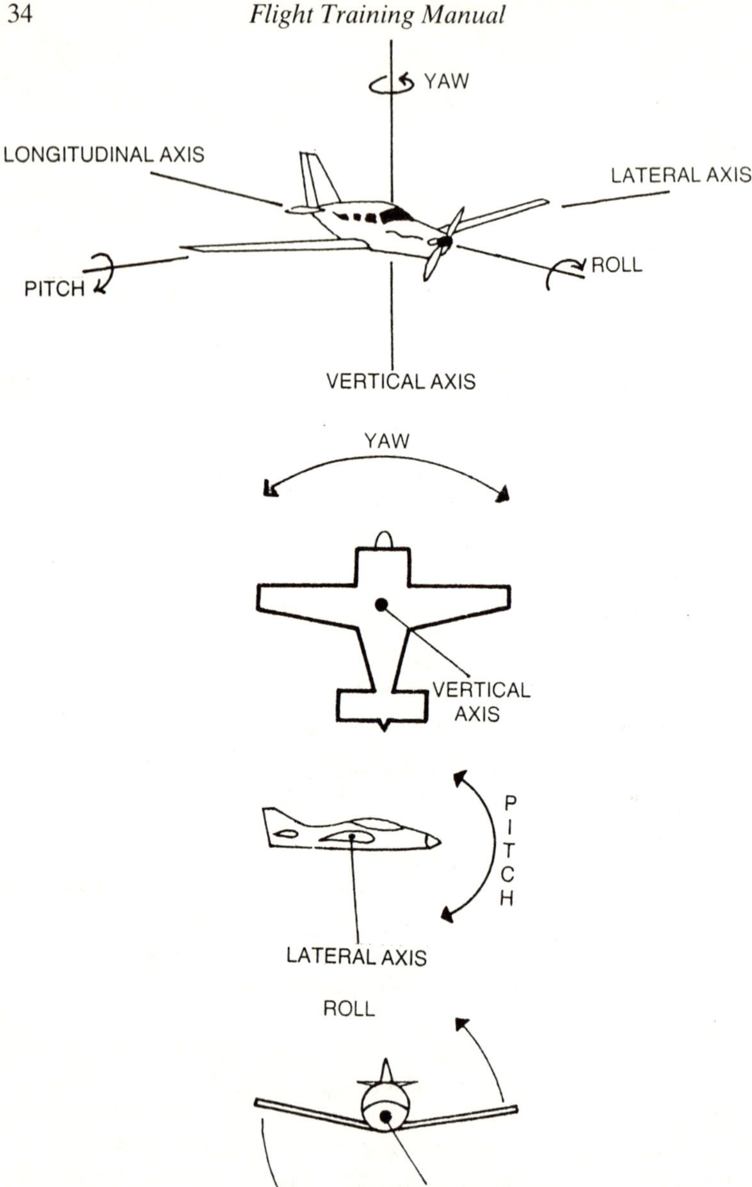

Fig. 25

Fig. 26

The following notes explain how stability is achieved about each operating axis in modern light training aeroplanes.

Longitudinal stability and the relationship of the four forces

When lift equals weight and thrust equals drag an aeroplane will be in equilibrium. However, although each pair of opposing forces may be equal, their lines of action will be different. Additionally, due to changes in angle of attack and airspeed the position of the centre of pressure will change. Similarly, changes of the aeroplane's disposable load in flight will shift the position of its centre of gravity and the deployment of flaps or undercarriage will alter the position of the drag line. (In single-engined aeroplanes the thrust line is fixed.) Furthermore, the strengths of all the forces will be subject to variations.

The combined result of this will be to produce turning moments in the pitching plane which must be balanced and countered within the design of the aeroplane as well as controlled by the pilot to suit changing flight configurations.

Conventional aeroplanes are designed with the centre of gravity acting ahead of the centre of pressure, so that a stable nose-down moment is produced, as shown in Figure 27.

Whenever possible, the thrust and drag couple is arranged to cause a nose-up moment. However, since lift and weight are the greatest of the forces acting on an aeroplane, the nose-down moment will predominate. In flight, with the fuselage length providing the leverage, this nose-down tendency will be balanced by the force produced by the tailplane (often called a horizontal stabilizer), which is set at a negative angle of attack to produce a download (negative lift).

Through the use of the elevators or stabilator the pilot will be able to control the amount and direction of the tailplane force to balance changing moments that arise from normal variations of the four forces. Thus, in a trimmed flight condition there will be no tendency for pitching moments to occur and the aeroplane will possess positive longitudinal stability.

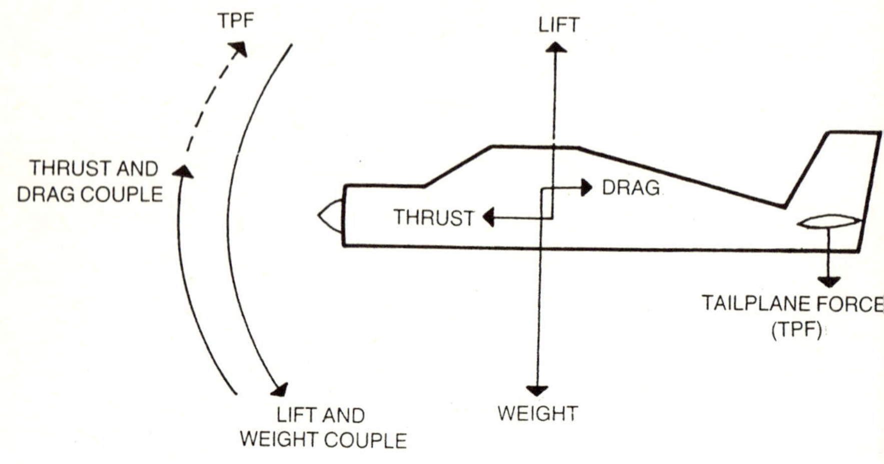

Fig. 27

This arrangement of the forces is considered stable because a stability disturbance will induce a change in the effective angle of attack, which causes a lift change that tends to rotate the aeroplane back to its trimmed state.

When an aeroplane experiences a nose-up disturbance, for a short time it will continue on the same flight path due to inertia. The new angle of attack thus created will cause the tailplane to decrease the negative lift produced or convert it to positive lift, which in either case will result in the tail rising and the nose lowering again, as illustrated in Figure 28.

NOSE UP DISTURBANCE

Fig. 28

On the other hand, a nose-down disturbance will increase the negative angle of attack of the tailplane, producing a greater download and returning the nose to its original position, as shown in Figure 29.

Fig. 29

Additionally, this arrangement of the forces is considered stable because any reduction in thrust, especially in the event of an engine failure, will cause the aeroplane automatically to adopt a nose-down attitude, so assisting the pilot in maintaining airspeed and reducing the likelihood of a stall.

If the distance between the centre of gravity and the centre of pressure increases or decreases, both stability and control will be affected. Movements of the centre of pressure are designed to be within closely defined limits. However, since the centre of gravity can be controlled by the pilot, care must be taken to load the aeroplane strictly according to its Flight Manual. If the weight or centre-of-gravity limits are exceeded serious stability and control problems will result.

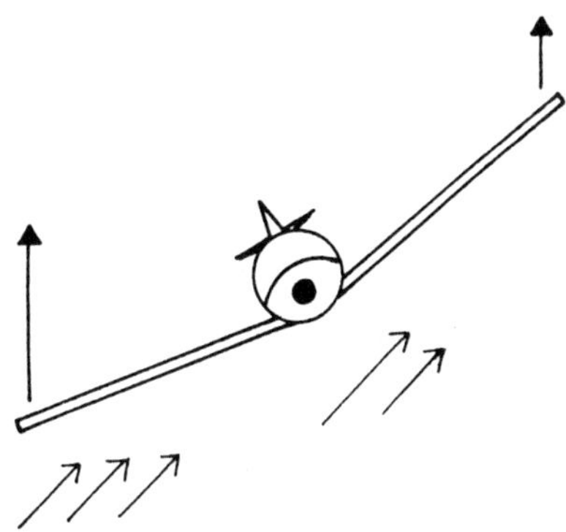

Fig. 30

Lateral stability

This refers to the ability of an aeroplane to return to wings-level flight following a disturbance.

When a wing drops, an aeroplane has a natural tendency to sideslip towards the lower wing (explained fully in 'Effects of Controls' p. 50). As illustrated in Figure 30 the relative airflow experienced as a result of this increases the angle of attack and the lift of the lower wing and reduces the angle of attack and decreases the lift of the raised wing. This differential in lift starts a rolling moment that raises the low wing.

The stabilizing effect of sideslip can be increased by arranging the wings to produce an angle to the plane of symmetry (geometric dihedral), as shown in Figure 31.

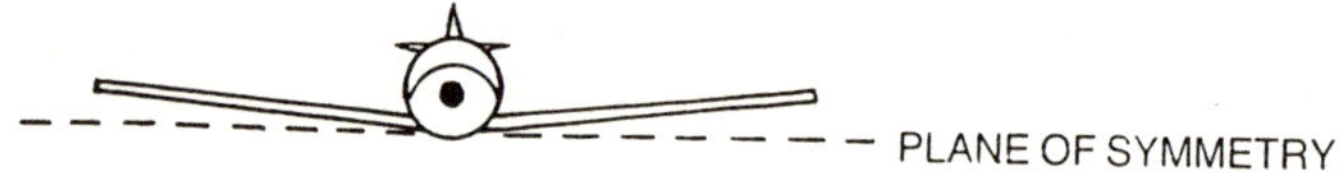

Fig. 31

This will increase the lift differential during a sideslip.

Another method of improving lateral stability is to arrange for a high wing in relation to the centre of gravity, so that a pendulous movement is produced, tending to return the aeroplane to wings-level flight whenever it is displaced by atmospheric disturbances, as illustrated in Figure 32.

Directional stability

This refers to the ability of an aeroplane to remain stationary about its vertical axis.

When a disturbance causes an aeroplane to yaw and sideslip, it must have a natural tendency to return to equilibrium (straight flight). This is normally done by ensuring that the fuselage length behind the centre of gravity is greater than that ahead of it, so that a weathercocking effect is created as the aeroplane sideslips. However, since this is usually insufficient, a fin (vertical stabilizer) is added. This is symmetrical aerofoil capable of producing lift in either direction, similar to the tailplane.

As the aeroplane yaws, due to inertia it will continue on its original flight path for a short time. This causes the fin to

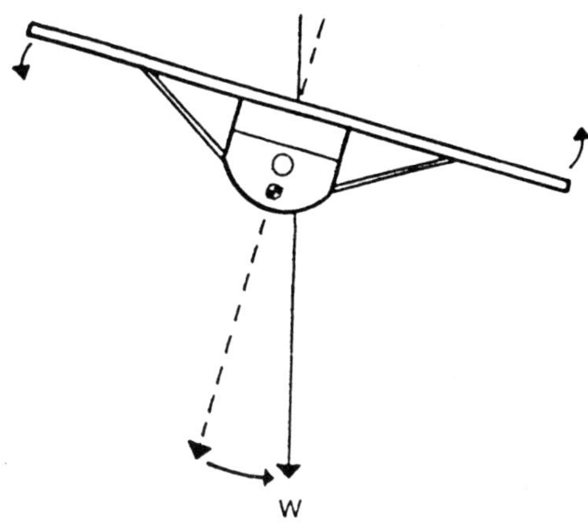

Fig. 32

experience an angle of attack which produces a horizontal lift force that returns the aeroplane to equilibrium, as illustrated in Figure 33.

Spiral instability and Dutch Roll

Due to the relationship between yaw and roll, in that when a yaw is created a roll will follow (covered in detail under 'Effects of Controls', p. 50), there will inevitably be a relationship between lateral and directional stability.

When a wing drops the sideslip produced also disturbs directional stability. With a tendency for strong directional stability the aeroplane attempts to correct directionally before correcting laterally. The sideslip initiates the weathercocking effect which induces further yaw and roll and resulting in the flight path becoming a descending spiral. This is known as **spiral instability** and once the lowered wing is raised the spiral stops.

On the other hand, with strong lateral stability the sideslip angle caused by the lowered wing tends to correct the bank before correcting the direction. The combined effects of inertia and the roll and sideslip created in the opposite direction as the aeroplane corrects causes the other wing to drop. As further corrections take place, a lateral oscillation is developed, known as Dutch Roll.

Most aeroplanes are designed with directional stability slightly stronger than lateral stability, so that a lowered wing causes a

FLIGHT PATH
POSITIVE YAW CORRECTION
HORIZONTAL LIFT
CENTRE OF GRAVITY
FIN

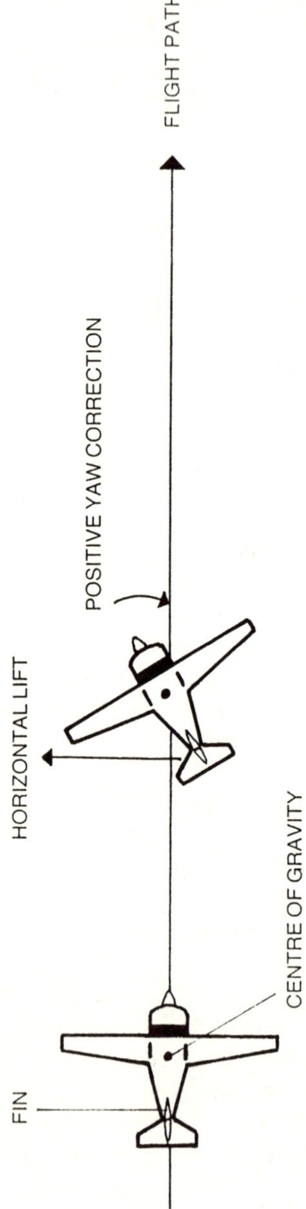

Fig. 33

tendency to enter a slight spiral rather than Dutch Roll, since lateral oscillations can lead to control problems. As mentioned earlier, the spiralling descent is stopped simply by the pilot raising the lowered wing.

Exercise 1

AIR EXPERIENCE

Objectives

To introduce the student to the sensation of flight in the training aircraft. Air experience flights, or trial lessons as they are usually called, are often given at flying schools as an introduction to the sensation of flying. For many people a trial lesson is their first experience of flying in a light aircraft, or even of flying itself. It is essentially a pleasure flight during which the instructor describes scenery, local landmarks and other points of interest. You will be seated in the front left-hand seat, which is normally the captain's position. At some stage you will be given the opportunity to handle the flying controls yourself. Usually no instruction will be given, but you will discover that the controls need to be operated very lightly for the aeroplane to respond. The instructor will usually describe what is taking place during the flight, pointing out the altitude of the aeroplane, the airspeed, the power used and so on. Since you will be seated in the student's position this will be a good time to determine whether you are comfortable, able to reach the controls easily and also see adequately out of the cockpit. You will then have a good idea of what adjustments to make when you begin serious instruction.

While watching the instructor on this flight you might think that learning to fly will be a very difficult task, but it isn't really: with regular instruction and dedication on your part you may well be flying solo in a matter of hours.

Exercise 2

AIRCRAFT FAMILIARIZATION

Objectives

To familiarize the student with the systems and operation of the training aircraft. In order to operate safely, both in the air and on the ground, all pilots must have a thorough knowledge of systems of the particular aeroplane they intend to fly. Additionally, in the cockpit they must be able to locate and operate the flying controls instinctively as well as items like switches, engine controls, instruments, radios and so on.

There are several different types of training aircraft in use today and it is not the intention of this manual to describe the systems of each one of them. Students must start familiarizing themselves with the Flight Manual of the particular aeroplane they are using as soon as possible. This will contain descriptions and operational information for the specific aeroplane it is published for.

On your first training session the instructor will begin to describe the features of the aeroplane you are to fly in. You will be shown the various parts of the airframe, including the positions of the fuel tanks, the type of undercarriage used for manoeuvring the aeroplane on the ground and also the engine compartment.

In the cockpit, the location of the flying and engine controls will be pointed out. Your instructor will also explain the layout of the instrument panel. Operation of the fuel system is of the utmost importance and the instructor will cover this in detail. The braking controls and the electrical system, including the radios and the ignition system, will be described. You will also be acquainted with such items as seat and harness adjustments, location and operation of the fire extinguisher and first-aid kit and the use of the cockpit heating and ventilation controls. Particular attention will be paid to make sure you understand how to secure doors or hatches.

This may seem quite a lot to absorb on your first training session, but you will not be expected to have memorized everything by your next lesson. As you progress through your course and begin to operate the various controls and switches yourself, your familiarity with the aeroplane will come naturally. However, by the time you are ready to go solo your instructor will expect you to have a thorough knowledge of the aeroplane. Therefore, you are advised to gain as much exposure as you can to your aeroplane and its systems.

Exercise 3

PREPARATION FOR AND ACTION AFTER FLIGHT

Objectives

To familarize the student with the procedures to be carried out before and after flight. Learning the proper procedures to follow both before and after a flight will be a very important part of your training. There are several things to be learnt and your instructor will be guiding you through them during the initial stages of the course. By the time you are ready to start solo flights, you must be able to cope with these procedures yourself.

Preparation before Flight

The safe conduct of all flights will depend to a large extent on the decisions and preparations the pilot makes prior to entering the aeroplane.

As far as making decisions are concerned you must determine first that you are fit both physically and mentally to fly and are not under the influence of drugs or alcohol. Secondly, you must ensure that the weather conditions are within your own flying abilities and those of the aeroplane. In addition to these, navigational planning and aircraft weight limits must also be considered.

As a student pilot, any weather-related decisions will be the responsibility of your instructor. However, you will be shown where and how to obtain useful weather data since eventually as a licensed pilot you will have to make such decisions yourself. Navigational planning and aircraft weight considerations will also be left to your instructor until the later stages of your course when they will become your responsibility.

Once the decision to proceed with a flight has been made the next few steps will be to follow the flight authorization procedures, check the aeroplane's documents and finally check the aeroplane itself.

All flights must be recorded on a suitable recording sheet and your instructor will describe the type you will be using. You will also be shown the following aircraft documents:

1. The Certificate of Airworthiness
2. Maintenance documents
3. Aircraft Weight Schedule
4. Aircraft Technical Log.

These must be checked for validity, any special conditions and to ensure that any required maintenance has been carried out.

Aeroplane Checks

These must be done with the aid of a checklist written specifically for the aeroplane you are about to fly. Your flying school will normally provide you with one or, alternatively, you may use the checklist contained in the aeroplane's flight manual.

Checklists are extremely thorough and ensure an organized and systematic inspection of the aeroplane. Their instructions must be followed in detail if they are to be effective.

The notes which follow will give you an idea of the general nature of aeroplane checks.

External checks

The external checks will begin by ensuring first that the aeroplane is in a position where it can be safely started and taxied out of the parking area. It may be necessary to tow the aeroplane to a more suitable position. Before examining the general condition of the aeroplane it is important for safety reasons to check that the ignition system is switched off. At this point the fire extinguisher and first-aid kit is normally checked and the master switch turned on to test the stall-warning system, the pitot heater, the various lights of the aeroplane and also to check the fuel gauges. For a thorough inspection, the flaps must be lowered as well.

While walking around the aeroplane you will be looking for any signs of damage, cracks and corrosion. The condition of the undercarriage, including the tyres and brakes, must be examined. The security of cowlings, hatches, fuel and oil caps must also be checked. A visual check of the fuel and oil contents should always be made and compared with the gauge indications.

An aeroplane that has been left unused for any length of time may accumulate water in the fuel tanks. This must be checked for and cleared by draining fuel from strainers attached to the tanks. This is normally done before the first flight of the day. The procedure will be covered by your instructor.

The condition of the propeller must also be checked, making sure that you keep clear of its plane of rotation as a safety precaution.

Aircraft are often secured to the ground by tie-down ropes. These must be removed before taxi-ing. Other items such as chocks, pitot covers and control locks must also be removed.

Internal checks

Inside the cockpit you must make sure that you are seated comfortably and can easily reach the flying and engine controls. Your instructor will explain how to secure and adjust the seat belt or harness of the particular aeroplane. Once this has been done the internal checks can begin, using the checklist. These will include checking for full and free movement of the flying and engine controls. A visual check-out of the windows must be made to ensure that the flying controls, including the flaps, are working correctly. If your aeroplane has a nosewheel steering system full deflection of the rudder pedals may not be permitted until you start to taxi. The instruments should be checked for service-ability and any signs of damage. Such items as fuses, circuit breakers and the alternate static source must also be checked.

The pre-start checks and starting instructions given by the checklist must be strictly followed. The most important pre-start checks will be firstly to ensure that the brakes are securely on, secondly to switch off any radio equipment to prevent damage, and thirdly to make a warning shout to alert any people in the vicinity to keep clear of the aeroplane. It will be a good idea, particularly at busy airports, to switch on the rotating beacon as a sign that the aeroplane is operational.

Once the engine has started you must immediately check that the starter warning light, if fitted, has gone out. If it is still on, the engine must be shut down immediately to prevent damage to the starting mechanism. A low power setting is normally set afterwards, followed by a check that the oil pressure has started to rise. If it does not rise within 30 seconds of starting, the engine must be stopped immediately.

While the engine is warming up a scan must be made of the fuel pressure, oil temperature, suction and ammeter to make sure they are indicating as expected. The gyro instruments should be checked to ensure that they are erecting properly.

By selecting each of the two magneto positions in turn, any malfunction in the ignition system can be determined. If the engine stops when a single magneto position is selected or continues to turn when the OFF position is set, the engine must be shut down.

Once these checks have been completed and found satisfactory, the radios will be switched on and tested with a call to the Air Traffic Service Unit (ATSU) for current airfield information and taxi instructions. Important details such as wind velocity, pressure information and active runways must be written down. This will be handled by your instructor until you have learnt the proper radio procedures. While taxi-ing the efficiency of the brakes must be tested and various other taxi-ing checks carried out. These will be covered under the heading 'Taxi-ing' (p. 77) and will also be explained by your instructor.

Power checks

At the designated holding area the aeroplane should be parked into wind and the engine run-up checks carried out. These are designed to give you a more accurate indication of the condition of the engine and its systems. Another fuel tank must be selected to test the fuel system and then the RPM increased to the amount stated in the checklist. If the brakes are not securely on, the aeroplane will start to move, in which case the throttle must be immediately closed and the handbrake re-applied. Temperatures, pressures and other gauges must then be checked that they are within limits. This will be followed by another magneto check, during which you will be observing the decrease in RPM as each magneto is selected. Checklists normally give two figures relating to the RPM decrease. The first one is the maximum permitted decrease when a single magneto is selected and the second figure is the maximum permitted difference in RPM decrease between the two magnetos.

The carburettor heat system must also be tested. A drop in RPM will be observed if it is functioning correctly. Finally, the throttle must be closed to check the idling speed of the engine.

If all these checks have proved satisfactory, a low RPM is set and the aeroplane is prepared for take-off. The pre-take-off checks are included in the checklist. Particular emphasis will be placed on ensuring that seat belts and doors are secure, there is full and free movement of the flying controls and that the compasses are synchronized correctly.

Your instructor will be guiding you through all these stages and you should not hesitate to ask any questions. When you are given the responsibility of carrying out aeroplane checks yourself, you must report immediately to an instructor if you recognize any malfunction or have any doubts about the condition of the aeroplane.

Action after Flight

Once back in the parking area after a flight the correct running down procedures must be followed. After the brakes have been firmly applied the engine must be allowed to cool at an even rate, so a low RPM reading should be set for a few minutes. During this, a final magneto check is normally made and such items as radios, lights and fuel gauges are switched off. The exact procedure for shutting down the engine will be given in the checklist. However, you must always ensure before leaving the cockpit that the ignition and master switches are turned off. Additionally, the mixture control must be in the idle cut-off position and the fuel cocks switched off.

Before leaving you must remember that it will be your responsibility to check for any damage that might have occurred while you were in command of the aeroplane. Depending on weather conditions or the procedures used by your flying school, it may be necessary to replace chocks, control locks and pitot covers. In strong wind conditions you will have to secure the aeroplane with tie-down ropes. Your instructor will brief you fully on what to do.

After the aeroplane is safely parked you will be required to sign the flight authorization sheet giving details of the length and nature of the flight. Finally, any defects must be recorded and reported.

Pilots very quickly become creatures of habit. Developing good habits from the very beginning is a sure way of you turning out to be a responsible and competent aeroplane captain.

Exercise 4

EFFECTS OF CONTROLS

Objectives
This will be your first airborne lesson and it will have two purposes:

1. To teach you the effects of the primary flying controls of an aeroplane in flight. You will also be taught the correct method of using the controls to change the attitude of the aeroplane.
2. To teach you the effects of the secondary and ancillary controls of an aeroplane. You will also be shown the correct procedures to adopt when operating these controls.

THE PRIMARY FLYING CONTROLS

An aeroplane has three planes of movement in flight:

1. The pitching plane about the lateral axis. Movement in this plane is controlled by the **Elevators**.
2. The rolling plane about the longitudinal axis. The **Ailerons** control movement in this plane.
3. The yawing plane about the vertical axis. The **Rudder** controls the aeroplane in this plane of movement.

Effects of Controls
These planes of movement are considered to be fixed relative to the pilot and the aeroplane. This means that whatever the attitude of the aircraft, when the controls are operated it will continue to respond in the correct sense in relation to the pilot. For example, if the aeroplane is placed in a steep banked attitude, operation of the elevators will still produce a pitching motion, i.e. nose up, nose

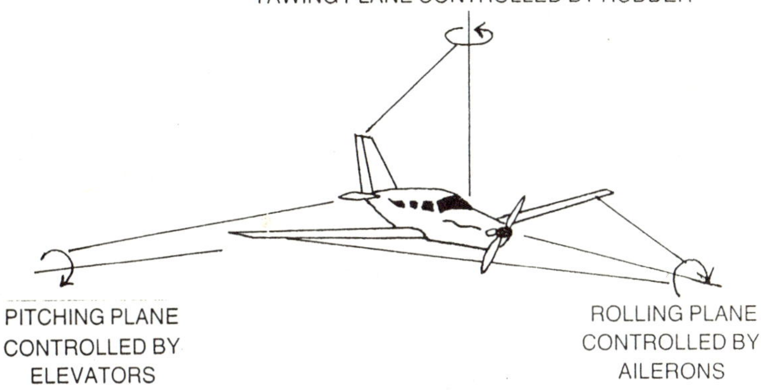

Fig. 34

down, relative to the pilot. Your instructor will demonstrate this to you during the lesson.

The elevators

These are used to adjust the aeroplane's nose attitude in pitch. There are actually two types of control surface that can be used for this purpose: conventional elevators, which are hinged aerofoils attached to the rear of the tailplane; or a stabilator, which is basically a complete tailplane unit that moves in one piece when operated. Stabilators serve as both elevators and tailplane combined. Since both types of control surface have the same results, conventional elevators are used in this book to describe how movement in the pitching plane is achieved.

The pilot operates the elevators by forward and backward movement of the control column. This movement is transmitted to the elevators via a system of cables and pulleys. When the control column is moved forward the elevators lower, as shown in Figure 35.

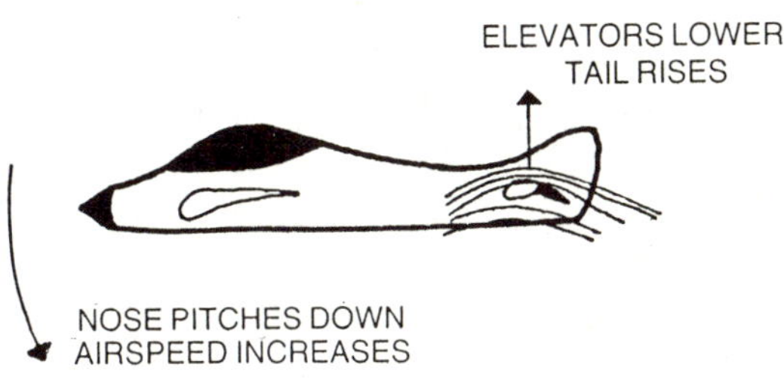

The increase in camber of the tailplane will modify the airflow and consequently the tail rises and the aeroplane's nose pitches down. When this happens the angle of attack of the wings decrease resulting in a reduction of drag, which combined with the effect of gravity causes an increase in airspeed. The opposite happens when the control column is moved backwards. The elevators are raised, the nose pitches up, increasing the angle of attack as well as the drag and results in a decrease of airspeed (see Fig. 36).

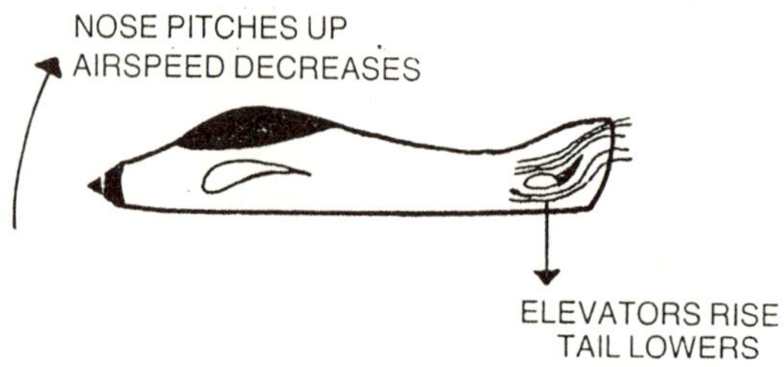

Fig. 36

So, by using the elevators it can be seen that the pilot can select different nose attitudes to suit his purposes. It must be emphasized here, however, that the primary function of the elevators is *not* to make the aeroplane climb or descend, although they can be used for this purpose to a very limited extent during cruising flight. The ability of an aeroplane to make efficient changes in altitude will depend on the power being used in addition to the angle of attack of the wings. The pilot uses the throttle to control the power and the elevators to control the angle of attack using airspeed as a reference, since changes in angle of attack also affect airspeed, as mentioned above. The relationship between power, angle of attack and speed will be made clearer in future lessons and the important thing to understand at this stage is that while the primary effect of the elevators is to alter pitch attitudes, their primary function is to control airspeed in flight. Furthermore, it must be noted that there is a limit to the operation of the elevators or stabilator. Continual raising of the aircraft's nose will eventually result in a stall, when the nose will start to drop of its own accord. On the other hand, continuous forward pressure on the control column may increase the airspeed to an extent where structural failure of the airframe is possible.

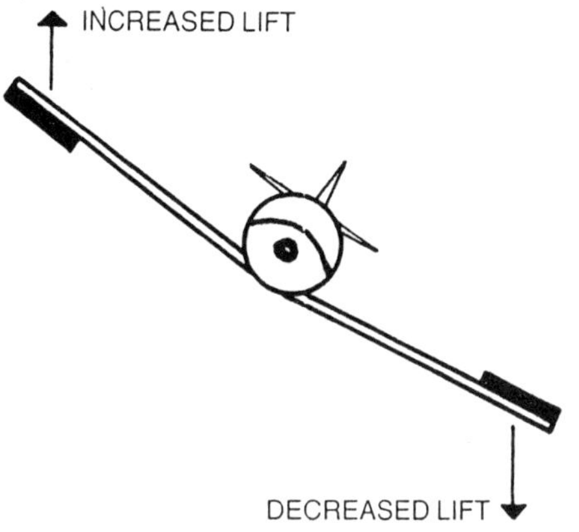

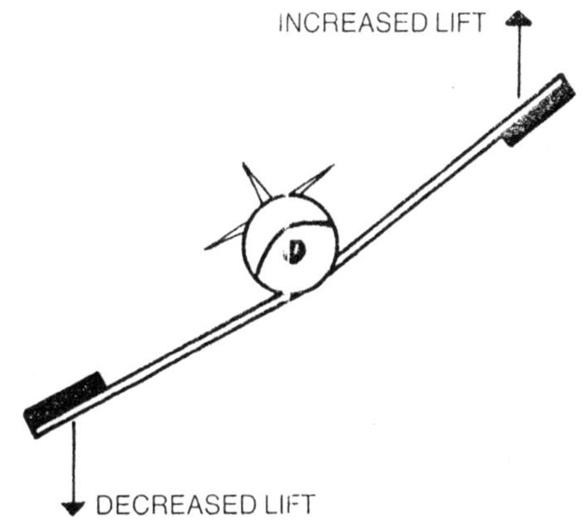

Fig. 37

The ailerons
These are hinged control surfaces, attached to the outboard trailing edge of the wing and are used to control the aeroplane in the rolling plane.

The pilot operates the ailerons by rotating the control wheel to the left or right. When a control stick is fitted, a sideways movement is used. The aileron system is such that when the right aileron is raised, the left one lowers and vice versa. This is done to create a lift differential between the wings which will induce the aeroplane into a banked attitude.

When the control wheel is rotated to the right, the left aileron lowers and the right aileron rises. This causes an increase in the mean camber and angle of attack of the left wing. The consequent increases in the lift created will cause the left wing to rise. At the same time the right wing will lower due to the reduced lift and added parasite drag caused by the raised aileron. The exact opposite will happen when the control wheel is rotated to the left (see Fig. 37).

Aileron differential/drag

If both ailerons are designed to be deflected through the same number of degrees, the lowered aileron will produce more drag (induced drag, as a result of the increase in mean angle of attack) than the raised one. The result of this drag difference will be to cause an adverse yaw. This is a movement about the vertical axis in the opposite direction to which the aeroplane is rolling. Adverse yaw is reduced by designing the system so that the downgoing aileron moves through a smaller number of degrees than the upgoing one, as in Figure 38.

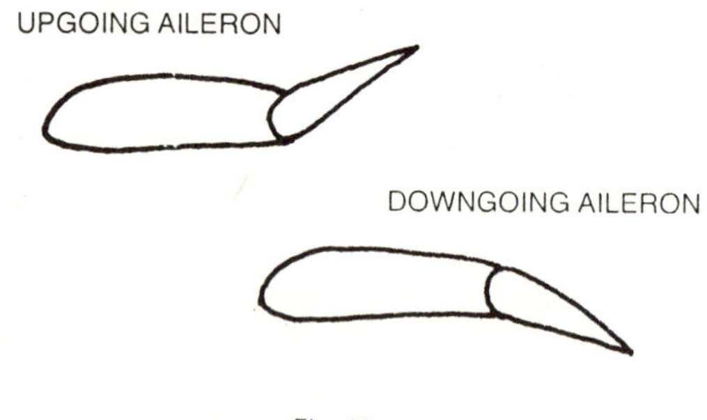

Fig. 38

In addition to this, the leading edge of the upgoing aileron can be designed to protrude into the airstream to create additional parasite drag, as shown in Figure 39. When this arrangement is used they are called Frise ailerons.

However, despite these methods, there will still be a slight

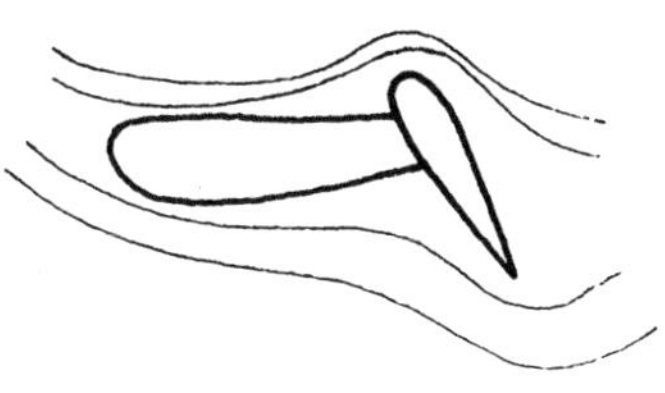

Fig. 39

adverse yawing tendency due to the lift force on the upgoing wing being inclined backwards and on the downgoing wing slightly forward. This variation in the direction of the lift force occurs because each wing experiences a different relative airflow, as shown in Figure 40.

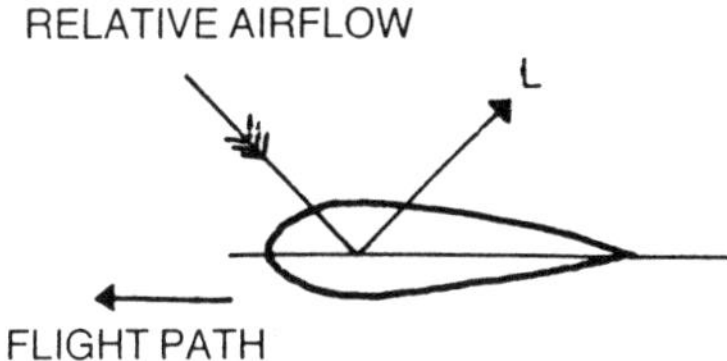

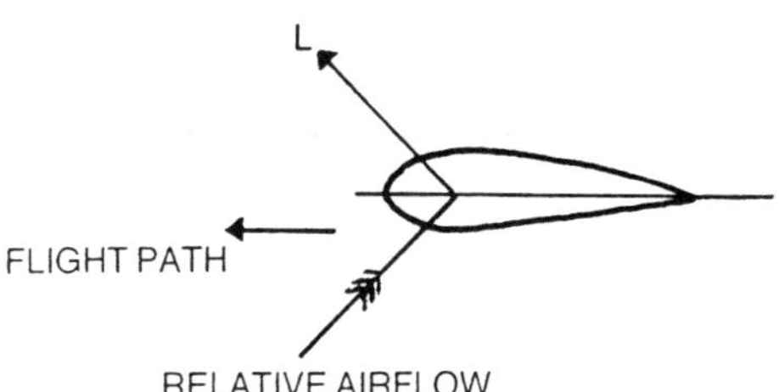

The result of this is to create an adverse yawing effect whenever the aeroplane is banked.

The primary effect of operating the ailerons, therefore, is for the aeroplane to roll and the pilot uses this rolling motion to initiate a

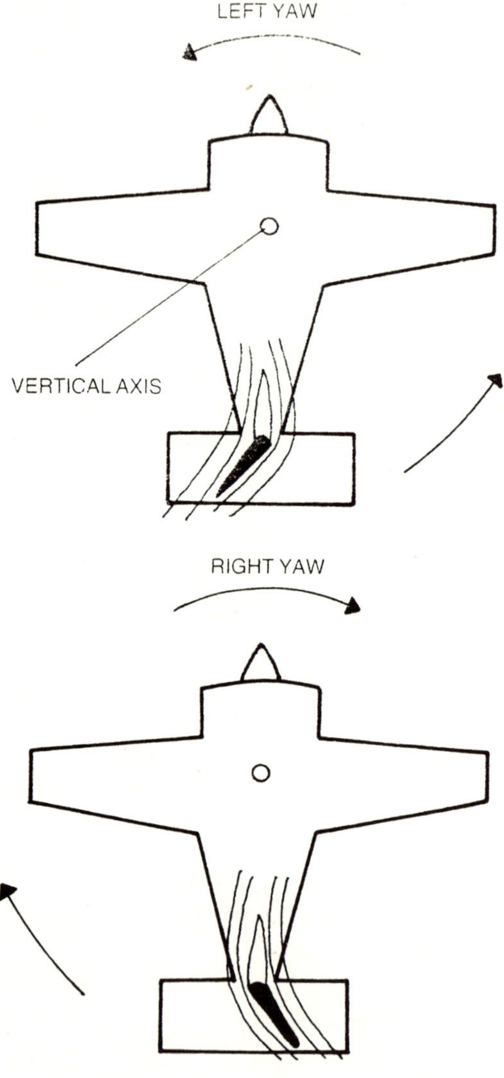

Fig. 41

turn. Once the ailerons have been operated the aeroplane will continue to roll until the pilot neutralizes them by centralizing the control wheel. The aeroplane will then tend to stay in a banked attitude. The ailerons will work in this way regardless of the fore and aft position of the control column.

The rudder

This is another hinged control surface which is attached to the rear of the fin of the aeroplane. It is used to prevent or control any yawing motions that occur. The rudder is operated by depressing pedals which are situated on the floor by the feet of the pilot. By depressing the right pedal, the rudder moves to the right, causing the aeroplane to yaw to the right. The opposite happens when the left pedal is depressed.

Whenever the rudder is deflected, the camber of the fin is changed. This modifies the airflow pattern and causes a horizontal lift force that induces the yawing motion of the aeroplane, as illustrated in Figure 41.

However, the rudder is not normally used to manoeuvre the aeroplane like this in flight. Its function, as mentioned earlier, is to prevent or control the yawing motions that occur. Due to its aerodynamic design an aeroplane will be made to yaw of its own accord whenever the power setting is changed or turning manoeuvres are made. Turbulence can also cause an aeroplane to yaw. The use of rudder to control yaw and achieve a balanced flight condition in these types of situations will be covered in later lessons. In this lesson your instructor will be demonstrating the effects of rudder operation only.

Further Effects of Ailerons and Rudder

Again, due to the aerodynamic design of an aeroplane, there is an inevitable relationship between operation of the ailerons and rudder, in that the long-term or secondary effect of aileron movement is to cause yaw, and the long-term effect of rudder is to cause roll.

Ailerons

When an aeroplane is made to roll, the main lift force is tilted and the remaining vertical component will be insufficient to balance the weight. This will cause the aeroplane to sideslip in the direction of the lowered wing (see Fig. 42).

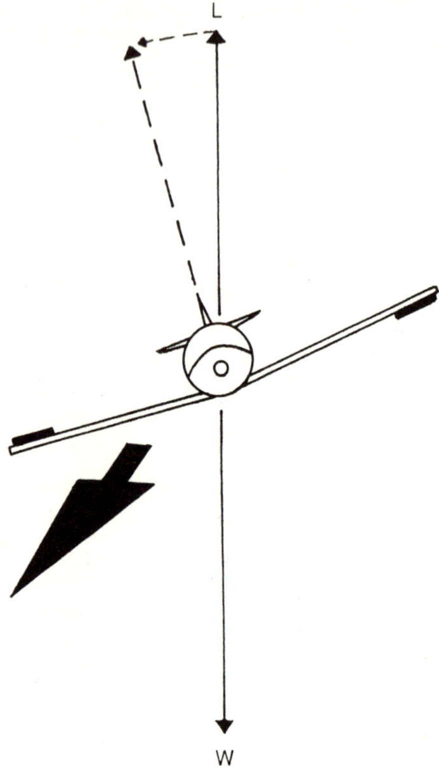

Fig. 42

As this happens, the air strikes the sides of the aeroplane and since the fuselage area behind the centre of gravity is greater than that ahead of it, a weathercocking effect is started and the aeroplane yaws in the direction of the sideslip. If left to develop, a

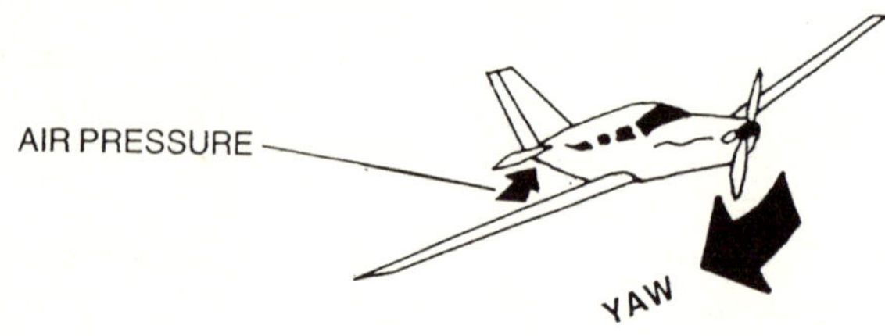

Fig. 43

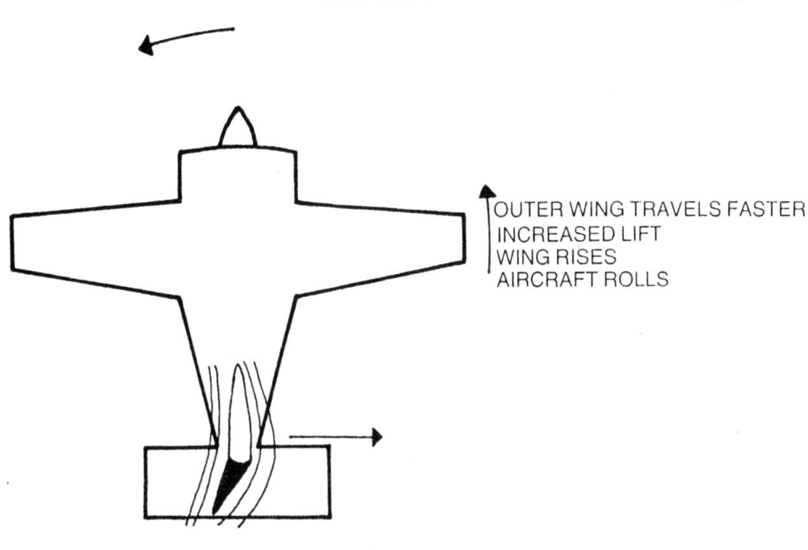

Fig. 44

spiral descent will follow.

In the flight lesson your instructor will operate the ailerons leaving the rudder pedals untouched and you will be able to observe these effects yourself.

Rudder

When an aeroplane is made to yaw, whether it is through the use of the rudder or any other reason, a rolling action will always follow. This is because during the yaw the outer wing will be travelling faster than the inner wing. This, in addition to the larger angle of attack caused by a different relative airflow, will result in the outer wing creating more lift and consequently rising. As you will discover during the lesson, this rolling action occurs quite quickly. When a rudder pedal is depressed, a rolling action will follow almost simultaneously.

Rudder operation will also result in a spiral descent if the situation is left to develop. The roll, induced by the yaw, will cause a sideslip. The sideslip, as explained earlier, will create more yaw which creates more roll and so on, leading to a spiralling descent.

An appreciation of the inter-relationship between the ailerons and the rudder is very important, since this is the reason for the co-ordinated use of the flying controls in flight, which will be emphasized throughout your future lessons.

Effects of Airspeed on the Controls

The effectiveness of the flying controls will depend on the speed of the airflow passing over them. At relatively low airspeeds they become light and sloppy and the pilot will have to make large control movements for the aeroplane to respond. As speed is increased the controls become increasingly more firm and effective, requiring much smaller movements for response.

Effects of Slipstream

Slipstream is the spiralling airflow generated by the propeller, as shown in Figure 45.

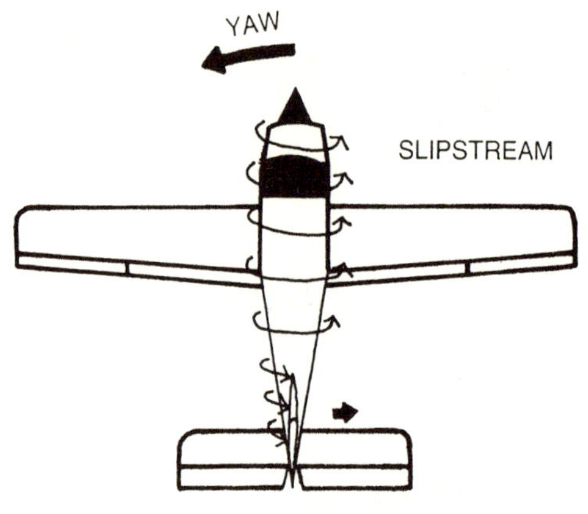

Fig. 45

On the conventional single-engined aircraft it increases the effective airflow over both the rudder and elevators. The ailerons are unaffected since they lie outside the slipstream envelope. It follows therefore that elevator and rudder effectiveness increases with high power settings due to the increased airflow and decreases at low power settings due to the decreased airflow.

An important point to remember for future lessons is that slipstream causes the fin to experience an angle of attack that produces a horizontal lift force which results in a yawing motion of the aeroplane. The direction of yaw will obviously depend on the direction of propeller rotation. Since this is clockwise (when viewed from the cockpit) on most modern training aircraft, the aeroplane will yaw to the left, as shown in Figure 45.

The degree of yaw will depend on both the RPM of the propeller as well as the airspeed of the aeroplane. A combination of low airspeed and high power setting, such as during climbing manoeuvres, will produce the greatest yawing effect. This is because at low airspeeds the slipstream spiral will be tighter, like the coils of a spring. This will increase the angle of attack of the fin and consequently the horizontal lift force. As airspeed is increased, the slipstream spiral elongates resulting in the effects of yaw becoming much less pronounced.

Effects of Power

Changes in throttle setting induce very definite responses from an aeroplane. When power is increased the strength of the thrust and drag couple is also increased. This, together with the increased effectiveness of the tailplane, causes the aeroplane to pitch up. In addition, the effects of increased slipstream will induce a yaw followed by roll. The opposite happens when power is reduced. The lift and weight couple becomes dominant, causing a nose-down movement and the reduced slipstream results in a yaw and a roll in the opposite direction. Even small changes in power will produce these responses. This means that the pilot will have to use all the flying controls in a corrective sense to maintain a steady flight condition whenever any power adjustments are made.

THE SECONDARY CONTROLS

The Flaps

These are another set of hinged aerofoils, which are normally attached to the inboard trailing edge section of the wing. On training aeroplanes they are usually operated manually or electrically, depending on the aeroplane type.

Flaps are used to increase the lift generating capabilities of a wing and also when required to increase the drag substantially. The pilot is able to select varying degrees of flap, depending on the desired result. Use of optimum flap settings increases the camber of the wing to result in effective increases of lift. This is particularly useful since sufficient lift can be produced at slightly lower than normal airspeeds, enabling the aeroplane to take-off safely and land using shorter distances. As flap settings are increased, the amount of drag created also increases. During a descent this can be very useful, since it results in a steeper glide angle without the need to increase airspeed. The operational use of flaps will be covered later. In this lesson you will be shown the effects of operating the flaps on your particular aeroplane in terms of changes in pitch attitude and airspeed.

Whenever the flaps are lowered an aeroplane will experience a pitching movement followed by a decrease of airspeed. The reasons why this occurs are as follows:

1. The centre of pressure moves aft as the flaps are deployed, increasing the effect of the lift and weight couple. This will cause a noticeable nose-down pitching tendency on most low-wing aeroplanes.
2. The downwash angle over the tailplane is also altered. On high-wing aeroplanes this deflection of the airflow may be sufficient to overcome the effects of the centre of pressure movement and cause a pitching-up tendency.

Other factors such as the increase in drag and the lowering of the drag line also affect the pitching movement of the aeroplane. It is actually the interaction of all the above factors that determines the ultimate pitch change. In this lesson you will be shown exactly how your particular aeroplane will respond to flap extension.

If the elevators are used to maintain a constant attitude while lowering the flaps, a further decrease in airspeed will result. It is worth while remembering that when raising the flaps the pitching movement will be reversed. This is especially important during take-offs and overshoot situations, when correct flap operation procedures must be carried out. These will be covered at the relevant stage in your training. A further point to remember is that to prevent excess stress on the airframe, flaps must only be lowered when at or below the flap limiting speed (Vfe). This is shown on the airspeed indicator as the bottom of the white arc, or it can be found in the Flight Manual.

There are several types of flap that are used on light aeroplanes, and Figure 46 illustrates four common designs.

Trimming Controls

These are used to relieve the pilot of sustained control loads on the flying controls in flight.

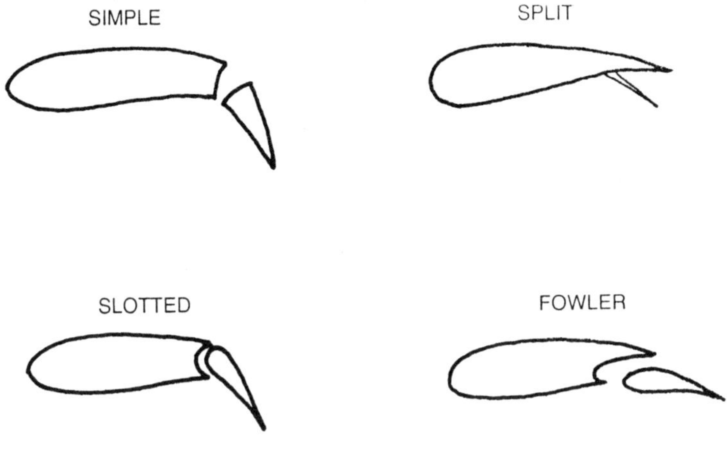

Fig. 46

Use of the elevator trim control will result in the aeroplane's being able to maintain a constant attitude in pitch without the need for the pilot to apply continuous pressure on the control column. Some aeroplanes are fitted with a rudder trim as well, which will relieve the need for constant pressure on the rudder pedals to prevent yaw. Training aircraft are not normally fitted with aileron trimmers.

It must be emphasized here that the trimming controls are not used to change the attitude of the aeroplane. The correct procedure is to select and maintain the attitude required using the primary flying controls, then operate the trimmer until no more pressure is required to hold the new attitude. The aeroplane will then fly 'hands off'.

There are two types of trimming control systems in common use today. These may be operated electrically or manually, depending on the aeroplane type. The spring-loaded trimmer simply adjusts the tension of a spring and holds the control column in the desired position. An aerodynamic trimmer takes the form of a small, movable auxiliary aerofoil attached to the trailing edge of a main control surface. Once a main control has been operated, the use of its trimming control will adjust the position of the auxiliary aerofoil and the resultant modification of the airflow will maintain the

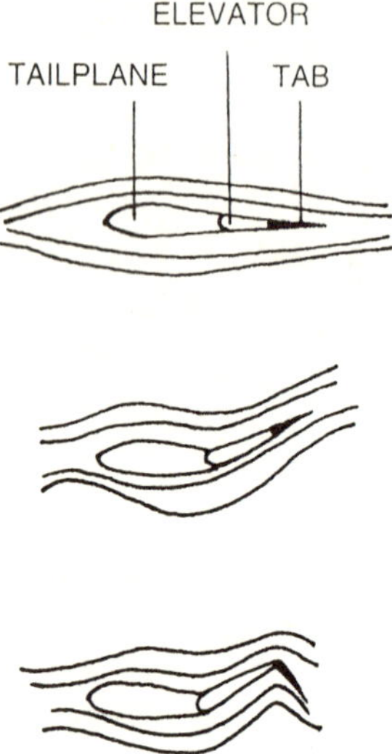

Fig. 47

control in its new position without any pressure required by the pilot, as shown in Figure 47.

The elevator trim control is the most frequently used in flight. Proper use of it will result in easier and more accurate flying. The trimmed condition of an aeroplane will have to be adjusted whenever the power setting or airspeed is changed. Additionally, further adjustments will have to be made as a result of changes in the aircraft's weight and centre of gravity in flight. These are due to fuel consumption, or the dropping of parachutists and other similar actions.

The **balance tab** is a slight variation of the aerodynamic trimmer described above. As the main control is moved the auxiliary aerofoil (tab) moves in the opposite direction and so assists the pilot in moving the main control surface. Once the desired attitude is achieved, the tab position can be adjusted to trim the aeroplane using the trimming control in the normal way.

Stabilators are usually fitted with a similar type of tab, only this time it moves in the same direction as the main control surface to form a resistance and so dampen its movement. This is necessary because stabilators are very sensitive controls. Again, the tab, now called an **anti-balance tab**, can function as a trimmer as well.

In order to correct any permanent out-of-trim effects of an

aeroplane fixed tabs are fitted to the main control surfaces. These are simply small metal strips that are adjusted on the ground.

Aerodynamic balance

On the subject of balance it will be worth while mentioning another design method which assists the pilot in moving the controls and also one that prevents dangerous vibrations of the flying controls occurring in flight.

HORN BALANCE

By arranging part of a control surface to protrude into the airstream ahead of its hinge line, the resulting air pressure will assist the pilot in moving the control surface, as illustrated in Figure 48.

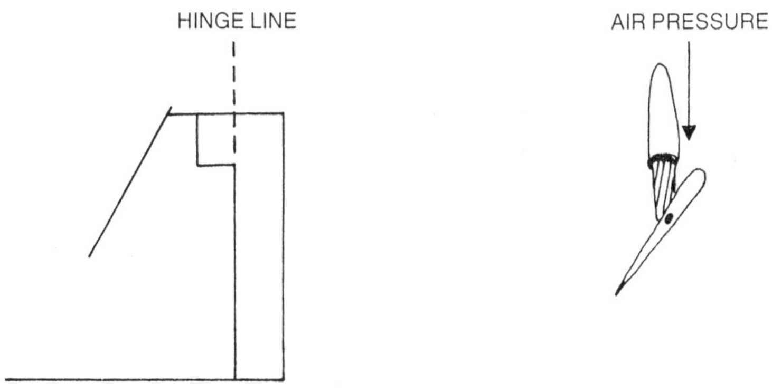

Fig. 48

MASS BALANCE

Although aeroplane wings are made strong and quite rigid, a certain amount of flexing will occur due to the changing air loads experienced in flight. In fact, this applies to the whole aeroplane structure. The result of this will be to start violent oscillations of any flying control that is not properly balanced. This is called flutter and will eventually cause structural failure. To prevent this, each control is balanced by ensuring that its centre of gravity is forward of the hinge line. This is usually done by integrating small weights into the leading edge of the particular control surface, as shown in Figure 49.

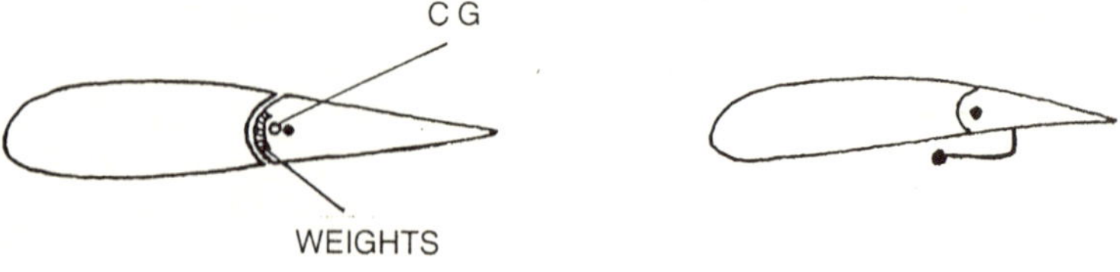

Fig. 49 *Fig. 50*

Alternately, a small weight attached to an arm that extends ahead of the hinge line will have the same effect (see Fig. 50).

The Mixture Control

Briefly, this control is used to adjust the fuel/air ratio entering the engine cylinders to give a more efficient and economical use of fuel.

Among other things, aero engines require the correct combination of fuel and air to operate efficiently. However, they are designed to run with a slightly fuel rich mixture to reduce the possibility of overheating, detonation or pre-ignition occurring. Since this is unlikely at normal cruise power settings, it is permissible for the mixture strength to be adjusted by the pilot for economy. In addition, since air density decreases with height, unless an adjustment of the fuel/air ratio is made the mixture will be too rich and a power loss will result. This will be indicated by rough running of the engine and a drop of RPM on aircraft fitted with fixed pitch propellers (which is the case on most modern training aeroplanes).

The mixture is adjusted by moving the mixture control knob from the fully rich position slowly towards the fully lean position, using the RPM gauge or exhaust gas temperature gauge (if fitted) to determine when the correct fuel/air ratio is obtained. This is called **leaning the mixture** and the exact procedure for your aeroplane will be explained in the Flight Manual. Too lean a mixture will cause rough running and overheating of the engine and care must be taken not to place the knob in the fully lean position since this will cut off the fuel supply to the engine. This position, called the **idle cut-off**, is only used during the engine shut down procedure.

The Carburettor Heat Control

Under certain conditions ice will form in the carburettor system of an engine and if left uncleared will result in engine stoppage. The accumulation of ice will be indicated by a drop in RPM (on aeroplanes fitted with fixed pitch propellers) and rough running of the engine. Operation of the carburettor heat control will divert hot air into the carburettor to melt the ice. As the control is operated further, rough running and another drop in RPM will occur. Once the ice has melted, the RPM will increase slightly and when the control is placed back in the OFF position the original RPM and smooth running will be restored.

Partial use of carburettor heat is not normally recommended since this can, under certain conditions, increase the chances of ice forming. Usually full heat must always be used and after the ice has cleared the system must be turned completely off.

During prolonged, low-powered descents and any flight condition that requires the throttle to be completely closed, such as during power-off glides, carburettor heat must be used to prevent any ice occurring. On the other hand, during full power operations it must be turned fully off to prevent any power loss. Normally, carburettor heat is not used while taxi-ing, due to the danger of dust and dirt entering the system and causing damage. However, if ice is suspected it must certainly be used, particularly just prior to take-off. The complete range of carburettor heat operations will be contained in the Flight Manual.

Carburettor icing has resulted in fatal accidents in the past; therefore frequent checks must be made to prevent its occurrence.

AIRMANSHIP

Lookout – Orientation – Engine Considerations – VFE Handing over and taking Control

Lookout

This will be the most emphasized airmanship point throughout your training.

The only sure way of avoiding a mid-air collision in visual flying conditions will be to maintain a constant lookout for all types of other aircraft and take adequate separation measures if a potential collision course exists. Due to increasing aerial, traffic and high airspeeds, the need for continuous lookout by all pilots is absolutely vital to prevent fatal accidents.

Your instructor will explain the Clock Code method of reporting other aircraft to each other during flights.

The nose of your aeroplane is always taken as the 12 o'clock position and the horizontal position of any other aircraft is reported in relation to it. The vertical position of another aircraft is described as high, low or level if it is flying at the same altitude as you are.

CLOCK CODE

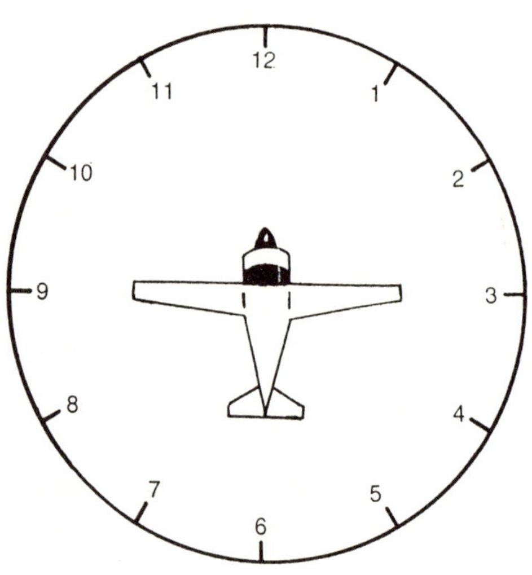

Fig. 51

Orientation

It is very important on all flights to be absolutely sure where you are. Straying into Controlled Airspace can cause serious problems and be potentially dangerous. On this and the next few flights your instructor will be responsible for any navigation.

Engine considerations

In this lesson you will be shown the effects of power, carburettor heat and the mixture control. It is a good idea to get into the habit of scanning the engine instruments, i.e. temperatures and pressures, just before operating any engine controls.

Flap limiting speed (Vfe)
Before lowering any flaps the airspeed must be checked to be within the stated limits in order to prevent any unnecessary stress on the airframe. In addition, once the flaps have been lowered care must be taken not to exceed the airspeed limits.

Handing over and taking control
It is very important on any flight to establish exactly who is handling the controls of the aeroplane at any particular time.

The normal procedure during training flights is basically for the instructor to demonstrate and explain something to you, then allow you a chance to practise it by handing over control and saying, 'You have control.' You must confirm this by taking hold of your controls and saying, 'I have control.' When the instructor wishes to resume control he or she will say, 'I have control', and you must confirm this by saying 'You have control' and taking your hands and feet off the controls. If for any reason you want the instructor to take over you simply say, 'You have control', wait for the confirmation, then leave the controls free.

Your instructor will often tell you to 'follow through' on the controls. This simply means that you can very lightly handle the flying controls to feel the kind of movements and pressures the instructor uses while flying the aeroplane.

AIR LESSON

This lesson is usually spread over two flights, the first one dealing with the primary flying controls and the second with the secondary and ancillary controls of the aeroplane.

The take-off and landing on this flight will be handled by your instructor and you will probably be asked to follow through on the controls. You will be flying a few miles away from the airfield to a clear area where instruction can begin. Once the aeroplane is flying level at a chosen altitude the instructor will point out the attitude of the aeroplane, i.e. the position of the nose and wings in relation to the natural horizon. In fact, the aeroplane will be in the normal cruise flight configuration (straight and level) and you will be shown the airspeed being flown and the power setting used. Next, the instructor will explain the correct method of holding the control column and placing your feet on the rudder pedals.

Effects of Elevators (from straight and level flight)
The elevators are controlled by a fore and aft movement of the control column.

Note the position of the nose in relation to the natural horizon.

By applying a backward pressure on the control column the nose of the aeroplane will begin to rise above the horizon. It will continue to rise until the movement of the control column is 'checked'. This is a very slight reverse movement (forward in this case) of the control column which results in a constant nose-up attitude. Note the decrease in airspeed.

When a forward pressure is applied to the control column the nose will begin to lower. It will continue to lower until the control column is checked (a slight backward pressure) when the aeroplane will tend to maintain a constant nose-down attitude. Note the increase in airspeed.

Effects of Ailerons (from straight and level flight)
The ailerons are controlled by rotating the control wheel.

By rotating the control wheel to the right, the right wing lowers and the aeroplane will roll to the right. It will continue to roll until the control wheel is centralized when the aeroplane will tend to remain in a constant banked attitude. To return to the level flight attitude rotate the control wheel to the left and as the wings become level with the horizon centralize the wheel again.

Repeat to the left.

Effects of Rudder (from straight and level)
The rudder is operated by depressing the rudder pedals.

Pick a reference point in the distance straight ahead.

Depress the left rudder pedal and the nose of the aeroplane will swing (yaw) to the left. When the pressure on the left pedal is relieved and the pedals centralized, a slight yaw to the right will normally occur due to the weathercocking effect, and then the aeroplane will continue to fly in a straight line again.

Repeat to the right.

Remember, although rudder can create yaw, it is normally used to prevent or control it.

All Movements are Relative to the Pilot

Place the aeroplane in a shallow banked attitude, then operate each control in turn and note that the aeroplane will continue to respond in the correct sense.

Further Effects of Ailerons (from straight and level)

Taking your feet off the rudder pedals, commence a roll to the left using the aileron. Notice that as the aeroplane banks, it will yaw towards the left wing of its own accord, developing into a spiral dive.

Return to the level flight attitude, using the controls in the normal way and repeat to the right.

Further Effects of Rudder (from straight and level)

Leaving the control wheel free, depress the right rudder pedal. The yaw created will be followed immediately by a roll in the same direction and then a spiral dive.

Return to the level flight attitude and repeat to the left.

NOTES

1. All control movements must be smooth and progressive. Harsh or jerky movements must be avoided.
2. The rate of aeroplane response is proportional to control deflection.

Effects of Airspeed

The aircraft will be set up to fly at a faster than normal airspeed. By operating each control in turn you will feel how much more firm and effective they become.

The aeroplane will then be set up to fly at a lower airspeed and you will notice how ineffective and sloppy the controls are, requiring larger movements for the aeroplane to respond.

Effects of Slipstream

Slipstream increases the effectiveness of the control surfaces it envelops.

The aeroplane will be set up to fly at a relatively low airspeed with the throttle closed. By operating each control in turn you will find that all of them are sloppy and ineffective.

The aeroplane will then be set up to fly at the same airspeed but with full power. By operating each control in turn, the elevators and rudder will be found to be much more responsive, but the ailerons will remain ineffective since they lie outside the slipstream envelope.

Effects of Trimmer

The trimmer is used to relieve sustained loads on the flying controls in flight.

With the aeroplane trimmed for normal cruising flight, raise the nose slightly with a backward pressure on the control column, then release this pressure and the nose will lower of its own accord and after a few small oscillations it will return to its original attitude.

Next, raise the nose again and operating the elevator trimmer in the correct sense, trim the aeroplane until no pressure is required to hold the new attitude. The aeroplane will now stay in a nose-up attitude without any effort required by yourself. To return to and maintain the original attitude from this will require a forward pressure on the control column, which can be relieved again by use of the trimmer once the desired attitude is achieved.

If your aeroplane is fitted with a rudder trimmer, a similar demonstration will be given.

You will be given several opportunities to practise the correct use of the trimming controls, which is very important to understand. Remember, first select the attitude required using the main flying controls, then use the trimmer to relieve any sustained pressure required.

Effects of Flaps

From the normal cruising flight attitude check that the speed is within the flap operation limits and then, leaving the control column free, lower one stage of flaps. Note the direction and amount of pitch change and also the decrease in airspeed. Use the elevators to return to the original attitude and note another decrease in airspeed.

Lower full flap and note the further change in pitch attitude and decrease of airspeed. Maintaining the original attitude will reduce the airspeed still more.

Next, start raising the flaps in stages and note that the pitch changes will be in the opposite direction and that airspeed will begin to increase.

Finally, practise raising and lowering the flaps while maintaining the cruising flight attitude constant.

Effects of Power (from straight and level flight)
Check the temperatures and pressures, ensure that the mixture is in the fully rich position, then select maximum power with the throttle while leaving the flying controls free. The aeroplane will respond by pitching up, followed by a yaw and roll.

Return to normal cruising flight, then close the throttle, leaving the controls free. The aeroplane will now respond by pitching down, followed by a yaw and a roll in the opposite direction.

Practise maintaining a constant attitude while changing power settings, using all the flying controls to counteract the pitching, yawing and rolling effects.

The Mixture Control (from straight and level at normal cruise power)
Scan the temperatures and pressures, note the RPM, then gradually move the mixture control towards the lean position. The engine will soon start to run roughly and the RPM will drop slightly. At this point, start moving the mixture control slowly back towards the fully rich position until the engine runs smoothly again and the RPM has restored. Care must be taken not to select the fully lean position in flight since the engine would then stop.

The Carburettor Heat Control
The presence of carburettor ice can be recognized by a drop in RPM and rough running of the engine.

Check the engine instruments, note the RPM, then place the carburettor heat control fully into the hot position. Note the drop in RPM. If there is any ice present there will be a large drop in RPM and further rough running of the engine. When the ice has melted the RPM will increase slightly, then the cold position can be selected and the original RPM will be restored.

Cabin Heating and Ventilation Controls
The operation of these controls, including the windscreen demister if fitted, is usually covered in this lesson. The important thing to remember is to open fresh air vents whenever any heating control is used in order to reduce the effects of fumes entering the cockpit should the heat exchanger unit be defective.

Instructor's Guide
Exs. 1,2,3, and 4

Lesson Plans
The lesson plans in this manual do not prescribe a specific period of instruction or flight time. They can be looked at as one unit of flight training. Each plan includes the objectives, contents of the lesson and completion standards (where a lesson is in more than one part the completion standards are given at the end of the last part). Obviously, instructors are not expected to stick rigidly to these plans. They should be used essentially as guides and adapted to suit the training situation.

LESSON PLAN

Aircraft familiarization/Preparation before and after flight/Effects of controls Part One (the primary flying controls)

Objectives
To familiarize the student with the training aeroplane, its servicing, its operating characteristics, cabin controls, instruments, systems, preflight procedures, use of checklists and safety precautions to be followed; to acquaint the student with the sensations of flight and the effect and use of the primary flying controls; and to familiarize the student with the local area and airport.

Contents
1 Preflight briefing
Discuss the main elements of the air lesson, i.e. the effects of the primary flying controls. Introduce airmanship considerations (lookouts and the clock code, handing over and taking control and orientation). Explain the three axes of the aeroplane, the method of operating the controls and the primary and secondary effects of each control. Explain: (a) that control movements must be smooth and progressive; (b) the aircraft will continue to respond until the

controls are centralized; (c) the rate of response will be proportional to control deflection; and (d) all movements are relative to the pilot. Discuss the effects of airspeed and slipstream.

2 Flight lesson

(a) Aircraft servicing (introduce the student to the various aircraft documents that must be checked before flight; and the method of booking in and out).
(b) Explain the purpose of preflight checks.
(c) Demonstrate the visual checks, emphasizing the importance of checklists.
(d) Demonstrate the engine starting procedure.
(e) Carry out the radio communications procedure.
(f) Taxi-ing (student to follow through on the controls).
(g) Demonstrate the engine run-up checks and pre-takeoff checks.
(h) Take-off (student to follow through).
(i) Circuit departure, climbout and level-off.
(j) Demonstrate the effects and use of controls etc. Student-practice (See 'Air Lesson' (p. 69) for full description of flight exercise).
(k) Familiarize the student with the local area.
(l) Talk about collision avoidance and wake turbulence avoidance.
(m) Circuit rejoin, approach, landing and parking (student to follow through).
(n) Ground safety (use of chocks, tie-down ropes etc.).

3 Postflight discussion and pre-view of the next lesson

LESSON PLAN

Effects of controls Part Two (the secondary and ancilliary controls)

Objectives

To acquaint the student with the secondary and ancilliary controls of the aeroplane.

Content

1 Preflight briefing

Briefly revise the previous lesson, discuss the objectives. Introduce airmanship points (lookouts, engine considerations, Vfe). Discuss effects of power and flaps, the use of the trimmer, mixture control, carburettor heat control and other controls (heating, lighting etc.).

2 Flight lesson
Review:

(a) aeroplane servicing
(b) visual inspection
(c) engine starting procedure
(d) radio procedure
(e) taxi-ing
(f) power checks, pre-takeoff checks
(g) take-off and circuit departure; then: *Revise previous lesson. Demonstrate the use and operation of the secondary and ancilliary controls. Student practice (see air lesson for full description of flight exercise).*
(h) Circuit rejoin, approach and landing and safe parking.

3 Postflight discussion and preview of the next lesson

Completion Standards
These two instructional periods will have been successfully completed when the student understands how to check the aeroplane's documents, how to book in and out, the use of the checklist for the visual inspection, starting procedure and the power checks and pre-takeoff checks; displays an understanding of the operation and use of the aircraft's controls; and has a reasonable familiarity with the local area and airfield. A short oral test can be given to test the student's knowledge after each lesson.

Exercise 5

TAXI-ING

Objectives

1. To teach you how to control the aeroplane on the ground.
2. To teach you to cope with emergencies (brake and steering failure).

Taxi-ing is not normally taught as a separate lesson in itself. Since every flight involves taxi-ing of some kind, your instructor will use these as opportunities to introduce you to the various procedures and methods used to taxi the aeroplane.

Control

An aeroplane is manoeuvred on the ground through the use of engine thrust (throttle), rudder pedals and brakes. These are used separately or combined, depending on the circumstances.

The throttle is used to move the aeroplane forward and is the primary control for speed on the ground.

The rudder pedals control direction on the ground. On tricycle undercarriage designs, which is the case on most modern training aircraft, the rudder pedals are linked to the nose wheel steering system.

The brakes are primarily used to slow down and stop the aeroplane but may also be used for manoeuvring.

Before Taxi-ing

Before you begin to taxi the necessary clearance must be obtained from the Air Traffic Service Unit (ATSU). You must then ensure that the direction you intend to taxi in is sufficiently clear of obstructions and that there is adequate room to manoeuvre. Remember, the length of the wings and tail must be taken into consideration before making any turning manoeuvres.

Use of the throttle

A considerable amount of power may be needed initially to move the aeroplane from standstill, particularly when on a grass surface. Once the aeroplane is moving, power must be reduced to prevent excess speed building up. While taxi-ing in the parking area or in the vicinity of buildings and hangars, or when near other taxi-ing aircraft strict speed control must be maintained. This is normally between 5 and 10 mph, or a fast walking pace. However, if taxi-ing on a clear, wide and long taxiway it is permissible to increase speed slightly to aid engine cooling and also to save time. Normally a power setting is chosen that will give a constant and safe speed.

While turning, taxi-ing up an incline or when operating on uneven surfaces, it may become necessary to increase power.

Closing the throttle will slow down the aeroplane and the brakes may be used to assist when required.

Direction Control

Depressing the right rudder pedal will make the aeroplane turn to the right and depressing the left pedal will make it turn to the left.

Sharp changes in direction should only be made at very slow speeds to prevent a swing building up which can be difficult to control. When making turns near obstructions ensure there is sufficient clearance for the wing and tail surfaces.

Use of the Brakes

Normally, the brakes are tested at the earliest opportunity, usually immediately after moving off. This is done by closing the throttle and firmly applying the brakes. To stop the aeroplane always close the throttle first then smoothly but positively apply the brakes. Once the aeroplane has stopped, apply the handbrake then set the throttle to about 1,000 RPM.

Many modern aeroplanes have the brake pedals situated above the rudder pedals, so an even pressure must be used when stopping or slowing down the aeroplane. With this arrangement, differential braking can be used to turn the aeroplane in confined spaces. Normally power should never be used against the brakes, but in these circumstances it may be required to overcome the effects of friction. Care must be taken to avoid locking a wheel, since this can cause stresses on the undercarriage and damage to the tyres.

Effects of Wind

The speed and direction of the wind will affect the control of an aeroplane on the ground. While taxi-ing directly into wind or downwind presents no problem, crosswinds attempt to weathercock the aircraft into wind. In strong crosswind conditions differential braking may be necessary to maintain direction. Additionally, proper use of the flying controls will assist in maintaining control of the aeroplane. Figure 52 shows the correct positioning of the controls during strong wind conditions.

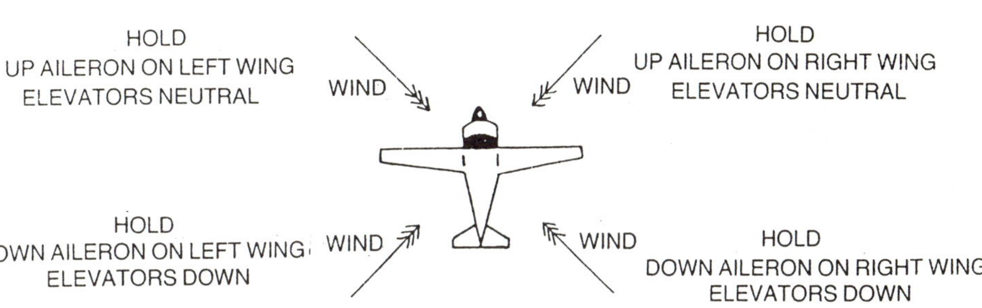

Fig. 52

Taxi-ing Tailwheel Aeroplanes

Special care must be taken when operating these types of aircraft. Although most of the information already given also applies to tailwheel aeroplanes, the following notes must be considered in addition.

Due to the reduced forward visibility of these types during taxi-ing, a satisfactory lookout can only be maintained by weaving from side to side.

Whenever power or brakes are used the control column should be held back to prevent a nosing-over tendency. Additionally, care must be taken not to apply the handbrake while the aeroplane is still in motion, since this can have the same result. Unlike tricycle undercarriage designs tailwheel aeroplanes rely on the rudder to initiate turns. Therefore, very positive and firm applications are required. Braking assistance may also be necessary.

While taxi-ing on soft grass or rough and uneven ground the control column must be held back (good practice on tricycle types as well), so that the tail remains firmly down to counteract any tendency to nose over.

When taxi-ing downwind, the control column should be held forward to prevent a possibility of the wind lifting the rear of the aeroplane. Strong crosswinds are more difficult to handle in tailwheel types and the use of brakes and rudder will be required to maintain direction.

Taxi-ing Checks

While taxi-ing it is normal procedure to carry out various instrument checks. These are designed to give you an accurate indication of the serviceability of the flight instruments, in particular the attitude indicator, the magnetic compass, the direction indicator and the turn and balance indicator. When the aeroplane is in a clear area shallow turns are made and the indications of the instruments observed. If any instrument is not indicating as expected the flight may have to be cancelled unless it is decided that the instrument is not required for that particular flight.

Aeroplanes with nosewheel steering must have a full and free rudder movement check. Again, this must be done in an area free of obstructions and a good lookout always maintained.

AIRMANSHIP

Remember, as a pilot you must exercise the responsibilities of a captain on the ground as well as in the air.

A constant lookout for obstacles, other aircraft, holes and ditches in the ground etc. must be maintained at all times while taxi-ing. In addition, you must watch out for light signals from ATC or marshalling signals from ground crew, particularly at busier airfields. Details of these signals can be found in the Air Navigation Order (ANO). Your flying school will have a copy which you can consult. A listening watch for radio messages must also be maintained.

Start familiarizing yourself with collision avoidance and right of way rules and also airfield ground markings and signals. These, too, are contained in the ANO.

In addition to normal taxi-ing checks, monitor the condition of the engine. While taxi-ing keep your hand on the throttle ready for instant action in the event of an emergency.

TAXI-ING PRACTICE

Moving Off and Brake Test

Once clearance to taxi has been obtained, look-out first, loosen the throttle friction nut for easier movement, release the handbrake, then increase power until the aeroplane starts to move forward. Now close the throttle immediately and firmly apply the brakes to check that they are functioning correctly. If dual brakes are fitted, both sets should be tested in this way.

Stopping Procedure (from slow forward motion)

1. Close the throttle.
2. Smoothly and firmly apply the brakes.
3. When the aeroplane has stopped completely apply the handbrake.
4. Reset the power to approximately 1000 RPM.

General Taxi-ing

Have a good lookout and ensure the direction you intend to taxi in is clear. As you taxi forward use the rudder pedals to control direction and the throttle to control speed, keeping your hand on the throttle at all times.

Use power according to the nature of the ground surface, increasing power when on grass or rough ground and when going uphill and decreasing power when on concrete and going downhill. Make sure you keep clear of ditches and loose stones, which can damage the propeller and flaps (these must be retracted while taxi-ing). When crossing from one surface to another, such as from grass to concrete, do so at about a 45 degree angle.

Keep a constant lookout for obstacles and maintain a strict control on speed. On tailwheel types turn from side to side to improve visibility.

At a slow speed practise making turns using the brakes and power.

Checks

In a convenient area make a shallow turn to the left and ensure that the compass and direction indicator are both decreasing in direction, the turn indicator shows a turn to the left and the balance indicator shows a skid to the right. Repeat these checks to the right observing opposite indications. During these turns the attitude indicator must remain level, responding only when the aeroplane tilts or rocks.

Check for full and free movement of the rudder by depressing each pedal fully in turn. When possible, look out behind the aeroplane to check rudder deflection.

EMERGENCIES

At some stage during training a simulated brake and steering failure exercise will be given.

Brake Failure

In the event of the brakes failing while taxi-ing the following procedures must be carried out:

1. Close the throttle and switch the magnetos off.
2. Steer the aeroplane away from obstacles into a clear area.
3. If a danger of collision exists shut down the engine immediately (mixture to idle cut-off, ignition, fuel and master switches to OFF). Otherwise, wait for the aeroplane to stop and shut the engine down in the normal way.

Steering Failure

Should the steering system fail carry out the following procedure:

> Use differential braking if available to control direction and proceed to a clear area. If this is not possible, stop the aeroplane and shut down the engine.

In both types of emergency inform ATC immediately and wait for assistance or if necessary secure the aeroplane and obtain assistance yourself.

Instructor's Guide
Ex. 5

Taxi-ing is not normally taught as a separate exercise. Since every flight involves some taxi-ing it is taught gradually during the early lessons. The lesson plans which follow outline the main items that need to be covered.

LESSON PLAN

General taxi-ing

Objectives
To teach the student to control the aeroplane on the ground.

Content
1 Before taxi-ing explain:

(a) how the aeroplane is manoeuvred on the ground
(b) the use of power
(c) the use of the rudder pedals
(d) the use of the brakes.

2 Moving off. Explain:

(a) the need for taxi clearance.
(b) lookouts
(c) brake tests (student practice)
(d) stopping procedure (student practice)
(e) taxi-ing checks (student practice)
(f) general taxi-ing (lookouts, speed control, turning, use of power on different surfaces, effects of wind etc.) *See* 'Taxi-ing Practice' (p. 80) *for full description of exercise.*

LESSON PLAN

Taxi-ing emergencies

Objectives
To teach the student to handle brake and steering failures.

Content

(a) Fully explain emergency procedures
(b) Simulate brake failure.
(c) Demonstrate safety procedure (student practice).
(d) Simulate steering failure.
(e) Demonstrate safety procedure (student practice). *See* 'Taxiing Practice' *for full description of exercise.*

Completion Standards

The student must demonstrate the ability to taxi the aeroplane safely and cope with emergencies on the ground with the absolute minimum assistance by the instructor before going solo.

Exercise 6

STRAIGHT AND LEVEL

Objectives

1. To teach you to fly the aeroplane at normal cruising airspeeds maintaining a constant height and direction with the aeroplane in balance (straight and level).
2. To teach you to fly straight and level, at different airspeeds and with flaps.

You are likely to spend a great deal of time flying straight and level and there are several factors that affect an aeroplane in this mode of flight which all pilots must understand.

FACTORS AFFECTING STRAIGHT AND LEVEL FLIGHT

The Forces

To fly straight and level the forces acting on an aeroplane must be in equilibrium, i.e. lift must equal weight and thrust must equal drag, with the tailplane force balancing the moments produced, as shown in Figure 53.

If power is increased, thrust will become greater than drag and the aeroplane will accelerate until the forces reach equilibrium again. As this occurs, the airspeed increases, producing more lift and causing the aeroplane to climb. The opposite happens when thrust is reduced, the aircraft decelerates, reducing lift and causing a descent. In fact, a change in any one of the four forces will result in a change in the others.

Relationship between Power, Airspeed and Angle of Attack

The normal cruising speed of an aeroplane is obtained at a given power setting and angle of attack, which in turn will result in level flight.

If the power setting is correct but the angle of attack is too large or too small, the desired airspeed will not be achieved and the

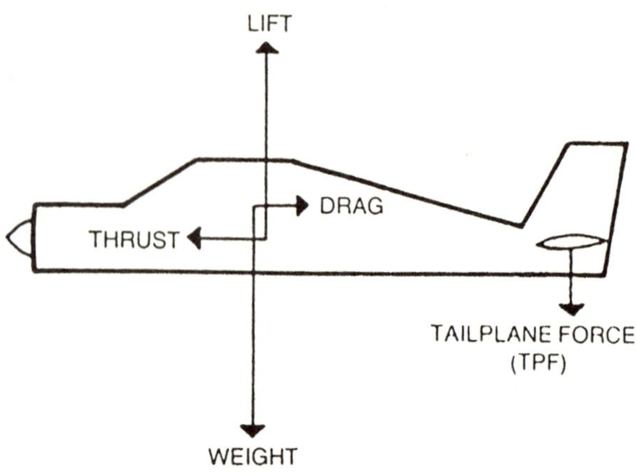

Fig. 53

aeroplane will climb or descend. The same is true if the angle of attack is correct and too much or too little power is used. So, in other words, for level flight at a given speed in a given aeroplane, there is only one combination of power and angle of attack that can be used.

To fly level at different airspeeds requires changes in both power and angle of attack. To increase, airspeed power must be increased while at the same time reducing the angle of attack to maintain level flight, until the maximum airspeed is obtained at full power. To decrease airspeed, power must be reduced and angle of attack increased. However, there is a point when power must be increased to maintain level flight at low speeds and eventually the slowest speed will be achieved at maximum power. The reason for this is explained below. This will also be demonstrated during the flight lesson.

Relationship of Power Required to Airspeed

Figure 54 illustrates a typical power curve. The lowest point on the curve is the maximum endurance speed (MES). Power required and hourly fuel consumption at this speed is at a minimum and the aeroplane will remain airborne for the longest period of time. Notice that at speeds above MES, increased power is required. This is due to the increase in parasite drag produced. Speeds below the MES also require increased power, due to the increase in induced drag.

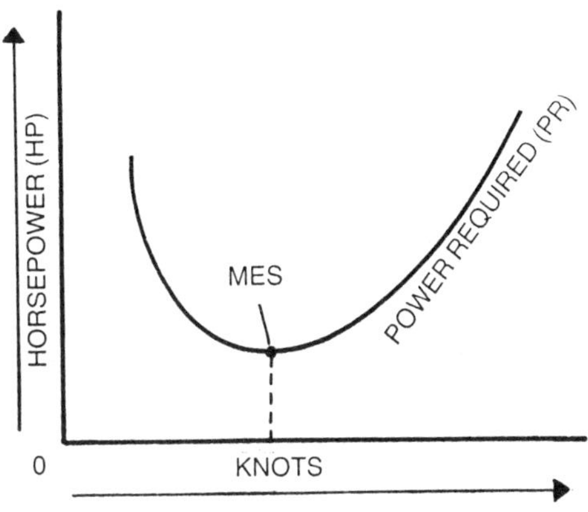

Fig. 54

Notice also that two airspeeds can be achieved at one power setting: Figure 55 clarifies this.

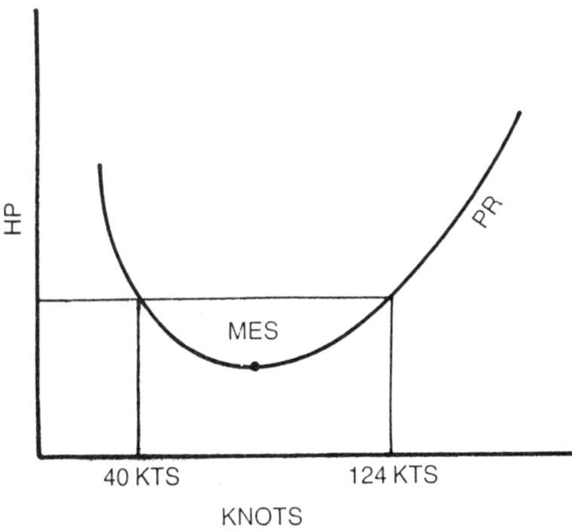

Fig. 55

The lower of these speeds occurs at high angles of attack. Although in level flight the difference in angle of attack is clear, this is not so during steep banks. Therefore, never confuse the aeroplane's pitch angle with the angle of attack.

The Maximum Range Speed is the speed above the MES which gives the greatest increase in speed for the lowest increase in power. At this speed the aeroplane flies further per gallon. Note, however, that range will be affected by winds, and the reduced air density experienced as altitude is increased.

The performance section in the Flight Manual will contain all the necessary information regarding the range and endurance of your aeroplane.

An aeroplane's behaviour changes significantly when operating at speeds below the MES. This change is important to understand and will be covered in detail under Stalling.

Straight and Level in Different Configurations

Lowering of flaps or undercarriage increases the drag. Therefore power must be increased to maintain level flight at any given airspeed. This is shown on the graph in Figure 56.

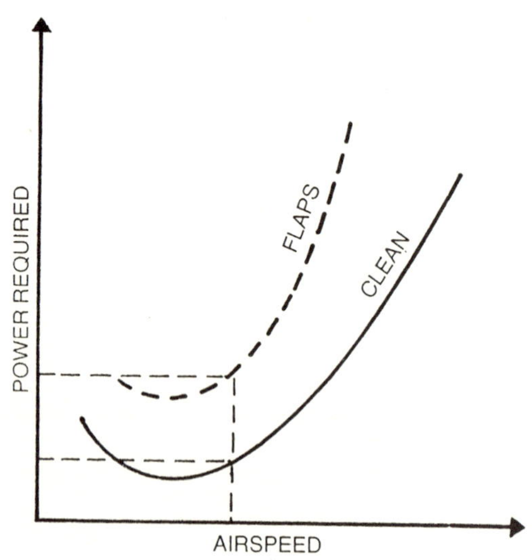

Fig. 56

FLYING STRAIGHT AND LEVEL

Maintaining Heading

To fly in a constant direction with the aeroplane in balance, the wings must be kept absolutely level with the horizon using the ailerons. Tendencies to yaw (unbalance) must be controlled with rudder. Once the wings are level, any unbalance will be indicated by a gradual change in heading and also by the ball on the balance indicator, which will be out of its central position. Balanced flight can be attained by applying rudder in the same direction that the ball has moved. For example, if the ball has moved to the right, apply sufficient right rudder pressure to return it to the centre.

Fig. 57

Take care to avoid flying with crossed controls. It is possible to fly straight with one wing low, using opposite rudder pressure to oppose the yaw produced and so maintain a constant direction. This is an inefficient flight condition that results in a decrease of airspeed. Balanced flight is defined as a condition where the aeroplane's flight path is in line with its longitudinal axis.

When the wings are level and the ball is in the middle a constant heading will be maintained. Due to the relationship between the roll and yaw, while making heading corrections with the ailerons, rudder pressure is also used, normally in the same direction, to counteract any adverse yawing effects and to maintain balanced flight. In fact, the direction and amount of rudder pressure required will also be affected by factors such as power setting, airspeed and the direction of propeller rotation. Therefore, always refer to the balance indicator to determine the exact requirement for balanced flight.

Maintaining Level Flight

To attain a condition where a constant height is maintained at the normal cruising airspeed, first the power required must be selected using the throttle and referring to the RPM gauge. Next, the straight and level pitch attitude must be adopted using the elevators. When the airspeed has settled down, the aeroplane can then be trimmed for hands-off flight.

During the air lesson the aeroplane will initially be set up for normal cruise flight and the instructor will describe the straight and level flight attitude in relation to the natural horizon and various parts of the aircraft, emphasis placed on noting the position of the nose. With experience and practice you will soon learn the correct pitch attitude to adopt.

Once the power and attitude have been selected, a scan of the altimeter should be made to check if level flight is being achieved. If the aeroplane has a tendency to climb or descend the power setting, attitude or both are likely to be incorrect and adjustments will have to be made and the aeroplane retrimmed. A check that the desired airspeed is being flown must also be made and further adjustments and retrimming may be necessary. It must be appreciated that due to inertia an aircraft will take a little time to accelerate or decelerate to a different speed, so allow the airspeed to stabilize first before attempting any corrections.

If deviations of up to 100 feet from the chosen altitude occur, it is permissible to raise or lower the nose slightly as required to return to the original altitude, the small changes in airspeed being acceptable. However, if the corrections required are over 100 feet, power adjustments will be necessary as well. Increase power and raise the nose slightly to regain height and decrease power and lower the nose to lose height. As the original altitude is reached, the normal straight and level power and attitude must be reselected.

Straight and Level at Different Airspeeds

To fly level at different airspeeds both power and attitude must be changed. If power is increased and the attitude held constant, the aeroplane will climb. If power is reduced and the attitude held constant, the aeroplane will descend. Therefore, both power and attitude (elevator angle/angle of attack) must be adjusted at the same time if level flight is to be maintained while changing airspeed.

Remember the effects of power changes, i.e. pitching, rolling and yawing, which will require co-ordinated use of the flying controls to maintain steady and balanced flight during airspeed changes.

Straight and Level in Different Configurations

Whenever the flaps or undercarriage are lowered, the increase in drag will cause a reduction in airspeed. Therefore, to maintain level flight at a preselected airspeed when either or both of these are extended will require an increase in power and also a lowering of the pitch attitude. Care must be taken not to exceed the flap limiting speed.

For efficiency in cruising flight aeroplanes are usually flown in the clean configuration, i.e. with both flaps and undercarriage (if the aircraft is fitted with retractable landing gear) retracted. However, in deteriorating weather conditions, flying at a slow safe airspeed with partial flap is useful due to the improved visibility that results from the lower nose attitude. This will be demonstrated during the air lesson.

Trimming

The key to accurate straight and level flight and, indeed, to other modes of flight as well, is frequent and good use of the trimming controls. An aeroplane that is well trimmed tends to remain in a steady flight condition, requiring only small control pressures and adjustments by the pilot to maintain it. Each time power and airspeed are changed, retrimming will be necessary.

Reference to Instruments

To achieve accurate height and heading control, it will be necessary to monitor the flight instruments, particularly the altimeter, the compasses, the airspeed indicator, the balance indicator and the RPM gauge. Provided they are serviceable, aircraft instruments are very accurate and reliable. However, it must be emphasized that reference to instruments must not be made at the expense of a good lookout. The correct method of monitoring the performance achieved is briefly to scan the instruments required, assessing the need for corrections, then immediately to revert to normal visual references outside the cockpit while carrying out any adjustments, making the occasional quick glance at individual instruments as required. The time spent looking inside the cockpit must be kept to an absolute minimum.

The altimeter will give almost immediate indications of height deviations and owing to its design the most recent pressure readings will have to be set to ensure that the aeroplane is actually flying at the altitude chosen.

Regarding heading control, direction is maintained by using outside references such as roads, chimney stacks and the like, as well as the compasses, mainly the direction indicator (DI) which is a gyro-controlled instrument. Since most training aeroplanes are fitted with a basic DI this will have to be periodically synchronized with the magnetic compass, usually every ten to fifteen minutes or so.

AIRMANSHIP

The pilot's workload during straight and level flight will be to concentrate on maintaining height and heading, navigation, ATC liaison and management of the aircraft's systems (cruise checks). A good lookout must be maintained throughout. The cruise checks which are often given the mnemonic FREDA, consist of regularly checking and managing the fuel system (F), ensuring the correct radio frequencies are set and any required radio calls are made (R), monitoring the engine systems and checking for carburettor ice (E), synchronizing the DI and magnetic compass (D) and making sure the altimeter setting is correct (A).

By this lesson you are advised to have learnt the collision avoidance and right of way rules. You must also be familiar with the privileges of the Private Pilot's Licence, especially regarding the visibility regulations. Your instructor will ensure that the aeroplane is operated in a responsible manner and according to normal procedures, so that most of your attention can be concentrated on the air lesson. Remember, however, that your instructor's task is to train you into a competent aircraft captain and so throughout future lessons as you learn new things and become accustomed to the aeroplane and its environment, more and more of the responsibilities of being a pilot will be entrusted to you, until you are eventually capable of having complete command of the aeroplane for solo flight.

AIR LESSON

The aeroplane will initially be set up to fly in the normal cruise configuration and the instructor will begin to describe the various conditions required for this mode of flight, pointing out the power being used, the wings-level and nose attitudes, the altitude, airspeed and heading. The aircraft will then be displaced from this condition and you will be shown how to assume straight and level flight. After you have had a chance to practise this, the lesson normally continues with demonstrations on how to fly at different airspeeds and with flaps. Other exercises such as level flight at maximum speed and a slow speed/maximum power demonstration are likely to be given. Cruise checks and leaning procedures will be introduced at appropriate stages.

The Straight and Level Flight Condition at the Normal Cruise Airspeed

Observe the following:

1. the power being used
2. the position of the nose and the relationship of the horizon to the windscreen
3. the wings-level attitude (level with the horizon)
4. instrument indications (height, heading and airspeed constant and the balance ball central)
5. the trimmed condition results in steady flight being maintained.

Power + Attitude = Performance (demonstration)
The instructor will increase power slightly while maintaining the original straight and level attitude and note that a rate of climb commences. The power will be reduced while still maintaining the original attitude and observe that a rate of descent now begins. Normal cruise power will be reselected and this time a nose-high attitude will be held and you will notice that the aeroplane climbs. Next a nose-low attitude will be adopted at normal cruise power and the aeroplane will start to descend. Similarly, when shallow banked attitudes are held you will observe that the heading starts to change and unbalance is likely to occur.

Therefore, it can be seen that to achieve a performance of straight and level flight at the cruise airspeed, the correct combination of power and aircraft attitude must be selected.

Attaining Level Flight

The power setting and pitch attitude will be changed by your instructor.

To assume level flight:

1. Select cruise power with the throttle.
2. Select the straight and level pitch attitude with the elevators.
3. Trim.
4. Check the altimeter and airspeed.
5. Adjust power and/or attitude if necessary and retrim.

Attaining the Wings-Level Attitude and Balanced Flight

The aeroplane will be placed in a banked attitude and out of balance.

To assume the lateral level attitude and balanced flight:

1. Roll the wings level with the ailerons.
2. Prevent yaw with the rudder (co-ordinated use of the controls).
3. Pick an outside reference point on which to maintain direction.
4. Check the DI.
5. Check the balance indicator.

The power setting and both the pitch and lateral level attitudes will be changed and you will be practising assuming the complete straight and level configuration.

Height Corrections

The aeroplane will be allowed to descend from the reference altitude and you will be practising using the elevators and power, if required, to regain height while at the same time maintaining heading and balance.

Heading Corrections

The aeroplane will be allowed to wander a few degrees off the chosen heading and you will begin practising the co-ordinated use of the ailerons and rudder to bank the aircraft in the direction required to return to the original heading. As the chosen heading is reached, level the wings in the normal way.

Remember, by keeping the wings level and the ball in the middle, the heading will remain constant.

Straight and Level at Selected Airspeeds (from normal cruise flight)
For a given increase in airspeed, first estimate the power and pitch attitude required then:

1. Select the power with the throttle.
2. Lower the pitch attitude as required to maintain height, keeping the wings level and maintaining balance.
3. Trim.
4. Allow the airspeed to settle then make any adjustments necessary and retrim.
5. Check for straight and level (constant height, heading and airspeed and balanced flight).

For a given reduction in airspeed, estimate the power and attitude required and then:

1. Select the power, maintaining direction and balance.
2. Raise the pitch attitude as required to prevent a descent.
3. Trim.
4. Allow the airspeed to stabilize, then make any corrections and retrim.
5. Check for straight and level (altimeter, airspeed indicator, DI and balance indicator).

NOTES
It is likely that your instructor will tell you what power settings are required for different airspeeds, otherwise a good guide for estimating the power requirement is to increase or decrease power by approximately 100 RPM for every 10 knots/mph of airspeed change. Also, once the speed has stabilized recheck the RPM setting. A re-adjustment may be necessary since airspeed changes tend to affect the RPM of fixed pitch propellers.

Always remember that the effects of any power change will require the use of elevators, ailerons and rudder to maintain steady and balanced flight.

Good use of the trimming controls will result in easier and accurate flying.

Straight and Level Flight with Flaps (from normal cruise)
Check the airspeed is below Vfe.

Lower one stage of flaps and note the pitch change and airspeed decrease.

Increase power and lower the pitch attitude to prevent a climb and retrim. Note the amount of extra power required to maintain level flight at the cruise airspeed. Notice also the lower pitch attitude that results.

Practise adopting selected airspeeds with flaps lowered while remaining straight and level.

If retractable landing gear is fitted a similar exercise will be given.

Instructor's Guide
Ex. 6

LESSON PLAN

Straight and level flight Part One

Objectives
To teach the student to achieve, maintain and regain straight and level flight.

Content
1 Preflight briefing
Revise previous lessons. Discuss the objectives of this lesson, defining the straight and level flight condition. Introduce airmanship points (lookouts, cruise checks etc.). Introduce the formula, Power + Attitude = Performance, and the normal cruising speed. Explain how to achieve, maintain and regain straight and level flight.

2 Flight lesson
Review:

(a) aircraft servicing
(b) visual checks
(c) engine starting procedure
(d) radio procedure
(e) taxi-ing
(f) power and pre-takeoff checks
(g) take-off
(h) circuit departure; then describe the straight and level flight condition at the normal cruise speed. Demonstrate that Power + Attitude = Performance. Demonstrate how to achieve, maintain and regain straight and level flight, perform cruise checks etc. Student practice. *See* 'Air Lesson' (p. 93) *for full description of flight exercise.*
(i) circuit rejoin, approach and landing, parking.

3 Postflight discussion and preview the next lesson

LESSON PLAN

Straight and level flight Part Two

Objectives

To develop the student's skill in flying straight and level; and understanding of the formula, Power + Attitude = Performance by introducing straight and level flight at different airspeeds and with flaps.

Content

1 Preflight briefing

Revise previous lessons, discuss airmanship points and explain the formula P + A = Perf in relation to different airspeeds and configurations (emphasize the changes in pitch attitudes and correct use of the trimmer).

2 Flight lesson

Review:

(a) all preflight procedures
(b) engine starting procedure
(c) power and pre-takeoff checks
(d) take-off and circuit departure
(e) revise straight and level part one, then: *Demonstrate straight and level flight at selected airspeeds and with flaps. Student practice. See* 'Air Lesson' (p. 93) *for full description of flight exercise.*
(f) circuit rejoin, approach and landing, parking.

3 Postflight discussion and preview of next lesson

Completion Standards

These lessons will have been completed successfully when the student is able to fly straight and level maintaining altitude within ±100 ft, airspeed within ±10 kts and heading within ±10° and is able to change airspeed smoothly with the minimum assistance from the instructor.

Exercise 7

CLIMBING

Objectives

1. To teach you to enter and maintain a climb at the normal climbing airspeed and to level off at selected altitudes.
2. To teach you to enter and maintain a climb with flaps extended. You will also be taught the correct technique for retracting the flaps while in a climb.

This lesson is likely to be integrated with an exercise on descending, so you are advised to study both chapters beforehand.

The Forces in a Climb

The maximum climbing performance of an aeroplane does not result from excess lift production but from excess thrust. When the thrust line is inclined upwards from the horizontal, part of the

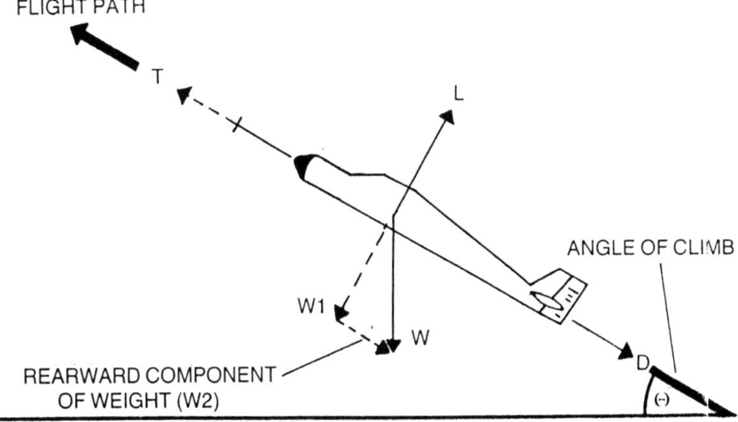

Fig. 58

thrust produced balances the drag and part overcomes a component of weight, which results in a climb, as illustrated in Figure 58.

When an aeroplane is in a climb, thrust and drag remain as forces parallel to the flight path, while the vertical component of lift acts at right angles to the flight path. However, weight, which always acts downwards towards the Earth, will be at an angle to the flight path and by reference to Figure 58 it can be seen that the result of this is for the weight to act in two directions, the primary component (W1) acting perpendicular to the flight path and equal and opposite to lift, and the secondary component (W2) parallel to the flight path and opposite thrust. For equilibrium to be maintained excess thrust, i.e. thrust not required to overcome drag, will be necessary to balance the rearward component of weight (W2). The actual climb is a result of the excess thrust moving the rearward component of weight upwards.

Climbing Performance

This is discussed in terms of the maximum rate of climb and the best angle of climb that can be achieved.

Maximum rate of climb

Figure 59 illustrates power curves typical for light propeller driven aircraft.

Provided the aeroplane is flown between airspeeds A and B, a positive rate of climb can be obtained. This is because there is more power available than is required to maintain level flight at these airspeeds. However, when climbing, an aeroplane tends to be flown most of the time at an airspeed that will achieve the maximum rate of climb. This speed, called the best rate of climb speed (Vy), occurs at the point where the greatest difference between the power available and the power required exists. If the aeroplane is flown at speeds either side of Vy, a reduced rate of climb will result. At both the maximum level flight speed and the slowest level flight speed a rate of climb cannot be obtained because maximum power is used just to maintain altitude. The best rate of climb speed will be found in the Flight Manual and is used whenever it is desirable to gain the maximum altitude in the minimum amount of time.

Best angle of climb

For a given aeroplane weight, the maximum angle of climb that

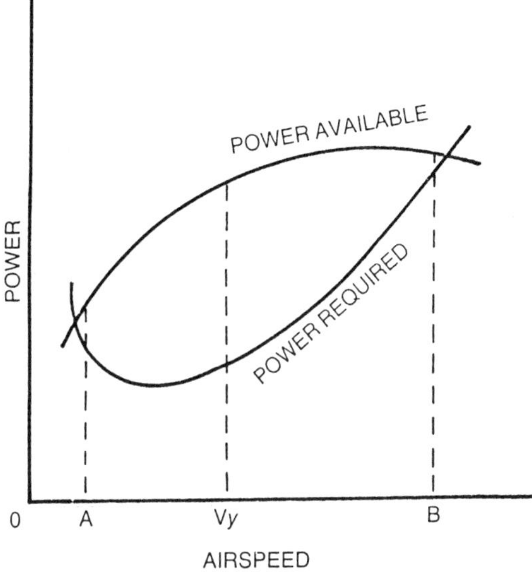

Fig. 59

can be achieved will depend on the surplus thrust available after the requirement for level flight has been met. At this point it would be worth while clarifying the difference between power and thrust. Whereas power is the work performed by an engine, thrust is a force produced to overcome drag, i.e. an engine works by turning a propeller, which in turn produces a force by accelerating the air backwards.

Figure 60 illustrates thrust curves in relation to airspeed. The thrust available curve indicates that propeller thrust is highest at low airspeeds and decreases as airspeed increases. Maximum excess thrust is therefore obtained at the point where the greatest difference between the thrust required and the thrust available exists. This point will determine the best angle of climb airspeed (Vx). This speed, which is lower than the best rate of climb airspeed results in a steeper climb angle that causes the maximum altitude to be gained in the minimum forward distance.

The best angle of climb speed can be found in the Flight Manual and is normally used when there are obstacles at the end of a runway that must be overflown after take-off.

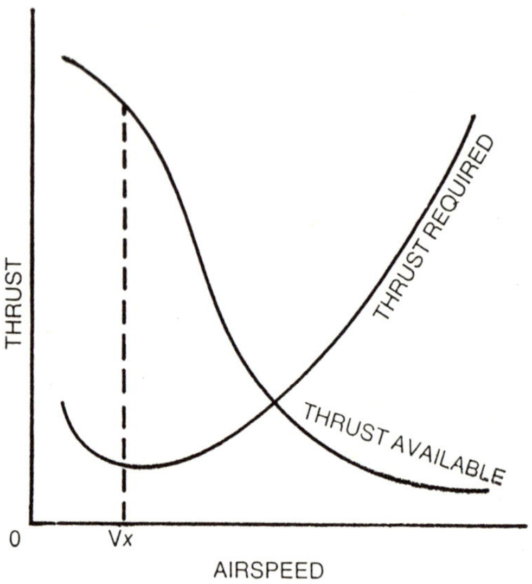

Fig. 60

Factors Affecting Climbing Performance

Weight
Changes in weight will affect both the rate of climb and the angle of climb achieved. However, provided the limitations are not exceeded, any variations in weight will not seriously affect climbing performance.

Airspeed
For a given weight, a specific airspeed is required to achieve maximum performance. Therefore, the larger the variation in speed from that required, the larger the variations in performance that will result.

Altitude
As altitude is increased, air density decreases. This will affect both the power required and the power available. Due to the reduced air density, a higher angle of attack will be required to produce the necessary lift. This will increase the drag and consequently more power will be needed for level flight. However, since a normally

aspirated engine requires relatively dense air to function effectively, increases in altitude reduce power output, i.e. a decrease of power available. So, as more power is required to maintain level flight as altitude is increased, it follows that there will be less excess power (and thrust), available, hence both rate of climb and angle of climb performance will be reduced.

In fact, as height increases the speed for the best rate of climb reduces and the best angle of climb speed increases. Eventually a point is reached where power available equals the power required and the two speeds converge. When this happens, the aeroplane has reached its absolute altitude (ceiling) and is capable of level flight at one airspeed only, having no surplus power to produce a climb performance.

In practice, an aeroplane is not operated at altitudes at or near its absolute ceiling. However, when climbing from 5,000 feet above sea level upwards, in order to maintain the maximum climb rate reduce Vy by approximately one knot/mph for every 1,000 feet in altitude gained (this rule will only apply to aeroplanes fitted with normally aspirated engines).

Flaps

During a climb, lowering of flaps decreases airspeed and causes a reduction in the rate of climb. Therefore, when normal climbs are executed flaps are not deployed. However, when obstacles need to be overflown after take-off, the best angle of climb speed is used, normally in conjunction with an optimum flap setting. Since optimum flaps can produce sufficient lift at lower speeds, the aeroplane can take-off using shorter distances, so increasing the net climb angle. Normally, when the obstacles have been cleared the flaps are raised and the best rate of climb speed adopted.

THE CLIMB

Entering a Climb

It is vital that before entering a climb the various airmanship considerations (described later) are taken care of. At this stage it is likely that you will be positively sharing the responsibility for lookouts.

During training the mnemonic PAT is often used as an aid to

learning the correct method of placing the aeroplane in the climbing configuration. To enter a climb, therefore, first select climbing power with the throttle (P). Then, keeping the wings level and maintaining balance, place the aeroplane in the climbing attitude (A) with the elevators. Once the speed has stablized trim for hands-off flight (T).

The climbing attitude will be demonstrated by your instructor and again, with practice, you will learn the correct attitude to adopt.

Maintaining the Climb

Since light training aircraft tend to use maximum power during normal climbs, airspeed changes are made by small adjustments to the pitch attitude using the elevators. As usual, allow the airspeed to settle before making corrections, otherwise you will be consistently readjusting the pitch attitude (chasing the airspeed). Once the aeroplane is properly trimmed, a constant airspeed will be held.

As far as maintaining direction is concerned, again, by keeping the wings level and the balance ball central, the heading will remain constant. Due to the low airspeed and high power combination during a climb, the slipstream effect will be quite strong, so positive rudder pressure will always be required throughout climbing manoeuvres. Since the view of the ground straight ahead will be restricted, a feature to one side of the aeroplane is normally used in conjunction with the heading indicator when maintaining a specific direction.

Returning to Straight and Level (levelling-off)

Once again a mnemonic, APT, is used as a learning aid. To return to straight and level flight from a climb first select the straight and level attitude with the elevators (A). Allow the speed to increase to the normal cruising airspeed then select cruise power (P) and trim (T).

In order to avoid overshooting a selected altitude it will be necessary to start the level-off a short while before the chosen height is reached. By using 10 per cent of the rate of climb achieved, you will arrive at a figure that can be used as a guide as to when the level-off should begin. For example, if the rate of climb is 500 feet per minute, begin the level-off 50 feet before your chosen altitude. In this way a smooth transition from climbing to level flight will be achieved.

The Cruise Climb

Often during cross-country flying the need to climb to the cruising altitude in the shortest time is not always necessary. This is when the cruise climb airspeed is used. At this speed, which usually works out to be approximately 20 knots/mph above the best rate of climb speed, the aeroplane maintains an acceptable climb rate while enjoying the time-saving and economical benefits that arise from the increase in forward speed. Your instructor will tell you the exact airspeed used for the cruise climb in your aeroplane.

Reference to Instruments

The instruments that need to be scanned quite regularly during a climb are the airspeed indicator (ASI), the DI, balance indicator, altimeter, vertical speed indicator and, of course, the engine instruments. Again, it must be emphasized that this must not be done at the expense of a good lookout.

AIRMANSHIP

Aircraft operate at several altitudes, therefore always have a good lookout all around before entering a climb. This will include looking above into the direction of the intended climb as well as to the sides and also behind the aeroplane if possible. Once in the climb the high nose attitude will reduce forward visibility, so it will be necessary to lower the nose regularly or make gentle turns from side to side ('S' turns) to check the area ahead. Remember to keep clear of clouds.

Due to the presence of controlled airspace it is vital that a pilot is well orientated. Airways and other controlled areas exist at selected altitudes above sea level, or at given flight levels (these will be indicated on your topographical charts) and extreme care must be taken not to inadvertently climb into them. Always ensure that the correct pressure reading is set on the altimeter so that you will be able to determine your exact vertical position in relation to controlled airspace.

Prior to selecting climbing power make sure that the mixture is in the fully rich position and the engine instruments are indicating normally. While in the climb the temperatures and pressures must be checked regularly. Due to the combination of low airspeed and high power setting overheating of the engine may result and if this occurs it will be necessary to increase airspeed and reduce power to allow the engine to cool before continuing the climb.

Due to the power loss that results as altitude is increased it is normally recommended that the mixture control is used to improve engine efficiency when climbing above 5,000 feet above mean sea level (amsl).

AIR LESSON

Entering a Climb (from straight and level)
To enter a climb:

1. *Lookout.*
2. Check the temperatures and pressure and set the mixture to fully rich.
3. Keeping the wings level, select climbing power with the throttle (*power*).
4. Adopt the climbing attitude with the elevators (*attitude*).
5. Allow the airspeed to settle and trim for hands-off flight (*trim*).

Maintaining the Climb

1. Maintain lookouts.
2. Maintain airspeed with the elevators and retrim after every adjustment.
3. Maintain direction with the ailerons using the heading indicator and outside references.
4. Maintain balance with the rudder by checking the balance indicator.
5. Check the engine instruments regularly.
6. When climbing from 5,000 feet upwards use the mixture control for engine efficiency.

Note the constant rudder pressure required for balance flight, and also the rate of climb that is achieved.

Returning to Straight and Level
Anticipate the selected levelling-off altitude, then:

1. Adopt the straight and level attitude with the elevators (*attitude*).
2. Allow the speed to increase to the normal cruising airspeed then reduce power to the normal cruise RPM (*power*).
3. When the speed has stabilized trim for hands-off flight (*trim*).
4. Recheck RPM.
5. Check for and maintain straight and level flight (constant height, heading, airspeed and balance).

Climbing with Flaps Lowered (best angle of climb)
From a normal climb select the optimum flap setting, trim to maintain the normal climbing airspeed and note the reduced rate of climb. Reduce the airspeed with the elevators to the best angle of climb speed, retrim and note a slight increase in the rate of climb. Notice also the higher nose attitude compared with a normal climb.

To return to the normal climb from this:

1. Check the airspeed is not below the best angle of climb airspeed.
2. Raise the flaps while at the same time adopting the normal climbing attitude with the elevators.
3. When the speed has stabilized, retrim.

Practise entering climbs with different flap settings at the best angle of climb speed, then raising the flaps in stages returning to a normal climb, following the techniques just described.

NOTES
When operating the flaps manually, make sure this is done smoothly and always be prepared for the resulting pitch changes. Similarly, do not make abrupt power changes with the throttle. In other words, all control movements must be smooth and progressive.

The Cruise Climb
From a normal climb, increase the airspeed to that recommended for a cruise climb.

Note that the decrease in climb rate is small compared to the increase in forward speed.

Note: the Instructor's Guide for climbing is combined with the one on descending at the end of the next chapter.

Exercise 8

DESCENDING

Objectives

1. To teach you to enter and maintain a glide descent at the normal gliding speed and to level off at selected altitudes.
2. To teach you how to use engine power to control the rate of descent.

Other exercises such as descending with flaps, entering a climb from a descent with flaps and sideslipping are likely to be given at some stage during this lesson.

An aeroplane can be made to descend either by closing the throttle completely, adopting the best gliding speed and accepting whatever rate of descent is achieved, or, more usually, by using power to control the rate of descent at selected airspeeds according to requirements.

Forces in the Glide

In the section on 'Stability' (p. 33) it was explained that due to the arrangement of the four forces, a reduction of thrust would cause the aeroplane automatically to adopt a nose-down attitude, so assisting the pilot in maintaining airspeed and control. In other words, an aeroplane can still fly and remain controllable without engine power provided sufficient airspeed is maintained. A glide, therefore, is a flight condition where there is no engine thrust, as is the case with gliders and sailplanes. Knowing that weight has two components whenever the flight path is inclined from the horizontal, it can be seen from Figure 61 that the W2 component of weight acting parallel to the flight path will substitute for engine thrust whenever the aeroplane is placed in a glide and, provided a steady airspeed is maintained, a constant rate of descent will be achieved and there will be equilibrium.

Gliding Performance

The gliding performance of an aeroplane is discussed in terms of

FORCES IN THE GLIDE

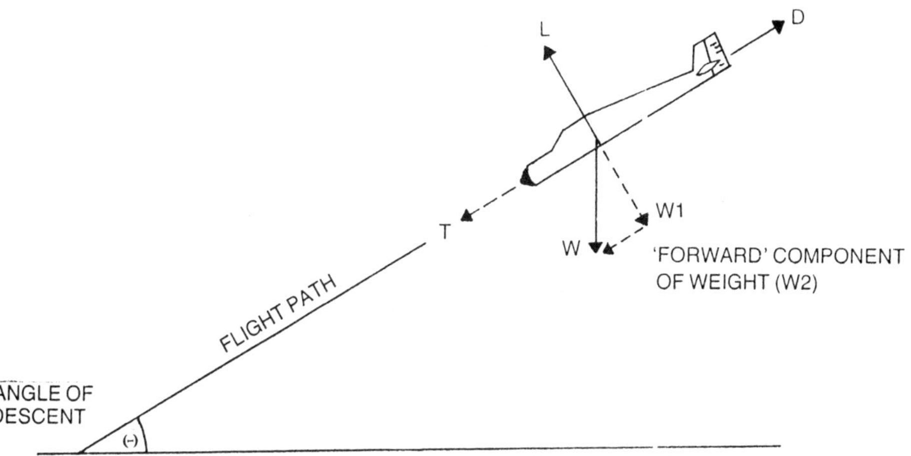

Fig. 61

the maximum range and the maximum endurance that can be achieved during a glide.

Maximum range glide (minimum glide angle)

The main objective during a glide, particularly in the case of an engine failure, is usually to obtain the maximum forward distance for the loss in altitude experienced as the aeroplane descends; in other words, to fly at the flattest possible angle. In light aircraft (without the use of flaps) this angle corresponds with a particular airspeed and angle of attack that gives the best lift/drag ratio. This airspeed, called the best gliding speed, will be given in the Flight Manual and will result in a maximum range glide (in zero wind conditions).

Maximum endurance glide (minimum rate of descent)

In the event of an engine failure, use of the minimum rate of descent speed will result in the aeroplane remaining airborne for a slightly longer period of time than if the best gliding speed is used. This can be useful, especially when the need for maximum range is not urgent (such as when at high altitudes over relatively gentle terrain) as the pilot will have a little more time to deal with the situation. The minimum rate of descent that can be achieved without any power available will occur at the angle of attack and airspeed that will produce a condition of minimum power required. In practical terms, the airspeed to be used for a maximum endurance glide usually works out to be approximately 75 per cent of the best gliding speed.

Factors Affecting Glide Performance

Airspeed

To obtain the maximum gliding range the aeroplane must be flown at the airspeed specified in the Flight Manual. At speeds both above and below the best gliding speed gliding range will decrease. Although it may appear that a glide can be 'stretched' if the nose attitude is raised slightly and the airspeed allowed to reduce, this is *not* the case. Any variation from the best gliding speed will reduce the gliding range and therefore it is very important that accurate speed control is maintained throughout a glide.

GLIDING SPEED AND RANGE

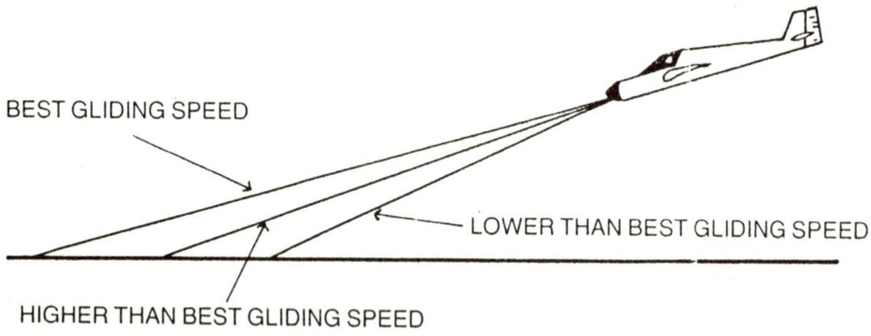

Fig. 62

Flaps

Any increase in drag, such as lowering flaps or undercarriage, will increase the rate of descent and reduce range, so aeroplanes are usually flown in the clean configuration during a glide. However, during a landing approach lowering of flaps can be very useful since the increase in drag produces a steeper descent angle.

Additionally, it can be seen from Figure 63 that when flaps are lowered the speed for a maximum range glide decreases, so if the airspeed is reduced slightly in this configuration, the rate of descent will decrease and the pilot will be able to maintain a steeper descent angle without the need to increase airspeed.

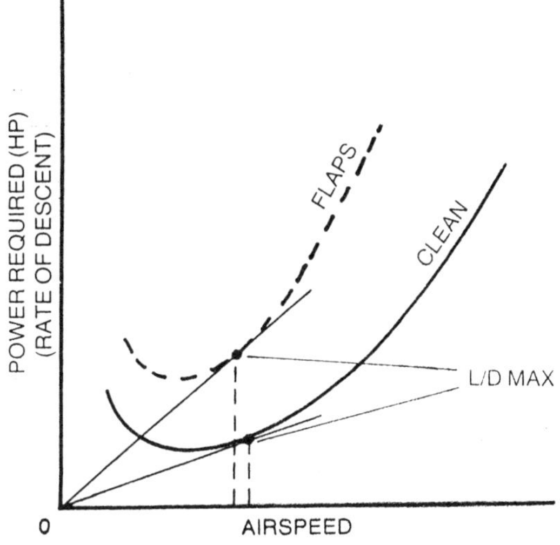

Fig. 63

Other benefits of using flaps during a landing approach will be the slower touchdown speed that will result, which reduces the landing distance and also the inevitable pitch change that occurs whenever flaps are lowered, which will give the pilot a better view of the landing area once the aeroplane is properly trimmed.

Weight

The effect of additional weight during a glide will be to cause the aeroplane to fly faster down its descent path. But, provided an airspeed that gives the best lift/drag ratio is maintained, the gliding range will not be affected. The glide speed specified in the Flight Manual will be based on the maximum authorized weight of the aircraft and since the variations in weight carried in light single-engined aeroplanes are relatively small there will not really be any need to make adjustments to the airspeed given.

Wind

The direction and strength of the wind relative to an aeroplane has a very significant effect on gliding performance. Basically, headwinds reduce range and tailwinds increase range.

In a strong tailwind situation it can be beneficial to decrease airspeed slightly to reduce the rate of descent and therefore extend the airborne time. In this way the tailwind can be used to maximum advantage. On the other hand, in strong headwind conditions it will be necessary to increase airspeed in order to make maximum progress against the wind.

Pilots must always be aware of the prevailing wind conditions during a glide, since in an engine failure situation the wind will play a major role in determining whether a safe landing can be made.

THE GLIDE

Entering a Glide

As in the lesson on climbing, mnemonics are likely to be used as aids to learning the correct methods of descending an aeroplane.

Apart from the usual lookouts that must be made, certain engine considerations should also be taken care of just before entering a descent. Since air density will start to increase when the aircraft descends, it will be necessary to ensure that the mixture control is placed in the fully rich position, so that when the throttle is opened again the engine will not be running with too lean a mixture. Once this has been done, the carburettor heat system must be turned on to clear any icing that may be present. If it is appropriate for your aeroplane the carburettor heat system should be left on throughout descents as with certain types of engine there is a greater possibility of icing occurring at low power settings, particularly during glides, when the throttle is closed.

Provided these actions are done before entering a descent and in the order described above, i.e. first checking that the mixture is rich before applying carburettor heat, you will have eliminated the risk of mistaking the mixture control for the carburettor heat control and operating the idle cut-off. If this is done during a glide the error will only become apparent if the need to use power arises. This is because the propeller will continue to windmill at normal gliding speeds. Such a situation may turn into an emergency if an engine restart is unsuccessful or there is insufficient altitude to attempt one.

Having carried out the above actions a normal glide is entered by first smoothly closing the throttle (*power*). As usual, be prepared for the effects of a power reduction. Next, keeping the wings level and maintaining balance, allow the aeroplane to decelerate to the recommended gliding speed, then adopt the gliding attitude (*attitude*). Once again, as in the climbing lesson, this pitch attitude will be demonstrated to you and described in relation to the horizon and various parts of the aeroplane. When the speed has stabilized, trim for hands-off flight (*trim*).

Maintaining the Glide

While in the glide lookouts must be maintained and care taken not to descend below the minimum safety altitude (described later). Airspeed corrections are made by small adjustments to the pitch attitude with the elevators, allowing the speed to settle down first as usual. Direction is maintained in the normal way using the ailerons and an outside reference point, in conjunction with the heading indicator. Due to the effects of reduced slipstream, a slight rudder pressure will be required to keep the aeroplane in balance. Regular checks of the engine instruments should be made and every minute or so the throttle must be opened to the halfway position for a few seconds so that the engine continues to produce sufficient heat to clear any icing and also to prevent spark-plug fouling and large variations in engine temperature.

Returning to Straight and Level (levelling-off)

In a similar manner to the climbing manoeuvre anticipate levelling-off at selected altitudes by 10 per cent of the rate of descent achieved.

To level off, first turn the carburettor heat to the OFF/COLD position, then select normal cruising power (*power*) while at the same time adopting the straight and level attitude with the elevators (*attitude*). Both these actions must be smooth and co-ordinated and be prepared for the strong forward pressure on the control column that will be required to maintain the straight and level attitude (due to the effects of increased power). As the aeroplane accelerates to the cruising speed trim for hands-off flight (*trim*) and proceed with the normal techniques for maintaining straight and level flight.

POWERED DESCENTS

Using Power to Control the Rate of Descent

In a normal gliding descent the pilot will have to accept whatever descent rate is achieved, being able to vary it to a limited extent through the use of flaps, small adjustments to airspeed or sideslipping (described later). However, by using engine power the rate of descent can be accurately controlled at selected airspeeds according to the needs of the pilot.

If power is added during a normal glide, the aeroplane will start to accelerate along the descent path due to the thrust supplementing the forward component of the weight. But if the original airspeed is maintained through the use of the elevators, the rate of descent will decrease and the resultant descent angle will become flatter. By varying the amounts of power used it can be seen that the pilot can have a great deal of control over both the rate and angle of descent.

Entering and Maintaining a Power Assisted Descent

It was explained in the lesson on 'Straight and Level Flight' (p. 85) that for a given airspeed a particular power setting is required to maintain level flight. Therefore, if the airspeed is maintained but the power selected is insufficient for level flight, the aeroplane will descend, i.e. a rate of descent will be achieved (the value of which will depend on the amount of the power deficiency). So, provided the level flight RPM of the airspeed chosen for the descent is known, a useful rule of thumb for estimating the power setting for a given rate of descent at that airspeed will be to reduce power by approximately 100 RPM for every 100 feet of descent rate required. For example, if the level flight power setting for 80 knots is 2,000 RPM, to descend at 400 feet per minute at 80 knots reduce power to 1,600 RPM.

So, to enter a powered descent first decide the airspeed to be flown and the rate of descent required. Then, once the airmanship and engine considerations have been looked after, select the estimated RPM, adopt the pitch attitude to maintain the selected airspeed and trim in the normal way. Next, check the vertical speed indicator (VSI) to see if the desired rate of descent is being achieved. If the descent rate is too great, increase power (in small increments) and raise the nose slightly to prevent the airspeed increasing above the chosen figure and retrim. Be ready to apply a positive forward pressure on the control column to prevent the nose rising too high due to the effects of increased power. If the rate of descent is insufficient, reduce power and this time lower the nose to maintain the original airspeed and retrim. Continue to make small adjustments in power and attitude in this way until the desired rate of descent is achieved. Note that this technique further emphasizes the fact that power controls rate of descent and the elevators control airspeed.

A cruise descent is simply a powered descent made at normal cruising airspeeds. It is normally used during the final stages of a cross-country flight when the need for a steep angle of descent is not important. A gradual rate of descent is commenced a few miles from the destination and the higher forward speed is both time-saving and economical.

The Sideslipping Manoeuvre

This manoeuvre was originally developed for aeroplanes not equipped with flaps as a means of rapidly losing height without increasing airspeed, especially in situations where the aircraft is found to be too high during an approach to land.

From a normal descent, if the wings are banked to one side and the natural tendency of the aeroplane to turn is prevented by using rudder pressure in the opposite direction, while at the same time the pitch attitude is adjusted to maintain the original airspeed, the aeroplane will continue to fly in a constant direction but the rate of descent will be greater. This increase in the descent angle is a result of the aeroplane's descending slightly sideways, exposing more surface area to the airflow and creating more drag.

To recover from a sideslip and return to a normal descent, the wings must be levelled and the rudder pedals centralized, while at the same time readjusting the pitch attitude to maintain airspeed. These control actions must be co-ordinated and positive.

The sideslip is not used very often in newer types of aeroplane, since flaps achieve the same result without the need to fly with crossed controls. However, during training you are likely to be given some practice in sideslipping as this is a good handling exercise in itself and can be useful in the event of a flap failure.

On certain types of aeroplane the use of flaps during a sideslip will be prohibited (see the Flight Manual). This is due to the very high rate of descent that will occur and the reduced effectiveness of the elevators and rudder.

Entering a Climb from a Descent with Flaps (Overshoot Procedure)

During a landing approach, due to misjudgement by the pilot or the current airfield traffic conditions, it may become necessary to execute a missed approach or what is usually called a 'go around' or overshoot. This basically means that the pilot will immediately have to enter a climb from the descent, level-off at the circuit height and proceed around the airfield again for another landing approach. Now it is very likely that the initial approach will be made with flaps lowered and in an overshoot situation it is essential that the correct procedure for entering a climb in this configuration is followed. In preparation for such situations you will be given plenty of opportunity to practise this at safe altitudes and away from the airfield until you are proficient in the technique.

With the aeroplane trimmed for a descent (glide or powered) with full flaps lowered, to enter a climb, first turn the carburettor heat control off. Then, keeping the wings level, select climbing power while adopting the pitch attitude for a climb with flaps down. Maintain this attitude (strong forward pressure on the control column will be required), and soon after a safe airspeed is obtained start raising the flaps in stages to reduce the drag. At a safe height with a steady rate of climb indicated, raise the flaps completely, adopt the attitude for the best climbing speed and trim. Then proceed with the usual techniques for maintaining a climb. Remember to anticipate the pitch changes that occur when the flaps are operated, and the rudder pressure for balanced flight when climbing power is selected.

Reference to Instruments

The instruments that need to be monitored to ensure that the expected performance is being maintained during the descent will be the ASI, DI, altimeter and balance indicator. During a powered descent the RPM gauge and VSI will become more important. Engine instruments must be checked occasionally to ensure they are indicating normally.

Once again it must be emphasized that any reference to instruments must be brief, and a return to normal visual references outside the cockpit made as soon as the indications on the instruments have been interpreted.

AIRMANSHIP

Before entering a descent have a good lookout all around, especially below the aircraft and particularly in the direction of the intended descent. In low-wing aeroplanes the wings should be banked slightly to each side so that the area immediately below the aeroplane can be viewed. In the vicinity of an airfield you must be particularly alert, since the danger of a collision is much greater due to the increased traffic density. Listen out for messages on the radio, which will give you a good idea of the positions and movements of other aircraft.

On flights away from the airfield it is usual procedure for minimum cruising altitudes to be worked out based on the height of obstacles along the route. Care must be taken not to descend below these altitudes (minimum safe altitudes) unless you are absolutely sure of your position in relation to any obstacles. On this flight, of course, your instructor will ensure that the flight is conducted safely, but in future always remember your minimum safe altitudes while descending. In addition, ensure the correct pressure datum is set on the altimeter.

AIR LESSON

Entering a Glide (from straight and level flight)
To enter a glide descent:

1. *Lookout.*
2. Check the temperatures and pressures and set the mixture control to the fully rich position.
3. Turn on the carburettor heat control if applicable.
4. Close the throttle (P).
5. Maintain the straight and level attitude to allow the aeroplane to decelerate to the normal gliding speed, then adopt the gliding attitude (A).
6. Trim (T).

Maintaining the Glide

1. Maintain lookouts and make shallow turns to each side to increase the view below.

2. Maintain airspeed with the elevators, retrimming after every adjustment.
3. Maintain direction with the ailerons, using the heading indicator and an outside reference.
4. Maintain balance with the rudder by reference to the ball.
5. Every minute or so open the throttle to the halfway position for a few seconds to keep the engine 'warm'.

Note the rate of descent achieved and the amount of rudder pressure required to maintain balance due to the reduced slipstream.

Levelling Off

1. Anticipate the chosen levelling-off altitude.
2. Turn the carburettor heat to cold.
3. Select cruising power with the throttle (P) while simultaneously adopting the straight and level attitude with the elevators (A).
4. Maintain attitude and as the aeroplane accelerates to the cruising airspeed trim for hands-off flight (T).
5. Check the altimeter and RPM gauge.
6. Proceed with normal straight and level flight techniques.

Gliding with Flaps

From a glide at the best gliding airspeed, lower optimum flaps and adjust the pitch attitude to maintain airspeed. Once the aeroplane is trimmed note the increase in the rate of descent and the lower nose attitude that results compared to a clean glide. Next, reduce the airspeed to the recommended speed for gliding with optimum flaps, retrim and note the slightly reduced rate of descent that results. Now raise the flaps while at the same time adjusting the nose attitude for the normal gliding speed.

Practise lowering all the flaps in stages while simultaneously adopting the pitch attitude for the flaps down gliding speed. Next, practise raising the flaps in stages while adjusting the pitch attitude to return to the clean glide.

Powered Descents (Demonstration)

Enter a clean glide at the normal gliding speed and once the aeroplane is properly trimmed note the rate of descent. Then start adding power in small increments of about 100 RPM at a time, readjusting the pitch attitude to maintain airspeed and retrimming. Note how much the rate of descent decreases with each 100 RPM increase in power and also the flatter nose attitude that results.

Entering and Maintaining a Power Assisted Descent

To enter a powered descent:

1. *Lookout.*
2. Decide the airspeed and the rate of descent required.
3. Check the temperatures and pressures and set the mixture to the fully rich position.
4. Apply carburettor heat if applicable.
5. Select the estimated RPM with the throttle.
6. Adopt the approximate pitch attitude to maintain the selected airspeed.
7. Trim.
8. Check the VSI.
9. If the rate of descent is too much, increase power and raise the nose slightly and retrim. If the rate of descent is insufficient reduce power and lower the nose slightly and retrim.
10. Check the VSI and continue to make corrections as required until the desired performance is achieved.

The level off is executed in the same way as for a glide descent, i.e. power – attitude – trim.

Practise entering powered descents at different airspeeds and descent rates and also with flaps lowered.

Sideslipping

From a glide at the normal gliding speed, adopt a shallow banked attitude with the ailerons while using rudder in the opposite direction to prevent a change in heading. Due to the increase in airspeed that results in this flight condition, it will be necessary to raise the nose slightly to maintain the normal gliding airspeed. Note the increase in the rate of descent.

To recover from a sideslip, roll the wings level while at the same time centralizing the rudder pedals and adjusting the pitch attitude for a normal glide.

Practise entering and recovering from different degrees of sideslip.

Entering a Clinb from a Descent with Flaps (Overshoot Procedure)

From a normal glide with flaps, to enter a climb:

1. Turn off the carburettor heat.
2. Select full power with the throttle.
3. Adopt the pitch attitude for the flaps down climbing speed.
4. Trim.
5. Once a safe airspeed has been obtained start raising the flaps in stages.
6. At a safe height raise the flaps completely and trim the aeroplane for a normal clean climb.
7. Continue with normal climbing flight techniques.

Practise entering climbs from powered descents with flaps lowered in the same way.

Instructor's Guide
Exs. 7 and 8

LESSON PLAN

Climbing and descending (Part One)

Objectives
To develop further the student's skill in straight and level flight; to teach the student how to enter, maintain and level-off from a climb; and to enter, maintain and level-off from a glide descent (including sideslips).

Content
1 Preflight briefing
Revise previous lessons, discuss objectives of this lesson, introduce airmanship points (lookouts, engine considerations, altimeter settings, MSAs etc). Discuss the forces in the climb and descent and introduce the flight technique for each. State the speeds to be used.

2 Flight lesson
Review:

(a) preflight procedures (include weather report checks)
(b) engine starting procedure and radio communications
(c) taxi-ing and power and pre-takeoff checks
(d) take-off and circuit departure to training area
(e) revise straight and level exercises, then: *Demonstrate the techniques for climbing and gliding flight. Student practice. Emphasize attitude and trim control, lookouts and engine considerations. (See* 'Air Lesson' (p. 106) *for full description of flight exercise.*
(f) circuit rejoin, approach, landing and parking.

3 Postflight discussion and preview of next lesson.

LESSON PLAN

Descending (Part Two)

Objectives

To develop further the student's skill in the manoeuvres learnt so far (straight and level, climbing and glides) and to introduce the technique for controlling the rate of descent through the use of power and flaps; then to teach the student to use this technique during a landing approach.

Content

1 Preflight briefing

Revise previous lessons and discuss the objectives of this lesson. Discuss airmanship considerations. Explain the use of the formula P + A = Perf in relation to controlling the rate of descent at the normal descent speed. Specify power settings for given rates of descent. Discuss the effects of flaps on the rate of descent. Explain the use of power and flaps during a landing approach.

2 Flight lesson

Review:

(a) preflight procedures
(b) engine starting and radio procedures
(c) taxi-ing and power and pre-takeoff checks
(d) take-off and circuit departure
(e) revise previous manoeuvres, then: *maintaining the descent speed demonstrate how power and flaps affect the rate of descent. Demonstrate how to use this technique to vary the approach path. Student practice. (See* 'Air Lesson' (p. 117) *for full description of the flight exercise)*
(f) circuit rejoin, approach, landing and parking.

3 Postflight discussion and preview of the next lesson

LESSON PLAN

Climbing and descending with flaps

Objectives

To develop the student's handling of the aeroplane during low speed operations (climbing and descending speeds) by introducing the technique for entering a climb from a descent with flaps lowered (overshoot procedure).

Content

1 Preflight briefing

Revise previous lessons, discuss objectives of this lesson and airmanship considerations; explain the overshoot procedure.

2 Flight lesson

Review:

(a) preflight procedures
(b) engine starting procedure and radio communications
(c) taxi-ing and power and pre-takeoff checks
(d) take-off and circuit departure
(e) revise previous manoeuvres, then: *demonstrate the overshoot procedure. Student practice. (See* 'Air Lesson' (p. 117) *for description of flight exercise)*
(f) circuit rejoin, approach, landing and parking.

3 Postflight discussion and preview of the next lesson

Completion Standards

These lessons will have been successfully completed when the student uses the techniques correctly and can smoothly enter, maintain and level-off from climbing and descending flight, has a reasonable understanding of how to adjust the approach path and can smoothly carry out the overshoot procedure.

Exercise 9

TURNING

Objectives

1. To teach you to enter and maintain a level turn and to roll out on to specific headings.
2. To teach you to enter and maintain climbing and descending turns.

Forces in the Turn

'Every body continues in its state of rest or of uniform motion in a straight line unless compelled by an external force to act otherwise' (Principle of Inertia).

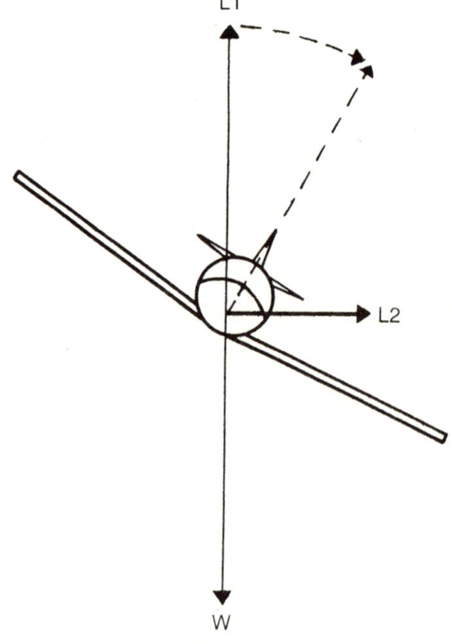

Fig. 64

From the above statement it can be seen that for an aeroplane to turn, i.e. to follow a curved path, a force must be present acting towards the centre of the turn that will induce the aeroplane away from maintaining a straight flight path. Such a force, called the centripetal force, is produced in flight by placing the aeroplane in a banked attitude and tilting the lift line. When this happens the lift force will have two components acting at right angles to each other, as illustrated in Figure 64.

The L2 component acts horizontally and provides the centripetal or turning force that accelerates the aircraft towards the centre of the turn. The L1 component acts upwards to support the weight. Now, it was explained in earlier lessons that whenever the lift force is tilted the vertical component will be insufficient to balance the weight causing the aeroplane to sideslip and descend. So, to maintain a constant height during a turn additional lift will have to

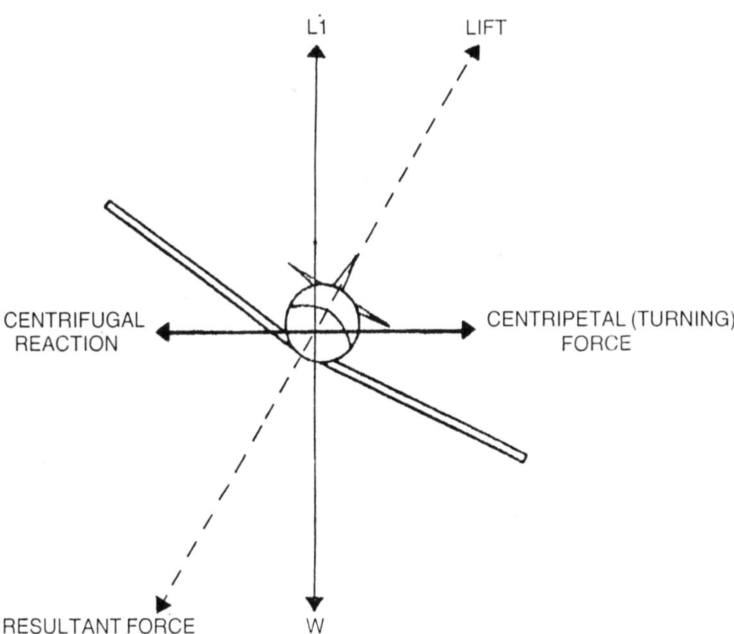

Fig. 65

be produced and this means either angle of attack or airspeed will have to be increased. During a level turn the vertical component of lift will balance the weight, as shown in Figure 65 and the centrifugal reaction indicated, is an equal and opposite reaction to the centripetal force.

Due to the centripetal acceleration that forces the aircraft to follow a curved path, an aeroplane in turning flight will not be in a condition of equilibrium.

In practice, the additional lift is produced by increasing the angle of attack with a slight back pressure on the control column when the angle of bank is 30 degrees or less. For steeper angles of bank power must be used in addition to maintain a safe airspeed. Figure 66 shows that the steeper the angle of bank, the greater the amount of additional lift required.

Load Factor

This is the proportion between the lift produced and the aircraft's weight and is determined by the following equation:

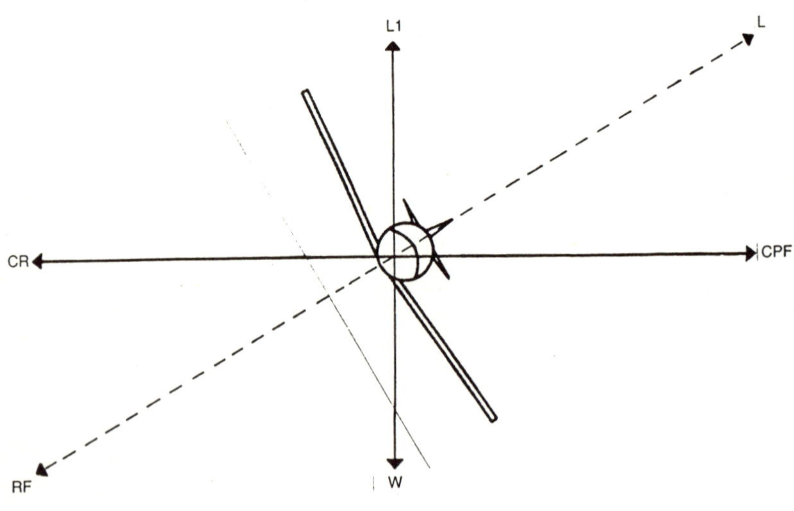

Fig. 66

$$n \text{ (load factor)} = \frac{\text{lift}}{\text{weight}}$$

In straight and level flight the lift produced equals the weight; therefore the aeroplane experiences a load factor of 1. During a steady turn, however, the aircraft must produce more lift than its weight and the load factor increases, the actual value being determined by the bank angle. The steeper the angle of bank, the greater the load factor. For example, during a level turn at 60 degrees angle of bank, the wings will have to produce twice as much lift than is required for straight and level flight (load factor of 2).

Any increase in wing loading will increase the speed at which an aeroplane stalls, therefore load factor is an important consideration during manoeuvring flight and will be covered in more detail under 'Stalling and Advanced Turning' (pp. 140-254).

Turning Performance

The performance of an aeroplane in a steady turn is discussed in terms of turning rate and radius and these are determined by the following equation:

$$\text{rate of turn (degrees per second)} = \frac{1{,}091 \times \text{tangent of the bank angle}}{\text{true airspeed (knots)}}$$

$$\text{Turn radius} = \frac{(\text{true airspeed})^2}{11.26 \times \text{tangent of bank angle}}$$

It can be seen from the two variables in these equations that both rate of turn and turn radius are quite simply functions of airspeed and bank angle. Basically, this means that provided the airspeed and bank angle are constant during a turn, the rate of turn and turn radius will be the same for all aircraft, regardless of type or weight.

For a given airspeed the rate of turn will depend on the amount of centripetal force. Therefore, the greater the bank angle (the more the lift force is tilted) the greater will be the rate of turn. In addition, the turn radius will decrease as bank angle increases. Similarly, for a given angle of bank the turn radius will be the least at the lowest airspeed at which the aeroplane can be flown. The operational use of small radius turns, however, is usually limited to manoeuvring around an airfield in conditions of bad visibility, and in such a situation extreme care must be taken while handling the aeroplane, since, as mentioned earlier, stalling speeds increase with an increase in bank angle.

Standard Rate Turns

A standard rate turn or rate one turn as it is usually called is often used in flight and gives a rate of turn of 3 degrees per second.

A useful rule of thumb for estimating the bank angle for a rate one turn is to use 10 per cent of the indicated airspeed, then add 7 for knots or 5 for miles per hour. For example, if your airspeed is 90 knots, the bank angle for a rate one turn will be 16 degrees (9 + 7 = 16). The Turn and Slip Indicator will give you an indication if a rate one turn is being achieved. At 3 degrees/sec. a 360 degree turn will take 2 minutes to complete.

The medium-level turn takes place at about 30 degrees angle of bank and is also often used in flight, particularly during instruction. At a 30 degree bank angle a faster rate of turn is achieved, usually without any need to use additional power to maintain a safe airspeed.

The Magnetic Compass and the Direction Indicator

The magnetic compass basically consists of a rotating compass card suspended on the tip of a needle inside a small bowl filled with liquid. When left undisturbed it will always align itself to magnetic north, thus indicating the magnetic heading towards which the aeroplane's nose is pointing. However, due to the nature of its construction, whenever the magnetic compass is disturbed, such as when the aircraft accelerates or decelerates or when the wings are banked to either side, it has peculiar reactions. In addition, when turbulence is experienced it will be very difficult to maintain a constant heading using the magnetic compass. It is quite likely that you will have noticed this behaviour during earlier flights.

So, in order to fly headings accurately the pilot uses the Direction Indicator. This instrument is gyro-controlled and consists of a rotating compass card that can be manually set to any direction. It gives accurate and instantaneous indications of any turn of the aeroplane and does not suffer from the errors of the magnetic compass. However, since it does not incorporate any north-seeking properties it can only be used practically if it is synchronized with the magnetic compass. Additionally, the DI does have errors of its own. Therefore, in flight it will be necessary to resynchronize the two instruments quite often, usually every fifteen minutes or so. This is a very important procedure so get into the habit of periodically checking both instruments on every flight.

When synchronizing the instruments in flight it will be necessary to keep the wings absolutely level, with the aeroplane in balance and the airspeed constant so that the magnetic compass can settle down to a steady reading. In this way accurate synchronization will be possible.

Turns using the magnetic compass

Although aircraft instruments are very reliable a possibility always exists of one or more of the instruments failing in flight. If the DI should become unserviceable the pilot will have to steer the aeroplane using the magnetic compass and this will require a thorough knowledge of its errors and how to compensate for them. It must be pointed out here that the magnetic compass and DI rotate in opposite directions during turns, which may confuse you initially.

Errors of the magnetic compass

On easterly and westerly headings whenever the aeroplanes accelerates or decelerates, for a brief period the magnetic compass will show an apparent turn towards north, although the direction is kept constant. The opposite happens when the aircraft decelerates, an apparent turn towards south will be indicated. These indications must be ignored, and once the airspeed has settled down the compass will return to a true reading.

A more important error that must be remembered when steering by the magnetic compass is the turning error. Whenever an aeroplane banks on northerly and southerly headings the magnet system has a tendency to tilt. This means that during turns towards north or south the magnetic compass will give incorrect indications of the headings through which the aircraft passes. To compensate for this, when turning on to north, it will be necessary to begin the roll out of the turn about 30 degrees *before* north is reached. The opposite must be done when turning on to south; begin the roll out 30 degrees *after* south has been passed through. In both cases the action of levelling the wings will swing the compass system towards the correct reading. Once the compass has settled down it may still be necessary to make small corrections to the heading using gentle turns. These errors are maximum on north and south headings and progressively reduce until they are non-existent on east and west headings. This means that the 30 degree allowance factor should be reduced slightly when turning on to headings approaching north or south. Note that these errors refer to the Northern Hemisphere only and the effects will be reversed south of the Equator.

Heading orientation is very important in flight and you are advised to become thoroughly familiar with the compass rose (Fig. 67).

THE COMPASS ROSE

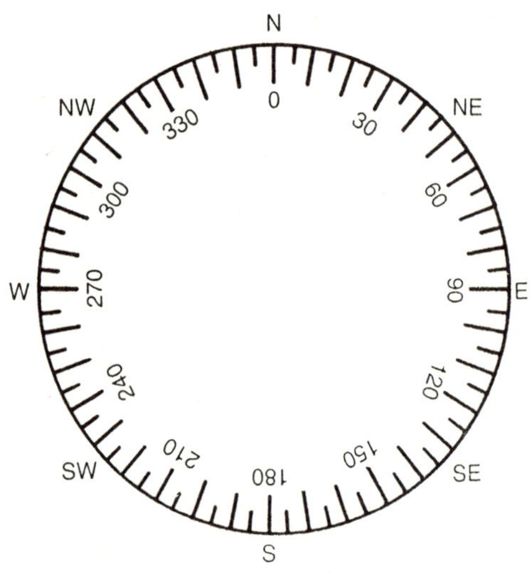

Fig. 67

THE TURN

Entering a Level Turn

After the airmanship considerations of lookout have been taken care of, a medium level turn is entered by rolling the aircraft to the required bank angle with the ailerons while applying rudder pressure in the same direction to prevent adverse yaw, and raising the nose attitude slightly with back pressure on the control column to prevent a sideslip and loss of height. These control actions must be made simultaneously.

The rate of roll will depend on the amount of aileron deflection and when the required bank angle is reached the ailerons must be neutralized and then used during the turn to maintain the bank angle. You will learn the exact amount of rudder application and back pressure on the control column required after some practice. Your instructor will demonstrate a few turns so that you become accustomed to the aircraft's attitude.

Remember, all control movements must be smooth but positive – no jerky movements are necessary.

Maintaining a Turn

During a turn the selected bank angle must be maintained by the ailerons, the pitch attitude for level flight maintained by the elevators and balance controlled by the rudder.

Throughout a turn a certain amount of rudder pressure will normally be required to maintain balanced flight. The actual direction and exact amount will depend on various factors, such as the direction of propeller rotation, airspeed and power setting. This can be determined by checking the balance indicator and then applying sufficient pressure in the direction indicated to bring the ball back to the central position. It is this need for constant rudder pressure that is the primary cause for the bank angle to be continually monitored during a turn. Remember, the further effect of rudder is roll. Therefore, depending on the direction of rudder pressure applied in a turn, a tendency for overbanking or underbanking will exist and this must be controlled by using the ailerons in order to maintain a constant bank angle.

During a level turn the pilot aims to maintain a constant height. Now, since the use of the three flying controls are closely related during a turn, this means that whatever the bank angle chosen the pitch attitude must be correct and the aeroplane in balance for steady level flight to be achieved. If the bank angle desired is being maintained but the back pressure on the control column is insufficient the aeroplane will descend. On the other hand, if the back pressure is too much the aeroplane will climb. Similarly, if the back pressure is correct and the bank angle is allowed to increase, the aeroplane will descend. If, on the other hand, the bank angle is allowed to decrease a climb will result. It must be noted that since turning is a transitionary manoeuvre, the elevator trimmer is not normally used to relieve the back pressure.

So turning, as with other modes of flight, requires continuous monitoring if the desired performance is to be achieved and maintained. The correct sequence for monitoring a turn will be first to check the bank angle and make any corrections required. Next, check the altimeter and readjust the pitch attitude (back pressure) if necessary to maintain height. Finally, ensure that the aeroplane is in balance. Throughout the turn keep a good lookout for other aircraft.

The correct execution of a turn requires the co-ordinated use of all the flying controls and this comes with practice and experience. On aircraft fitted with side by side seating the pilot's view of the aeroplane's attitude in relation to the horizon will differ during left and right turns, but, once again, with practice you will become accustomed to this.

During medium level turns make a note of the airspeed reduction that results from the back pressure. This usually amounts to about 5 knots, which is acceptable during these types of turn. At steeper angles of bank the airspeed reduction will be greater requiring an increase in power in order to maintain a safe margin of airspeed, as you will discover in the lesson on advanced turns.

Rolling Out of the Turn (returning to straight and level)

The return to straight and level flight is achieved by rolling the wings level with the ailerons, while maintaining balance with the rudder and releasing the back pressure from the control column. Once again, these control actions must be simultaneous.

During the roll out, the rudder pressure must be applied in the same direction as the control wheel is rotated when levelling the wings, i.e. control wheel right – right rudder; control wheel left – left rudder. As the wings become level with the horizon centralize the controls and continue with normal straight and level flight techniques.

When turning on to specific headings using bank angles of 30 degrees begin the roll out 10 degrees before the desired heading is reached. At greater or lesser angles of bank this lead allowance must be varied accordingly. When a roll out is executed correctly these lead allowances will result in a smooth transition from turning flight to straight flight on the desired heading, i.e. the wings should become level with the horizon just as the aeroplane arrives on the selected heading.

Climbing Turns

A climbing turn is entered in the same way as a level turn except that bank angles are limited to a maximum of 20 degrees. The roll out is also accomplished in the same way.

During a climbing turn the pilot aims to maintain a sufficient rate of climb as well as an adequate rate of turn. When an aeroplane is placed in a banked attitude during a climb the nose has a tendency to drop, requiring the pilot to apply a slight back pressure on the control column to maintain the climbing speed (thus increasing the angle of attack and consequently the drag). Now, since most light training aircraft use maximum power during a climb, there will be no surplus thrust available to balance the additional drag and this results in a reduced climb rate. The greater the angle of bank during a climbing turn the more the climb rate will be reduced and this is why the bank angle is limited.

Now, during a straight climb a certain amount of rudder pressure is required to maintain balanced flight. On most modern training aircraft this will be to the right. This means that during a climbing turn to the left it is likely that right rudder pressure will still be required, but to a smaller extent. In other words, when entering a climbing turn to the left, instead of applying left rudder reduce the amount of right rudder pressure slightly. Refer to the balance indicator for the exact requirement for balanced flight. During a climbing turn to the right positive right rudder pressure will be required throughout.

During a climbing turn, the flight path of the aeroplane will be describing an upward spiral. This results in the two wings each experiencing a different relative airflow and consequently angles of attack. This, in addition to the outer wing travelling slightly faster than the inner wing will cause a tendency for the aeroplane to overbank. So, during a climbing turn it will be necessary to 'hold off' the bank by rotating the control wheel away from the direction of the turn slightly in order to maintain a constant bank angle.

Descending Turns

Descending turns are also entered in the same way as level turns and this time bank angles of up to 30 degrees may be used. The roll out is also accomplished in the same manner.

During a descending turn the pilot will be concerned with the rate of descent and the rate of turn. As in the case of climbing turns, whenever the aeroplane is banked during a descent, the tendency for the nose to drop will require a slight backward pressure on the control column to maintain the desired airspeed. This will result in an increase in the rate of descent. The greater the angle of bank, the greater the rate of descent. In a gliding turn the pilot will have to accept this increase. However, during a powered descent by adding extra power the original rate of descent can be maintained.

During a descending turn the flight path of the aeroplane will now be a descending spiral and this time the larger angle of attack experienced by the inner wing will override the effects of the faster speed of the outer wing and will cause a tendency to underbank. This will require the pilot to 'hold on' bank in order to maintain a constant bank angle. The reduced effects of slipstream during a descent will make the use of the rudder more straightforward in a descending turn.

The Slipping Turn

The slipping turn is a variation of the sideslip manoeuvre described in the lesson on descending. It is used whenever it is desirable to lose height rapidly during a turn without increasing airspeed.

During a straight sideslip, the wings are banked but the aeroplane is prevented from turning by applying sufficient opposite rudder. To accomplish a change of heading during a sideslip, the wings must be banked in the normal way but this time insufficient rudder pressure applied so that a rate of turn is achieved. For any given angle of bank, the rate of turn will, of course, be less than during a straightforward turn. If the original rate of turn is required, a greater angle of bank will be necessary.

Since the nose tends to lower during a slipping turn, slight back pressure will be required on the control column to prevent the airspeed increasing. During slipping turns and sideslips there are likely to be errors in the ASI readings due to the position of the pressure vents, particularly with aircraft fitted with static vents on the sides of the fuselage.

Slipping turns were also developed originally for aircraft not equipped with flaps and therefore are not recommended to be used with flaps lowered. Proper execution of slipping turns requires good co-ordination of the flying controls and they are used often during training as an exercise to develop handling skill.

Reference to Instruments
During a level turn the main instruments that need to be monitored to ensure that the desired performance is being achieved are the altimeter and the balance indicator. The attitude indicator should also be referred to occasionally for precise bank angle indications and the DI scanned to monitor progress towards the selected heading. When a rate one turn is required the turn indicator must be checked. During climbing and descending turns the ASI and VSI and also the engine instruments will need to be scanned in addition.

AIRMANSHIP

Before entering a turn, begin the lookout by first checking that the area behind the aircraft in the opposite direction to the intended turn is clear of traffic. This should be followed by looking out across the horizon, above and below the aeroplane and then into the direction of the intended turn.

By now you will have realized that lookouts are a very important part of flying procedures. Remember, at a time when you are in full command of the aeroplane, you alone will be responsible for separation from other aircraft, so get into the habit of maintaining lookouts at all times.

While flying the aeroplane there is a tendency for pilots to keep looking at the cockpit instruments in the effort to fly accurately. Now, to prevent this becoming a habit you must discipline yourself to make any reference to instruments as brief as possible and *never* change the flight path of the aeroplane without having a good lookout first.

All lookouts must be a conscious effort to look for potential collision courses.

AIR LESSON

Entering a Level Turn (from straight and level)
To enter a medium level turn:

1. Look out all around the aeroplane.
2. Roll the wings to the required bank angle while applying

rudder pressure in the same direction to maintain balance and raising the nose slightly with back pressure on the control column.
3. As the selected bank angle is reached neutralize the ailerons.

Maintaining a Turn

1. Keep a good lookout.
2. Maintain the bank angle with the ailerons (check the attitude indicator).
3. Maintain balance with the rudder (check ball).
4. Maintain height with the elevators (check the altimeter).

Remember, *select* and *maintain* the attitude.

Rolling out

To roll out of a turn:

1. Look out.
2. Anticipate the roll out by 10°.
3. Roll the wings level with the ailerons while maintaining balance with the rudder and releasing the back pressure from the control column.
4. Continue with straight and level flight techniques.

Practise entering both medium-level and rate one turns to the left and right and rolling out on to different headings.

Climbing Turns

From a normal climb, look-out then enter a turn to the right at 20° angle of bank and note:

1. the need to adjust the pitch attitude to maintain the climbing speed
2. the reduced rate of climb
3. the rudder pressure required for balanced flight
4. the need to hold off the bank.

Increase the bank angle and note the further decrease in the climb rate.

Enter a climbing turn to the left and note particularly the rudder requirement for balanced flight.

Practise entering climbing turns to the left and right and rolling out on to selected headings.

Next, practise levelling off at selected altitudes while continuing the turn.

Descending Turns

From a normal glide, lookout then enter a medium turn at 30° angle of bank and note:

1. the need to adjust the nose attitude to maintain the gliding speed
2. the increased rate of descent
3. the rudder pressure required for balanced flight
4. the need to hold on bank.

Increase the bank angle and note the further increase in the rate of descent.

Practise descending turns to the left and right on to selected headings.

Next, practise levelling off from the descent while continuing the turn.

Then enter a power-assisted descent and practise using power to maintain the rate of descent while turning.

Finally, practise entering descending turns with flaps lowered.

Slipping Turns

At a safe height and after a good lookout, enter a straight sideslip then reduce the amount of rudder pressure so that a rate of turn is achieved and note:

1. the need to adjust the pitch attitude to maintain the airspeed
2. the increased rate of descent
3. the rate of heading change.

To return to a normal straight glide from a slipping turn:

1. Level the wings while readjusting the rudder pedals for balanced flight and the elevators for the gliding speed.
2. Continue with normal gliding flight techniques.

Notice that during medium-level turns the elevators are used to maintain height, and during climbing, descending and slipping turns they are used to control airspeed.

Once you are reasonably proficient in executing turns, to develop your handling skills further a series of exercises which will combine all the manoeuvres and procedures you have learnt so far is likely to be given.

Instructor's Guide
Ex. 9

LESSON PLAN

Turning

Objectives

To develop further the student's skill in straight and level flight and climbing and descending flight; to introduce the student to basic turning manoeuvres and to develop the student's orientation in relation to the compass rose (headings).

Content

1 Preflight briefing

Revise previous lessons and discuss the main objectives of this lesson. Discuss airmanship points emphasizing lookouts. Explain the forces in the turn and the technique for entering, maintaining and rolling out of a turn (including climbing, descending and slipping turns). Emphasize attitude control and the co-ordinated use of the ailerons and rudder.

2 Flight lesson

Review:

(a) all preflight procedures
(b) engine starting and radio communications
(c) taxi-ing and power and pre-takeoff checks
(d) take-off and circuit departure
(e) revise previous manoeuvres, then: *Demonstrate how to enter, maintain and roll out of medium level turns and climbing, descending and slipping turns. Student practice. (See* 'Air Lesson' (p. 135) *for description of flight exercise)*
(f) circuit rejoin, approach, landing and parking

3 Postflight discussion and preview of the next lesson

Completion Standards

This lesson will have been successfully completed when the student can execute a steady turn and has a reasonable standard of heading orientation.

Exercise 10

STALLING, STALL AVOIDANCE AND SLOW FLIGHT

Objectives

This lesson is of the utmost importance and has three purposes:

1. to teach you the symptoms of an approaching stall
2. to teach you to execute a safe recovery from a stall with minimum height loss
3. to teach you to handle the aircraft at very slow airspeeds.

The Stall

Among other factors the lift produced by an aerofoil depends to a very important extent on the smoothness of the airflow passing around it. Now, air, like every other mass, possesses inertia, i.e. it can only make gradual changes in direction. So, provided the angle at which the airflow meets the wings (angle of attack) is not too great, the air will be able to flow smoothly around it, as shown in Figure 68.

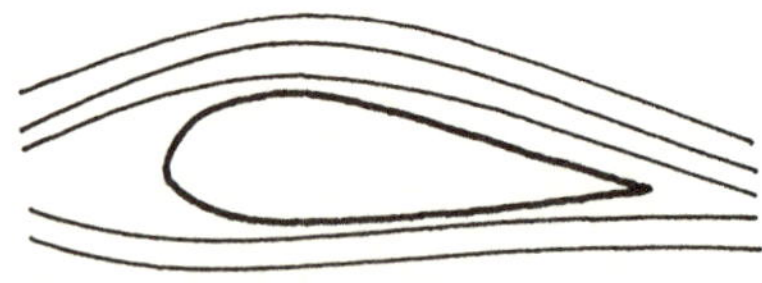

Fig. 68

However, at a specific angle of attack, which will vary for different types of wing, the air will not be able to negotiate the change in direction around the wing quickly enough and the smooth streamlined airflow will break down and become turbulent, as illustrated in Figure 69.

This condition is known as a **stall** and will result in large losses in lift and an increase in drag.

Now, the elevators control the angle of attack and with it the

Fig. 69

pilot is able to determine the angle at which the air meets the wings. As the control column is moved backwards the angle of attack increases. When sufficient back pressure is applied to the control column the angle of attack will increase to a critical angle (stalling angle) when the air can no longer flow smoothly over the wings and the aeroplane will stall. In this condition the aeroplane will be unable to continue flying, its nose will usually drop and rapid losses of height will occur. Other undesirable characteristics are also likely.

A stall can only result from an excessive angle of attack and an aeroplane can be made to stall at any airspeed while being flown in any attitude and configuration. If the excessive angle of attack is maintained for any reason it is very likely that the aeroplane may then enter a spin.

The above statements are very significant and must be appreciated by all pilots.

A stall in itself need not necessarily be a dangerous manoeuvre. In the air lesson you will actually be entering full stalls and you will discover that provided the correct recovery techniques are employed, safe, controllable flight will be resumed in a short time. It is when a stall is left to develop, or occurs at low altitudes, such as during a landing approach when there is likely to be insufficient height in which to execute a recovery, that stalling can be fatal.

To avoid entering a stall situation the aeroplane must be flown strictly according to the operating procedures you have been taught, particularly regarding handling techniques and airspeed control. These have been designed so that the aeroplane is kept safely within its angle of attack limitations. However, through mishandling of the flying controls or weather conditions such as wind shear and severe turbulence, the angle of attack limits may be exceeded and the aeroplane will stall. Therefore, all pilots must be taught to cope with stall situations. So, with the emphasis on stall avoidance you will be trained to recognize automatically the onset of a stall and to initiate a safe and prompt recovery.

Relationship of Stalling Angle to Airspeed

The stalling speed of an aeroplane is the speed at which the aeroplane will reach its critical angle of attack and stall. Now, it might be assumed that since increasing angle of attack (back pressure on the control column) is usually associated with reducing airspeed, an aeroplane will stall only at low airspeeds. However, this is not always the case.

Factors Affecting Stalling Speed

Since the amount of lift being developed to maintain controllable flight is dependent on a minimum airspeed being maintained, the stalling speed of an aeroplane will be the minimum speed below which controllable flight is impossible. The basic stalling speed of an aeroplane is the speed at which it will reach its critical angle and stall from level flight, with the throttle closed, flaps retracted and the control column being moved slowly aft until the stall occurs. However, the basic stalling speeds quoted for any particular aeroplane will not be the only speeds at which stalling will occur. The actual stalling speed will depend on the aircraft's weight, load factor, configuration (flaps) and the power being used.

Weight

For level flight to be achieved the lift produced must equal the weight of the aeroplane. Any increase in weight will require an increase in lift for level flight to be maintained. So, for any given angle of attack greater airspeed will be required to produce the necessary lift. This means that as the angle of attack is increased the aeroplane will reach the stalling angle at a higher airspeed. In other words, an increase in weight will increase the speed at which the aeroplane stalls. This is another reason why weight limitations must never be exceeded.

In addition to weight, the location of the centre of gravity will also affect the stalling speed. In the section on 'Stability' (p. 33) it was explained that the lift and weight couple (the centre of gravity acting ahead of the centre of pressure) produces a nose-down tendency that must be balanced by the download provided by the tailplane. This means that the wings must in fact produce sufficient lift to balance the weight of the aeroplane as well as the effect of any aerodynamic download. Forward movement of the centre of gravity will require a greater download on the tailplane which must be balanced by additional lift from the wings. So, again, for any given angle of attack greater airspeed is required to produce the extra lift and, consequently, stalling speeds are increased. This emphasizes the need to load the aeroplane so that its centre of gravity is within the stated limits (see Flight Manual).

Load factor (manoeuvring flight)
It was mentioned in the previous lesson that manoeuvres such as turning require the wings to produce more lift than its weight. The effect of this on stalling speeds is similar to the effect of increased weight, in that the greater the load factor the higher will be the stalling speed. The table in Figure 70 illustrates the percentage increase in stalling speeds and the load factors (g) experienced at different angles of bank. The figures are valid for any type of aeroplane.

BANK ANGLE IN TURN	0°	10°	20°	30°	40°	50°	60°	70°	80°	90°
LOAD FACTOR	1.0g	1.02g	1.06g	1.15g	1.31g	1.56g	2.0g	2.92g	5.76g	INFINITE
STALL SPEED INCREASE	0%	1%	3%	7%	14%	25%	41%	71%	140%	INFINITE

Fig. 70

Notice that for bank angles of up to 30° the increases in load factor and stalling speeds are relatively small, but for greater angles of bank the increases are quite substantial.

Sudden changes in pitch can also increase the load factor considerably, particularly during an abrupt pull-out from a dive. In this case, due to inertia, the aeroplane continues on the same flight path for a short while despite the change in pitch attitude. As this happens, the angle of attack can increase quite considerably and a high-speed stall is likely to occur.

Flaps

The lowering of optimum flap increases the lift producing capabilities of a wing. Therefore, at any angle of attack a given value of lift can be produced at a lesser airspeed. Thus, stalling speeds are correspondingly reduced. Flaps have a very significant effect on the stalling characteristics of an aeroplane, which is discussed later.

Power

The amount of power being used will also reduce the stalling speed of an aeroplane. This is because at high angle of attack the vertical component of thrust will augment the lift being produced, as shown in Figure 71.

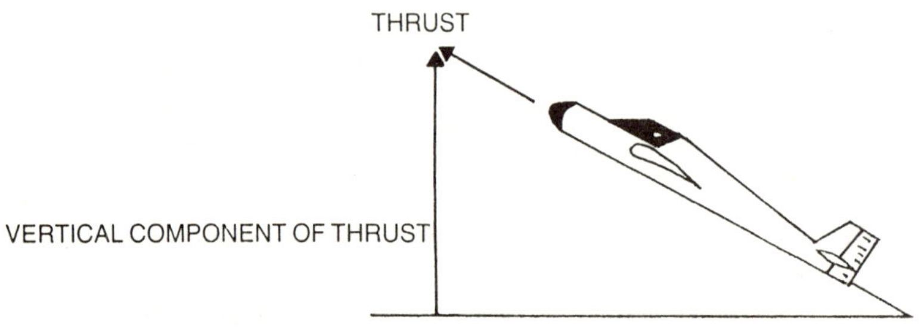

Fig. 71

In addition, the slipstream from the propeller will increase the airflow over the inboard wing sections, preserving the lift in these areas. Power also has a significant effect on stalling characteristics.

Stalling Characteristics

The stalling characteristics of an aeroplane refer to its behaviour when close to and during the stall. Each type of aeroplane behaves differently during stalled flight and even individual aircraft of the same type are likely to exhibit slightly differing behaviour.

When an aeroplane stalls there is usually a tendency for the nose to drop. Now, in normal flight the downwash from the wings helps produce the download on the tailplane. During a stall, however, the downwash becomes insufficient, causing the tail to rise and the nose to drop. In effect, this is a form of longitudinal stability which assists the pilot in the recovery (discussed later).

Another likely tendency during a stall is wing dropping. For various reasons one wing may stall before the other, causing the aeroplane to bank sharply with the risk of spin entry.

Stalling characteristics with flaps

When an aeroplane approaches the stall with flaps lowered its lateral stability is weakened significantly. This means that any wing-dropping tendency will be quite emphatic. (The method of dealing with a wing drop is explained later.) Figure 72 illustrates the lateral distribution of lift about a wing with flaps lowered.

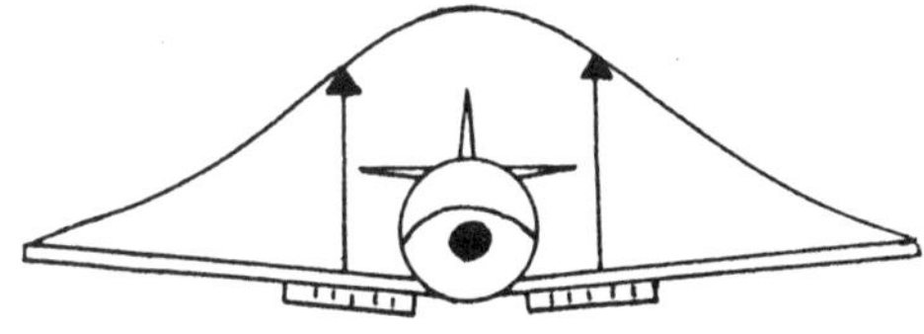

Fig. 72

The centre of pressures tend to move closer together when flaps are lowered and this is responsible for the weakened lateral stability of the aeroplane.

Stalling characteristics with power

When an aeroplane is approaching a stall with power on, the slipstream will preserve the lift over the wing sections within its envelope and also maintain the effectiveness of the tail surfaces for a longer period. As a result of this the aeroplane can be forced into a fuller stall involving more wing area. As the stall progresses a considerable wing area will be losing lift and consequently the lateral stability of the aircraft will reduce quite substantially. When this happens the aeroplane tends to exhibit strong rolling movements towards the wing that is more deeply involved in the stall and very sharp wing dropping is possible. If flaps are used during a power-on stall rapid wing dropping is likely. Figure 73 illustrates the difference between power-on and power-off stalls.

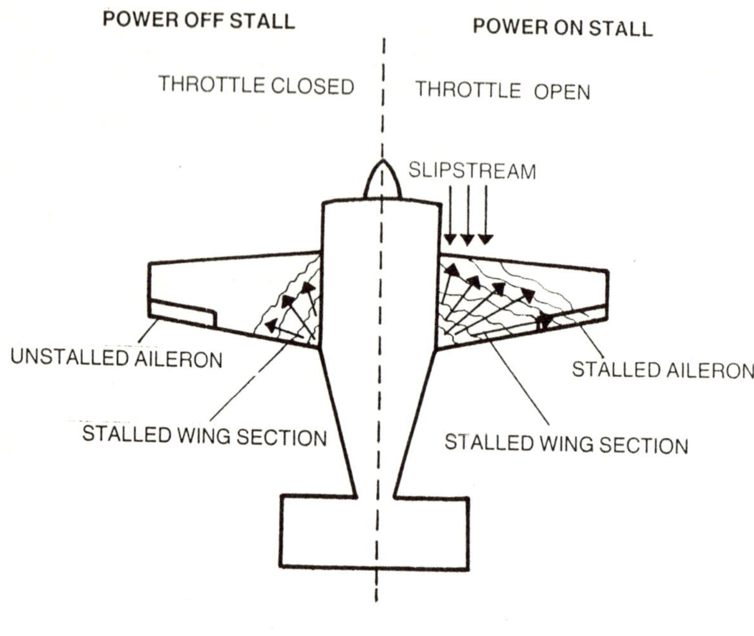

Fig. 73

Stalling characteristics in the turn

When an aeroplane stalls during turning flight, a wing drop is highly probable. During a climbing turn the outer wing is at a slightly higher angle of attack than the lower wing. If the aeroplane is stalled in this condition the higher wing usually stalls first and results in an abrupt reversal of bank attitude. On the other hand, during a descending turn the lower wing is at a larger angle of attack, so when the aircraft stalls the lower wing will drop usually, leading to a sharp increase in bank angle.

In reality, without experience in a particular aeroplane it is very difficult to predict which wing will drop during any stalled flight condition, since even seemingly minor factors such as small dents or dirt on the leading edges may induce one wing to stall before the other. Although wing dropping cannot be prevented entirely, aircraft are usually designed with one or more methods of maintaining a degree of lateral stability as the stalling angle is approached.

Stall Propagation

As an aeroplane reaches its critical angle of attack the entire wing sections do not stall, although this is suggested by the behaviour of the aeroplane. A stall develops progressively and the wings will always be producing some lift. The way a stall develops along a wing is determined largely by its shape, although additional design features incorporated in the wings have a significant influence. Figure 74 illustrates the stall patterns on four typical wing plan forms.

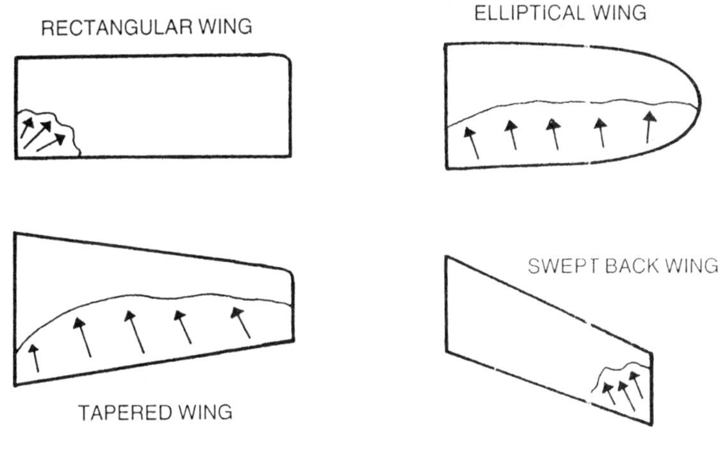

Fig. 74

Note particularly the stall pattern on the rectangular wing, which is a commonly used design on most light training aircraft. The stall begins at the wing root at the trailing edge of the wing and propagates outward. This is an ideal stall pattern since the turbulent airflow from this section of wing usually strikes the elevators causing a tail buffet (a shuddering of the aeroplane) which provides the pilot with an early warning symptom of the impending stall. In addition, the wingtips are able to remain flying for a longer period, allowing the ailerons to maintain a degree of effectiveness.

On the other hand, a tip stall, as indicated on the swept wing, may not provide a warning buffet, since the tail surfaces do not lie directly behind the stalled portion of the wing. In addition, the ailerons become ineffective early on in the stall and the chances of a rapid wing drop are increased.

The root stall is by far the most desirable characteristic and therefore aircraft wings are generally designed to exhibit optimum root stall patterns. There are four methods commonly used to achieve this.

Washout

With this design method a wing is twisted slightly along its length so that the inboard section is always at a higher angle of attack than the outboard section. This will force the wing root to stall before the wingtip.

Variable airfoil wings

This method is similar to washout, except that the wing is made up of two or more aerofoils. The aerofoils near the root are designed to have smaller stalling angles of attack than those at the tip. Again, the result is a root stall.

Stall strips

These are narrow lengths of metal, usually of triangular cross section, which are attached spanwise along the leading edge of a wing. As the angle of attack increases a stall strip interferes with the airflow, inducing the wing section directly behind it to stall. In this way the initial stall pattern can be placed almost anywhere along a wing.

Slats

These are movable aerofoils attached to the leading edge of a wing. They are operated manually or automatically.

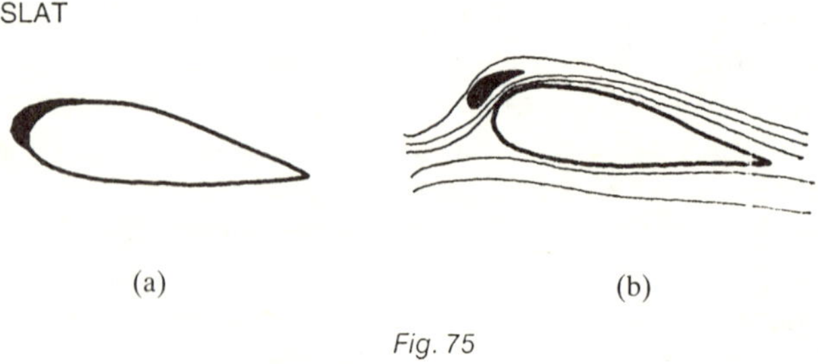

Fig. 75

When the slat is in the closed position, as in (a), it forms the leading edge of the wing. In the open position a gap (slot) is formed between the actual leading edge and the slat (b). This results in a venturi-type effect being created; the increased airflow velocity at the leading edge preserving the lift in the section directly behind the slat. It can be seen that if the slats are incorporated within the outboard sections of the wings a root stall is likely to occur first and any wing-dropping tendency delayed. Also, aileron effectiveness is maintained for longer.

Slots have the same effects as slats, except that they are integrated into the wing structure normally near the leading edge. Both these design features help reduce the stalling speed of the aeroplane.

On the subject of wing design, it must be noted that the stalling angle of a wing will depend on its overall shape and aspect ratio. The lower the aspect ratio the higher the stalling angle. For most modern training aircraft the stalling angle is usually about 20°.

If you have not done so already, it will be well worth having a good look at your aeroplane to find out what design features are employed.

Symptoms of a Stall

Whatever the factors that may induce an aeroplane to stall there will always be warning symptoms present. To avoid a stall pilots must be able to recognize these symptoms instinctively and take recovery action as soon as the situation is interpreted. Listed below are six symptoms that indicate an approach to a basic stall (with the throttle closed and flaps up) from the level flight attitude:

1. reducing airspeed and high nose attitude
2. reducing effectiveness of the controls
3. stall warner. (Most training aircraft are fitted with a device that gives an audible and/or visual warning inside the cockpit that comes into operation 5-10 knots before the stall)
4. Buffeting. This is the turbulent airflow striking the elevators and is felt through the control column
5. nose drop although the control column is held fully back, and possible wing drop
6. rapid loss of height

It must be noted that these symptoms may not all be present during every situation an aeroplane can stall in. For example, if an aeroplane is flown too slowly with insufficient engine power, it will start to sink. The relative airflow will approach from below and the

CONFIGURATION	RATE OF SPEED REDUCTION	NOSE ATTITUDE	STALLING SPEED	WING DROP
BASIC STALL (POWER OFF AND FLAPS UP)	NORMAL	NORMAL (HIGH)	NORMAL (AS INDICATED)	POSSIBLE
BASIC STALL WITH FLAPS (POWER OFF)	FAST	LOWER THAN NORMAL	LOWER THAN NORMAL	MORE POSSIBLE
POWER ON STALL (NO FLAPS)	SLOW	HIGHER THAN NORMAL	LOWER	MORE POSSIBLE
POWER ON STALL WITH FLAPS	NORMAL	NORMAL	LOWER	PROBABLE
STALL IN TURN	FAST	LOW	HIGHER THAN NORMAL	POSSIBLE

Fig. 76

stalling angle can easily be reached while the aircraft is maintaining a level flight attitude. The aeroplane will be losing height rapidly without the feeling of a stall. The recognition of a stall, or potential stall, requires you to be aware that things may not be quite what you expect them to be.

Stalling in Different Configurations

The chief differences from the basic stall when stalling with power-on, with flaps or in a turn will be in the nose attitude at the stall, the rate of speed reduction as the stalling angle is approached, the stalling speed and the possibility of a wing drop. The table opposite can be used as a guide to these differences, which are compared to the basic stall. In the air lesson you will be practising stalling in various configurations and you will be able to observe the exact differences in your own aircraft.

Stalling at steeper angles of bank will be covered under 'Advanced Turning' (p. 254).

Slow Flight

Prior to commencing stall training you are likely to have a session of slow-flight practice. Slow flight is defined as flight below the maximum endurance speed to just above the stalling speed. This is a very important exercise since it will develop your skill in handling the aeroplane at the very slow airspeeds that occur during the take-off and landing phases. In addition, it will help develop your ability to recognize a potential stall.

Aeroplane behaviour during slow flight

Figure 77 illustrates a typical power required curve.

Note that to fly at speeds above the maximum endurance speed (in the region of normal command) extra power is required to maintain level flight. To fly at speeds below the maximum endurance speed (in the region of reversed command) additional power is also required for level flight. Now, an aeroplane's behaviour will change significantly when flying on either side of the power curve and it is very important to recognize these differences.

When flying in the region of normal command an aeroplane has what is known as speed stability, i.e. the tendency to return to its trimmed state whenever the speed fluctuates (provided the power setting is constant). However, when flying in the region of

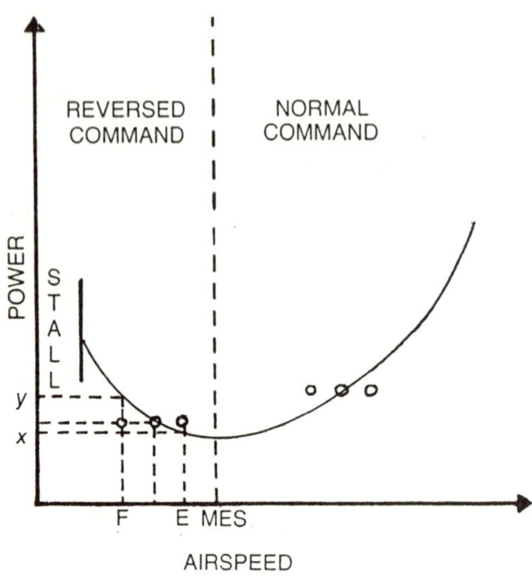

Fig. 77

reversed command, if the nose is lowered the airspeed will increase (E) and to maintain this higher speed a lower power is required (x) or the aeroplane will climb due to the excess power. In other words, at speeds below the maximum endurance speed lowering the nose will cause a climb. On the other hand, if the nose is raised the airspeed will decrease (F) and more power (y) will be required for level flight or the aeroplane will descend due to the power deficiency. In other words, in the region of reversed command raising the nose causes a descent. It can be seen that to arrest a sink rate when flying below the maximum endurance speed will require an increase in power and lowering of the nose. In addition to these characteristics a high-nose attitude and greatly reduced effectiveness of the controls will be present.

AIRMANSHIP

The airmanship checks before performing manoeuvres such as stalling are usually carried out using the mnemonic HASELL.

Height

Since stalling practice involves considerable loss of height, it is normal practice to ensure that the aeroplane is able to recover with at least 3,000 feet above ground level as a safety margin.

Airframe
Check that the brakes are off and select the flaps and/or slats as required. Ensure the aircraft is properly trimmed and the gyro instruments are caged if necessary.

Security
Check that the hatches/doors and seat belts are secure and that there are no articles such as maps, headsets etc. lying loosely around the cockpit.

Engine
Check that the temperatures and pressures are normal and ensure that the mixture control is in the fully rich position. Check for carburettor icing and leave the control on throughout the manoeuvre if recommended for your aeroplane. Switch on the fuel booster pump if necessary.

Location
Always ensure that stalling practice takes place well clear of controlled airspace. In addition, ensure that you are not above towns, active airfields or other aircraft.

Lookout
This should be done by making clearing turns and looking out all around, especially below the aeroplane.

AIR LESSON

Slow Flight
From normal cruising flight start reducing airspeed while maintaining level flight. For speeds within the normal range, reductions in power will be required. However, at a certain point increases in power will be necessary to maintain level flight.

Trim the aeroplane to fly level at a speed a few knots above the stalling speed. Note the positive use of rudder pressure that is required for balanced flight and the larger control movements needed to obtain a desired response from the aeroplane. Note the pitch attitude of the aircraft.

Carry out climbs, descents and turning manoeuvres at this airspeed.

Repeat this exercise with flaps lowered.

Symptoms of a Stall (Demonstration)

Your instructor will enter a basic stall with the flaps retracted in the following way and point out the symptoms as they occur.

1. HASELL.
2. Close the throttle.
3. Keeping the wings level and the aeroplane in balance start raising the nose in order to prevent a loss in height and note the rate of airspeed reduction and the reducing effectiveness of the flying controls.
4. Maintain the back pressure and be alert for the stall warner. The pre-stall buffets should be felt soon afterwards and this will normally be followed by a nose drop.
5. Note the rate of height loss.

The Recovery without Power

Once the aeroplane has stalled your instructor will demonstrate that by simply easing forward on the control column the aeroplane will start to accelerate and once a safe airspeed has been achieved fully controllable flight will be resumed again. Note, however, the considerable height loss.

The Standard Stall Recovery

After performing the HASELL checks note the height then enter a basic stall in the same manner as above, then, as soon as the nose begins to drop:

1. Apply full power while easing the control column gently forward. Be ready to counteract the effects of power.
2. At a safe airspeed proceed into a climb or straight and level flight as required.

Note the reduced height loss compared to a recovery without power and also that the control column does not need as much forward pressure during the recovery.

You will be practising several stalls and recoveries and once you are proficient in the technique the emphasis will be on recovering with a minimum loss of height.

Dealing with a Wing Drop

Use **opposite rudder** to prevent yaw when a wing drops. The wings can be levelled in the usual way once a safe airspeed has been achieved.

An attempt to raise the dropped wing using the ailerons is likely to cause the wing to drop further. (The lowered aileron increases the mean angle of attack of the stalled wing.) The aim is initially not to raise the wing immediately but to prevent the further effect of yaw.

Stalling with Power

After carrying out the HASELL checks approach a stall with a little engine power on, and note the slower rate of speed reduction and the steeper nose attitude at the stall. Be prepared for a wing drop. Note the lower stalling speed.

Recover using the standard stall recovery.

Stalling with Flaps

Carry out the HASELL checks and approach a power-off stall with flaps lowered. Note the faster rate of speed reduction and the nose attitude at the stall. A sharper nose drop is likely and the stalling speed will be lower. Be prepared for a possible wing drop.

Recover using the standard technique and note that positive pressure on the control column is required.

Stalling with Power and Flaps (in the Approach to Land Configuration)

HASELL

Enter a normal powered descent with full flaps lowered and trim. Start raising the nose slowly until the aeroplane stalls. Be ready for a wing drop. Note particularly the nose attitude at the stall.

Recover using the standard stall recovery.

Stalling in a Turn

Enter a medium gliding turn with flaps lowered and move the control column backwards until the aeroplane stalls. Be prepared for a wing drop. Note the fast rate of speed reduction, the higher stalling speed and the pitch attitude at the stall.

Recover using the standard stall recovery.

Practise stalling in the turn with different amounts of power.

Recovery at the Incipient Stage of a Stall

HASELL

Note the height and approach a basic power-off stall in the normal way. As soon as the pre-stall buffets are felt carry out the normal recovery action, and note the height loss.

Approach another stall and this time recover as soon as the stall warner is activated. Note the height loss.

Repeat this exercise while approaching a stall in all the configurations so far practised (with power, flaps, in turns etc.).

Remember, the objective of stall training is *stall avoidance*. In order to avoid an inadvertent stall, recovery action must be taken as soon as the earliest symptom is recognized.

Instructor's Guide
Ex. 10

LESSON PLAN

Stall awareness

Objectives

To introduce the student to flight at minimum controllable airspeed (slow flight); to teach the student to recognize the symptoms of an approaching stall; to teach the student the stall recovery technique; to train the student to carry out the recovery actions instinctively as soon as the earliest symptoms are recognized; and ultimately, to instil in the student the dangers of mishandling the flying controls.

Content

1 Preflight briefing

Revise previous lessons and discuss the importance of stall awareness; discuss the airmanship considerations (HASELL), slow flight and aircraft handling, the symptoms of a stall, stalling speeds and the recovery technique (Standard Stall Recovery) including how to deal with a wing drop.

2 Flight lesson

Review:

(a) all preflight procedures
(b) engine starting and radio communications
(c) taxi-ing and power and pretake-off checks
(d) take-off and circuit departure
(e) revise previous manoeuvres, then: *Demonstrate flight at minimum controllable airspeed. Student practice. Perform HASELL checks then demonstrate the symptoms leading to a stall, and a full stall. Demonstrate the recovery technique. Student practice. Demonstrate how height loss can be minimized when the recovery is made at the incipient stages of the stall. Student practice. (See the* 'Air Lesson' (p. 153) *for a*

full description of the flight exercise.)
(f) circuit rejoin, approach, landing and parking.

3 Postflight discussion and preview of the next lesson

LESSON PLAN

Stall awareness Part Two

Objectives
To develop further the student's stall awareness by introducing stalls in different flying configurations.

Content
1 Preflight briefing
Revise previous lessons, discuss objectives and airmanship considerations of this lesson, explain the differences between the basic stall and stalls in different configurations.

2 Flight lesson
Review:

(a) all preflight procedures
(b) take-off and circuit departure
(c) revise previous manoeuvres, slow flight and basic stalls and recoveries, then: *Demonstrate stalling and recovering from the various flight configurations (with power and flaps, during turns etc.). Student practice. (See the* 'Air Lesson' (p. 153) *for a full description of the exercise)*
(d) circuit rejoin, approach, landing and parking

3 Postflight discussion and preview of the next lesson

Completion Standards
These training sessions will have been successfully completed when the student can perform manoeuvres at minimum controllable airspeed to a reasonable standard; can recognize stall indications and can execute safe and prompt recoveries with minimum height loss.

Exercise 11

SPINNING

Objectives

1. To teach you to recognize the early stages in the development of a spin and to execute a safe recovery.
2. To teach you to recover from a fully developed spin.

In the previous lesson it was explained that when an aircraft stalls it is in a condition of uncontrollable flight until recovery action is taken by the pilot. Rapid losses of height will occur and such a situation is likely to be fatal at low altitudes, particularly if the stall is allowed to develop into a spin. Under controlled conditions and at high altitudes a spin is a very safe and exciting manoeuvre. However, if an aeroplane spins inadvertently at low altitudes such as during the approach to land phase, there will be insufficient height in which to execute a recovery and a fatal accident is probable. In the air lesson you will discover just how much height is lost during a spin and its recovery, and you will appreciate this effect should a spin occur at low altitudes. The underlying objective of this lesson is to ensure you understand that, in order to avoid accidents occurring, you must fly the aeroplane strictly according to the techniques and procedures you have been taught which have been designed to avoid dangerous flight conditions.

Development of a Spin

The spin

A spin is a condition of stalled flight during which the aeroplane is continually pitching up, rolling and yawing (relative to the horizon) while describing a spiralling descent path involving considerable loss of height. An aeroplane will continue to spin until recovery action is taken by the pilot. A spin can only develop when an aircraft is at or close to a stall. In normal flight conditions an aeroplane will not enter a spin. However, any situation which brings an aeroplane close to its stalling angle, either intentionally or through incorrect handling of the flying controls, the chances of a spin entry are increased. Therefore, in order to avoid an inadvertent spin you must avoid flying the aeroplane close to a stall.

Spin entry

It was explained in the lesson on stalling that as the critical angle is approached, for various reasons one wing may drop. If the recovery actions are not taken a sideslip and yaw will take place in the direction of the dropped wing. The relative airflow experienced by the dropped wing causes it to become further stalled, while the upgoing wing becomes partially unstalled. The resultant increase in bank will induce more sideslip and yaw, the aircraft will pitch downwards and the continuing inequality of lift of the two wings will produce an automatic rolling action known as autorotation. The aeroplane will now have entered the incipient stages of a spin and will be out of control until the correct recovery action is taken.

Spinning Characteristics

The behaviour of an aeroplane during a spin depends on various complex factors which are not discussed in this manual. It is difficult to make generalizations which are true for all aircraft, since one aeroplane may behave in a particular way during a spin and another completely differently under the same conditions. It can be said, however, that if the aerodynamic and inertia forces and their moments can achieve a state of equilibrium during a spin, an aeroplane will settle down into a stable spin with a steady rate of descent and rate of rotation.

The pitch attitude adopted by an aeroplane during a spin will depend largely on design characteristics and the position of the centre of gravity. Basically, an aeroplane with large heavy wings and a small fuselage tends to adopt a flat pitch angle and spins at a faster rate. The recovery action may be difficult in such an aircraft. On the other hand, an aeroplane that has a long fuselage with short wings will tend to have a steeper pitch angle and a slower spin rate, which makes recovery easier. A forward centre-of-gravity position will also cause a steep spin and a faster rate of descent. The recovery will also be easier with a forward centre-of-gravity position since the spin tends to be less stable. In certain cases an extreme forward centre of gravity may prevent the aeroplane entering a true spin, the aircraft instead entering a very steep spiralling descent (autorotative spiral). An aft centre of gravity, however, causes a flatter spin, during which the rate of descent is less. Such a spin tends to be more stable, making recovery action difficult. An extreme aft centre-of-gravity position can result in a very stable spin from which an aircraft may not be able to recover.

It must be mentioned here that in some aeroplanes spinning is prohibited altogether, whereas in others it is permitted only under certain weight conditions. Consult the Flight Manual to obtain this information.

Due to their design characteristics, some aircraft resist entering a true spin despite deliberate attempts by the pilot. In such cases the aeroplane will tend to enter an autorotative spiral, during which the airspeed and rate of descent will be increasing.

Inducing a Spin

In the air lesson your instructor will demonstrate a spin and recovery so that you become accustomed to the manoeuvre. The aeroplane will be brought close to a stall with the power off and the flaps retracted. Just before the stall occurs, usually at the buffeting stage, full rudder will be applied in the direction of the intended spin and the control column will be held fully back. The aeroplane will now enter a spin. During the spin the pressure on the control column and rudder pedal must be maintained. Your instructor will point out the high rate of descent as indicated on the altimeter and VSI, the tendency of the airspeed to remain at a low figure and the spin direction as indicated on the Turn Indicator, which always gives the true direction of a spin in case of any doubt. As the aeroplane spins, vibrations and buffeting may be felt.

The Recovery

After a few rotations the instructor will carry out the recovery actions. Now, since yaw is the primary cause of the spin this must be removed by applying full rudder in the opposite direction to the spin, i.e. if the aeroplane is spinning to the left apply full right rudder and vice versa. Always check the Turn Indicator for confirmation of spin direction. Then, after a short pause to allow the rudder to become effective, the control column must be moved forward to unstall the wings until the spin stops. Note that the amount of forward movement of the control column will vary according to the stage of the spin. A fully developed spin is likely to require full forward movement to effect a recovery while the incipient stages may only require partial movement. Just before the spin stops the rate of rotation may increase. This is an indication that the correct recovery action has been taken. When the spin stops the rudder pedals must be centralized. The aeroplane will now be in a dive, from which the pilot must level the wings in the normal way and gently proceed into a climb, or straight and level flight, as required. While coming out of the dive, care must be taken not to make abrupt movements of the control column to avoid a secondary stall occurring.

The technique described above is known as the Standard Spin Recovery and you are advised to memorize the control actions (presented clearly in the 'Air Lesson' section (see p. 164).

In some aeroplanes the recovery actions may be different, so consult the Flight Manual to determine the exact spin recovery procedure for your aeroplane.

In the event of the aeroplane entering an autorotative spiral (which will be recognized by increasing airspeed) the recovery action is the same as for a spin except that a lesser amount of both rudder pressure and forward movement of the control column will be required to effect a recovery.

Effects of Power during a Spin and Recovery

When entering an intentional spin in training aircraft power is not normally used because the effects of yaw on the slipstream path may increase the rate of rotation during the spin. Additionally, since the aeroplane will be established in a dive following the recovery, there is a greater risk of exceeding structural limitation speeds (Vne) and also the engine speeds (red line on the RPM gauge). For the same reasons power is not used to assist the recovery, unless specifically stated in the Flight Manual.

However, since power may indeed be on in the event of an inadvertent spin, a check that the throttle is closed completely will be the first control action in the recovery procedure (see 'Air Lesson' (p. 164)).

Effects of Flaps

Spinning with flaps lowered is strictly forbidden in most aeroplanes due to the risk of exceeding the flap limiting speed during the recovery. Additionally, flaps tend to affect the airflow striking both the rudder and the elevators and may subsequently reduce their effectiveness during the recovery. Therefore, a check that the flaps are raised must also form part of the recovery procedure.

The Incipient Spin and Recovery

This will be a very important exercise as it will develop your ability to recognize the conditions which may lead to a spin entry and also train you to take immediate recovery action.

The aeroplane will be brought close to a stall in the normal way, usually with a little power on to simulate an approach configuration. Then, just before the stall occurs, rudder pressure will be applied in the desired direction and the control column will be moved back slowly. These actions will produce a marked wing drop and the beginnings of a spin. Then, as the nose drops, the following recovery actions must be taken – move the control column forward to unstall the wings, centralize the rudder pedals and use to prevent further yaw and add power to assist the recovery if required. The aeroplane will then be established in a dive from which a return to normal flight conditions can be made by the co-ordinated use of the elevators, ailerons and rudder.

The amount of power to be used during the recovery will depend on the pitch attitude adopted by the aeroplane following the spin entry. A relatively flat nose attitude will require full power. Use of full power when the nose attitude is steep, however, may result in an excessive speed build-up. Therefore, in such a case power should only be added once the aeroplane has come out of the dive.

AIRMANSHIP

The HASELL checks are also used before carrying out spinning manoeuvres. Particular emphasis will be placed on lookouts, since during a spin the aeroplane will be losing height rapidly and will also be out of control and therefore unable to take collision avoidance actions.

Spinning practice should take place at high altitudes, aiming to recover with a safety margin of at least 3000ft agl remaining as in the lesson on stalling.

Care must be taken to keep well clear of controlled airspace and any other areas which may have a lot of aerial traffic. Prior to entering a spin a landmark is usually chosen for orientation purposes.

The Flight Manual must be consulted before the flight to check that the aeroplane is cleared for intentional spins and also if there are any weight and balance requirements to be considered before spinning takes place.

Finally, it must be noted that in order to conform to the ANO regulations a safety harness must be worn throughout spinning manoeuvres.

AIR LESSON

Entering a Spin

1. HASELL.
2. Approach a clean power-off stall in the normal way.
3. Just before the stall occurs apply full rudder smoothly in the direction desired and at the same time hold the control column fully back. The aeroplane will now enter a spin.

During the spin demonstration note the high rate of descent, the low airspeed indication and the direction of the spin shown on the Turn Indicator.

The Standard Spin Recovery

To recover from a spin:

1. Check – throttle closed and flaps up.
2. Check – Turn Indicator then apply full opposite rudder.
3. Pause.
4. Move the control column forward until the spin stops.
5. When the spin stops, centralize the rudder pedals.
6. Level the wings and ease out of the dive.
7. Proceed into a climb or straight and level flight.

You will be practising entering and recovering from spins from climbing, descending and turning flight – the main objective here being to show you how easily an aeroplane may enter a spin through incorrect handling of the flying controls.

The Incipient Spin and Recovery

Approach a normal clean power off stall and just before the stall occurs apply progressively increasing rudder pressure in the desired direction and slowly move the control column backwards until a wing starts to drop (incipient spin).

To recover:

1. Move control column forward and centralize the rudder pedals.
2. Power on as required.
3. Apply sufficient rudder pressure to prevent further yaw.
4. Level the wings and return to normal flight.

You will be practising entering and recovering from incipient spins from climbing, descending and turning flight.

Instructor's Guide
Ex. 11

LESSON PLAN

Incipient Spin Recognition and Recovery

Objectives
To develop further the recognition of stall indications; to demonstrate the effects of a full stall being allowed to develop (incipient stages of a spin) and how to recover from this condition.

Content
1 Preflight briefing
Revise previous lessons, discuss objectives and airmanship points of this lesson, discuss the incipient stages of a spin and the recovery actions.

2 Flight lesson
Review:

(a) all preflight procedures
(b) take-off and circuit departure
(c) revise slow flight and stalling exercises, then; *demonstrate the incipient spin and the recovery. Student practice.* (*See* 'Air Lesson' (p. 164))
(d) circuit rejoin, approach, landing and parking.

3 Postflight discussion and preview of the next lesson

LESSON PLAN

Full Spin and Recovery

Objectives
To introduce the student to the sensations and symptoms of a full spin and to teach the recovery technique.

Content

1 Preflight briefing

Revise the incipient spin exercise, discuss the objectives of this lesson, explain the entry to a full spin, the symptoms of a spin (high rate of rotation, low airspeed etc.) and the Standard Spin Recovery.

2 Flight lesson

Review:

(a) all preflight procedures
(b) take-off and circuit departure
(c) revise slow flight, stalling and incipient spin recoveries, then: *demonstrate a full spin and the recovery. Student practice.* (*See* 'Air Lesson' (p. 164))
(d) circuit rejoin, approach, landing and parking.

3 Postflight discussion and preview of the next lesson

Completion Standards

These lessons will have been successfully completed when the student can perform flight at minimum controllable airspeed, maintaining the assigned speed within ± 10 kts, with minimum assistance from the instructor; can instinctively recognize and recover from incipient and full stalls, and incipient and full spins.

Circuit Training

Having covered the basic handling exercises the next few hours of training will be spent teaching you to take off and land the aeroplane. It is quite likely that you have already received some instruction in this on previous flights. However, these lessons will concentrate specifically on teaching you the various techniques

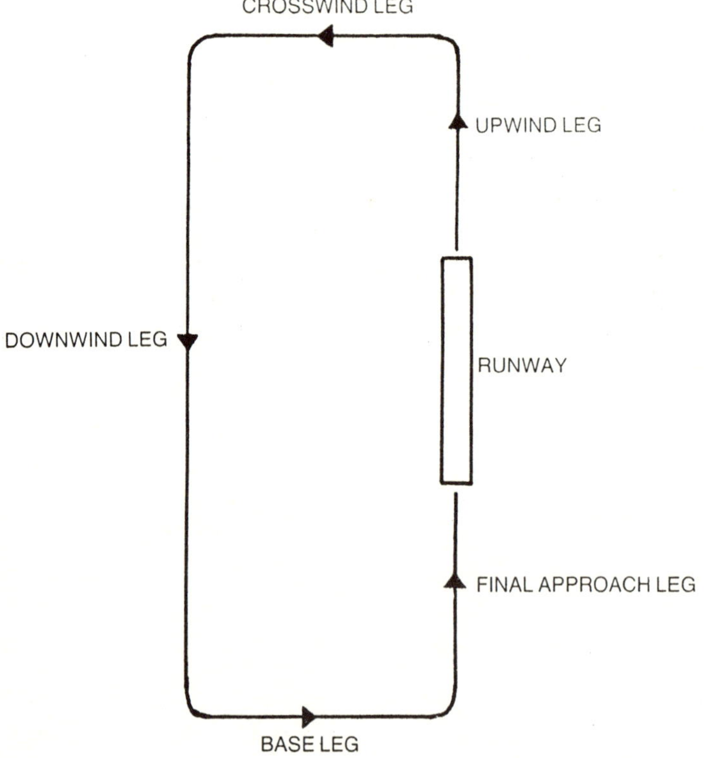

Fig. 78

and procedures that are used. Additionally, you will be taught how to fly in the airfield traffic pattern, or circuit as it is commonly called (see Fig. 78).

Flying in the circuit will require all the handling skills and procedures you have learnt so far, apart from stalling and spinning, of course. Climbs, descents, straight and level flight and turns will all be brought together in a very practical exercise which will sharpen your flying skills as you will be required to fly the aeroplane very accurately. This is also likely to be the first time you will be flying the aeroplane and positively orientating yourself around a ground reference (the airfield and runway) and you will be learning how to make allowances for the effects of wind. At some stage you will also be taught how to cope with engine failures after take-off and abandoned take-offs.

During circuit training you will become more familiar with the airfield layout, regarding runways, taxiways, unusable areas and so on, and also general aerodrome procedures. Emphasis will be placed on airmanship considerations, particularly lookouts, due to the density and proximity of other traffic, both in the air and on the ground. Once you are proficient in taking-off and landing the aeroplane and your performance around the circuit is satisfactory, you will be sent on a first solo flight.

The factors affecting a take-off and various take-off techniques will be covered in the next chapter entitled 'The Take-Off and Initial Climbout'. Similar information on the landing phase of a flight is covered under the chapter entitled 'The Approach and Landing', which will follow a detailed section on flying in the circuit.

Exercise 12

THE TAKE-OFF AND INITIAL CLIMBOUT

Objectives

1. to teach you to take the aeroplane off the ground under a variety of different surface and wind conditions
2. to teach you to cope with an engine failure after take-off.

The Take-Off

In order to become airborne an aeroplane's wings have to produce sufficient lift. This means the aircraft must be accelerated to a speed which will create the required lift, then through the use of the elevators it must be gently induced to leave the ground. This is the basic take-off method.

The speed at which the lift-off takes place must be sufficient for the pilot to maintain control of the aeroplane immediately after leaving the ground and is worked out as 1.15 times the stalling speed of the particular aeroplane. Once airborne, the aircraft must be allowed to accelerate naturally to climbing speeds before adopting normal climbing attitudes.

Factors Affecting the Take-Off

During any take-off there are two main objectives:

1. to take the aeroplane off the ground safely within the available distance
2. to overfly safely any obstructions in the immediate climbing path.

In order to take off within the available distance the aeroplane must be accelerated as quickly as possible to the lift-off speed. In most aircraft this will require the use of full power. The shorter the take-off run, the greater will be the net angle of the initial climbout, thus increasing the clearance in the climbing path (see Fig. 79).

Therefore, it can be seen that the aim during any take-off should be to get airborne as quickly as possible. Now, there are four main

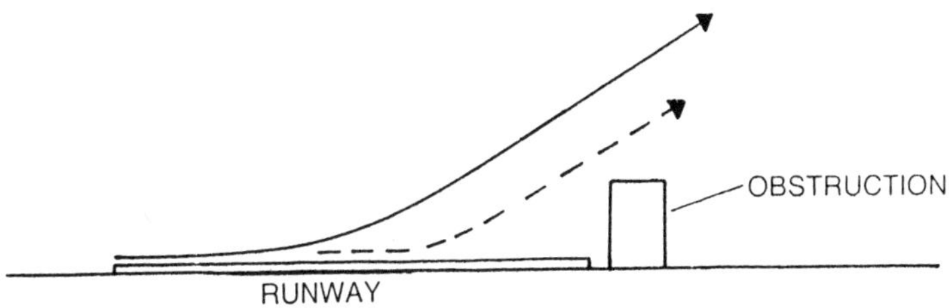

Fig. 79

factors that influence the length of the take-off run and hence the angle of the initial climbout which must be understood by all pilots.

Ground surface

The nature of the ground surface will have a significant effect on the take-off run and may therefore require adjustments to the take-off technique. Soft surfaces such as grass or sand will increase the take-off run appreciably and if such surfaces are wet the increases can be quite considerable. The runway gradient will also affect the length of the take-off run. Upslopes increase the distance and downslopes decrease the distance.

Wind

The strength and direction of the wind will have the most significant effect on both the length of the take-off run and obstacle clearance during the climbout. When an aircraft takes off into a headwind it is able to reach its lift-off speed at a lower ground speed, thus reducing the ground run. Additionally, climbing out into a headwind increases the climbing angle thereby increasing obstacle clearance. On the other hand, a tailwind requires the aeroplane to reach a higher ground speed in order to attain its lift-off speed. This means that a longer take-off run will be required and during the climbout the angle of climb will be shallower.

From this it can be seen that for the best results and for added safety take-offs should always be made as much into a headwind as possible. When the wind direction and the take-off run are out of line, there will be a tendency for the aeroplane to yaw into the wind. This will require an adjustment to the take-off technique. Additionally, the wing on the side from which the wind is coming will have a tendency to rise. In such conditions the rudder and the ailerons will have to be used to counter these effects during the ground roll so that direction and control is maintained.

Weight

Since the take-off speed of an aeroplane is calculated as 1.15 × the stalling speed of the aeroplane, any increase in weight (which increases the stalling speed) will also increase the take-off speed. This means that the length of the take-off run will increase and is another reason why weight limitations must never be exceeded.

Air temperature and pressure (density altitude)

The efficiency of an aeroplane's wings in producing a given value of lift and the efficiency of an engine and propeller in producing power and thrust will depend significantly on the density of the surrounding air. For any given angle of attack the less dense the air is, the greater must be the true airspeed achieved for a given value of lift to be created. Additionally, the power output from the engine, and hence the thrust, will reduce as air density decreases. The combined result of this during a take-off will be to increase the length of the take-off run. Now it is extremely important that you are able to determine the effects of the prevailing air density on the take-off performance of your aeroplane, especially when operating out of high-altitude airfields and/or under hot and humid conditions. In order to do this you must work out the density altitude. This is the current pressure altitude corrected for non-standard temperature variations. Having determined the density altitude you then can proceed on to working out the take-off distance, taking into consideration the factors already mentioned (wind, weight and ground surface). Detailed information of such calculations will be contained in the performance section of the Flight Manual which will include various graphs, tables and also some examples for your understanding. You are advised to become thoroughly familiar with this section of the Flight Manual.

Aircraft Behaviour during the Take-Off

The application of take-off power, which is maximum power or full throttle in training aeroplanes, will cause a yawing tendency during the take-off run. The direction of yaw will depend on the direction of the propeller rotation and since this is clockwise in most training aircraft the yaw will be to the left. The two main reasons for this are slipstream and torque reaction.

The yawing effects of slipstream have already been discussed in earlier chapters and this becomes more pronounced during a take-off due to the application of maximum power.

Torque reaction is quite simply a reaction of propeller rotation. The propeller rotates in one direction, causing the aeroplane to attempt to rotate in the opposite direction. In the air this effect is not noticeable since the lateral stability of the aeroplane tends to oppose it. On the ground, however, the effect of torque will cause one main landing gear to experience more pressure than the other, producing a slight yawing tendency. Again, the direction of yaw will depend on the direction of propeller rotation and is usually to the left (see Fig. 80).

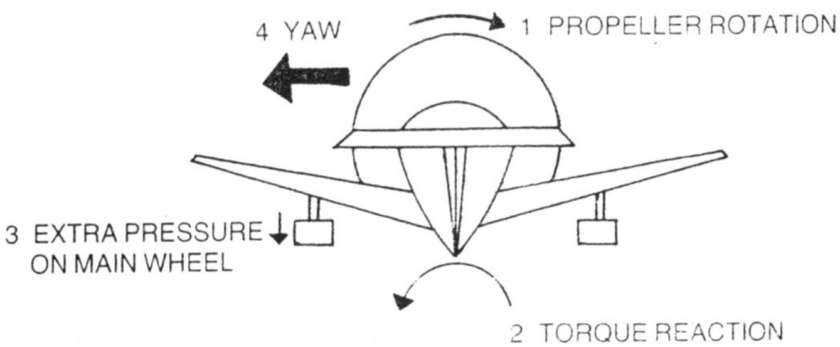

Fig. 80

In addition to torque and slipstream there are two more factors that produce a yaw during the take-off roll. These are propeller precession and asymmetric propeller thrust.

Briefly, since a rotating propeller is essentially a gyroscope, it will possess gyroscopic properties and will therefore be affected by a turning tendency known as precession. Gyroscopic precession is a deflection that arises when a force is applied to a spinning object. The reaction to a force applied to a gyro will take place about 90° from the point of application in the direction of the rotation. For example, imagine a stationary upright disc spinning clockwise freely in mid-air. Applying a force to the top of the spinning disc will not simply tip it over as might be expected, but will cause it to turn to the left as if the force were applied to the right side of the disc. So, in the case of a propeller, this means that whenever an aeroplane is moved rapidly from a nose-high to a nose-low attitude, precession will cause a tendency for a yaw to the left to occur (on aeroplanes with clockwise propeller rotation). This effect is more apparent on tailwheel aircraft as the tail rises during the take-off roll.

When a propeller-driven aircraft is flown at high angles of attack, the thrust produced by the right side of the propeller is greater than that produced on the left (asymmetrical propeller thrust) causing a yaw to the left. Briefly, this is because the downgoing blade on the right side of the engine has a greater angle of attack than the upgoing blade on the left, so producing more thrust. Again, this reaction is more prevalent in tailwheel aircraft during the initial stages of the take-off roll. In normal cruise flight asymmetrical thrust does not occur because both propeller blades are at the same angle of attack and producing equal thrust.

So, in order to maintain direction and control during the take-off run these yawing tendencies must be countered by positive use of the rudder. As speed increases and the rudder becomes more effective, the pressure on the pedals must be adjusted accordingly.

TAKE-OFF TECHNIQUES

Prior to every take-off the power and pre-take-off checks must be fully completed using the checklist. Before taxi-ing on to the take-off area clearance must be obtained from the Air Traffic Service Unit (ATSU), if applicable. Before you taxi into position, ensure that both the landing approach path and the climbout direction are safely clear of traffic.

The Normal Take-Off

A normal take-off is described as a take-off in dry conditions directly into a headwind, i.e. when the wind is blowing directly down the runway, and when the take-off distance required is well within the runway length available (see Fig. 81).

After obtaining the necessary clearance from the ATSU the aeroplane should be positioned in the centre of the runway with the nose or tailwheel straightened. During the ground run ensure

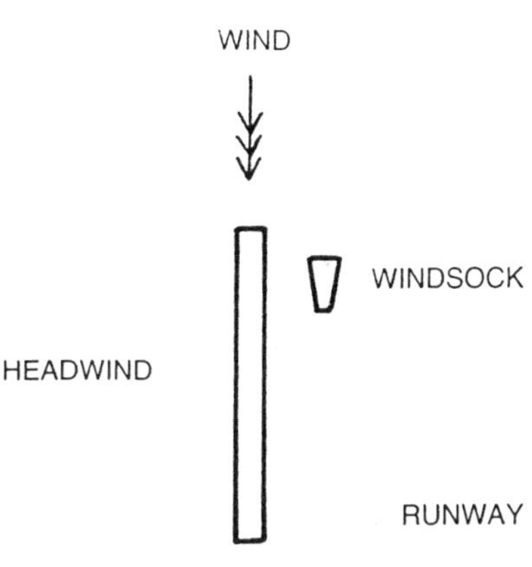

Fig. 81

that your heels are resting on the floor and the balls of your feet are placed firmly on the rudder pedals and well clear of the toe brakes.

The take-off begins with the smooth application of maximum power. Anticipate the swing that will occur as power is applied. Keep your hand on the throttle throughout the take-off. Direction on the ground is to be maintained using the runway centreline, or, if this is not available, a suitable reference feature in the distance can be used. The converging sidelines of the runway will also be useful.

As speed increases start applying a slight back pressure on the control column to ease the weight off the nosewheel. At an early stage during the ground run check that the temperatures and pressures are within normal limits. At the correct lift-off speed apply a positive but gentle backward movement of the control column to lift the aeroplane cleanly into the air. Do not adopt a climbing attitude straight away. Hold an attitude slightly higher than the level flight attitude to allow the airspeed to increase naturally to the required figure, then proceed into a normal climb.

Remember the need to apply constant rudder pressure for balanced flight during the climbout and trim the aeroplane properly.

Ground Effect

When an aeroplane is flown very close to the ground, such as during the take-off and landing phases of flight, a reduction of induced drag will occur. This will significantly affect both the performance and the behavioural characteristics of an aeroplane.

Now, one way of reducing induced drag would be to reduce the amount of upwash ahead of the wing. Fig. 82(a) illustrates a wing flying close to the ground.

IN GROUND EFFECT

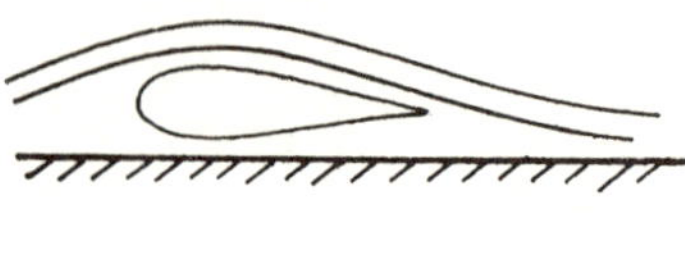

A

ABOVE GROUND EFFECT

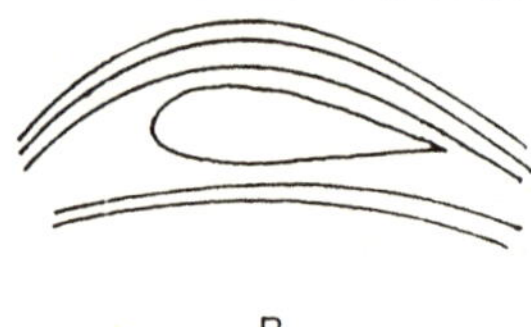

B

Fig. 82

Notice that the amount of upwash in (a) is much less than that in (b). This is because near the ground the air has insufficient room in which to develop any significant vertical movement. Notice also that there is less downwash in (a) – the air from the trailing edge being forced to flow parallel to the ground. Now, the result of this alteration of the airflow will be firstly to reduce the diameters and velocities of wingtip vortices hence reducing induced drag and, secondly, it will modify the downwash angle over the tailplane. The reduction in induced drag will improve aircraft performance in that the aeroplane will be able to lift off at a slower speed. However, it must be noted that although an aeroplane can lift off at a lower speed this does not mean that it can climb above the influence of the ground (the depth of the ground effect area is roughly equal to the span of the aeroplane's wings; above this the ground has no significant influence). Remember, induced drag will increase as the aircraft leaves ground effect and additional power will be required to compensate for this. But since the engine will already be developing maximum available power during the take-off, the increase in drag may induce a stall if a climb is attempted at too slow an airspeed. Additionally, the downwash angle over the tailplane will increase as the aeroplane climbs out of the ground effect and will cause a slight pitching-up tendency, which you may have noticed already. This will further aggravate a slow-speed climb attempt and can also be critical if the aeroplane is loaded at or beyond its aft centre-of-gravity limits.

Now, you will notice that all the take-off techniques described in this manual will stress the need to allow the aeroplane to accelerate naturally to climbing speeds before attempting a normal climb. This is to take advantage of ground effect, since an aeroplane can accelerate more rapidly due to the reduction of induced drag. When the required speed has been reached a normal climb can be safely assumed. This technique is much more efficient than forcing the aeroplane into a premature climb.

All these factors must be borne in mind before every take-off, especially when operating conditions are marginal. The influence of ground effect on landings will be covered later in this book.

The Crosswind Take-Off

This technique is used whenever the wind is blowing at an angle to the runway (crosswinds), as shown in Figure 83.

The method is essentially the same as a take-off into the wind,

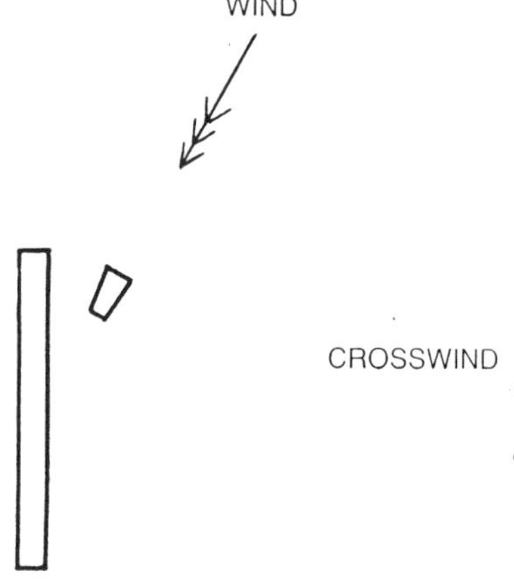

Fig. 83

except with the addition of positive aileron deflection to counter the weathercocking and leaning tendencies (wing rise) caused by the crosswind. The safe and successful execution of a crosswind take-off will depend largely on the pilot's assessment of the strength of the crosswind and accurate control co-ordination.

Pilots must always be aware of the wind direction and speed and also the crosswind component prior to commencing a take-off. Get into the habit of looking at the windsock just before applying take-off power. Also air traffic control will state the wind velocity

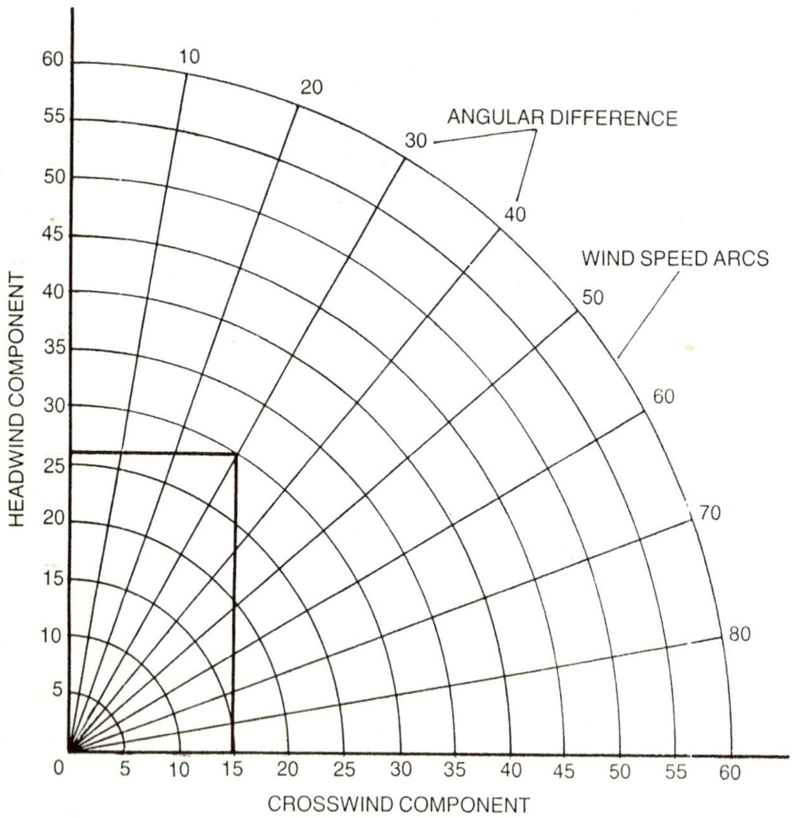

Fig. 84

after giving you take-off clearance, which is helpful.

The crosswind component is that portion of the wind which acts at 90° to the runway and is expressed in terms of velocity. It can also be described as that portion of the wind which will apply a sideways force to the aircraft during the take-off run. Now, it is very important that pilots are able to determine crosswind components, especially when surface wind conditions are strong. This is because aircraft have limiting crosswind components (which will be given in the Flight Manual).

Computing the crosswind component

When the wind is blowing at an angle to the runway it will have two components – a headwind component and a crosswind component. For a given windspeed, the strength of these components will depend on the angular difference between the runway direction and the wind direction. For example, if the runway directions is 270° and the wind is blowing from 300° at 30 knots, the angular difference is 30°. Using this information on the chart in Figure 84 the crosswind component can be found out to be 15 knots and the headwind component to be 26 knots.

A useful rule-of-thumb method for computing an approximate crosswind component is given in the table below (Fig. 85).

		CROSSWIND COMPONENT
ANGULAR DIFFERENCE	30°	½ WIND SPEED
	45°	¾ WIND SPEED
	60°	9/10 WIND SPEED
	90°	TOTAL WIND SPEED

Fig. 85

For example, with a wind velocity of 045/20 kts and a runway heading of 090°, using the table the crosswind component can be worked out to be approximately 15 knots (angular difference of

45° = ¾ wind speed). Notice that when the wind is at 90° to the runway the crosswind component is equal to the total windspeed, i.e. there is no headwind component.

Use of controls during the crosswind take-off

The ailerons are the main controls that are used to counteract the weathercocking and leaning tendencies during a crosswind take-off. The ailerons must be deflected into wind, i.e. the aileron on the side the wind is coming from must be raised. Aileron deflection into wind will, firstly, offset any leaning tendency by keeping the upwind wing down and, secondly, it will help counteract weathercocking by increasing the drag.

The ground run

At the start of the take-off run a large deflection must be applied to the ailerons to prevent the upwind wing from rising. As the speed increases and the controls become more effective, the aileron deflection must be progressively reduced but never fully released until after the lift-off. Rudder pressure is used in the normal way to maintain direction.

Proper use of the elevators is also very important to ensure a successful and safe crosswind take-off. They should be held almost neutral to allow a higher speed to be obtained before lift-off. A higher than normal lift-off speed will reduce the possibility of sudden gusts of wind lifting the aeroplane prematurely off the runway before it has attained sufficient airspeed to remain airborne. Unlike the normal take-off the aircraft should remain on all three wheels (nosewheel aircraft) until the lift-off speed is reached, i.e. the nosewheel should not be completely eased off the runway. This is because the action of the nosewheel on the ground will aid directional stability on the runway and therefore help prevent weathercocking. However, extreme care must be taken not to apply any excessive forward pressure on the control column because of the stresses that will be imposed on the nosewheel as the aeroplane accelerates. Too much forward pressure and excessive airspeed is likely to result in 'wheelbarrowing' which is a dangerous condition where the mainwheels have lifted off the runway, leaving the nosewheel still on the ground.

The lift-off and climbout

When the lift-off speed is reached the aeroplane should be rotated firmly off the runway in the normal way. Immediately after becoming airborne the wings must be levelled and the aeroplane headed into wind a few degrees (crab angle) to avoid being blown away from the initial take-off direction (Fig. 86). Allow the aeroplane to accelerate naturally in the ground effect to climbing speeds before establishing a normal climb.

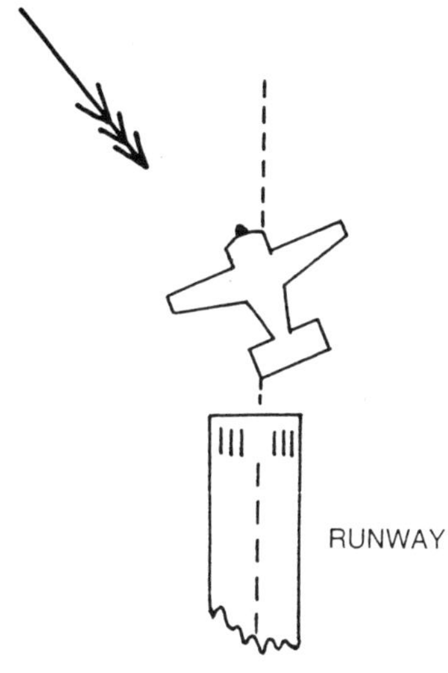

Fig. 86

MAXIMUM PERFORMANCE TAKE-OFFS

Once you are reasonably proficient in straightforward take-offs you will be introduced to the soft field and short-field take-off techniques, which are designed to obtain the maximum performance out of an aeroplane when conditions are marginal. Indeed, you may have to learn these techniques at the start if your airfield requires them to be employed.

The Soft-Field Take-off

This technique is used whenever conditions are wet, particularly on grass runways and especially after snow and heavy rainfall when the ground is likely to be very soft and soggy. Unless the proper take-off method is used in these conditions the lift-off speed may not be attained in the ground run available.

So, the objective of the soft-field take-off is to transfer the weight of the aircraft from the landing gear to the wings as quickly as possible. Basically, in order to do this the aeroplane must be accelerated in a nose-high attitude, which means the nosewheel must be raised off the runway during most of the ground run. This is necessary to avoid the nosewheel sinking into the ground and will allow a quicker acceleration to the lift-off speed. Optimum flap settings are also usually required to obtain a lower lift-off speed and hence reduce the ground run (see the Flight Manual).

Remember also, while taxi-ing prior to take-off the proper soft-field procedures must be followed, i.e. the control column must be held fully back (full up elevator) and a small amount of power used to keep the aircraft moving.

The ground run

In very soft conditions it is advisable that the aeroplane is transitioned from taxi-ing to the take-off roll without stopping in order to maintain momentum and hence decrease the total take-off distance. However, speed must be controlled carefully during the turn on to the centreline and if the fuel level is low in the tanks a running, turning take-off should be avoided.

Once positioned for take-off smoothly apply full power and hold the control column fully back to raise the nosewheel from the runway surface. Hold the appropriate aileron deflection if a crosswind exists. As the aeroplane accelerates and the elevators become more effective a reduction in back pressure will be necessary to maintain a constant pitch attitude. If the back pressure is not reduced the aeroplane will adopt a very high nose attitude which may cause the tailskid to scrape the ground. Furthermore, a premature lift-off will be induced, which is likely to be followed by the aeroplane settling down back on the runway as an attempt is made to readjust the pitch attitude. Your instructor will demonstrate the correct attitude to be held in the air lesson. Direction is maintained by the rudder and remember to anticipate the swing as full power is applied.

The lift-off and climbout

If the proper pitch attitude is established during the ground run the aeroplane should lift off at or close to the power-off stalling speed (see the Flight Manual). Once the lift-off has been accomplished the back pressure must be reduced until the normal level flight attitude is achieved. The aeroplane should be allowed to accelerate like this in the ground effect to climbing speeds before establishing a climb (see Fig. 87).

At a safe height, usually about 300ft agl, start raising the flaps slowly in stages, readjusting the pitch attitude in the normal way to maintain airspeed. Remember to anticipate the pitch changes that occur as the flaps are raised. Rudder pressure will also have to be readjusted for balanced flight.

SOFT FIELD TAKE-OFF

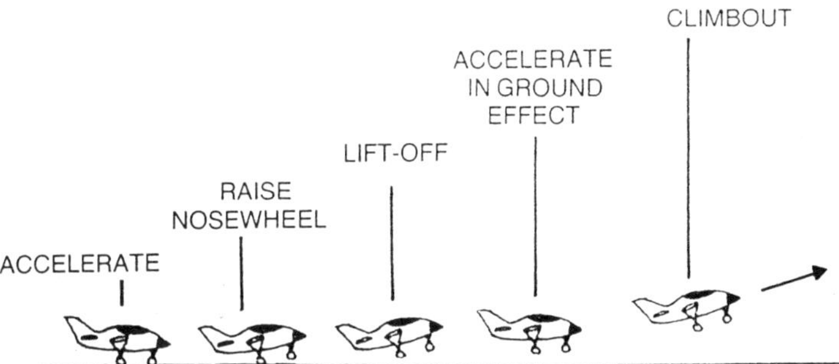

Fig. 87

The Short Field Take-Off

This technique is used in marginal runway conditions and when there are obstructions at the end of the runway that need to be overflown. This will mean that the aeroplane must become airborne in the shortest possible ground run and a climb initiated at an angle (speed) that will give the greatest gain in altitude for the forward distance travelled. A short field take-off needs careful planning and all the factors affecting take-offs must be considered with detailed reference to the Flight Manual. The short field take-off data given in Flight Manuals will be given in terms of the distance taken by the aeroplane to climb over a fifty foot obstacle (called the take-off distance).

Since wind is a very significant factor in determining the actual angle of climb achieved, a short field take-off should always be made as much into a headwind as possible. Optimum flaps may also be recommended (see Flight Manual). Then a safe early lift-off followed by a climbout at the best angle of climb speed (Vx) will ensure safe obstacle clearance if the take-off run available is worked out to be sufficient for the manoeuvre.

The ground run
When lining up for take-off the aeroplane must be positioned as far back on the runway as conditions will permit, so that all the available length of the runway can be used for the ground run. Full power must be smoothly applied and the elevators held neutral, with the appropriate aileron deflection if a crosswind exists. Some short field techniques dictate that the aeroplane be held on the brakes as power is applied until maximum RPM is achieved, after which the brakes are released. See your Flight Manual. The elevators should be held neutral during the ground run and care taken not to apply too much forward pressure, otherwise unnecessary loads will be imposed on the nosewheel.

The lift-off and climbout
Just before the lift-off speed is reached, increase the back pressure slightly and at the required speed apply firm back pressure to rotate from the runway. This will ensure a smooth transition from the ground to the air. Once airborne reduce the nose attitude slightly and accelerate in the ground effect to Vx before assuming a climb. After the obstacle has been overflown at Vx, readjust the

SHORT FIELD TAKE-OFF

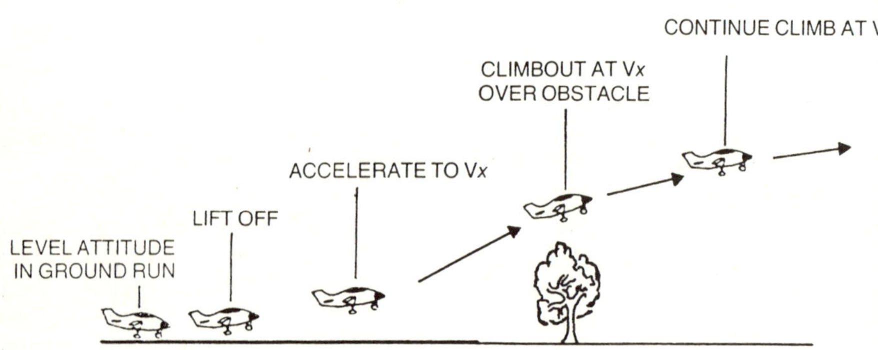

Fig. 88

pitch attitude to continue the climb at the best rate of climb speed (Vy) and retract the flaps (see Fig. 88). During the initial climbout over the obstacle the best angle of climb speed must be maintained, otherwise obstacle clearance will be hampered.

Observation of Proper Airspeeds during Take-Offs

Take-off speeds for various conditions will be given in the Flight Manual and you must memorize them. It is vital that these speeds are strictly adhered to. Premature lift-offs will usually result in the aeroplane settling back on to the ground. On the other hand, delaying the lift-off will impose stresses on the landing gear and unnecessarily increase the ground run. Similarly, during the climbout, if too slow a speed is used climb performance will deteriorate.

Taking-Off in Tailwheel Aircraft

Tailwheel aeroplanes tend to be more prone to the swing that results as full power is applied for take-off, so be prepared to anticipate this with the rudder. As maximum power is set and the aircraft moves forward, apply a slight forward pressure on the control column to raise the tail so that the take-off run is made in the level flight attitude. This will place the wings at the correct angle of attack for lift-off and reduce the drag. As speed increases back pressure will now have to be applied to the control column to maintain a constant pitch attitude, otherwise the nose will start to lower and the propeller will strike the ground. Positive use of the rudder will be required to counteract any yaw and to maintain direction. At the lift-off speed apply slightly more back pressure to rotate the aeroplane off the ground and, keeping the wings level, accelerate in ground effect in the normal way before entering a climb.

EMERGENCIES DURING THE TAKE-OFF AND CLIMBOUT

During any kind of emergency that occurs while the aeroplane is close to the ground the time available for actions to be taken will be very short indeed and it is only with thorough training and alertness of the pilot that such situations can be handled safely.

The Abandoned Take-Off

There are many reasons why a flight may have to be abandoned during the take-off run. The most likely reason will be an engine malfunction, such as misfiring, rough running, or maximum power not being developed. This is why the engine instruments must always be checked during the ground run. Other reasons could be control failures, bird strikes, burst tyres, doors or windows opening and the like. So, as soon as you recognize anything that may affect the safety of a flight, close the throttle and apply the brakes firmly to slow down the aeroplane. Taxi clear of the runway if possible and notify ATC. It may be necessary to shut down and secure the aeroplane and look for assistance. You will have several simulated aborted take-offs during the rest of your course.

Engine Failure after Take-Off

Should the engine fail completely after take-off, the pilot's immediate action should be to lower the nose to maintain flying speed (the best gliding speed) and to select a suitable landing area, preferably into wind to glide towards.

Now, it is not possible to give a particular course of action that will guarantee success in every engine failure situation since the options available to the pilot will be determined largely by the altitude of the aeroplane following the failure. Other factors such as wind and terrain will also affect a course of action.

If the engine fails immediately after take-off a landing straight ahead on any remaining runway may be possible. Otherwise, if the aeroplane is too high a landing site such as a field must be selected straight ahead or to one side. Remember, the rate of descent will already be very high in such situations and will increase during turns, together with an increase in stalling speeds. Therefore, maintain the best gliding speed at all times and limit bank angles to a maximum of 45° to avoid a stall-spin accident. If there are too many obstacles all around, a controlled crash landing may have to be the only option.

At some airfields an adjoining runway or taxiway may be available. However, turns back towards the airfield are not advised unless there is sufficient altitude to complete the turns and to make a safe landing. At altitudes below 1000ft agl a turn back is not advised unless the surrounding terrain makes this the only course of action. It must be remembered that the margin for error is very small with this type of manoeuvre and there are too many factors involved for it to be possible to state a minimum turn-back altitude. But, if you are absolutely sure that you can safely make it back to the airfield, then by all means do so. You are more accessible to emergency services on the airfield than anywhere else, if they are needed.

Once the aeroplane is under control and headed towards the selected landing area an engine restart may be possible if time permits. Otherwise the checks appropriate for an emergency landing must be carried out. These will be contained in the checklist and must be memorized as soon as possible.

Fortunately, modern aircraft engines are very reliable and the required regular maintenance and inspections ensure that they remain so. Engine failures, therefore, do not occur very frequently. Nevertheless, pilots must be able to deal with them and also do whatever is in their power to prevent them occurring in the first place. Statistics indicate that the most frequent causes of engine failures is fuel starvation rather than mechanical defects. So, during the time prior to take-off, make sure you follow the checklist thoroughly. Operate the fuel systems correctly to ensure the fuel supply to the engine is unrestricted. Checks for carburettor icing must not be forgotten. During the power checks and the initial stages of the take-off run listen carefully to the engine for rough running, misfiring and any unusual noises. If you are in doubt about the condition of the engine do not continue with the flight. Return immediately to the parking area and get the problem rectified.

Knowledge of the terrain immediately surrounding an airfield is advised so that you have an idea of what to expect should the engine fail after take-off. At your base airfield your instructor will point out possible emergency landing areas. When travelling to unfamiliar airfields study the surrounding terrain. Study your topographical maps and also any useful information given in the Air Pilot and other airport directories on obstructions in the vicinity of an airfield.

By taking all the necessary precautions prior to take-off it is quite probable that you will enjoy a flying career free of such emergencies. However, after several uneventful take-offs it can be easy to become complacent and not even acknowledge the possibility of an engine failure. This is where the danger lies. An unprepared pilot who is faced with an engine failure will lose vital time and altitude before he realizes what is happening and decides what to do about it. Such a situation can be fatal. It is strongly suggested that the emergency checks you have memorized are simulated prior to *every* take-off, just after the pre-take-off vital actions have been carried out. This will serve both as a reminder of an engine failure possibility and also train you to instinctively locate the items on the emergency checklist. Mental alertness and preparation are critical factors in surviving any emergency. You will have several simulated engine failures during your course until your responses become instinctive.

AIRMANSHIP

Prior to take-off make sure the landing approach path and the climbout direction are safely clear of traffic. Ensure that the runway is also clear of traffic and any obstructions, particularly at those airfields without an active control tower. Remember the right of way rules contained in the ANO and obey ATC instructions at all times. Make sure you are thoroughly familiar with the ground signals and markings used at aerodromes and also the light signals that may be used by ATC (see ANO). Never neglect performance considerations regarding take-off distances, especially when conditions may be marginal.

AIR LESSON

The following actions must be carried out prior to every take-off:

1. Carry out the pre take-off vital actions and simulate the emergency checks.
2. Obtain clearance from ATC.
3. Lookout (the final approach path, climbout direction and runway must be clear of traffic).
4. Line up in the centre of the runway.
5. Check the wind direction.

NOTE

1. During a take-off be prepared to encounter turbulence, especially in windy conditions.
2. On grass and rough surfaces the noise level is likely to be fairly high.

The Normal Take-Off into Wind

1. Hold the elevators and ailerons neutral.

2. Apply full power in one movement. Keep your hand on the throttle and be ready to counteract the swing with the rudder.
3. As speed increases start applying back pressure on the control column.
4. Check the RPM, temperature and pressures.
5. Maintain the centreline with the rudder.
6. At the lift-off speed apply gentle back pressure to rotate from the runway.
7. Once airborne lower the nose slightly and keeping the wings level accelerate to the climbing speed.
8. At the correct speed adopt the climbing attitude and trim.
9. Maintain speed, direction and balance.
10. At 300 ft agl check the engine instruments.
11. Lookout.

The Crosswind Take-Off

1. Hold the appropriate aileron deflection (upwind aileron raised) and the elevators neutral.
2. Apply full power smoothly. Anticipate the swing with the rudder and keep your hand on the throttle.
3. As speed increases progressively reduce aileron deflection, keeping the elevators neutral and maintaining direction with the rudder.
4. Check the RPM, temperatures and pressures.
5. At a slightly higher than normal lift-off speed apply positive backpressure to rotate and neutralize the ailerons.
6. Once airborne lower the nose slightly and accelerate to climbing speeds while heading the aeroplane into wind a few degrees to prevent drift.
7. At the climbing speed adopt the climbing attitude and trim.
8. Maintain speed and balance and select a heading into wind to prevent drift.
9. At 300ft agl check the engine instruments.
10. Lookout.

Soft Field Take-Off (use flaps if required)

1. When lined up for take-off smoothly apply full power and hold the control column fully back. Hold the appropriate deflection if a crosswind exists.
2. As speed increases and the nose rises, relax the back pressure to maintain a constant pitch attitude.

3. Maintain direction with the rudder.
4. Check the RPM and the engine instruments.
5. At the lift-off speed rotate, then lower the nose slightly and accelerate to the climbing speed.
6. At the climbing speed proceed into a normal climb.
7. At 300ft agl check the engine instruments, retract the flaps slowly and retrim.
8. Lookout.

Short Field Take-Off (use flaps if required)
Line up as far back on the runway as possible then:

1. Apply full power smoothly maintaining the elevators neutral. Alternately, apply full power while holding the aeroplane on the brakes until maximum power is achieved, then release the brakes.
2. Check the engine instruments.
3. As speed increases hold the elevators neutral and rotate at the appropriate speed.
4. Accelerate to Vx.
5. Climb at Vx over obstacle.
6. After obstacle has been cleared proceed into a normal climb at Vy.
7. At 300ft agl check the engine instruments, retract the flaps and retrim.
8. Lookout.

Taking off in Tailwheel Aircraft

1. Select a suitable reference point for direction.
2. Apply full power in one movement while holding the control column fully back. Be ready to counteract the swing.
3. As the aircraft moves forward apply a forward pressure on the control column to raise the tail.
4. Use the rudder positively to maintain direction.
5. Check the engine instruments.
6. As the speed increases back pressure must be applied to prevent the tail rising too high.
7. At the lift-off speed apply slightly more back pressure to rotate off the runway.
8. Once airborne accelerate naturally to climbing speeds then continue in a normal climb.

9. At 300ft agl check the engine instruments, retract any flaps and retrim.
10. Lookout.

EMERGENCIES

Abandoned Take-off

Immediately you recognize any reason to abort the take-off:

1. Close the throttle.
2. Apply the brakes firmly to slow down the aeroplane.
3. Take avoiding action if necessary. If a collision is unavoidable operate the Idle Cut-Off, turn off the fuel, ignition and master switches.
4. Taxi clear of the runway if possible.
5. Secure the aeroplane and inform ATC.

Engine Failure after Take-off

In the event of an engine failure after take-off immediately:

1. Lower the nose and adopt the attitude for the best gliding speed.
2. Close the throttle.
3. Look for a landing area straight ahead or to one side.
4. Maintain flying speeds at all times and limit bank angles to a maximum of 45° during turns.
5. When committed to a landing carry out emergency checks.

NOTE

The instructor's guide for the take-off will be found at the end of the chapter on the 'Approach and Landing'.

Flying in the Circuit

The Circuit

The airfield traffic pattern is a safe, efficient and organized way of controlling aerial traffic arriving and departing from an airfield. Figure 89 illustrates a basic circuit pattern which must be firmly imprinted in your mind.

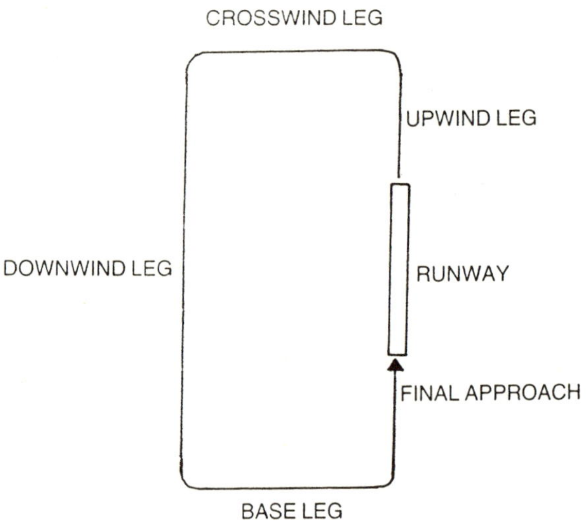

Fig. 89

Circuits may be left-handed or right-handed and may vary for different runways. The direction of circuit patterns are decided by airfield controlling authorities or air traffic control, who take into consideration local noise abatement rules and the proximity of controlled airspace and high terrain. Each airfield will have a specific height, called the circuit height, which must be maintained on the downwind leg of the circuit. Arriving aircraft usually join the circuit on the downwind leg or another leg as instructed by ATC, after having first descended to the circuit height. Aircraft departing an airfield make the initial climbout on the upwind leg (maintaining the take-off direction) before setting an en route course.

Circuit Practice

During circuit training you will be flying all the legs of the traffic pattern. After take-off the initial climbout is made on the upwind leg up to a height of about 500ft agl, when a climbing turn is made through 90° in the required direction (left or right) on to the crosswind leg. The climb is continued on this leg to the circuit height and at a suitable point not too far away from the airfield a medium-level turn is made through another 90° on to the downwind leg. Your instructor will point out useful ground references that can be used as turning points. The circuit height is maintained on the downwind leg at a slow cruising speed. At a convenient point another turn is made on to the base leg when a descent should be commenced. Then, at a suitable position and at about 600ft agl the turn on to the final leg is made and the descent is continued down to the runway for a landing.

Correcting for the Effects of Wind (drift)

The wind direction given on meteorological reports and by ATC is the direction a wind is *coming from* and *not* where it is blowing to. For example, a wind report given as 230°/20 kts means the wind is coming *from* the direction of 230° at a speed of 20 knots. This is very important to remember.

An orderly flow of traffic must be maintained at all times in the airfield pattern and this means you will have to fly neat and accurate circuits, making the necessary allowances for the effects of wind.

While flying around the circuit you must maintain specific ground tracks for each leg. So, to fly accurately and to correct effectively for wind you must know the headings for each leg of the circuit. These are simple to determine. For example, if a right-hand circuit is in operation, as in Figure 90 and the runway direction is 060°, then the heading for the upwind leg is obviously also 060°. Following this, each leg will require a turn to the right through 90°. This means that the crosswind leg heading will be 150° (060 + 90 = 150). The downwind heading will be the reciprocal of the runway direction making the heading to be flown 240° (or 150 + 90). To arrive on the base leg will require another turn through

90° on to the heading 330° (240 + 90) and the final turn will be back on to the runway heading of 060° (or 330 + 90). The headings for a left-hand circuit are also shown in Figure 90.

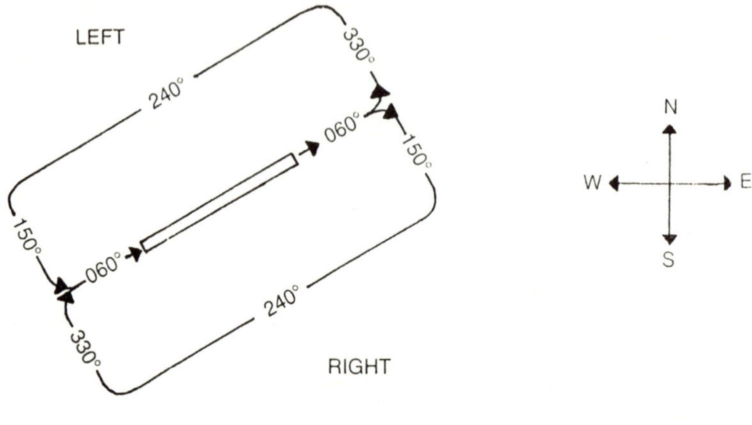

Fig. 90

Now, if these headings are flown accurately, then in zero wind conditions consistent ground tracks will be maintained resulting in a neat circuit. Work out the zero wind headings for each leg of all the runways at your base airfield.

When a wind exists, which is usually the case, adjustments to the zero wind headings will be required in flight in order to maintain the ground tracks. Additionally, wind will affect the ground speed of the aircraft which must also be taken into consideration while flying in the circuit. Before take-off make a note of the wind direction so that you have a good idea of the corrections required in the circuit. It must be borne in mind, however, that the winds at altitude will differ slightly and sometimes considerably from those at the surface.

Figure 91 illustrates the effect of a headwind on the different legs of the circuit.

Aircraft A, C and E will experience no drift. Aircraft B and D on the other hand will be blown away from the desired ground tracks, unless adjustments are made to the headings. In a headwind the heading flown on the crosswind leg should be a few degrees to the right (into wind) of the zero wind heading. In this example a heading of say 280° is likely to offset the drift and

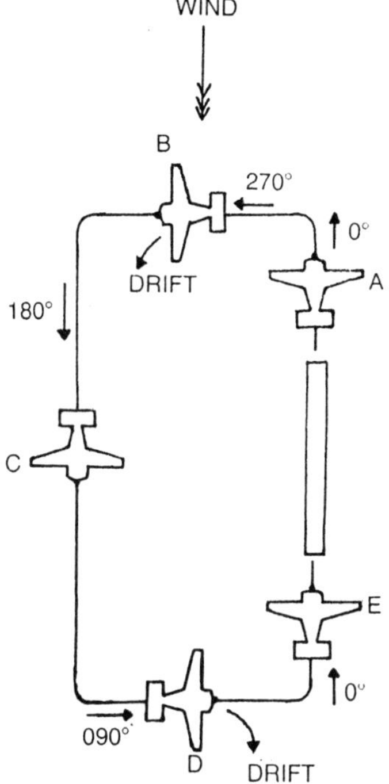

Fig. 91

maintain the ground track. The heading flow on the base leg should be to the left of the zero wind heading, say 080, as shown in Figure 92.

Figure 93 shows that in a 90° crosswind drift will be experienced on the upwind, downwind and final legs.

Once again, heading corrections must be made into wind to maintain the ground tracks on these legs. In the above example the ground speed on the base leg will increase thus reducing the time taken to reach the final leg. This is an important consideration as it will affect the descent path (covered in detail in the next chapter).

The crosswind conditions illustrated in Figure 94 will require heading corrections on all the legs of the circuit.

Each leg will also experience either a headwind or tailwind component.

Notice that in any wind condition the direction of drift will vary

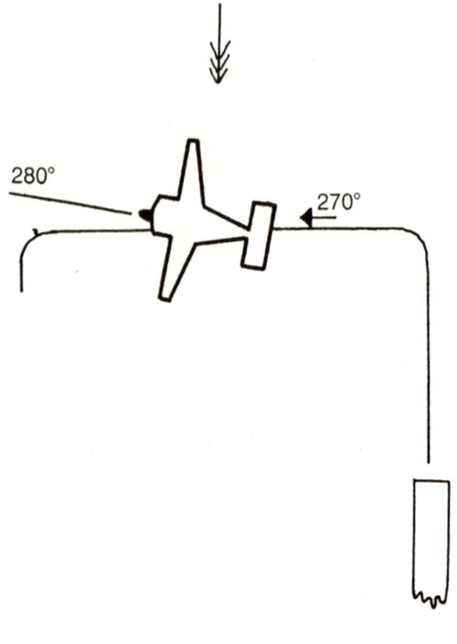

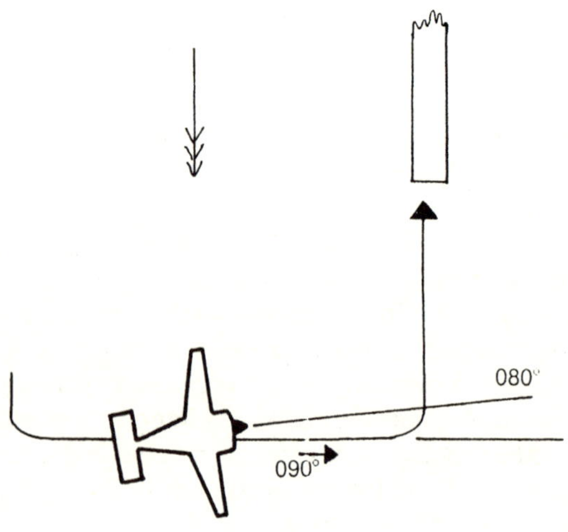

Fig. 92

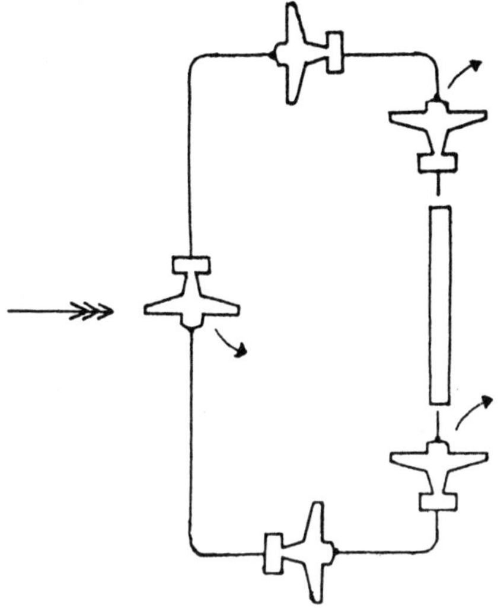

Fig. 93

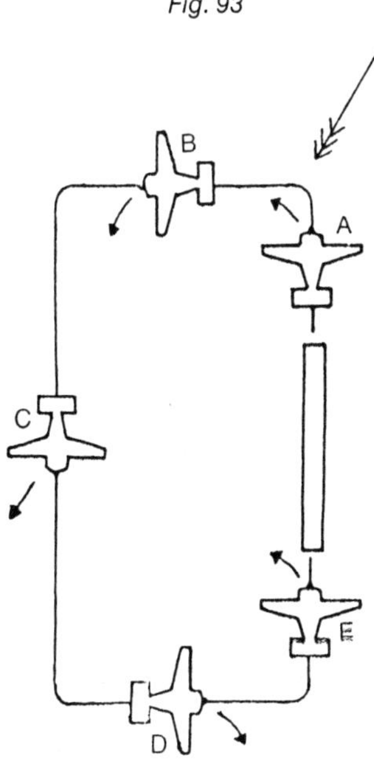

Fig. 94

around the circuit. The direction of heading corrections, therefore, also varies but will always be into wind. For example, in Figure 94 aircraft A, B and E will all experience drift to the left, requiring heading corrections to the right. However, aircraft C and D on the downwind and base legs experience drift to the right (relative to the pilot) and hence require heading corrections to the left. Always be aware of the changing effect of the wind whenever you change the flight path of the aeroplane. The amount of any heading correction will usually be around 10°, or more, depending on the wind velocity. The exact amount can be found out through trial and error which is good enough for normal visual flying in the circuit.

It may be difficult at first to determine the new angle of the wind once the aeroplane's heading has been changed, so the following method of assessing the wind angle by reference to the Direction Indicator will be very useful.

First of all you will need to know the direction the wind is coming from. Next, by noting this wind direction on the DI you will be able

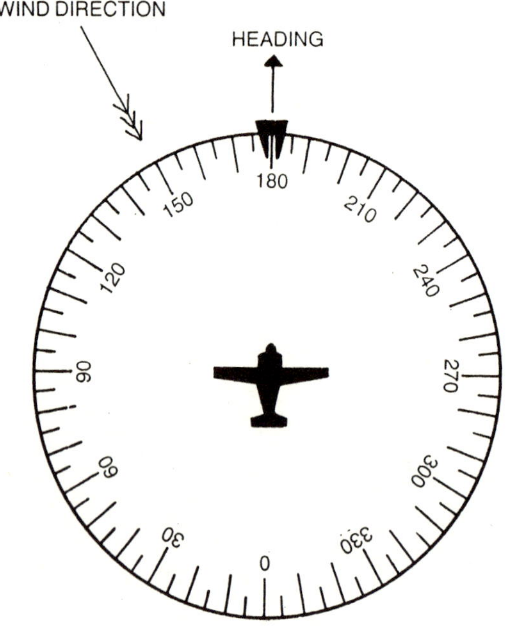

Fig. 95

to see the position of your present heading in relation to the wind. For example, if your heading is 180° and the wind is coming from 150° you can see on your DI that 150° lies to the left of 180°, meaning you have a wind coming from the left, as illustrated in Figure 95. As the wind is coming from ahead in addition there will be a headwind component.

Imagine now that you have turned on to North. The wind angle will be as shown in Figure 96.

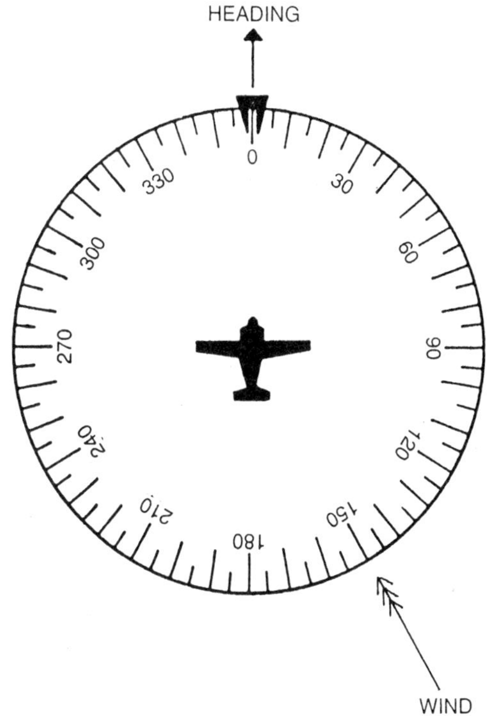

Fig. 96

You can easily see that although the wind is still from 150°, on a North heading it is now coming from the right and also from behind, meaning the aircraft will now be experiencing a tailwind component in addition. As long as you remember that the wind direction is the direction it is coming from, you will avoid confusion.

AIRMANSHIP

Aerial traffic is at its greatest in the vicinity of airfields and statistics reveal that the majority of mid-air collisions or near misses occur in these areas. Therefore, the importance of good lookouts cannot be overstressed while flying in the circuit. In addition, various safety checks must be carried out (after take-off checks and the downwind pre-landing checks). These are contained in the checklist and must be memorized immediately. Figure 97 illustrates the more important lookout points in the circuit.

AIRMANSHIP IN THE CIRCUIT

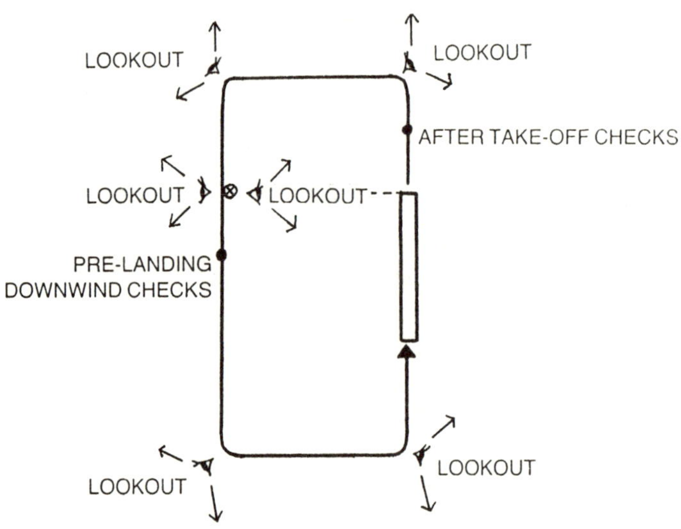

Fig. 97

The lookout at position X, made as the aeroplane passes the upwind end of the runway while on the downwind leg, is important as arriving aircraft often join the traffic pattern at this point. Also, listen out for joining instructions given by ATC to arriving aircraft and also to position reports given by other aircraft already in the circuit. By doing this you will know where to look for traffic. Adequate separation must be maintained at all times and it may be necessary occasionally to slow down or alter heading in order to do so. It may also 'be necessary to extend the downwind leg of the circuit on certain occasions due to traffic requirements. Circuit discipline is very important; do not attempt to cut in front of any aircraft.

It is standard procedure to make an R/T call once established on the downwind leg. Listen out for and obey ATC instructions at all times. You will be advised of your place in the order of landing and try to locate any aircraft ahead of you.

At airfields without an operating control tower pilots must be extra careful and even more so when visibility is not very good.

By now you will really begin to appreciate what is involved in being an aircraft captain. Before sending you solo your instructor will expect you to display good airmanship in addition to good handling of your aeroplane. At first things may seem a little intimidating, especially if the airfield is very busy. Everything will appear to be happening quite fast, but your instructor will be guiding you through. After the first few circuits you will soon get the feel of circuit flying.

By this stage of your training you will actively be going through the motions of a pilot, checking the aircraft, booking in and out and so on, although the final decisions still lie with your instructor.

Start getting yourself organized properly for your flight lessons. Carry some notepaper (preferably on a knee pad) and a pen to write down flight times, altimeter settings, radio frequencies etc. These are the sort of things you will have to do yourself when you fly solo, so the sooner you get used to doing them the better.

Exercise 13

THE APPROACH AND LANDING

Objectives

1. To learn to control the aircraft's rate of descent precisely in order to arrive in the desired landing area.
2. To land the aeroplane safely and under a variety of conditions.

The landing is a manoeuvre which will bring the aeroplane safely on to the ground at a slow airspeed and under control.

The Powered Approach and Landing

During the lesson on descending you were taught how to use power to vary the rate of descent while maintaining specific speeds. This technique is employed during a normal landing approach to control accurately the angle of descent so that the aeroplane will safely arrive in the desired area and in position for a landing (see Fig. 98).

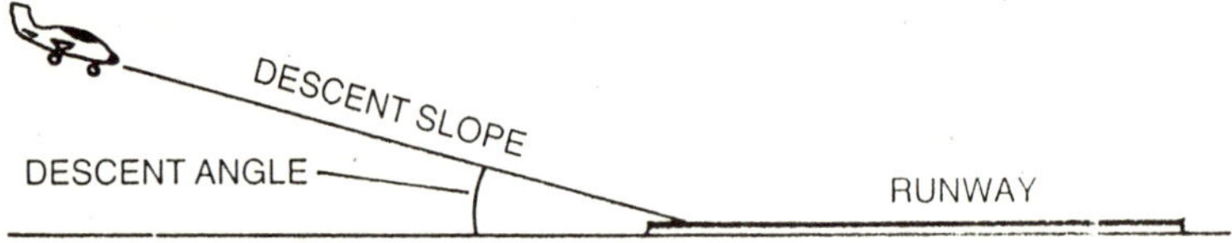

Fig. 98

Now, in a normal cruise descent accurate rate of descent control is not as important as during the approach and landing, when you will be aiming to bring the aeroplane into a relatively small and specific area of ground at a slow safe speed. This will require you to be able to assess your progress towards the landing area and make precise adjustments to the descent path to ensure you reach the runway safely. This in turn will require good control, co-ordination and judgement.

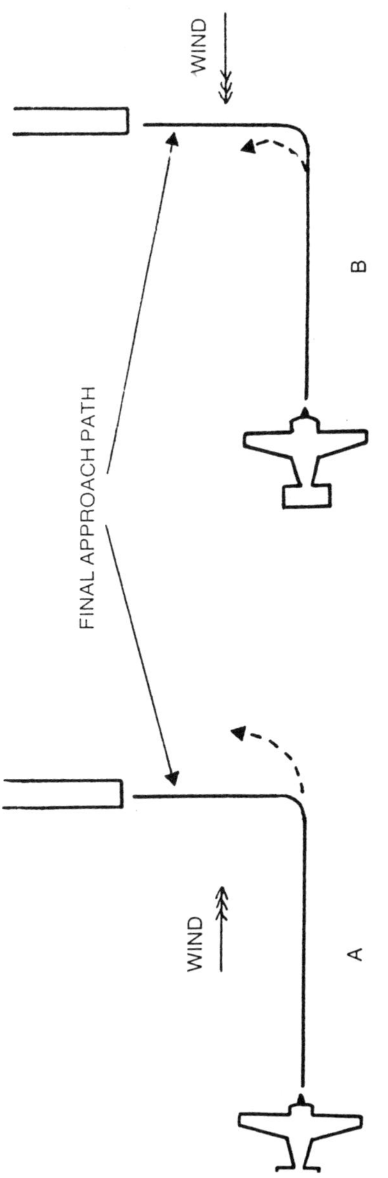

Fig. 99

Setting up a stablized approach

The descent for a landing usually begins once the aeroplane is established on the base leg. Power and airspeed are reduced and a rate of descent initiated (power, attitude, trim). Flaps are also selected at this stage. The aim is to lose a limited amount of altitude before making the turn on to the final leg. The power setting and rate of descent selected will vary according to both the distance away from the airfield and prevailing wind conditions. Your instructor will give you approximate figures for use in normal situations. Generally, if a tailwind is experienced on the base leg (increasing groundspeed) a higher ROD must be initiated so that the aeroplane is not too high when the final turn is made. When a headwind component is experienced a higher power setting and a lower ROD must be used.

Before the aircraft intersects the final approach path the final turn should be commenced and the bank angle varied so that the aeroplane arrives in line with the runway with the wings level. Timing for the commencement of this turn is important. With a tailwind on the base leg the turn will have to be started slightly earlier to avoid overshooting the final approach path (see Fig. 99 (a)). On the other hand, with a headwind the turn will have to be delayed slightly to avoid undershooting (see Fig. 99 (b)).

Should you mistime the turn small adjustments to the heading must be made to bring the aeroplane back in line with the runway (see Fig. 100).

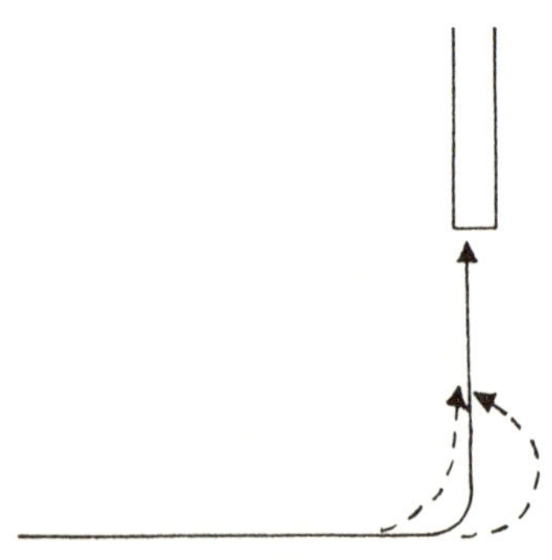

Fig. 100

Additionally, during the final turn care must be taken to limit the bank angle to a maximum of 30°. Airspeed must be maintained and controlled throughout the turn.

Having turned finals, full flaps are normally lowered and the airspeed reduced to the appropriate figure. To become properly established on the final approach a crab angle may need to be adopted.

As the aeroplane descends towards the runway you will have to assess whether the descent path being achieved is correct. In other words, you will have to decide whether your present descent path will result in the aeroplane arriving at the runway in position for a safe landing. This is done visually by noting the perspective of the runway and its surroundings. It may be a little difficult at first to assess your descent path and also make the necessary adjustments in good time, but your instructor will be talking you through the first few approaches until you are able to recognize when the approach is good. A useful hint to help you in this will be to note the position of the runway on the windscreen soon after you have turned finals. If the descent path is correct the runway should occupy the same space on the windscreen as you progress towards the airfield. However, if the aeroplane is too high on the approach the runway will start to move downwards and if the descent path is not steepened the aeroplane will overshoot the desired landing area. An approach that is too low will be recognized by the runway moving its position upwards on the windscreen. In this situation the descent angle must be flattened to avoid undershooting the runway.

Correcting a high approach

If the aeroplane is discovered to be too high during the approach the rate of descent (ROD) will have to be increased, so reduce power and lower the nose to maintain airspeed in the normal way and retrim. Remember from the lesson on descending that the nose-down couple comes into effect when power is reduced, so a slight back pressure will be required to prevent the nose lowering too much and the airspeed increasing.

Correcting a low approach

If the aeroplane is too low on the approach the ROD will have to be reduced, so increase power and raise the nose slightly to maintain airspeed and retrim. Again, remember the nose will have a tendency to rise anyway whenever power is increased, so be ready to apply a forward pressure on the control column to prevent the airspeed decreasing.

Accurate airspeed control is very important during the approach phase of a flight and this will require very good trimming. If the aeroplane is not trimmed correctly you will have a tendency to chase the airspeed. Erratic changes in the aircraft's pitch attitude must be avoided at this stage because the perspective of the runway will change, making it difficult to judge the descent path.

A stabilized approach is one where the aeroplane is accurately maintaining the approach track (an imaginary extension of the runway centreline), with the airspeed and ROD constant, requiring only small adjustments to maintain the descent path. This is what you should aim for during every landing approach. The key to achieving a stabilized approach is accurate trimming and early corrective action. On the base leg set up the descent with flaps lowered and ensure the aeroplane is well trimmed for the approach speed. As soon as you have turned finals assess your position both vertically and horizontally in relation to the runway and make any corrections immediately.

If the turn is made correctly only small heading adjustments may be necessary to maintain the approach track. Remember, keep the wings level and the ball central and the heading will remain constant. If the turn is made at around the correct height only small power adjustments (50-100 rpm at a time) will be necessary to maintain the descent path, unless wind conditions are strong and gusty. (In strong winds considerable power may be required to make progress towards the runway.) Remember, power (throttle) controls the ROD and the elevators control airspeed. Retrim after every power adjustment. Keep your hand on the throttle at all times except when carrying out other control actions, of course. If full flaps are lowered make sure this is done early on during the approach so that the aeroplane can be retrimmed for the appropriate speed in good time.

The Flareout, Hold-off and Landing

As the aeroplane descends to within about 20ft of the runway power must be gradually reduced and the descent checked by moving the control column backwards until the aeroplane is flying level and just above the ground (the flareout). During the flareout airspeed reduces and the back pressure must be continued to reduce the speed further and to keep the aeroplane airborne with the main wheels just off the ground (the hold-off). The aim is to touch down gently, main wheels first, at a slow airspeed with the aeroplane in a nose-high attitude (see Fig. 101). Just prior to touchdown the throttle must be closed completely.

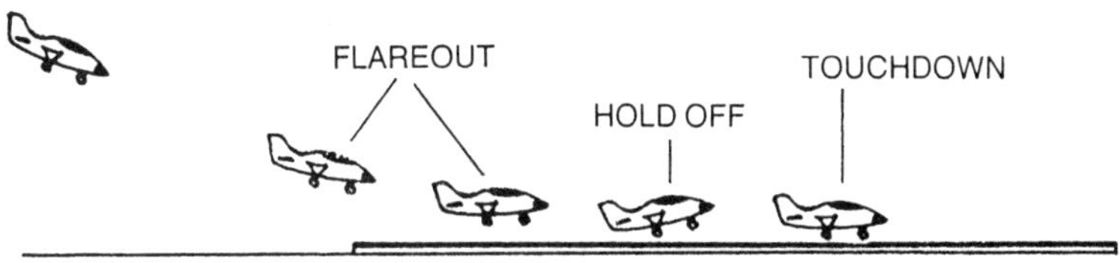

Fig. 101

Now, the height for the commencement of the flareout will be learnt through practice. During the flareout and hold-off you will have to direct your line of sight to the left of the nose in order to assess effectively your proximity to the ground. A useful tip is to get used to the aspect of the ground from your position in the cockpit during taxi-ing. This will help you when it comes to the landing.

The rate of backward movement should vary according to the aircraft's sink rate. If the sink rate is rapid, the control column must be moved back quickly, otherwise the aeroplane will land nose wheel first, which is hazardous. If the aircraft is sinking slowly move the control column back slowly.

Shortly after touchdown the nose wheel will lower and make contact with the runway. Back pressure must be maintained during the landing roll to keep the weight off the nose wheel. Direction is maintained by the rudder and the aeroplane must be slowed down and taxied clear of the runway to complete the after landing checks (see your checklist).

The workload is fairly high during the final approach, and the landing will require all your attention. Therefore, you must aim to have such items as flap lowering and speed and heading adjustments carried out in good time so that the aeroplane arrives at the runway in the desired landing configuration. A stable approach will help you predict the touchdown point and a good landing is likely to be the result of such an approach.

Factors Affecting the Approach and Landing

During every approach and landing the pilot will have two objectives:

1. to safely overfly any obstructions in the landing path and arrive at the runway in position for a landing
2. to land the aeroplane under control according to wind and ground conditions and come to a safe stop within the available distance.

Descent profiles

You will have noticed that following a landing the aeroplane will require a distance, which is determined by various factors, in which to decelerate and stop. When obstacles need to be overflown this will be an important factor in deciding the angle of descent to be adopted during the landing approach, especially when runway distances are also marginal. Figure 102 illustrates two descent profiles.

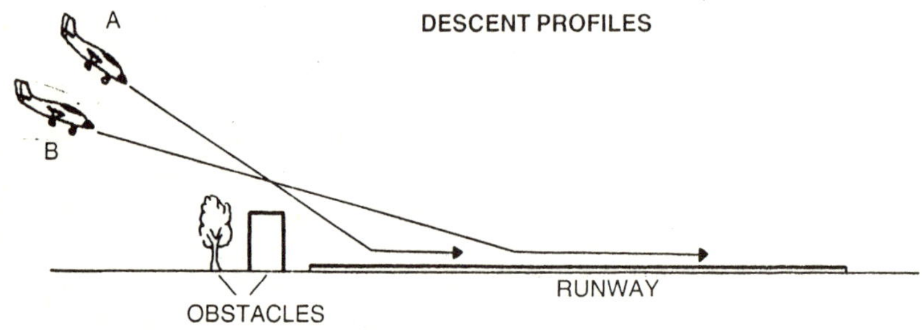

Fig. 102

It can be seen that although both descent paths clear the obstacle, the aeroplane on the steeper descent path (a) will have a greater distance in which to land, decelerate and stop safely. The aim, therefore, during every landing approach should be to adopt a descent profile that will result in the aeroplane touching down on the runway in a position with the maximum stopping distance available ahead.

The other factors that affect a landing approach and the length of the landing run are similar to those affecting the take-off. These must be understood by all pilots so that the appropriate techniques may be employed as required.

To help you understand some of the information which will follow it will be necessary to clarify a few points on the subject of aircraft speeds.

Indicated airspeed (IAS) and true airspeed (TAS)

The airspeed indicator is basically a sensitive pressure differential gauge calibrated in knots or miles per hour. However, a speed indicated on the ASI will not be the true or actual speed of the aeroplane through the air. True airspeed is determined by air density, which in turn is determined by altitude (pressure) and temperature. To calculate TAS, IAS must first be corrected for various technical errors inherent in the instrument, and then for temperature and height using a flight computer.

TAS is used primarily for navigational purposes to help determine the aeroplane's progress over the ground (groundspeed). The airspeed figures given in flight manuals, such as take-off, climbing and approach speeds, are all indicated airspeeds and therefore they must be achieved and maintained by reference to the ASI.

True airspeed and groundspeed (GS)

If an aeroplane is travelling at 100 kts TAS, in zero wind conditions its GS will also be 100 kts. However, if the aeroplane is flying in a headwind, its groundspeed will reduce by the value of the headwind or headwind component, as the case may be (see Fig. 103).

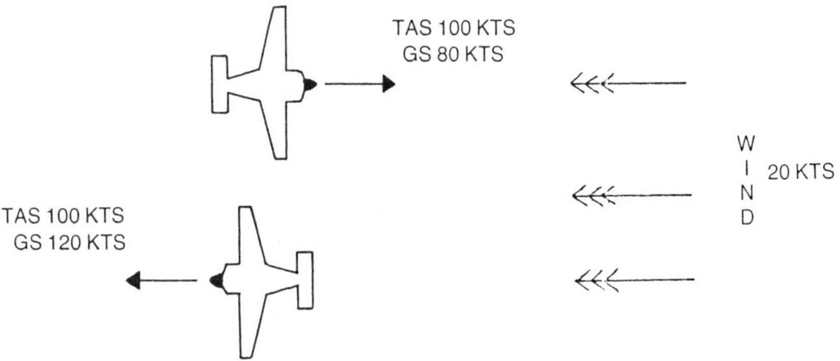

Fig. 103

Similarly, if a tailwind is experienced the GS will increase by the amount of the tailwind or tailwind component.

The subject of aeroplane speeds is covered in more detail later in this manual.

Wind

In relation to the landing approach a headwind will steepen the angle of descent. Figure 104 illustrates why.

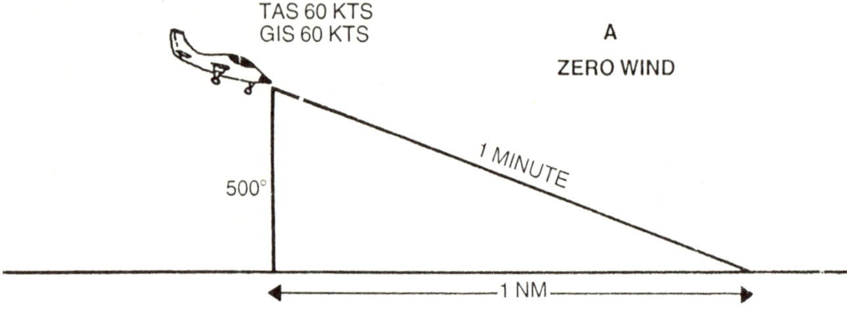

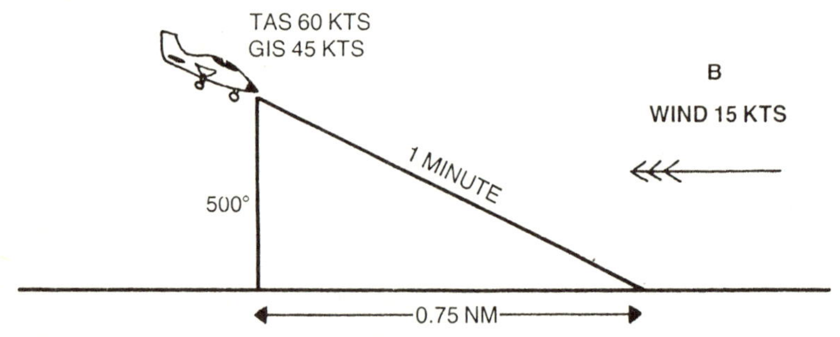

Fig. 104

At a descent rate of 500 fpm both aircraft will reach the ground after a period of one minute. However, due to a lower GS the aircraft in (b) will travel a shorter distance forward in this time, hence increasing the descent angle. Additionally, a landing into wind will reduce the length of the landing run. This is because the GS will be lower on touchdown. Landing with a tailwind increases the GS, therefore increasing the landing run. This is why landings must always be made as much into wind as possible.

Weight

It was explained in earlier chapters that stalling speeds are determined by various factors, weight among them. The airspeed figures given for low airspeed operations such as the landing approach are calculated to give optimum performance with safety. An increase in weight will increase the stalling speed. However, since optimum operating speeds are based on the maximum permitted all-up weight of the aeroplane, there will be no need to make any adjustments to an approach speed with variations in weight.

Now, what actually occurs during a normal landing is that as back pressure is applied during the hold-off period the angle of attack increases, airspeed reduces, rapid losses of lift occur followed by the aeroplane settling down on the runway. In other words, the aeroplane experiences a stall, or near stall, when within a foot or so of the runway. The speed at which the touchdown occurs will be at or close to the stalling speed of the aeroplane. So, an increase in weight will increase the touchdown speed and hence increase the distance required to slow down and stop the aeroplane. In general a 20 per cent increase in weight will result in approximately a 20 per cent increase in the landing run. Therefore, never exceed weight limitations.

Density altitude

If a high-density altitude exists the TAS on touchdown will be higher. Therefore, the landing run will be increased. This is an important factor which must be considered when operating out of high-elevation airports and/or under hot and humid conditions, particularly when runway conditions are also marginal. As for the take-off, the Flight Manual will contain landing performance information which should be consulted.

Ground surface and use of brakes

Compared to a smooth concrete runway, when an aeroplane lands on grass, soft ground and in slush and snow, the landing run will reduce. This is because of the increased friction caused by such surfaces.

The brakes are used to slow down further once direction is established following the touchdown. On a dry surface the brakes will be very effective. However, in wet conditions, especially on wet grass, extreme care must be taken when applying the brakes because of the risk of skidding, which can be difficult to control. At high speeds the brakes should be applied cautiously and intermittently. As speed reduces brake applications can be more firm.

A brake pressure check will form part of the pre-landing checks. This is so you will know what to expect during the landing roll if brake pressure is discovered to be very low or only partial (when toe brakes are fitted).

Use of flaps

Flaps are used during the approach and landing for two main reasons. Firstly, once the aeroplane has been trimmed following flap deployment, the change in pitch attitude will allow the pilot much better visibility of the runway and its surroundings. Secondly, since flaps will lower the stalling speed, the touchdown speed will be lower, so reducing the landing run. Additionally, since flaps also increase the drag, a higher ROD can be achieved without an increase in airspeed. This becomes more significant during glide approaches (covered later) when the descent path needs to be steepened. In strong wind conditions, however, full flaps should not be lowered.

The influence of ground effect on landings

Ground effect has already been explained in the previous chapter. When an aircraft enters the ground effect during the landing phase induced drag will decrease rapidly and will be noticed by a floating period, which may result in the aeroplane touching down beyond the estimated point. This float period will increase with an excessive approach speed.

Additionally, as the ground effect area is entered, the downwash angle over the tailplane will decrease and cause a slight tendency to pitch down.

LANDING TECHNIQUES

The techniques which follow are variations of the basic technique described earlier.

The Crosswind Landing

The aim during any landing should be to touch down on the centreline of the runway without imposing undue stresses on the landing gear. To accomplish this during crosswind conditions a crossed-controls technique is used which counteracts drift and results in the aeroplane landing with its longitudinal axis aligned with the centreline of the runway.

The crosswind approach

Having turned on to the final leg, a stabilized approach must be established. A crab angle will have to be used to maintain the approach track. It is important that this is done early during the approach so that you will have an idea of the amount of control pressures that will need to be used during the landing. When wind conditions are strong and gusty do not lower full flap and it is also advisable to increase the approach speed by 5-10 kts above the normal figure. This will improve control response and should not significantly increase the landing run because of the reduced groundspeed caused by the headwind component.

Control usage on touchdown and the landing run

The appropriate crab angle must be maintained throughout the flareout and hold-off. Just prior to touchdown the nose should be brought in line with the centreline of the runway using rudder pressure while at the same time keeping the wings level by raising the upwind aileron to prevent the upwind wing from rising due to the further effects of rudder. For example, if a crosswind from the left exists, the aeroplane will have to be headed into wind (to the left) to maintain the approach track. On touchdown this crab angle will have to be eliminated or the aeroplane will land sideways, imposing stresses on the undercarriage. So, just before the touchdown, apply sufficient right rudder to straighten the nose, and to prevent the left wing from rising as this is done, raise its aileron at the same time, i.e. rotate the control wheel to the left (into wind). The timing and co-ordination of these actions are both important. If they are executed too early the aeroplane will drift slightly before landing. If the opposite aileron is not used in time the aeroplane will roll slightly, making the touchdown awkward and if conditions are also gusty, the landing will be further compounded.

After touchdown the aileron deflection must be maintained to keep the upwind wing down, and the elevators held neutral so that the aeroplane rests firmly on all three wheels to aid directional stability. Slow down the aeroplane according to surface conditions and taxi clear of the runway.

The Sideslip Approach

This is another technique that may be used during a crosswind. Remember from the lesson on descending that during a sideslip the aeroplane will maintain direction despite the banked attitude. So, on the final approach bank the aeroplane into wind and use sufficient opposite rudder to prevent a turn and to maintain the approach track. These control pressures must not be released and will need to be varied in gusty conditions. If the control pressures are adequate the aeroplane will descend in a straight line with one wing low, as shown in Figure 105.

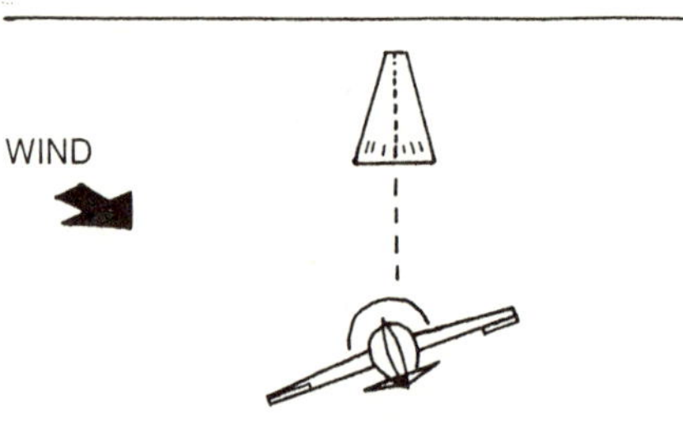

Fig. 105

In this configuration the aeroplane will land on one mainwheel first.

Landing

During the flareout the control deflections will have to be increased slightly due to the reducing effectiveness of the controls as airspeed reduces. The aeroplane should land on the upwind wheel first. The opposite mainwheel and the nosewheel will make contact with the runway shortly after. Upwind aileron deflection should be maintained during the landing run as usual.

Remember, during a sideslip the ROD increases, which will affect the descent angle. Also the pitch attitude will have to be adjusted to maintain airspeed.

The sideslip approach and landing will require very good control handling and judgement and will take time to master. In very turbulent conditions this technique is not advised, as a sudden gust of wind can easily cause a sharp increase in bank angle which can be dangerous near the ground.

The Soft Field Landing

Unless the correct technique is used to land on a soft surface the nosewheel will sink into the ground and may cause the aeroplane to come to an abrupt stop. The objective of the soft field landing is to transfer the weight of the aeroplane from the wings to the mainwheels as gently and as slowly as possible. If the landing is executed correctly during most of the landing run the weight will be on the mainwheels with the nosewheel clear of the ground.

Preparation for a soft field landing

The planning for this manoeuvre, as for all landings, should begin while the aeroplane is in the circuit. You must have it clear in your mind the objectives and techniques to be used. On the final approach to the runway a stabilized power approach with full flaps extended must be established.

Landing

Proper pitch and power control becomes a critical factor during a landing in soft field conditions. During the flareout the pitch attitude must be transitioned gradually from the descent attitude, through level flight to a nose-high attitude so that the aeroplane touches down on its mainwheels first (see Fig. 106). Now, in order to keep the nosewheel from making contact with the ground straight away, a small amount of power should be maintained throughout the manoeuvre, i.e. the throttle should not be fully closed on touchdown. The increased effectiveness of the elevators due to the slipstream will mean that the nose can be kept clear of the ground for a longer period, until the aeroplane slows down, when it will gently lower on to the runway. Unless runway distance is critical the throttle should not be closed. Premature power reductions will result in the nosewheel lowering immediately on to soft surface. The slipstream will also increase rudder effectiveness, which will compensate for the loss of the nosewheel steering capability while maintaining direction during the landing roll.

There will usually be little or no need to use brakes in soft field conditions and care must be taken if they are applied. Power should be left on to facilitate easier taxi-ing. This particular landing technique can also be used when landing on rough ground to prevent stresses on the nosewheel.

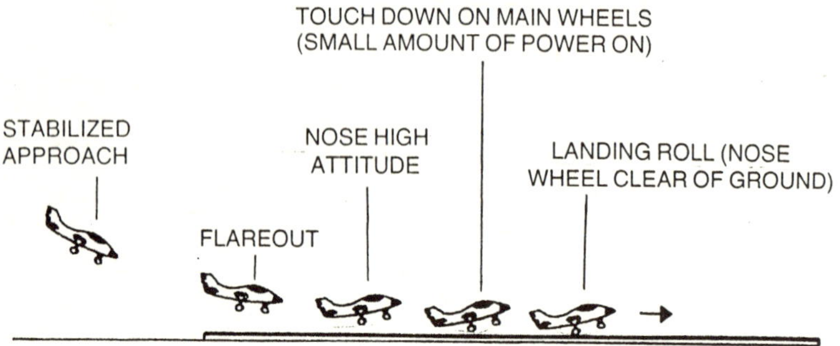

Fig. 106

The Short Field Landing

The objective of the short field landing is to land the aeroplane and come to a safe stop when landing distances are marginal. This means that the touchdown should be made at the slowest possible groundspeed, i.e. at or close to the stalling speed, with full flaps lowered and into a headwind if possible.

Planning the short field landing

Once again the preparation for this manoeuvre should begin in the circuit. When there are obstacles that need to be overflown in the landing path a steeper descent profile will have to be adopted. This means that the final turn should be made at a greater height than normal, so on the base leg the ROD initiated should be lower than usual. The descent profile adopted must be adjusted according to local conditions and a stabilized approach should be established with full flaps lowered and the aeroplane trimmed for the appropriate speed. Remember, if you have too many adjustments to make in a short time the accuracy and performance of a landing will suffer.

The correct descent profile is very important during a short field landing, as shown previously by Figure 102. The pilot should aim to touchdown with the maximum distance available ahead for stopping. When landing in a confined space an approach that is too flat can be hazardous, as illustrated in Figure 107.

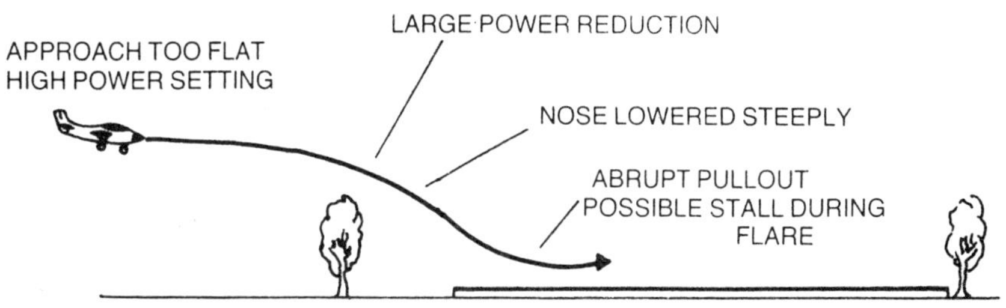

Fig. 107

A substantial amount of power will be required during the approach to overcome the drag created by the flaps and to reduce the ROD. Once the obstacle has been cleared the ROD will have to be increased considerably so that the aeroplane can touchdown in a suitable position. This means power will have to be reduced rapidly to produce a sharp increase in the descent angle. Then, in order to maintain airspeed, the pitch attitude will have to be lowered a large amount. This means that during the flareout the back pressure required to check the descent may increase the wing loading to an extent that an accelerated stall will occur. The effect is similar to an abrupt pullout from a dive. This is clearly an unsafe technique. Therefore, always plan for a steep descent when there are obstacles in the way.

Landing

As the aeroplane flies over the obstacle reduce airspeed by about 5 kts (the actual figure to be used will be given by your instructor). This reduction of airspeed will reduce the float period as the aeroplane enters ground effect. During the flareout, which should occur at about the same height as for a normal landing, reduce power smoothly to idle. During the hold-off aim to raise the nose as high as possible so that the touchdown occurs at the lowest speed possible.

Once the aeroplane is firmly on the runway the brakes should be firmly applied according to conditions to reduce the landing run further. Some techniques dictate that the flaps should be raised prior to brake application to increase the weight on the landing gear and so increase the braking action.

The Glide Approach and Landing

The practice of this manoeuvre will develop your judgement in relation to the assessment of wind effects and the adjustments to the descent path and also the prediction of the touchdown point. This is a very important technique, since it will have to be adopted in the event of the need to carry-out an emergency landing without engine power available (forced landing without power) as a result of engine failure.

The practice and planning for a glide approach and landing
As usual the planning for this manoeuvre should begin in the circuit. On the downwind leg look at the runway and select a touchdown point. On the base leg maintain the circuit height if necessary until you are in a suitable position and sure that the intended touchdown point can be reached. Then enter a glide in the normal way, trimming for the best gliding speed which must be maintained at all times. Now, at this point you will have two main items to bear in mind. Firstly, you are assuming that engine power is no longer available, so you will have a limited ability to control the ROD. Secondly, the wind will affect your groundspeed and hence the angle of the descent path. So, once you have trimmed the aeroplane on the base leg you will have to evaluate the effects of the wind and immediately decide what adjustments will have to be made to the remainder of the circuit pattern to ensure there is sufficient altitude to reach the touchdown point once the aircraft is

GLIDE APPROACHES

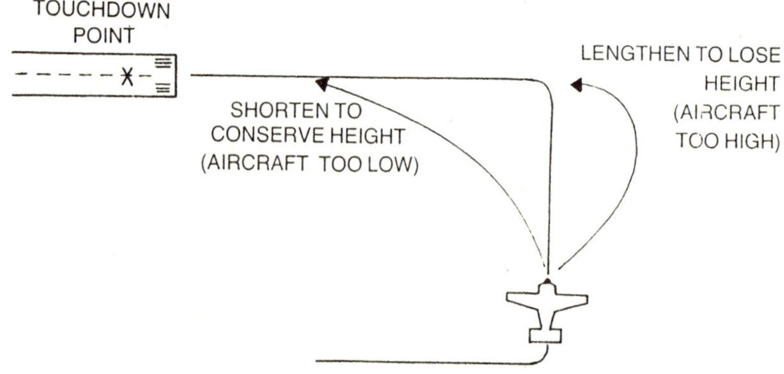

Fig. 108

established on the final approach. Figure 108 illustrates the type of adjustments that are likely.

Remember, the ROD is high during a glide and will increase during turns and since it is assumed that there is no engine power for use to flatten the glide path aim to arrive on the final approach at a greater height than normal, especially if a headwind is expected. Once established on the final approach there are various ways of losing excessive altitude if this becomes necessary in order to arrive at the touchdown point. Flaps will increase the ROD, but the use of full flaps should be delayed until you are absolutely certain of arriving in a safe position for landing. Shallow S turns (weaving turns), or moderate sideslips can also be used.

If the aeroplane is found to be too low during practice glide approaches, complete the approach using engine power, or overshoot. An attempt to stretch the glide by raising the nose will be ineffective and dangerous. Airspeed will reduce which will reduce glide range and this, combined with a lower groundspeed, will increase the descent angle and still result in the aeroplane undershooting the runway. Similarly, the raising of flaps to lower the descent rate is also not advisable. This is because the aircraft may sink due to the loss of lift.

If judgement and timing of actions are good, a stabilized approach can be achieved. Remember, engine considerations appropriate for a glide must not be neglected.

The landing

The landing should be executed in the normal way, but extra care taken during the flareout. This is because of the more acute angle which is a result of the steeper descent during a glide approach and the more rapid rate of speed reduction. Remember also that the reduced slipstream will make the controls less effective and therefore larger deflections of the rudder and elevators will be required to produce the desired responses.

The Flapless Approach and Landing

Due to mechanical or electrical failure, or strong winds, it may become necessary to land the aeroplane without flaps. Therefore, it is vital that you are aware that there are significant differences between a flaps down and a flapless landing.

Planning a flapless approach
Without flaps the descent path will be flatter. This will require a longer approach path, which means that the downwind leg will have to be extended as Figure 109 shows.

FLAPLESS APPROACH

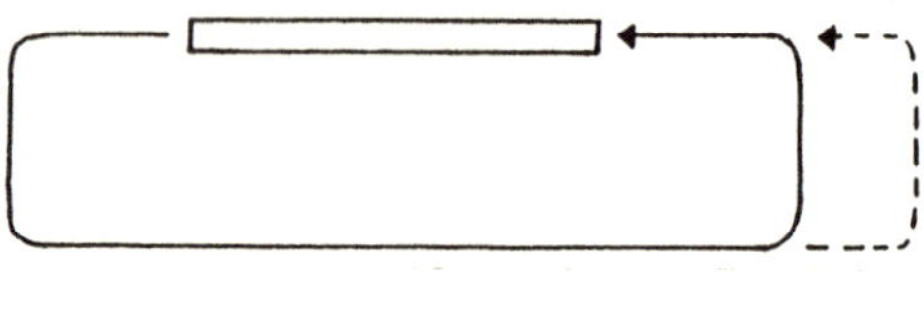

Fig. 109

Forward visibility is greatly reduced during a flapless approach, making it difficult to judge the approach path. A faster approach speed is normally used which maintains the safety margin because stalling speeds are higher without flaps.

Landing
The landing will be accomplished in the normal way but you will notice there will be little change in the aircraft's pitch attitude during the flareout and touchdown. Touchdown speeds will be higher and this, combined with the flatter descent path and prolonged float period, will produce an increased landing run.

Landing Tailwheel Aircraft
The approach and landing procedures already described will remain essentially the same for tailwheel aeroplanes, except for variations in the methods used to achieve the actual touchdown. There are two techniques that are used to land tailwheel aircraft.

The three-point technique will result in the aeroplane touching down on all three wheels simultaneously at a slow airspeed. To achieve this the hold-off period should be maintained as long as possible so that the aircraft is in the right attitude when touchdown occurs (see Fig. 110).

During the landing roll the control column should be held fully back.

THE '3' POINT LANDING

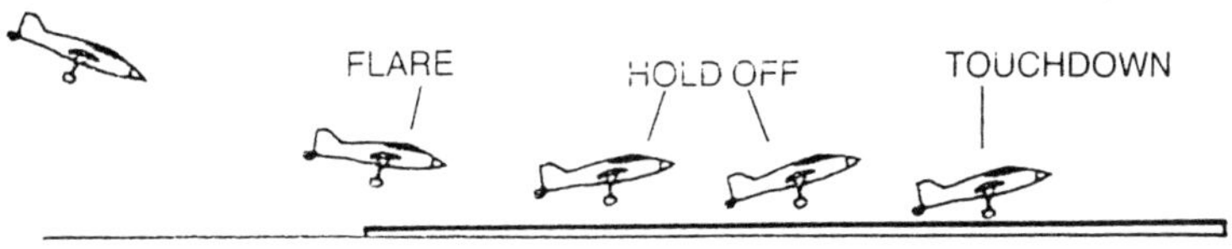

Fig. 110

In strong wind conditions the Wheel Landing technique is used. With this method touchdown must occur on the mainwheels first, as shown in Figure 111.

THE WHEEL LANDING

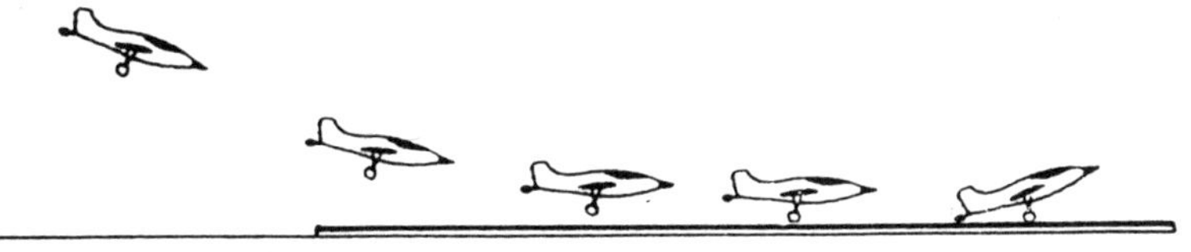

Fig. 111

The touchdown speed will be higher using the Wheel Landing, but this will improve control effectiveness in gusty conditions.

MISLANDINGS

Proper Pitch Control during Landings

Proper pitch control is vital during the landing flare. If the flareout is made too early the aeroplane will be too high above the runway and a hard touchdown will be the result. If the pitch attitude is raised too high and quickly during the flare-out the aeroplane will have a tendency to balloon, as illustrated in Figure 112.

If no corrective action is taken airspeed will dissipate rapidly and a hard landing will result. The recovery action will be to lower

BALLOONING

Fig. 112

the nose to the level attitude, add a small amount of power and land straight ahead (see Fig. 113).

BALLOONING RECOVERY ACTION

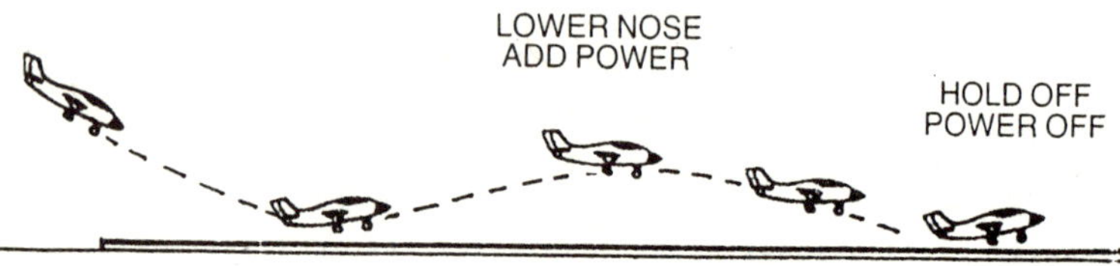

Fig. 113

It can be seen that the distance required for this may be quite considerable, so the safest course of action will be to overshoot and carry out another circuit.

If the nose attitude is not raised sufficiently during the flareout the aircraft will land either nosewheel first, or on all three wheels at a higher than normal speed which is likely to cause a bounce. There is nothing that can be done in these situations except to keep the wings level and allow the aeroplane to settle on the runway. In the case of a large bounce the recovery actions for ballooning may be used, but in any mislanding situation it would be better to overshoot.

Overshooting

Should you at any time have any doubts about the safe completion of a landing, the overshoot procedure must be carried out immediately. Your instructor must be sure of your ability to make prompt and sound decisions during the approach and landing before sending you solo.

The overshoot procedure was covered in the lesson on descending ('Entering a Climb from a Descent with Flaps' (p. 120)). Full power must be applied while at the same time raising the nose to the flaps lowered climbing attitude. Remember, strong forward pressure will be required to maintain the climbing speed. When a steady ROC is indicated start raising the flaps in stages, retrimming in the normal way. The procedure used for your aircraft must be carried out in the correct order and must be memorized. Once established in a normal climb continue to the circuit height and carry out another circuit as advised by ATC.

Touch and Goes

To save time during circuit training the aeroplane is usually not taxied back to the holding point of the runway for another take-off after every landing. Instead, provided the touchdown has taken place at the intended point leaving sufficient distance still available, the flaps are retracted, full power applied and the aircraft accelerated to take-off speed and then rotated, as illustrated in Figure 114. The flaps should not be retracted as the aircraft accelerates forward, as an unexpected pitch up may occur. The touch and go procedure will be covered in detail by your instructor.

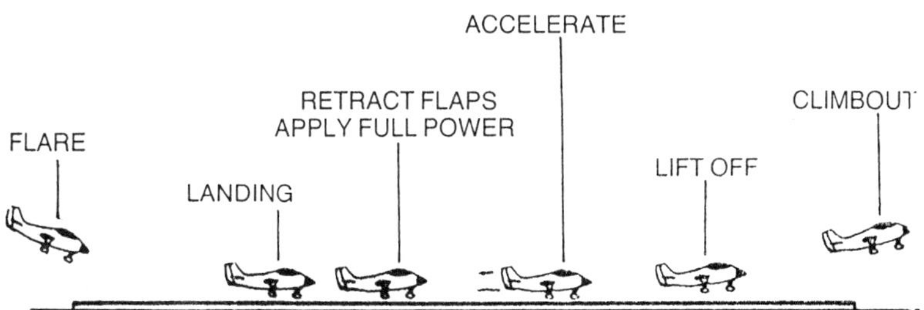

Fig. 114

If the touchdown occurs too far down the runway a touch and go should not be executed. Despite the forward momentum after the landing the aeroplane may not have sufficient distance to reach its lift-off speed. Or, if a lift-off is possible, safe obstacle clearance may not be. These are judgements you will have to make for yourself, but your instructor will give you guidelines based on local conditions.

EMERGENCY LANDINGS

Should the engine fail after take-off the pilot will have limited time and limited options. The immediate control actions have already been covered in the previous chapter. A landing may be possible in a long and relatively smooth field, or perhaps even on a road. On the other hand, a small and confined space may be the only area available. Be alert for overhead wires and cables. Do not prolong the flareout, land the aeroplane firmly if necessary and brake hard if required. If obstacles exist ahead take whatever avoiding action necessary. Strike any obstructions with the wings, not the nose. Aim to keep the fuselage intact to minimize the danger to occupants (information on the care and safety of passengers is contained in the section at the end of this book).

If there are too many obstructions around, a controlled crash landing will have to be carried out, again with the intention of minimizing fuselage damage. In dense woodland areas a tree landing may have to be made. The aim in this case should be to allow the wings and fuselage to make contact with the tops of the trees simultaneously at a slow speed and in a level attitude.

In these situations it is only possible to make generalizations. Only you can decide the best course of action to take in the circumstances, remembering two basic things; maintaining control of the aeroplane and minimizing injury to the occupants. Remember, also, a thorough pre-flight inspection will most probably prevent such an occurrence in the first place.

FURTHER EFFECTS OF WIND DURING LANDINGS AND TAKE-OFFS

No two landing approaches, or take-offs for that matter, are ever exactly the same. The main reasons for this are the prevailing wind/atmospheric conditions. The following pages will briefly describe the various conditions you are likely to encounter, the effects of which must be understood by all pilots.

Wind Shear

This is described as a change in wind speed and/or direction within a relatively short distance.

When two wind currents of different velocities meet friction will take place, which creates eddies (turbulent mixing of air) along a shallow zone called a shear zone (see Fig. 115).

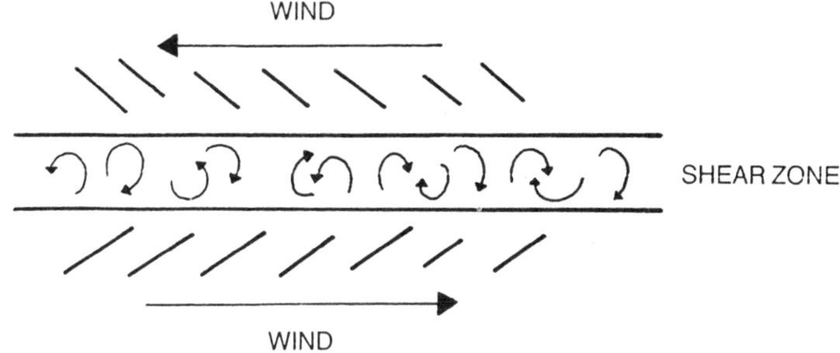

Fig. 115

When an aircraft flies from one wind current to another, as it passes through the shear zone bumpiness will be experienced and airspeed will be affected. This can be critical during low-speed operations, such as during the take-off and landing.

In order to understand why airspeed is affected when wind shear is encountered it will be necessary to remember the principle of inertia, i.e. the aeroplane will take time to adjust to a new environment. To use an extreme but illustrative example, imagine an aeroplane is trimmed to fly at 100 kts into a headwind of 100 kts. Its ground speed will, of course, be nil. Now, say the wind suddenly disappears. The aeroplane will have no forward momentum (ground speed), hence no airspeed. It will pitch downwards losing height (stall) until the forces of weight and thrust accelerate it back to its trimmed airspeed. The same thing would happen if the headwind were to suddenly change into a tailwind – the aeroplane would take time to propel itself to its trimmed airspeed, losing height in the process.

A more realistic example would be a situation where an aircraft suddenly encounters a tailwind during the initial climbout following take-off, as illustrated in Figure 116. Such a situation is not uncommon, but the atmospheric conditions that produce these winds are not covered in this book, as you will be learning about them when you come to study meterology.

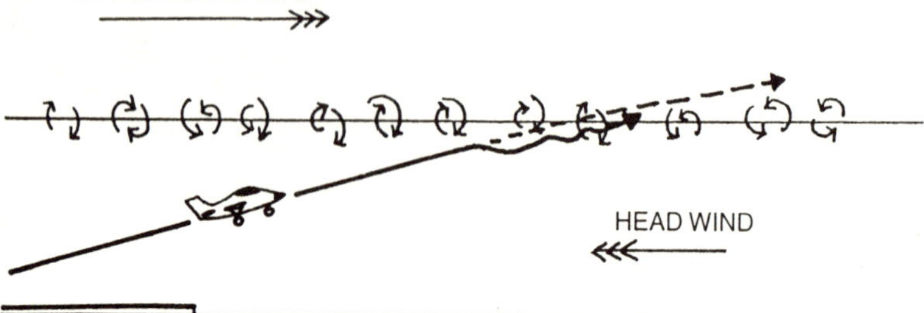

Fig. 116

The airspeed loss, combined with the turbulence as the aeroplane crosses the shear zone, could lead to a stall. For example, if the climbing speed is 80 kts and the headwind is 20 kts, as the aircraft enters the new wind current its forward momentum will be around 60 kts (remember the headwind now disappears). This brings the aeroplane closer to its stalling speed. Note also that the aircraft's gradient of climb will reduce as the tailwind exerts its influence. This could lead to the pilot subconsciously raising the nose to maintain the original angle of climb.

Similarly, an aircraft experiencing a sudden tailwind on the final approach may also lose sufficient airspeed to induce a stall (see Fig. 117).

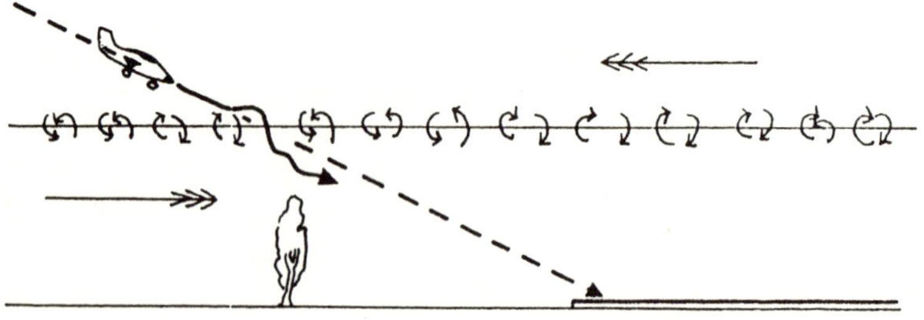

Fig. 117

Sudden decreases of headwind may also produce dangerous airspeed losses.

Obstructions to Wind Flow

Obstructions such as buildings, hangars, trees and uneven terrain around an airfield will disrupt wind flow, creating complex eddies (wind shears) which increase with the wind speed, as Figure 118 (a) and (b) illustrate.

OBSTRUCTIONS TO WIND FLOW

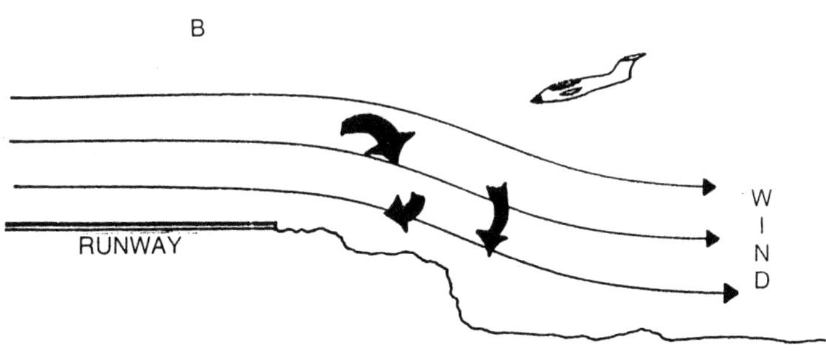

Fig. 118

If there are obstructions around a runway these can sometimes produce varying crosswinds and turbulence along different portions of the runway. All these effects can create serious problems during the take-off or landing approach. Make a special effort to note the obstructions in the immediate vicinity of an airfield, particularly at the ends of runways, so that you have a good idea of what may be expected.

The effect of wind shear will vary according to the strength of the different wind currents. The presence of wind shear, especially in the sort of situations described so far, is frequently undetectable until the turbulence at the shear zones is experienced. So, during low speed operations be ready with power and pitch control to maintain flying speed and prevent a stall.

Convective Currents

Briefly, these are caused by localized, uneven heating of the ground, producing up and down currents of varying velocities (gusts). An aircraft flying through gusty air is in fact encountering several wind shears. The effect on an aircraft will vary from mild bumpiness to severe jolts which can damage the aircraft, or injure the occupants. The aeroplane will be experiencing changing loads due to varying angles of attack and it is not unusual for the stall warner to operate. Turbulence on the approach can lead to abrupt changes in airspeed and a possible stall, so approach speeds must be increased by 5-10 kts. The airspeed needle may fluctuate wildly in these conditions, so concentrate on maintaining the correct pitch attitude and be ready to apply power if necessary. Sudden wing drops may also occur, and opposite rudder will have to be applied immediately to prevent further roll before levelling the wings.

If turbulence is felt early during the circuit you will know what to expect on the final approach. However, if the type of wind shears described at the beginning of this section exist, the aeroplane may well be flying through smooth air before suddenly encountering turbulence followed by a stall or near stall. So, whenever you are flying close to the ground be alert for the unexpected and be prepared for immediate reactions with power and pitch control. Also, depending on the direction of the new wind current, new drift may be experienced after flying through wind shear.

Wake Turbulence

In addition to natural turbulence caused by the weather, pilots must beware of the turbulence produced behind other aircraft, particularly larger aircraft. Fortunately there are more definite guidelines for avoiding the undesirable effects of this type of turbulence.

Going back to the basics, during lift production high-pressure air below the wing attempts to curl over the tip into the low-pressure region above it. When this air combines with the relative airflow above the wing a vortex is generated as shown in Figure 119.

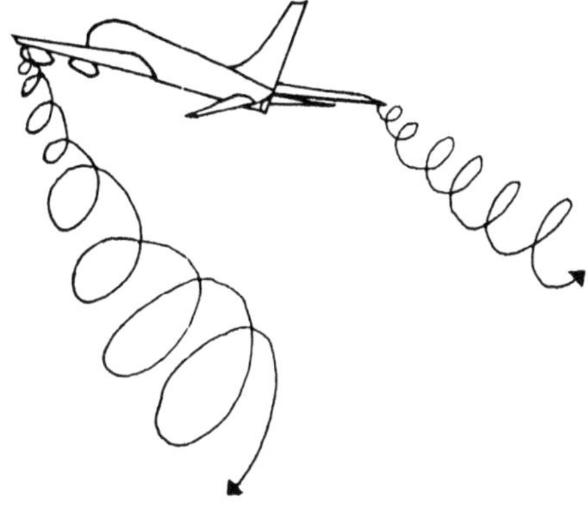

Fig. 119

These wingtip vortices are more intense behind large transport type aircraft, especially when they are flown at lower airspeeds. This is because at larger angles of attack the pressure differential is greater, producing a stronger vortex.

Vortices will spread outwards and downwards as they are generated and will drift with the wind, as illustrated in Figure 120.

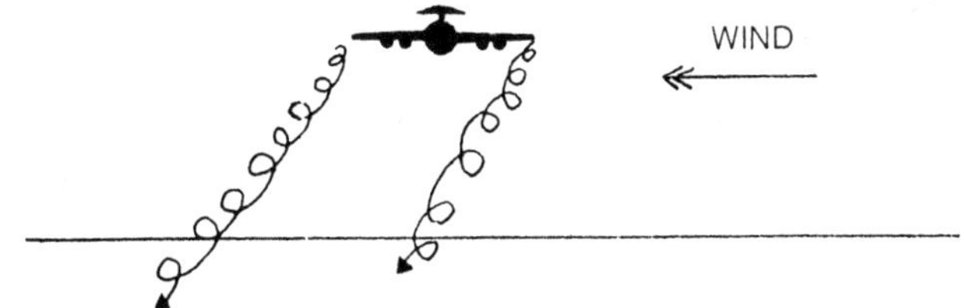

Fig. 120

During a ground run when most of the weight of the aeroplane is on the landing gear, and since the ground interferes with the airflow over the wings vortices will not develop. However, just before lift-off they will begin. Similarly, shortly after touchdown they will stop. An aircraft encountering vortices, especially those produced by larger aircraft, can easily be thrown completely out of control. Therefore, avoid flying close behind large aircraft.

Avoiding wake turbulence during take-off

Before taking off behind a larger departing aircraft ensure that you are able to become airborne well before its lift-off point, as shown in Figure 121.

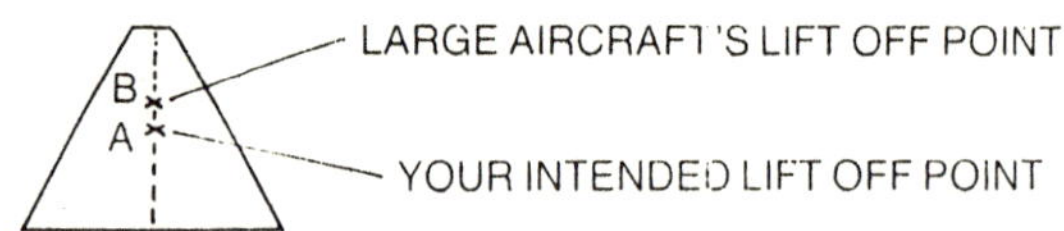

Fig. 121

It is also advisable to wait for a period of at least two minutes. In addition you must ensure that you are able to climb away above its climbing path (see Fig. 122)

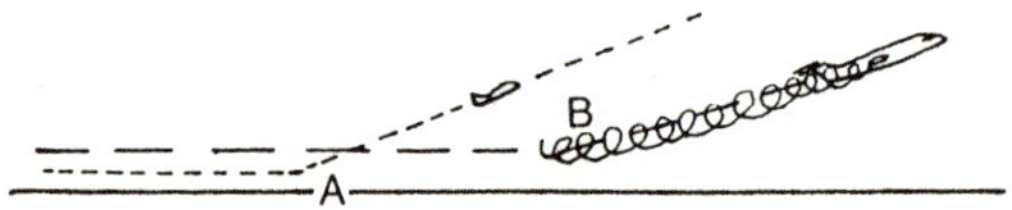

Fig. 122

Now, a take-off behind a landing aircraft is not advisable unless

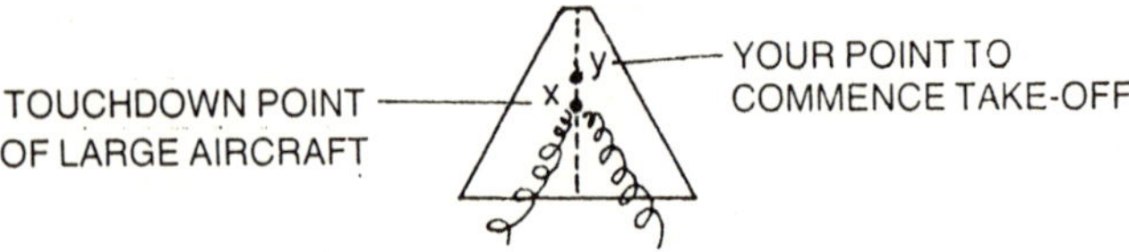

Fig. 123

you are able to start the take-off run beyond its touchdown point (see Fig. 123) and provided there is sufficient distance to do so.

If this is not possible you will have to wait for some time until the vortices dissipate or blow away.

Avoiding wake turbulence during the landing

When approaching to land behind a large aircraft maintain a safe distance behind it and adopt a descent profile that will result in a touchdown beyond that of the larger aircraft, as Figure 124 illustrates.

Fig. 124

When approaching to land behind a departing aircraft, aim to touchdown and stop before its lift-off point, as Figure 125 shows.

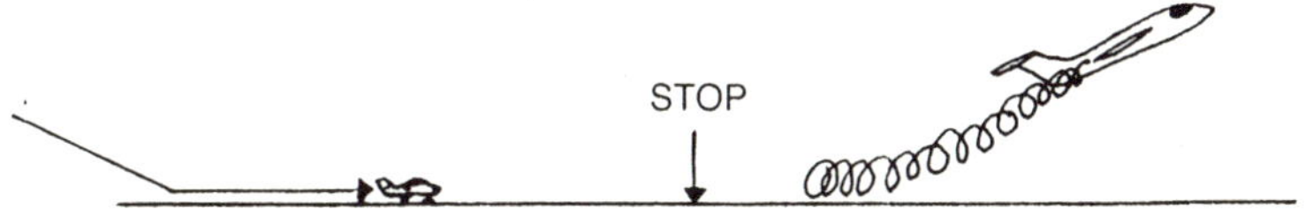

Fig. 125

The Effect of Crosswinds on Vortices near the ground

When a crosswind exists, it follows that the upwind vortices will be blown across the runway, as illustrated by Figure 126.

This is the main reason why a waiting period is necessary. If the crosswind is light, the drift rate of the vortices across the runway may be very slow and they may persist for a while. It is not possible to state a specific time, but a wait of several minutes is likely before it becomes safe for a take-off. If you are intending to land, another circuit may be necessary.

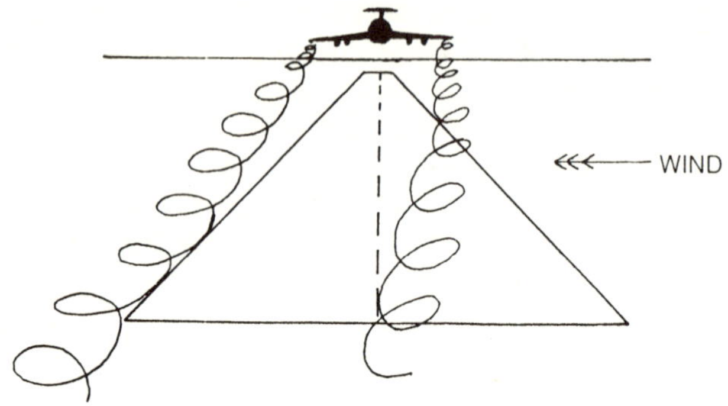

Fig. 126

AIRMANSHIP

Although concentration needs to be high during the approach phase, good lookouts must not be neglected. Aircraft often make long final approaches to the runway (straight-in approaches) so have a good lookout in this area before making the final turn. Aircraft on long and low final approaches can be difficult to locate against the ground and the situation illustrated in Figure 127 can occur if you are not careful.

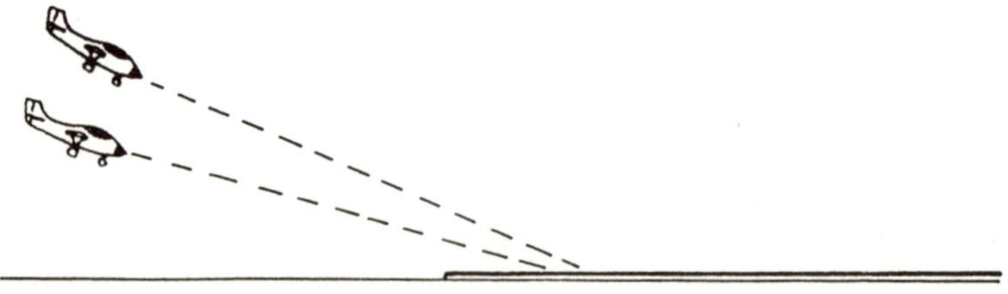

Fig. 127

So, lookout above and below as well.

Position yourself correctly and do not land close behind another aircraft that is landing or taking off. It is standard procedure to make a position report once the final turn is made. In bad visibility it is good practice to switch on the landing light so that you can be more easily located by ATC, and if severe turbulence is encountered on the approach report this so that other pilots will be made aware.

AIR LESSON

The Powered Approach and Landing

Establishing a stabilized approach
After turning on to the final approach:

1. Select a heading to maintain the approach track.
2. Lower full flap (if required).
3. Trim for the appropriate speed.

If the aeroplane is too high on the approach:

1. Reduce power (usually only small reductions are necessary).
2. Lower the nose to maintain airspeed.
3. Retrim.

If the aeroplane is too low on the approach:

1. Increase power.
2. Raise the nose to maintain airspeed.
3. Retrim.

Keep your hand on the throttle at all times and be alert for wind shear.

Maintain the appropriate speed at all times.

Maintain the approach track at all times, adjusting the aircraft's heading as required.

When using a sideslip descent remember the pitch attitude will have to be adjusted to maintain the airspeed, and the ROD will be greater.

Landing
As the aeroplane closes with the runway check the descent and fly level just above the ground by:

1. Moving the control column gradually backwards according to

the aircraft's sink rate while slowly reducing power. Keep the wings level.

2. Aim to touchdown in a nose high attitude on the mainwheels first and with the throttle fully closed.
3. As the mainwheels make contact with the runway close the throttle.

After touchdown:

1. Maintain the back pressure.
2. Control direction with the rudder.
3. Slow down the aeroplane and taxi clear of the runway for the after landing checks.

NOTE:
Remember to direct your line of sight to the left of the nose during the landing, focusing your eyes as required. You must be aiming to judge your proximity to the ground in order to anticipate the control pressures to be used to land the aeroplane correctly.

The Crosswind Landing (from a stabilized approach)
Maintain the necessary crab angle during the flareout and hold-off and just before touchdown:

1. Straighten the nose using rudder pressure.
2. Rotate the control wheel in the opposite direction as required (raise the upwind aileron) to keep the wings level.

These control actions must be simultaneous.

After touchdown:

1. Maintain aileron deflection.
2. Maintain elevators neutral (control column neutral).
3. Control direction with the rudder.
4. Slow down and taxi clear.

Landing from a Sideslip Approach
To maintain the centreline as airspeed reduces during the flareout and hold-off, slightly increase the control pressures used during the sideslip. Keep the aeroplane under control and aim to touchdown on the upwind mainwheel first. After touchdown neutralize the rudder pedals and use as required to control

direction. Maintain the aileron deflection during the ground roll, slow down and taxi clear.

The Soft Field/Rough Ground Landing

This manoeuvre is carried out from a stabilized approach with full flaps lowered with the aeroplane trimmed for the appropriate speed. The aim will be to touch down on the mainwheels like a normal landing except that during the landing run the nosewheel is kept clear of the ground for as long as possible. This is achieved by:

1. Leaving a small amount of power on as the aeroplane touches down.
2. Maintaining a nose-high attitude using the elevators as the aeroplane slows down. (When the aircraft has slowed down sufficiently allow the nose to gradually lower of its own accord.)

As the nosewheel makes contact:

1. Leave the power on.
2. Maintain the back pressure.
3. Slow down further with the brakes if required.
4. Taxi clear using soft field procedures.

The Short Field Landing

The objective of this manoeuvre is to land and stop safely in the shortest possible distance. It must be carried out from a stablized approach with full flaps lowered and with the aircraft accurately trimmed for the appropriate speed.

When there are obstacles in the landing path:

1. On the base leg select a suitable touchdown point on the runway.
2. Make the final turn at a higher altitude than normal so that a steeper descent angle will have to be initiated to reach the touchdown point and overfly the obstacle (beware of wind shear turbulence near the obstacle).

Landing

As the obstacle is overflown:

1. Reduce the airspeed by a small amount.

2. During the flareout reduce power to idle.
3. During the hold-off aim to reduce the speed as much as possible before the touchdown occurs, by increasing the back pressure.

After touchdown:

1. Ensure the aeroplane is firmly on the ground by holding the elevators neutral (depending on the surface conditions).
2. Raise the flaps if applicable, then apply the brakes according to surface conditions to slow down or stop the aeroplane as required.
3. Taxi clear of the landing area.

The Glide Approach and Landing

The practice of glide approaches begins on the base leg and you will be assuming that there is no engine power available with which to vary the ROD.

On the base leg:

1. Select a touchdown point on the runway.
2. Maintain the circuit height if necessary until you feel that the altitude will be sufficient to cover the distance around the remainder of the circuit and to the runway without the help of engine power.
3. Then enter a normal glide and trim for the best gliding speed.
4. Immediately evaluate the effects of wind on your progress towards the runway.

If you are too low while still on the base leg, start to turn towards the runway immediately to shorten the distance to be covered.

If you are too high, extend the base leg as required.

Maintain a crab angle if required to maintain the approach track.

If you are too high on the final approach lower flaps, but delay the use of full flaps until the later stages of the approach.

If you are still too high, sideslip or make shallow S turns.

Maintain the correct speed at all times, especially during turns, sideslips and flap operation.

Landing

The landing is made in the normal way but extra care taken in pitch control during the flareout. Once the aeroplane has been slowed down sufficiently taxi clear of the runway using power.

During practice glide approaches, if the aircraft is found to be too low to complete the landing, continue the approach using power, or overshoot.

Do not neglect engine checks during glide approaches.

The Flapless Landing

When a landing without flaps is intended extend the downwind leg to allow for a longer final approach.

On the base leg:

1. Trim the aeroplane for a slightly higher approach speed.
2. On finals establish a stabilized powered approach.
3. Note that forward visibility is reduced compared with an approach with flaps.

Landing

The landing is accomplished in the normal way, but note:

1. there will not be much change in the nose attitude during the flareout and hold-off
2. the higher touchdown speed
3. the extended float period and landing run.

Landing Tailwheel Aircraft

To achieve the three-point landing:

1. Flareout in the normal way and during the hold-off continue the back pressure until the aeroplane reaches the normal attitude it would be if it were on the ground. At this point it should touch down on all three wheels simultaneously.
2. During the landing roll maintain the back pressure and control direction with positive use of the rudder.

To achieve the Wheel Landing:

1. Flareout in the normal way but instead of aiming for a nose-high attitude control the pitch attitude so that the aeroplane touches down on the mainwheels first and in a slightly tail-down attitude.
2. On touchdown relax the back pressure slightly and allow the tail to lower naturally as the aeroplane slows down.
3. Do not use the brakes until the tail has made contact with the ground.

4. Use rudder positively to control direction during the landing roll.

Overshooting

The procedure for this has already been given in the air lesson section on descending.

Should you have any doubts about continuing an approach for a landing, or if a mislanding seems likely, or if instructed by ATC, overshoot immediately and carry out another circuit.

Touch-and-Goes

A touch-and-go should only be executed if the landing has been made safely and there is sufficient distance still available for a safe take-off to be made. Once direction is under control on the runway the basic procedure is as follows:

1. Retract the flaps.
2. Check the carburettor heat is set to COLD.
3. Apply full power smoothly.
4. Continue as for a normal take-off (checking engine instruments etc.).

SIMULATED ENGINE FAILURES AFTER TAKE-OFF

At a safe height during the initial climbout your instructor will close the throttle at unexpected moments to simulate an engine failure. Once the necessary actions have been completed (notably maintaining control of the aeroplane and selection of the landing site) the aeroplane is placed in a climb again and the circuit continued. This will be done several times during your course until your responses become instinctive.

Instructor's Guide
Ex. 12 and 13

LESSON PLAN

Normal and crosswind take-offs and landings; flying in the circuit

Objectives

To introduce and develop the following skills:

(a) normal and crosswind take-offs
(b) normal and crosswind landings
(c) aborted take-offs and engine failure after take-off procedures
(d) flying around the circuit and drift corrections
(e) overshoot procedures
(f) touch and go procedures.

Contents

1 Preflight briefing

Revise previous lessons and discuss the above objectives.

2 Flight lesson

Review:

(a) normal preflight procedures, then: *Demonstrate a take-off, circuit pattern and landing according to existing conditions. Student practice. Introduce engine failures, overshoots, touch-and-goes and aborted take-offs. (See* 'Air Lesson' (p. 188)).

3 Postflight discussion and preview of the next lesson

Completion Standards

This lesson will have been successfully completed when the student can execute normal take-offs and landings with minimum assistance and has a proper concept of the crosswind techniques during a take-off and landing. The student should have a reasonable standard of drift corrections in the circuit and be competent in emergency, overshoot and touch-and-go procedures.

LESSON PLAN

Maximum performance take-offs and landings

Objectives

To continue to develop the student's skills in normal and crosswind take-offs and landings, circuit flying, emergency procedures and overshoot and touch and go procedures by concentrated practice; to introduce short and soft field take-offs and landings, glide approaches and landings and flapless approaches and landings; to improve the student's ability to recover from poor approaches and mislandings.

Content

1 Preflight briefing

Discuss in detail the above objectives.

2 Flight lesson

Review:

(a) preflight procedures
(b) normal and crosswind take-offs and landings
(c) emergencies, overshoots and touch-and-goes
(d) circuit flying (emphasis on neat circuits) then: *Demonstrate short and soft field take-offs and landings and glide and flapless approaches and landings. Demonstrate how to recover from poor approaches and mislandings. Student practice.* (*See* 'Air Lesson' (p. 233))

3 Postflight discussion and preview of the next lesson

Completion Standards

These lessons will have been completed successfully when the student can demonstrate a degree of proficiency in normal and crosswind take-offs and landings and circuit patterns, which is considered safe for solo. The student should be able to perform maximum performance take-offs and landings without assistance and have instinctive and competent responses to emergency situations. The student should display sound judgement and proper techniques during overshoots, touch-and-goes and recoveries from poor approaches and mislandings.

Exercise 14

FIRST SOLO AND CONSOLIDATION

Your first solo flight will be the most important event in your training so far. For the first time you will be in sole command of the aeroplane.

Before going solo you must have completed a number of good take-offs and landings and your instructor must be satisfied with your ability to make safe decisions and cope with emergencies (apart from engine failures after take-off, aborted take-offs and various taxi-ing emergencies you must also be able to handle fire emergencies. The actions to be taken in the event of a fire will be contained in the Flight Manual and checklist and you must study them immediately if you have not already done so).

A first solo flight will consist of a normal circuit and landing, although you must not hesitate to go around again if you decide it is necessary. Your instructor will brief you fully beforehand. There will not be any significant differences in the aeroplane's performance on this flight, the most noticeable thing being the absence of another person in the cockpit.

After completing your first solo, your confidence will inevitably increase as this is the first proof of your ability to act as the captain of an aircraft.

Consolidation

Following the first solo, the next few flying hours will be spent in the circuit perfecting the various take-off and landing techniques with your instructor and also more solo flights. The period after this will be flexible, being basically an introduction to certain aspects of cross-country flying.

You will have to become more familiar with the surrounding area and more involved with local procedures.

If your airfield lies within controlled airspace, such as a control zone, special arrival and departure procedures will have to be carried out. Typically these are following entry/exit lanes and complying with ATC instructions. If your airfield lies outside such areas the procedures will be a little simpler. Your instructor will cover all the specific procedures required in your area. This type of information can also be found in the *Air Pilot*, which is a publication available at all flying schools and which you must become familiar with.

Airfield Arrival Procedures

It has already been explained that at certain airfields specific procedures will have to be followed. At airfields with an active ATSU arriving aircraft simply follow the instructions given. However, at airfields without such a service there is a standard procedure for joining the circuit pattern.

First of all you will have to overfly the airfield to determine the landing direction (runway in use) and circuit direction from the signals square. The height you fly over the airfield must be at least 2,000ft agl. Having done this, descend to the circuit height on the opposite side of the circuit pattern in operation (called the dead side), aiming to join the circuit on the downwind leg by crossing the upwind end of the runway, as illustrated in Figure 128.

STANDARD CIRCUIT REJOIN

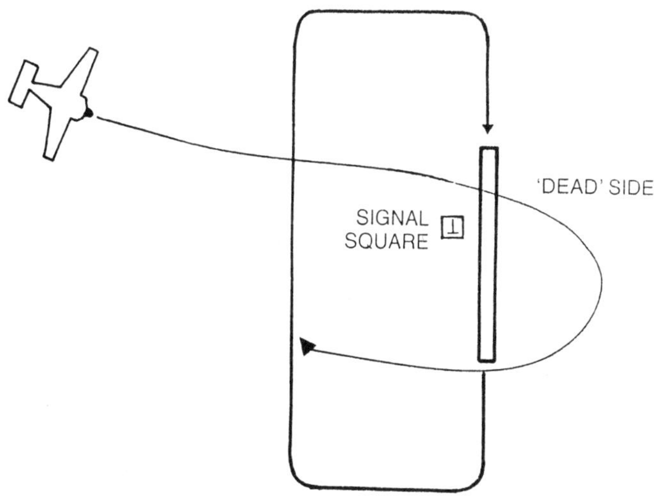

Fig. 128

Airfield Departure Procedure

At airfields with a traffic control service, departing aircraft usually have to proceed according to instructions. When departing from an uncontrolled airfield you will have to make your own decisions based on traffic conditions and your intended cruising direction, but you must aim not to conflict with the circuit pattern after the initial climbout.

Arrival and departure procedures are covered in more detail in the chapter on 'Pilot Navigation'.

Cruise Checks/Airfield Approach Checks

During the en route phase of a flight the systems of the aircraft must be monitored at regular intervals. These take the form of checks, often called FREDA checks:

Fuel

Check the fuel situation regularly. Where more than one fuel tank is fitted use them alternately so that fuel is consumed evenly from each one. Ensure the mixture is leaned according to the procedure for your aircraft. Readjust the mixture control whenever the power setting is altered or the cruising altitude is changed.

Radio

Check the radio frequencies selected are correct and adjust the volume and squelch controls if necessary. Make any radio calls required.

Engine

Check the temperatures and pressures and check for carburettor icing. Also check the ammeter and suction gauges.

DI and compass

Synchronize these instruments. Make sure the wings are level and the speed is constant when doing so.

Altitude

Check that you are maintaining the required altitude and that the correct pressure setting is set. Obtain a revised setting if necessary from ATC.

These checks should also be carried out during the final stages of a cross-country flight when approaching an airfield and before joining the circuit.

MAP READING

In addition to various operating procedures you must be able to locate the boundaries of the different types of airspace, such as control zones, special rules zones, military zones and danger areas, etc. The status of these types of airspace must be known and will be explained in the study of air law/legislation (not covered in this book). You will also have to be able to monitor your progress accurately along the ground. In order to do all this you will be learning how to orientate yourself using an appropriate map (obtainable from your school).

Locate your airfield on the map and study the area within a radius of, say, 20 miles. The legend at the bottom of the map will contain a description of the various symbols used. You must learn all these as soon as possible, so that map reading becomes easier and more rapid.

If your airfield is within a control zone, locate the entry/exit lanes, if any, and any suitable ground references that can be used in identifying their position. Locate the boundaries of any other nearby zones in the same way and make a note of the altitudes within which they are operant. Also, since many airfields are situated underneath terminal control areas (TMAs) make a note of the maximum altitudes that may be flown in such areas. These are all indicated on the map.

After the circuit consolidation period a short flight around the local area is usually made to give you an opportunity to practise map reading from the air. Using the aircraft's heading as a basis, monitor your progress along the ground by using suitable ground features to establish your position on the map. For example, if the aeroplane is flying away from the airfield on a heading of 090°, the ground features you come across will be located to east of the airfield location on the map. During this flight make a special note of the landmarks relatively close to the airfield as they will help you locate it more easily when returning from flights away.

ALTIMETER SETTINGS IN THE CIRCUIT AND LOCAL AREA

Circuit heights are given in feet above the ground (the airfield). Due to the design of pressure altimeters, which are used in most aeroplanes, it is vital that the prevailing atmospheric pressure at the surface of the airfield is set on the sub-scale of the altimeter so that the aircraft's height above the ground is indicated correctly. If the pressure setting is wrong the aeroplane will not be flying at the correct height, although the altimeter may indicate the required height. The pressure datum (setting) used to indicate height above the airfield is called the QFE (a term you have already heard by now) and is obtainable from ATC. When this is set the altimeter will indicate zero altitude when the aeroplane lands. However, the QFE can only be used safely and effectively in the circuit or airfield traffic zone.

The heights indicated on your maps, such as those of high ground, man-made obstructions, certain airspace limits and airfield elevations are all altitudes above sea level. Therefore, to overfly obstructions safely en route (terrain clearance) and orientate yourself vertically with respect to different types of airspace, a pressure datum that will indicate the aeroplane's altitude above sea level must be used. This is called the QNH and is also obtainable from ATC. Since atmospheric pressure changes with time and varies from one place to another, it will be necessary to update the QNH from time to time. The UK is divided into a number of altimeter setting regions and if you fly from one into another a revised QNH must be obtained. If you look on your map you will find the boundaries of various regions. When the aeroplane lands with the QNH set the airfield's altitude above sea level will be indicated.

You will probably have noticed the abbreviations FL (flight level) followed by a number, such as FL 60 for example, alongside the boundaries of certain types of airspace, mostly airways. When the altimeter sub-scale is set to the International Standard Atmosphere (ISA) pressure setting of 1013.2 mb (or 29.92 in. hg) an aircraft's vertical position is referred to in terms of flight levels. For example, with the ISA pressure datum set the aeroplane will be flying at FL 60 when the altimeter reads 6,000ft. Similarly, to reach FL 75 the aircraft will have to climb to 7,500ft. Now with this datum set the aircraft's altitude above sea level will not be indicated unless the prevailing pressure also happens to be 1013.2

mb, which is not often the case. This means that if an aeroplane operates at flight levels, reference must still be made to the QNH to ensure safe terrain clearance. The ISA pressure datum is used by aircraft operating under instrument flight rules and above 3,000ft amsl. Use of a standard datum will make aircraft separation more certain in instrument flying conditions regardless of barometric variations, since all altimeters will be synchronized.

As you will now be flying under visual flight rules you will be concerned mainly with the QFE and QNH pressure settings, but the ISA setting (often called the QNE) may be set when required to assess your proximity vertically in relation to controlled airspace when the limits are expressed in flight levels.

During circuit flying ensure that the QFE is set. When leaving the airfield set the QNH, revising it en route as required. When arriving at the airfield obtain and set the QFE before joining the circuit.

VERY HIGH FREQUENCY DIRECTION FINDING

Many airfields have equipment which can give bearings after analysing radio transmissions. These are listed in the *Air Pilot* under the 'Com' section.

The bearings given can be true bearings from the ground station (QTE) or magnetic headings (QDM) that can be used to steer to the ground station. These can be very useful in flight as they can be used to 'home in' to an airfield, although you will have to make the necessary corrections for wind.

To obtain a QDM, tune in the relevant frequency (following the proper radio procedures) and request one. The bearing given will include an accuracy classification. The various classes of bearing are as follows:

Class A – accuracy +/−2°
Class B – accuracy +/−5°
Class C – accuracy +/−10°
Class D – accuracy less than 10°

When a Class D bearing is given it should be treated with caution. For effective VHF bearings the aircraft must be high enough to allow the transmission to follow an uninterrupted 'line of sight' route to the ground station.

Having received the QDM turn on to the heading given and then request another one since the aircraft will have altered its horizontal position after the turn. The aeroplane will now be flying towards the station. Maintain the heading and continue to request more QDMs to assess your progress. If you find the QDMs constantly increasing or decreasing in heading, drift is being experienced. Now, by continually readjusting your heading as new QDMs are received the aeroplane will still arrive at the ground station although it will have followed a curved path (see Fig. 129).

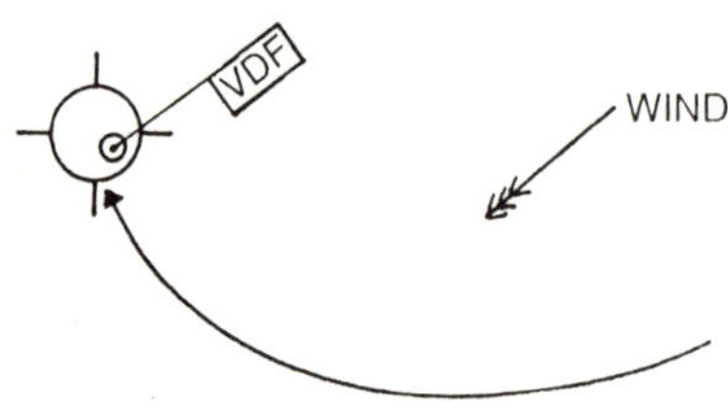

Fig. 129

To maintain a consistent ground track, a crab angle will have to be established to offset the drift. To do this you will have to determine the wind direction, if you do not know what it is beforehand. If the QDMs are increasing, i.e. you keep having to alter heading to the right, the wind is coming from the right and you are drifting to the left. So, on obtaining the next QDM instead of turning on to this heading select a heading a few degrees to the right of it, to offset the drift. For example, say the QDMs you received over a period of time were 270°, 280°, 290° and 300° respectively, the aeroplane is clearly drifting to the left, meaning the wind is from the right as Figure 130 illustrates.

Now, on receiving the QDM of 300° instead of turning on to this heading, a turn into wind on to a heading of, say, 310° is likely to offset some of the drift. If this correction is sufficient the QDMs received subsequently will not vary and the aeroplane will follow a consistent ground track to the station (see Fig. 131).

It may be that the crab angle is insufficient or too much, so you will have to make the necessary adjustments. If the QDMs are decreasing the method is the same. The wind is from the left, so drift corrections must be to the left.

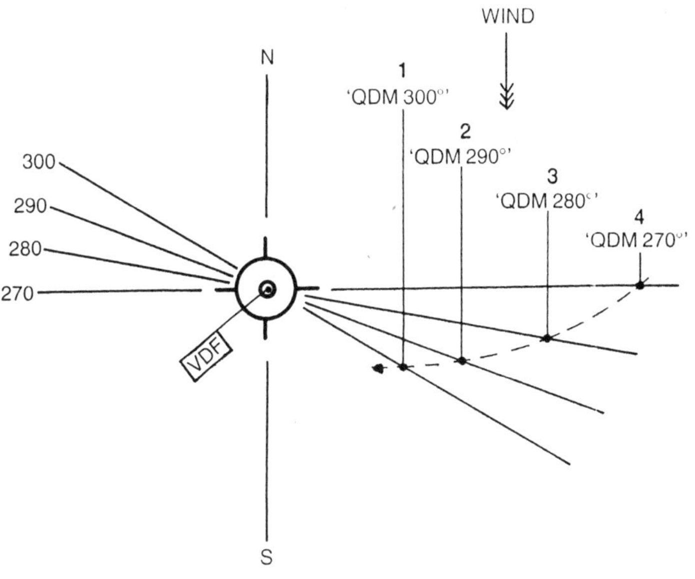

Fig. 130

You will have an opportunity to practise obtaining and using QDMs, but it is unlikely that you will have enough time to master the technique during the PPL course. VDF has many useful applications when it comes to advanced navigation procedures and these will be covered when you want to obtain higher flying qualifications. At this stage you are only required to have a basic understanding of how to use it to arrive within sighting distance of the airfield.

AIRMANSHIP

During your first solo flight for the first time lookouts will become your responsibility entirely. It is vital that you do not neglect them. Before each subsequent solo flight you will usually have a short dual check, when your instructor will be monitoring your performance to make sure you have not neglected your responsibilities or developed any bad habits.

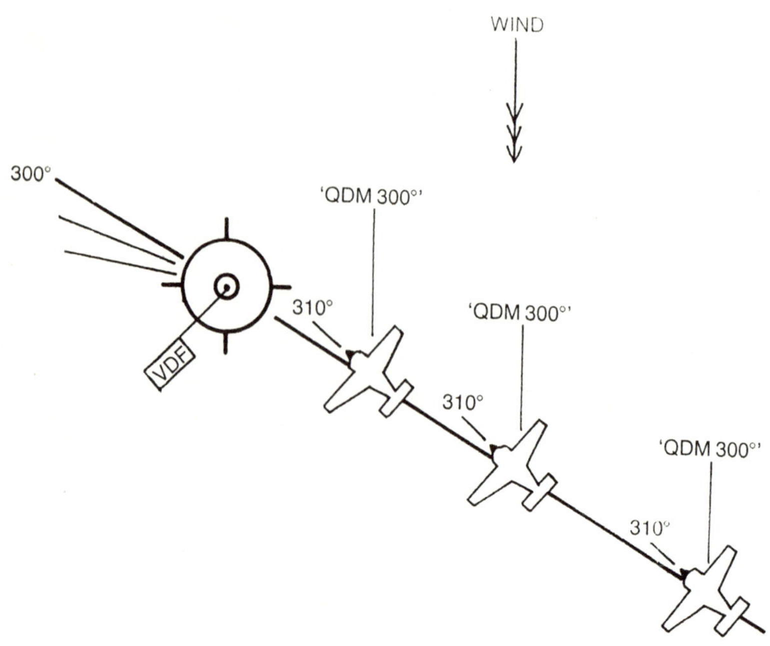

Fig. 131

AIR LESSON

As mentioned earlier, this period will be a mixture of solo flights and lessons with your instructor on local procedures, map reading, VDF procedures and also compass turns. This is a consolidation period so reread all the preceding chapters, making sure you thoroughly understand all the techniques and procedures you have been taught so far.

Ground Studies

The consolidation period after first solo really marks the end of your first stage in training. The second stage will consist of the following lessons – Advanced Turning, Operation at Minimum Level, Forced Landings, Pilot Navigation and an introduction to instrument flying. This will be followed by a revision period in preparation for a flight test. Ideally, before the start of the second stage you will have passed your air law and technical examination and have obtained an R/T licence; or at least you should have no doubts on these subjects. In this way you will be able to concentrate fully on the subjects of meterology and particularly navigation, which form the major part of the second stage.

Instructor's Guide
Ex. 14

LESSON PLAN

First solo flight

Objectives
To develop the student's competence to a standard which will allow the safe accomplishment of the first supervised solo flight in the circuit.

Content
1 Preflight briefing
Revise all circuit flying procedures.

2 Flight lesson
Review:

(a) take-offs and landings (according to existing conditions)
(b) overshoot procedures
(c) engine failure after take-off procedures
(d) recovery from poor approaches and mislandings.

Provided the student is up to standard he or she may be sent on a solo flight in the circuit.

3 Postflight discussion and preview of the next lesson

Completion Standards
This lesson will have been successfully completed when the student has safely completed a solo flight in the circuit.

THE CONSOLIDATION PERIOD

Objectives
1 To review pre-solo manoeuvres with the emphasis on achieving a higher standard of proficiency.

2. To develop further the student's familiarity with the local area and procedures.
3. To introduce the student to cross-country flying procedures (map reading, use of VDF, etc.).
4. To introduce elementary forced landings and send the student on more solo flights.

Completion Standards

This period of training will have been successfully completed when the student displays improved performance of the pre-solo manoeuvres; is able to determine position in the local area by reference to the map; and is confident in the use of VDF for homing purposes. The student's confidence should increase, and flying technique improve as a result of the solo flying periods.

Exercise 15

ADVANCED TURNING

Objectives

1. To learn to enter and maintain a steep level turn (between 45° and 60° angle of bank) and to roll out on to specific headings.
2. To learn to enter and maintain steep climbing and descending turns.

In addition you will be learning to recognize and recover from high-speed stalls, spiral dives and unusual attitudes.

The practice of steep turns is an excellent exercise for developing your control co-ordination and handling of the aeroplane. It requires accurate pitch, bank and power control. This is vital when increased turning performance is required, such as when taking extreme collision avoidance measures, or to get into a safe position for an emergency landing. An aeroplane in a correctly executed steep turn will be operating close to its performance limits. This is very important for you to understand, so before explaining the handling techniques the next few pages will go into the subject in some detail.

Manoeuvring Flight

The relationship between bank angle, load factor and stalling speeds has already been introduced in the chapters on 'Turning' and 'Stalling'. The types of turns you have been using so far (standard rate and medium level) use bank angles that produce adequate rates of turn with safe increases in load factor and stalling speeds and also safe reductions in airspeed due to the increase in induced drag. By reference to the Load Factor table in the chapter on 'Stalling' it can be seen that as bank angle increases above 30°, the load factor increases at a much faster rate, producing substantial increases in stalling speed. The amount of speed reduction is also much greater as bank angles are increased. This is due to the increased induced drag as more back pressure is applied to increase the angle of attack. In fact, the amount of speed reduction is related to the load factor. For example, a 60° banked turn at 2Gs would produce the same airspeed loss if the aircraft's weight were to double in level flight. So, since stalling speeds increase and airspeed decreases during a steep turn, the margin of airspeed between the two is reduced. To maintain a safe margin, therefore, power must be increased.

Load Factors

The load factor (G force) you will experience during a steep turn is called positive G. You have already felt the sensation while pulling out of a dive during spin training. Negative G on the other hand is loading produced in the opposite direction. You may have experienced this more unpleasant sensation if you have ever applied forward pressure on the control column too quickly.

Now, an aircraft structure like any other can only withstand a certain amount of loads and stresses before it weakens and collapses. An aircraft flying through severe turbulence or mishandled by the pilot can experience excessive load factors that can cause catastrophic structural failure in flight, or at least weaken it enough to cause failure on a later flight. Most modern training aircraft are designed to withstand positive load factors of +3.8G and negative load factors of −1.52G (limiting load factors). Although it may seem that the aircraft can withstand almost twice as much positive G than negative G, this is not the case. Remember, an aircraft in steady flight already experiences a load factor of 1. This means accelerations of only 2.8Gs are required to reach its positive limit and 2.52Gs to reach the negative limit.

The limiting load factors of your aeroplane will be given in the Flight Manual and these must not be exceeded. Nor must an aeroplane be exposed to numerous exposures of its limit, since this too will cause weakening, damage and eventual failure. In addition, excessive positive G will cause the pilot eventually to black out. This is caused by blood draining from the head and depriving the brain of oxygen. Similarly, excessive negative Gs can cause a red-out, when the tiny veins of the eyes burst as blood rushes to the head. Aircraft are not designed for negative G manoeuvres for this reason, although they can be produced in flight.

Relationship of load factor to airspeed

Now, the limiting load factor can only be exceeded if very severe turbulence is encountered, or the aircraft is mishandled at high speeds.

The greater the airspeed, the greater the forces exerted on the aircraft structure. If speed is allowed to increase above the aircraft's never-exceed speed (Vne), the loads experienced will cause structural failure. Similar dangerous loads can be produced at speeds below Vne by sudden increases in angle of attack (remember larger angles of attack will also increase the forces produced by an aeroplane). If an aircraft is certified to withstand 3.8G, this means the loads will have to be almost four times the aeroplane's weight before structural failure is possible. Since this limitation can be exceeded by excessive speed, it can also be exceeded by combinations of lower speeds and larger angles of attack. Therefore, as well as the Vne, it is important to establish the range of speeds where such combinations can occur.

So, since the forces experienced by an aircraft are determined largely by angle of attack and airspeed, it follows that the maximum load factor than can be produced at any particular speed will be achieved just before the stall (the largest angle of attack). Now, the lower the speed the smaller the loads imposed upon the airframe as a result of sudden accelerations. From this, another range of speeds can be established where the combination of speed and sudden accelerations will produce maximum load factors within the limiting load factors.

One way of preventing the limiting load factor from being exceeded is to ensure the aeroplane stalls first (stalling acts as a form of aerodynamic relief). So, as load factor capability increases with speed, a speed can be established where the aeroplane will stall at the limiting load factor. Figure 132 illustrates this.

This is a typical Vn envelope, which is a diagram used to illustrate the operating strengths and limitations of an aircraft. The maximum lift curves show that as airspeed increases so does the load factor capability and also that at given speeds the maximum load factor can be produced at the stall. It also shows that at a certain speed (Va) the aircraft will stall at the limiting load factor. The Va is called the design manoeuvring speed and will be given in the Flight Manual. The design manoeuvring speed is the dividing line between the two ranges of speeds previously mentioned. At and below Va abrupt and extreme control deflections are possible without exceeding the limiting load factor (although such actions are not advised). Above Va sudden accelerations will result in overstressing the airframe.

The Va given in the Flight Manual is, in fact, determined by

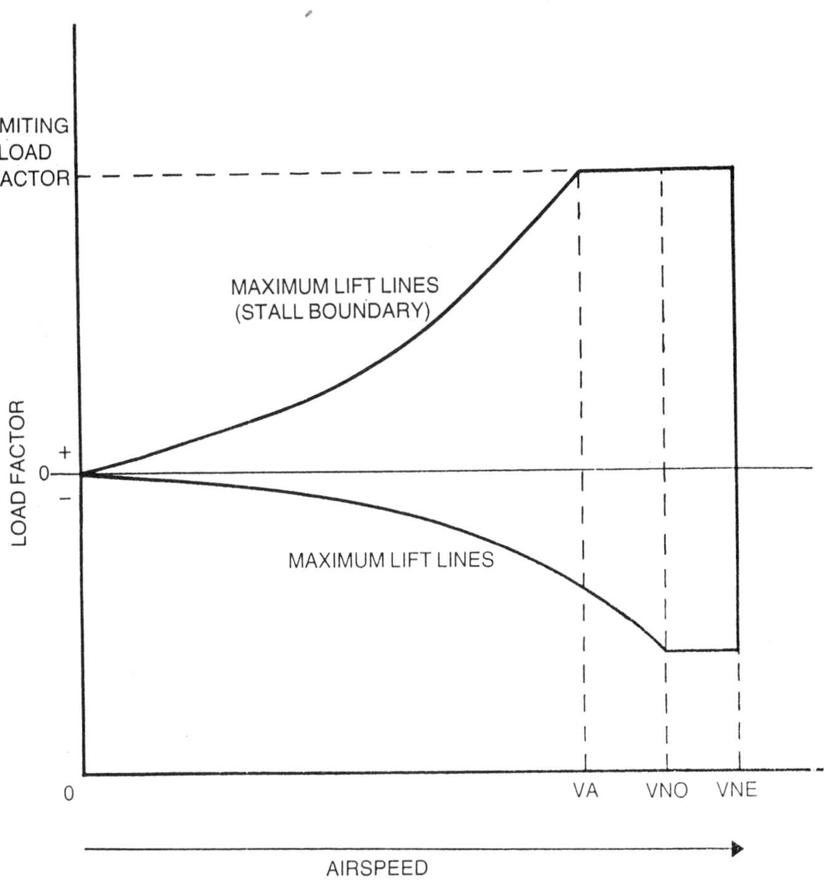

Fig. 132

multiplying the aeroplane's power-off, flaps up stalling speed (VS1) by the square root of the limiting load factor. However, remember that basic stalling speeds are based on the maximum permitted weight of the aeroplane, hence the actual stalling speed will be slightly lower if the aircraft is below maximum weight. Also, as you discovered a few lessons ago, stalling speeds reduce when power is used. All this means that if an aeroplane is flown at a reduced weight with power the actual Va will be somewhat lower than the figure published. For example, if an aircraft's limiting load factor is 3.8 G and its Va is 54 KIAS, the published Va will be 105 KIAS (54 × 1.95 [$\sqrt{3.8}$]). If, however, the actual stalling speed was 50 KIAS due to power and reduced weight, the actual Va would be 97.5 KIAS (50 × 1.95). This means that if the aeroplane is flown at its published Va when turbulence is encountered, or when abrupt control deflections are made, load factors exceeding 3.8 G can be produced. This may be a little difficult to understand at first, but the important thing to remember is that the design manoeuvring speed given in your Flight Manual must be used essentially as a guideline. In practice, when the aeroplane is flown at speeds approaching Va, care must be taken when operating the controls.

Airspeed Indicator Colour Codes

The colour codes on the ASI are related to the aircraft's Vn envelope. The speeds indicated by the colour bands are as follows:

1. bottom of white arc – Vso (flaps down stalling speed)
2. bottom of green arc – VS1 (flaps up stalling speed)
3. top of white arc – Vfe (flap limiting speed)
4. top of green arc – Vno (normal operating speed)
5. yellow band – Caution Range
6. red line – Vne.

Va, Vno, and Flight in Turbulence

When an aeroplane encounters turbulence it will experience varying airspeed fluctuations and load factors. A table describing turbulence intensities and their effects is given below.

Turbulence intensity	*Gust velocities*	*Airspeed fluctuations*	*Effect on aircraft*
Light	5–20 fps	5–15 kts	Mild bumpiness
Moderate	20–35 fps	15–25 kts	Jolts
Severe	35–50 fps	over 25 kts	Severe jolts – possible loss of control
Extreme	over 50 fps	well above 25 kts	Violent jolts, probable loss of control. Damage

It has already been explained that flight through turbulence at high speeds will impose increasing loads on the airframe. When an aircraft encounters a gust a new angle of attack is experienced, which increases the load factor (see Fig. 133).

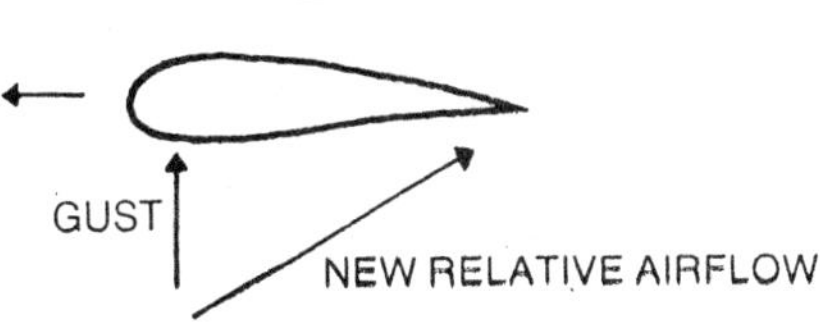

Fig. 133

The greater the intensity of the turbulence and the higher the airspeed, the greater are the chances of exceeding the limiting load factor. Pilots are warned not to fly when increasing turbulence is expected, such as in the vicinity of thunder clouds. However, if you inadvertently fly into such conditions it will be necessary to decrease airspeed to reduce the effects of gust encounters. Now, bearing in mind that airspeed fluctuates rapidly in turbulence (wind shear effects) flying at the published Va may still result in excessive load factors being experienced, so airspeed must be reduced substantially below Va. Turns in turbulent air should be made at shallow bank angles. The loads produced during steep turns will add to those created by the gusts and may cause damage or structural failure. In fact, any extreme use of the controls will have the same effect.

Now, the aeroplane's normal operating speed (Vno), or maximum structural cruising speed, is the maximum speed at which an aircraft can safely endure 30fps gusts. Such a gust is theoretically the most intense a pilot is likely to experience except when flying in moderate to extreme turbulence. This does not mean that you can safely fly at Vno in turbulent air. Speeds at and above Vno are strictly for smooth air conditions only.

So, to summarize. Airspeed will be your indication as to when structural limitations may be exceeded. If you observe airspeed increasing above Va and perhaps into the caution range, which may easily occur in a dive, you should be aware of the consequences of abrupt control deflections. Similarly, knowing the effects of gust encounters at such speeds you must ensure speed is reduced sufficiently in turbulence.

Increasing Turning Performance

Maximum turning performance is expressed in terms of the maximum rate and minimum radius of turn that can be achieved.

For a given bank angle the greatest rate of turn will occur at the slowest airspeed and for a given airspeed turn radius decreases as bank angle increases. This means that the maximum turning performance will be achieved at the steepest bank angle at the minimum airspeed. In theory an aircraft's maximum turning performance can be achieved by maintaining its Va and using the steepest angle of bank without inducing a stall or excessive load factor. The bank angle will be determined by the limiting load factor, so for aircraft certified for 3.8 G this will be around 75°. An aircraft in such a turn will be operating at its performance limits – on the verge of a stall at its structural limits. Any reduction of airspeed or increase in bank angle would result in a stall and any increase in airspeed may produce an excessive load factor. To maintain an aeroplane in such a turn will obviously be extremely difficult. In any case, however, most light aircraft are not capable of performing a maximum performance turn. At around 3.8 G an aeroplane effectively weighs close to four times its weight in level flight and to maintain altitude in this condition would require a considerable amount of power, more than many aircraft are capable of producing. So, for this reason, and also because operating an aircraft at its limiting load factor continuously is not advised, steep turns are normally carried out at between 45°– 60° angle of bank. In any case, maximum turning performance is not required for normal flying procedures. Aerobatic aircraft are designed to withstand higher load factors, up to 6 G in some cases, and therefore turning performance in such aeroplanes is substantially increased.

THE STEEP LEVEL TURN

To execute a steep level turn correctly a degree of advanced planning is required. The aim will be to establish a stabilized turn at the desired bank angle while maintaining a constant height. The rate and amount of power increase, as well as the amount of back pressure, should be anticipated. Use of the elevator trimmer will help greatly in maintaining the correct pitch attitude required to maintain height, but it must be remembered that strong forward pressure will be necessary during the roll out to prevent the nose rising and the aircraft climbing. Orientation is important during a steep turn due to the increased turning rate, so a suitable landmark should be chosen beforehand.

Entering and Maintaining a Steep Level Turn

A steep level turn should be entered at the normal cruising speed and power setting. After having a good lookout, the aircraft is rolled smoothly in the usual way using rudder to maintain balance. As the bank angle passes 30° start increasing power gradually and increasing back pressure to maintain height. Your instructor will usually give you an approximate RPM figure to use. The rate of power increase should be timed so that the required RPM is set when the desired bank angle is reached. At the chosen bank angle neutralize the ailerons in the normal way and use as required to maintain the bank angle.

Controlling pitch

Good pitch control is important during the steep level turn and is achieved by proper visual references and use of the trimmer. When the bank angle and height are constant, the back pressure will also be constant. Anticipation of the amount of control pressures required during a steep turn is important because then the back pressure can be applied smoothly. Failure to apply the correct pressures during the entry stage may result in height losses, which will then require large increases in back pressure to prevent further losses. You will learn the correct control pressures to be used during the air lesson. Once the appropriate back pressure is applied trim the aeroplane so that only small changes in pitch will be necessary to control height while maintaining the turn.

The correct pitch attitude for maintaining height in a steep turn will be established in the same way as for medium-level turns, i.e. by noting the position of the nose in relation to the horizon and maintaining this position. Remember, the attitude of the aeroplane will differ during left and right turns with a side-by-side seating arrangement.

Controlling bank

The tendency to overbank (due to the outer wing travelling faster than the inner wing) becomes more prominent during steep turns, so bank control becomes more emphasized. Once the desired bank angle is established you will find that some opposite aileron will probably be required to maintain it. Note that due to the effects of increased power (slipstream) more positive use of the rudder will be required for balanced flight, particularly during right turns. Remember also, as in the case of medium-level turns, if the bank angle changes so will the pitch requirements for level flight. Rudder pressure for balanced flight will also change.

Rolling out of a Steep Level Turn

The aim when rolling out of the turn will be to smoothly return to straight and level flight on a predetermined heading at the speed and power setting used at the entry. So, using a heading lead factor of half the bank angle used (30° for a turn at 60° angle of bank) the roll out begins by smoothly rolling the wings level while releasing the back pressure to maintain height and gradually reducing power to the normal setting. The rate of these control movements must be the same as during the entry. They must be timed so that the wings become level on the required heading when the straight and level pitch attitude and power setting are achieved.

Errors in the Steep Level Turn

The most common errors while executing a steep level turn are erratic changes in height and airspeed and improper pitch adjustments. If height is lost because of insufficient back pressure, simply increasing back pressure is not the correct method of checking the descent. Airspeed will have increased, so the application of more back pressure may result in a high speed stall, or structural damage. The correct technique for regaining lost height is first to reduce the bank angle. When this is done the load factor will decrease and the nose will rise. Raise the nose further if necessary to regain altitude. When the desired height is reached readjust the pitch attitude for level flight then return to the original bank angle, applying the required back pressure as bank angle increases.

STEEP DESCENDING TURNS

Steep spiralling descents will also be practised during the air lesson. They can be carried out from powered or glide descents and will be a valuable exercise in airspeed control. Bank angles of 60° may be used. However, descent speeds of up to 20 kts higher than normal must be established because of the increased stalling speeds. Remember, glide speeds are relatively slow anyway, therefore at steep angles of bank the safety margin from the stall is reduced substantially. Although the load factor experienced during a steady steep descending turn is less than a similar turn maintaining height, it can increase appreciably as a result of small increases in back pressure. For example, if the basic stalling speed of an aircraft is 50KIAS, at 60° angle of bank at a load factor of 2G this will increase by 41 per cent to about 70KIAS. Now, if the normal descent speed was, say, 75KIAS it can be seen that very little back pressure will be required to produce an accelerated stall. Your instructor will specify speeds to be used during steep descending turns.

Entering and Maintaining a Steep Spiralling Descent

The steep descending turn is entered in the same way as a steep level turn, after the airmanship considerations have been taken care of (lookouts and engine checks). Once the pitch attitude for the desired airspeed has been established, this must be maintained. Airspeed control is very important. If airspeed is allowed to increase, application of back pressure will increase the load factor and a high-speed stall may occur. So, reduce the bank angle first before adjusting the pitch attitude. Anticipate the underbanking tendency during the turn and note the higher ROD.

Rolling out

The aim during the roll out will be to resume a straight descent on a given heading at the normal descending speed. Again a lead factor of half the bank angle should be used and the roll out timed so that the wings become level on the desired heading at the same time that the pitch attitude is achieved for the normal descending speed. Rudder must be used accordingly to maintain balance.

The correct execution of a steep descending turn is vital, since it may determine the safe and successful outcome of a forced landing.

STEEP CLIMBING TURNS

Steep climbing turns are not required for any normal flying procedure, but they provide an excellent handling exercise for controlling an aeroplane at slow airspeeds and steep bank angles.

They are carried out at normal climbing speeds with full power. Bank angles of about 45° are used. The aircraft will be flying close to the stall and with full power, so very good control co-ordination will be required to maintain airspeed, bank angle and balance.

At climbing speeds the angle of attack is relatively large, and this, combined with an increasing angle of attack as bank angle is steepened, will produce substantial increases in induced drag. At 45° angle of bank, induced drag will more than double and hence the climb rate will be very small. If a bank angle of 60° is used induced drag will more than triple, and it is unlikely that sufficient power will be developed to produce a climb rate in light aircraft. In fact at a slow speed and such a bank angle the aeroplane may well start to descend with full power on. The effect may not be as dramatic as stalling but can be just as fatal close to the ground. In such a condition, an attempt to arrest the sink rate by raising the nose is likely to lead to a stall, so the recovery action should be to roll the wings level first. Awareness of the performance limitations of your aeroplane is very important, and failure to appreciate them will be very foolish indeed.

RECOVERING FROM A HIGH-SPEED STALL

The conditions that may produce a high speed stall have already been mentioned. Now, you have already been taught the pre-stall symptoms, so immediately you recognize the onset of a stall the necessary recovery actions should be taken. Remember, however, that during a steep turn the pitch attitude will not be very different at the stall and the stalling speed will be higher. Your main clues will be reducing airspeed, stall warner operation and buffeting.

At the incipient stage the recovery action will be simply to release the back pressure. Be ready for a wing drop. If a full stall develops, positive forward pressure will be required and power increased if necessary to assist the recovery. As speed increases level the wings and ease out of the descent in the normal way.

THE SPIRAL DIVE RECOVERY

If the nose is allowed to drop during a steep turn, especially during a descent, airspeed will start to increase. If this is not corrected in good time a steep spiralling dive with the airspeed continuing to increase will develop. Attempting to arrest the descent with back pressure alone in this high-speed condition will tighten the spiral further and probably overstress the airframe. The correct recovery action will be first to close the throttle, then level the wings positively. The aircraft will then be in a high-speed dive and careful use of the controls will be necessary to return to normal flight without inducing an accelerated stall or excessive load factors.

You will have the opportunity to practise entering and recovering from high-speed stalls and spiral dives during the air lesson.

UNUSUAL ATTITUDES

If the pilot becomes too occupied with activities inside the cockpit for a long period, the aeroplane may start to wander and eventually adopt an extreme attitude. Similarly, an unexpected strong wind shear or wake turbulence may also have the same result. The pilot will then have to react very quickly to prevent the situation developing into something more dangerous.

The type of unusual attitudes used during training will be varying degrees of steeply banked nose high attitudes (close to a stall) and steeply banked nose-down attitudes (spiral dives). What usually happens during the air lesson is that the instructor will ask you to close your eyes while the particular unusual attitude is selected. Then you will be told to open your eyes and take whatever recovery actions are necessary to bring the aeroplane under control. The recovery procedures for these types of situations have already been covered, but you must remember not to make abrupt control movements once you have interpreted the situation.

Reference to Instruments during Steep Turns

The steep turn must be maintained using visual references outside the cockpit, with only the occasional quick glance at the relevant instruments to determine bank angle, height, airspeed and balance. The reference to the DI can be increased slightly when approaching the desired rollout heading.

AIRMANSHIP

A very good lookout should be made, as is usual before entering any type of turn. When a change of altitude is intended lookout in the area below or above as required in addition.

Orientation is very important, so select a suitable ground feature to be used to establish your position and keep clear of controlled airspace and active airfields. During climbing and descending turns do not forget to check the engine condition frequently.

During the practice of high-speed stalls and spiral dive recoveries remember to do the HASELL checks beforehand and bear in mind the structural limitation speeds (Va and Vne).

AIR LESSON

Steep Level Turns (from straight and level flight at cruise speed)
To enter a steep level turn:

1. Lookout and choose a ground feature for orientation.
2. Start rolling in the chosen direction in the normal way and using rudder to maintain balance and back pressure to maintain height.
3. As the bank angle passes 30° start increasing power gradually and increase the back pressure.
4. Time your actions so that the bank angle is reached when the pitch attitude and power setting for the turn are achieved.
5. Trim. (During training, initially the trimmer may not be used. This is to develop further your feel for control pressures.)

Maintaining the turn

1. Keep a good lookout.
2. Maintain the bank angle with the ailerons.
3. Maintain the height with the elevators.
4. Maintain balance with the rudder.

During the turn anticipate a mild encounter with your own wake turbulence.

Height corrections
If height starts to decrease:

1. Decrease the bank angle.
2. Readjust the pitch attitude.
3. After height is regained resume the bank angle and back pressure.

Rolling out
To roll out of a steep level turn:

1. Lookout.
2. Anticipate the roll out heading by half the bank angle used.
3. Smoothly start rolling the wings level (maintaining balance with the rudder), while releasing the back pressure and gradually reducing the power to the cruise setting.
4. Time your actions so that the wings are level when the correct pitch attitude and power setting for straight and level flight are achieved.
5. Continue with normal straight and level flight techniques.

Steep Descending Turns
Enter a normal glide then:

1. Lookout.
2. Enter a steep turn in the usual way but increase speed by 10-20 kts as required.

Maintaining a Steep Descending Turn

1. Maintain lookouts.
2. Maintain airspeed, bank angle and balance in the normal way. Note the high ROD.

If the nose starts to lower (increasing airspeed):

1. Reduce bank angle.
2. Readjust pitch attitude.
3. When speed has stabilized return to required bank angle.

Rolling out
Anticipate the required heading by half the bank angle used and start rolling the wings level and readjusting the pitch attitude at the same time so that the aircraft resumes straight flight at the normal decent speed.

You will be practising steep spiralling descents with power and also with flaps lowered in a glide.

The High Speed Stall and Recovery
A high speed stall and recovery will be demonstrated in the air lesson.

To enter a high-speed stall:

1. HASELL.
2. Enter a normal steep level turn without increasing power.
3. Apply continuous back pressure until the stall occurs. Be ready for a wing drop.

Note the symptoms, the pitch attitude at the stall and the stalling speed.

To recover:

1. Apply positive forward pressure to unstall the wings.
2. Increase power if necessary.
3. As speed increases, level the wings and return to normal flight.

To recover at the incipient stage:

1. Release the back pressure.
2. Continue in the turn or return to normal flight.

The Spiral Dive and Recovery

A spiral dive and recovery will be demonstrated by your instructor.

To enter a spiral dive:

1. HASELL.
2. Enter a steep descending turn with reduced power.
3. Allow the bank to increase and the nose to drop.

Note the symptoms of a spiral dive:

1. Rapidly increasing airspeed.
2. Rapid loss of height.
3. Back pressure is insufficient to effect a recovery.

To recover:

1. Close the throttle.
2. Level the wings.
3. Gently ease out of the dive.

Steep Climbing Turns

The procedures for these turns are the same as for steep level turns, except bank angles are kept to a maximum of 45°. Due to the low airspeed and the effects of full power, good control co-ordination will be required for a balanced stable turn. Note the reduced rate of climb.

Instructor's Guide
Ex. 15

LESSON PLAN

Advanced turning

Objectives
To revise previous lessons and introduce the student to advanced turning manoeuvres, high speed stalls and recovering from unusual attitudes (including spiral dives).

Content
1 Preflight briefing
Revise previous manoeuvres and discuss objectives and airmanship considerations of this lesson; explain advanced turning performance and techniques, high-speed stalls and recoveries, and unusual attitudes and recoveries.

2 Flight lesson
Review:

(a) preflight procedures
(b) circuit departure to the training area, then: *Demonstrate steep level, climbing and descending turns, emphasizing pitch, bank and power co-ordination. Student practice. Demonstrate a spiral dive and the recovery. Student practice. Demonstrate high-speed stalls, unusual attitudes and recoveries. Student practice*
(c) map reading, circuit rejoin.

3 Postflight discussion and preview of the next lesson

Completion Standards
This lesson will have been successfully completed when the student can competently execute steep turns, understands how to correct errors in the turn and is able to recover effectively from spiral dives, high-speed stalls and unusual attitudes with minimum instructor assistance.

Exercise 16

OPERATION AT MINIMUM LEVEL

Objectives

1. To learn to operate an aircraft at low altitudes (between 500ft and 1500ft agl) and to appreciate that there will be some important differences from flights at higher altitudes.
2. To learn the procedures and precautions that must be followed if a flight at very low altitudes has to be made in deteriorating weather conditions.

Generally, the higher you are able to fly the better. At higher altitudes the engine operates more efficiently, navigation is easier, radio reception improved and more time will be available to sort out engine-failure situations. However, if your airfield is situated within a control zone a short low-level flight may be necessary, usually to and from an Entry/Exit lane so that you do not conflict with aircraft operating under IFR. Also, if weather conditions start deteriorating during a normal cross-country flight at cruising altitudes, it may become necessary to continue at much lower altitudes in order to keep clear of cloud and in sight of the ground. Whatever the reasons for flying at low levels you must be aware that such flights will be very different from those conducted at higher altitudes.

To help your understanding of this subject you are advised to combine your study of this chapter with the one on 'Pilot Navigation'.

Low Flying

Probably the first impression you will have during the demonstration of low-level flight is the increased sensation of speed over the ground. At low altitudes visual details are increased. Buildings, trees etc. not given much attention at higher altitudes appear to go by more quickly.

Your perspective of the ground will be more oblique. As height reduces, the shape of ground features looks less and less like their presentations on the map. Visual assessment of distances between them becomes difficult.

The nature of the terrain is more noticeable, i.e. undulations, ridges, hills etc. Ground features, particularly those behind high ground, which can easily be located from higher altitudes, can be encountered quite unexpectedly. Snow can change a landscape considerably. All these factors will make map reading and establishing your position more difficult.

Aircraft Handling at Low Altitudes

Speed

When flying at low altitudes, especially in bad visibility, speed should be reduced to a slow safe cruising speed with optimum flaps lowered. In this configuration forward visibility will be improved and navigation made easier due to the slower speed.

Effects of wind

When flying with a tailwind the effects of increased ground speed may initially give you the impression that the aeroplane is flying too fast. The temptation to raise the nose and decrease power to reduce airspeed must be resisted. If the aircraft is trimmed to fly at a slow cruising airspeed there will be no further need to reduce airspeed.

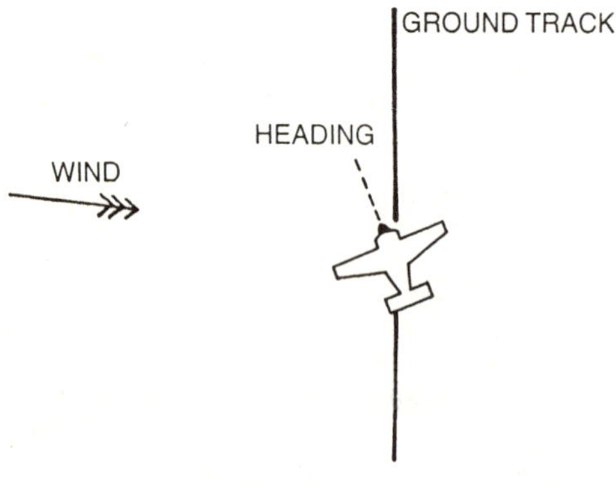

Fig. 134

Drift

The effects of a crosswind becomes more apparent at low altitudes as will the relationship between the aircraft's nose (heading) and the ground track when a crab angle is adopted, as shown in Figure 134.

Turning

Turns should be made at shallow bank angles normally. It must be appreciated that during a turn an aircraft has inertia and although this is less significant at higher altitudes, it must be borne in mind at lower levels when early decisions and actions must be taken to avoid obstacles.

When turning downwind, as in Figure 135 the effect of drift during the turn may give you the impression that the aeroplane is out of balance and slipping towards the centre of the turn.

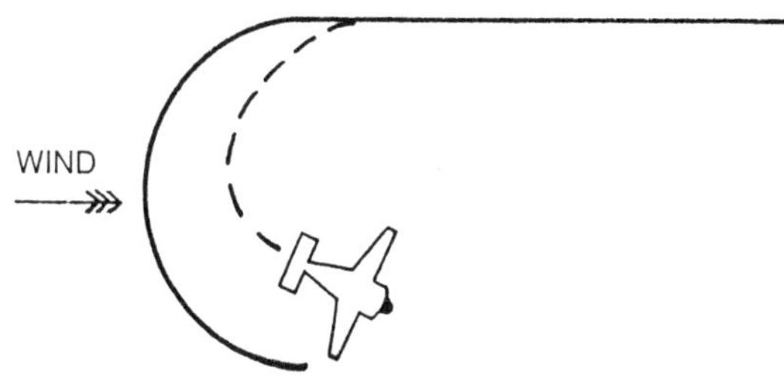

Fig. 135

When turning into wind the impression of skidding outwards will be given, as shown in Figure 136.

Both these situations may tempt you to start varying the amounts of rudder pressure to establish balance, but this must be resisted. A glance at the balance indicator will tell you the correct pressures to use.

Turbulence

Wind shear and the associated turbulence is much more dangerous near the ground and it must be expected whenever you fly low. Be extra alert in the vicinity of hills, ridges, forests and uneven ground. It is advisable to keep your hand on the throttle at all times except when other necessary actions are required, so that you will be able to react instantly with power should the need arise.

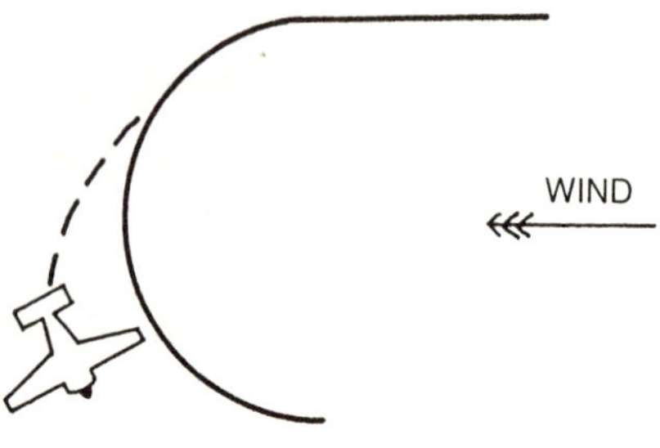

Fig. 136

Lookouts

When operating at lower levels your lookouts will have to be very good. Gliders, balloons, helicopters and microlight aircraft operate at these altitudes and will be difficult to locate against the ground. Be alert for high-speed, low-flying military aircraft. In the vicinity of control zones and entry/exit lanes remember that traffic density will be increased. Keep clear of pylons, television masts and high ground. Cables and wires will be difficult to see, so be careful.

Practical Considerations for Low Level Flight

If you have to operate in and out of a control zone there will be special procedures to follow, as explained in the chapter on 'First Solo and Consolidation'. You will have to bear in mind the dimensions of entry/exit lanes (see *Air Pilot*) and the visibility minimums for VFR flights in control zones (see ANO).

Whenever you anticipate flying at low altitudes you will have to consider the regulations for flights over built-up areas and the minimum low flying rule, (see ANO). When flying over built-up areas the aircraft should be high enough at all times to ensure it can safely glide clear in the event of an engine failure. If you are unable to do this, keep well clear of built-up areas.

The low flying rule basically states that an aircraft must not be flown closer than 500ft to any person, vehicle, vessel or structure.

During the flight lesson your instructor will ensure that the flight is conducted in accordance with the appropriate rules and you will be concentrating mainly on flying the aeroplane and becoming accustomed to map reading at lower levels. When you fly solo the responsibility for flying within the regulations will be yours entirely.

When a low-level flight has to be conducted within a control zone you will have good guidelines to follow in the form of specific procedures outlined in the *Air Pilot* and also instructions from ATC. In addition, if you operate frequently in and out of a particular control zone it is likely that the route you follow and the local terrain is very familiar to you. However, if an unplanned low-level flight has to be made in the middle of a cross-country detail, the situation is likely to be quite stressful and outrightly dangerous if you have not considered such an outcome during the pre-flight planning phase.

The flight planning involved for a cross-country flight is covered in detail in the chapter on 'Pilot Navigation'. Briefly, before undergoing such a flight you must obtain the latest weather information for the areas in which you intend to fly. The weather must firstly be within your flying limitations and secondly it must be forecast to remain that way for the duration of your flight. If the weather is found to be marginal, postpone the flight. Weather forecasts nowadays are usually very reliable. However, unforecast weather changes do occur from time to time and pilots must be prepared for such an eventuality. You will have to make a detailed study of your intended route(s), making a note of the heights of obstacles within 10 miles either side of your ground tracks. You will have to work out minimum safe cruising altitudes (MSA) for each section of your route which will ensure safe clearance from these obstacles. The type of terrain should be noted and alternative airfields must be selected in the event of the weather making it impossible for you to reach your destination or base airfield safely. Fuel allowances must be made for such diversions.

In flight the only unforecast weather you may encounter may be a cloud base that is slightly lower than expected, in which case the flight can usually be continued at a few hundred feet below the desired altitude. Localized rainfall can also be experienced but these can normally be seen from a distance and can be avoided. Now, weather does not deteriorate suddenly, but it can do so rapidly. However, there will always be clear indications. If you encounter a gradually lowering cloud base and progressively decreasing visibility, the weather is clearly worsening and you will have to make some instant decisions. To continue normally in the hope that conditions will improve ahead is positively dangerous. Without the proper training and qualifications and a suitably equipped aeroplane you may well find yourself in conditions beyond your flying ability and those of the aeroplane, with fatal results. Pilots too have a kind of inertia, i.e. the tendency to want to continue along the same course. This must be resisted.

You will have to decide whether to turn back and return to your departure airfield, or proceed to an alternate. Now, at this stage it is only possible to give broad guidelines and general advice, since the particular course of action you decide to take will depend on the extent and rate of weather deterioration, the lateness of your decisions, the proximity of available alternates and the nature of the terrain over which you have to fly.

It may be that you will be able to maintain at least the MSA back to your departure airfield or alternate and still be in sight of the surface and able to map read. If this is so, you are advised to proceed as fast as possible. However, if you envisage having to descend below the MSA, either immediately or at a later stage, the following actions should be taken:

1. (F) Check the fuel contents, switch to the fullest tank and turn on the electric fuel pump (if fitted).
2. (E) Check the engine condition and also scan the suction and ammeter gauges. Check for carburettor icing.
3. (D) Synchronize the DI and magnetic compass.
4. (A) Ensure the correct QNH is set on the altimeter.
5. (R) Check the radio frequencies and adjust the volume and squelch controls. Remember, radio efficiency deteriorates as height decreases. If you are in radio contact with anyone, inform them of your intentions. They may be able to offer assistance.
6. (P) Establish your position on the map.
7. (S) Secure hatches, doors and seatbelts and ensure loose articles are safely stored. Turn on the safety lights, i.e. the rotating beacon and navigation lights. (Strobe lights should not be turned on in precipitation, because the reflected light may cause disorientation.)

The workload will be high when you have to operate at lower levels and reduced visibility, so carry out the above actions while still at a reasonable altitude so that you can concentrate on flying the aeroplane and navigating. The procedures for making a diversion are covered under 'Pilot Navigation'.

Determining the height to fly (operation at minimum level)
The MSAs you calculate during pre-flight planning will give you the minimum safe clearance from the highest obstacles (including high ground) along different sections of your routes. If you have to descend below an MSA be extremely careful and keep a very good lookout. Even if you have established your position as being well clear of the highest obstacle on which the MSA was based, as you descend below this height you may well be in the vicinity of lower obstacles.

Now, it is very important to determine the minimum height you can descend to below the MSA. Above ground level this will be 500ft because of the low-flying rule, but since you will be using the QNH (altitude above sea level) a calculation will have to be made to ensure that you will be maintaining this minimum altitude above the ground. To do this you will have to locate the nearest contour line, spot height or airfield elevation to your position on the map and add 500ft to it. For example, say you locate a spot height of 400ft nearby, the lowest height you should fly in that particular area will be 900ft (QNH) in order to maintain a height of 500ft agl (500 + 400). Remember, at this minimum height you will have to steer well clear of built-up areas and keep a very sharp lookout for obstacles as you proceed to an airfield. All this makes it clear why a detailed study of your routes should be made prior to the flight.

Assessing Height
Although you will be maintaining specific altitudes using the altimeter, at lower levels the aircraft's height above the ground can really only be effectively assessed visually. It is important that you learn how to do this, especially when flying over uneven terrain. Height is assessed in a similar way as during a final approach. Look at the ground all around the aeroplane, focusing your eyes on the objects some distance away as well as those close to the aircraft. Looking directly below will not be enough.

Off-Airfield Landing Decisions
If the weather deterioration is such that a descent below 500ft agl has to be made, immediate forced landing preparations must be

made (covered in the next chapter). Your map will only contain positions of obstacles above 300ft agl. A descent below 500ft will mean you may encounter all sorts of obstructions not indicated on the map.

If the surrounding terrain is hilly, mountainous, gradually rising and just generally uneven, due to low cloud, rapidly rising ground and possible wind shear hazards, it will be impossible to maintain the minimum height continuously and safely, as Figure 137 illustrates. Only military aircraft equipped with terrain following radar can do this!

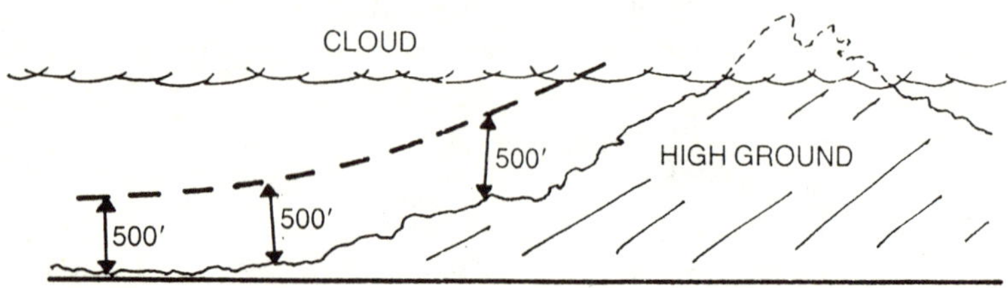

Fig. 137

If the minimum safe cruising altitude cannot be maintained in such areas (or if such areas have to be overflown in order to reach an airfield) the most sensible course of action will be to make a forced landing while visual conditions still exist.

You now have a good idea of the situation you will be in if a flight has to be made at minimum level in bad weather. By studying the latest weather reports and making sound decisions, you will probably never have to face such a situation. By thoroughly studying your routes, selecting alternates etc., at the very least you will be well prepared for low-level operation if unforecast weather is encountered.

Precipitation

When weather deteriorates precipitation of some kind may be encountered. This will reduce visibility further, particularly in heavy rain, hail, sleet or snow. Flying through hail will be very alarming and could cause damage to the aeroplane.

Whenever there is moisture on the windscreen the pilot's view outside the cockpit will be distorted. The effect is similar to driving a car in heavy rain, and can easily lead the pilot to think that he is too high on the approach and therefore adopt a descent path that is dangerously low. So be extra careful when flying in such conditions. As soon as you fly into precipitation switch on the windscreen wipers if fitted, as well as the demister and pitot heater.

Bad Weather Circuits

If the visibility at your departure, destination or alternate airfield has also reduced, you will have to carry out a low-level circuit and landing.

Try to establish contact with the airfield well before joining the circuit. Otherwise carry out a tight circuit, keeping fairly close to the runway so as not to lose sight of it. You are advised to time each leg of the circuit as well. The minimum height to be maintained in these situations will be the airfield's visual manoeuvring height (VMH), which gives a minimum of 300ft clearance from obstacles within a 4 nm radius of the airfield. This height can be requested from ATC if you have not obtained it from the *Air Pilot* during flight planning. If the visibility is such that you are unable to maintain the VMH (or if this minimum height is not available for any reason) you will have to be extremely careful. Obey ATC at all times and tell them immediately if you are unable to comply with their instructions.

When visibility is bad a suitably qualified pilot can navigate across country as well as descend for a landing in complete safety. An IFR pilot is trained to have complete control of the aeroplane in these conditions and follow special procedures. A VFR-only pilot cannot legally fly in weather that requires control of the aircraft by reference to instruments. If you encounter deteriorating weather at normal cruising altitudes you will have to descend to keep in reasonable sight of the ground. The underlying objective of this lesson is to impress upon you that low-level flight in bad weather is dangerous and not normal practice. You can only be taught what can be expected and given some guidelines to follow if you are forced into such a situation.

AIRMANSHIP

If you are forced to fly low because of the weather, it is likely that others will be in the same position, so keep a very good lookout.

At and around an airfield, traffic density will be greater, so added vigilance is required.

Do not neglect frequent engine checks and fuel management. Synchronize the DI and the magnetic compass regularly.

AIR LESSON

The air lesson will essentially be a simulated low-level operation in bad weather. You will be performing the various checks, flying the aeroplane and observing the effects of wind and learning how to assess height and map read.

The flight will usually be conducted in the local area, if conditions permit, so that you get to know the terrain surrounding the airfield. The return to your airfield may well be a simulated low-level/poor-visibility circuit rejoin. The flight will be made in normal visual flying conditions and you will soon appreciate how much more difficult things can become if visibility starts to reduce.

Instructor's Guide
Ex. 16

LESSON PLAN

Operation at minimum level

Objectives
To introduce:

(a) low level operations (entry/exit lanes etc.)
(b) aircraft handling at low altitudes (visual impressions, height assessment, effects of speed, inertia, wind and turbulence)
(c) map reading at low altitudes
(d) weather considerations (visibility, cloud base, precipitation)
(e) actions before making an unplanned descent
(f) bad weather circuit, approach and landing
(g) airmanship at lower levels (lookouts, low flying rule etc.).

Content
1 Flight lesson
This should consist of a low-level flight in the local area. The student should be allowed to fly the aeroplane while practising map reading and height assessment. Demonstrate the effects of turns at lower levels. The return to the airfield should be a simulated bad-weather circuit rejoin.

2 Postflight discussion and preview of the next lesson

Completion Standards
This lesson will have been successfully completed when the student displays an understanding of low-level operations and is able to map read to a reasonable standard while flying the aeroplane.

Exercise 17

FORCED LANDINGS

Objectives

1. To learn to cope with an engine failure in cruising flight and to make an emergency forced landing.
2. To learn to make a precautionary landing on or off an airfield with engine power available.

Engine Failure in Cruise Flight

If the engine fails in flight for whatever reason, immediate preparations will have to be made for an emergency landing. As you learnt during the circuit training period, an engine failure near the ground will mean you have very little time and few options. At normal cruising altitudes, however, there will be more time available and provided you have an organized plan of action, you can prepare for a landing as well as try to restart the engine.

Causes of engine failure

It has already been mentioned that mechanical defects are rare in modern aeroplanes and the most common cause of engine failure is the neglect of responsibilities on the part of the pilot. It has been emphasized that the safe outcome of any flight depends to an important extent on the pilot's preparations on the ground. Careful and thorough pre-flight preparations should reveal anything that may affect the safety of the flight. You must ensure that sufficient fuel of the correct grade for the engine is carried for the flight and plan for fuel stops on the way if necessary. Follow the checklists provided carefully and do not rely on memory alone. Assuming the ground preparations are carried out thoroughly, in flight you must manage the engine and fuel systems properly. Check frequently for carburettor icing and monitor the engine instruments regularly. Carburettor icing can occur rapidly in certain conditions. You must also monitor the fuel consumption, remembering, however, that fuel gauges can sometimes give misleading indications. If the fuel tanks are used individually make sure you follow the correct tank selection procedure for your aircraft. When operating the various switches in the cockpit make sure you do not inadvertently turn off the ignition switches.

Procedure when the engine fails

The immediate actions you must take when the engine fails, as always, will be to lower the nose and trim the aeroplane for the best gliding speed. If, however, you are travelling at fairly fast cruising speeds the excessive speed can be used to gain more altitude before adopting the gliding attitude. This is done by simply raising the nose slightly. The kinetic energy of the aircraft will cause a climb and as airspeed reduces to the best gliding speed lower the nose and trim. The extra altitude gained in this way will give you more time to sort out the situation. Having established positive control of the aeroplane, which is your first priority, try to assess the surface wind direction and select a suitable landing field. When trying to determine the wind, look for smoke or other signs on the ground. If these are not available assume the wind direction will be about the same as it was during the take-off at your departure airfield. This is why it is useful to make a note of the surface wind prior to take-off.

Choice of field

The field chosen for the landing should be as close as possible to the aircraft. Remember, without engine power range will be limited so you must choose a landing area that you are sure of reaching. The field should be as flat and as smooth as possible, and large enough for a landing. There should be no difficult obstructions in the approach path such as pylons or high-tension cables.

Assessing the ground surface will be difficult, but the colour of the field will be a good indication. Brown-coloured fields are likely to have very rough and hard surfaces, so it would be best to aim for grass fields if possible. Try to select a field near some habitation, or a road, so it will be easier to obtain assistance after landing. Ideally, the field should also be good enough for a take-off. It can be seen that the higher you fly the more choices you will have for a good forced landing field.

Your second priority after maintaining control of the aeroplane is the selection of a suitable field. But do not waste time aimlessly

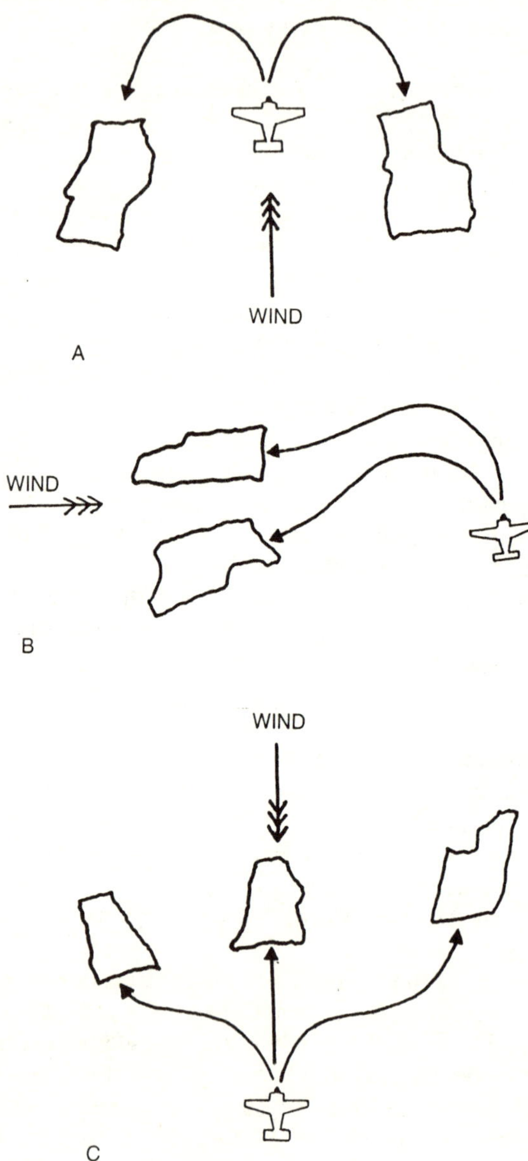

Fig. 138

looking around. Select a landing area immediately. Once you have made this decision you will be able to proceed in a more positive manner.

The Descent Plan

Having selected a field you must plan a descent towards it, aiming to land as much into wind as possible. The actual descent plan will vary according to the height available. Figure 138 illustrates the type of descent routes to the forced landing field that may be used from altitudes around 2,000ft agl.

At such altitudes the pilot has a short time to sort out the situation. If the engine fails at 2000ft agl and the rate of descent achieved is 1000 fpm, only two minutes of airborne time remains, assuming the ROD stays constant. The range will be determined by the ground speed, which in turn depends on the wind. Therefore, the field chosen has to be very close by. It can be seen that at these lower altitudes the choice of field and hence the descent route should also be determined by considering the wind direction. Landings should be made into wind, but tight spiralling descents from such altitudes in order to achieve this should be avoided, unless absolutely necessary. The ROD will be very high in such a manoeuvre.

At much higher altitudes the descent routes will be more like circuit patterns. Figure 139 illustrates the type of descent routes that may be followed.

Once again the wind plays an important part in the choice of field and descent route. Note that regardless of height, a continuous descending turn to position correctly on the final approach to the field is quite likely.

The frequent practice and experience of glide approaches will prove invaluable when a forced landing without power has to be made. During the practice of glide approaches the point where the throttle was closed was at a particular height and distance from the runway. At this key point you were certain of gliding safely to the runway, provided you correctly assessed your progress, extending or shortening the remaining legs of the circuit as required and lowering flaps at the right times. In a forced landing situation you must plan to arrive in a similar key position in relation to the forced landing field, as Figure 140 illustrates.

From your experience during glide approaches, you will know how close to the runway and how high the aircraft has to be in

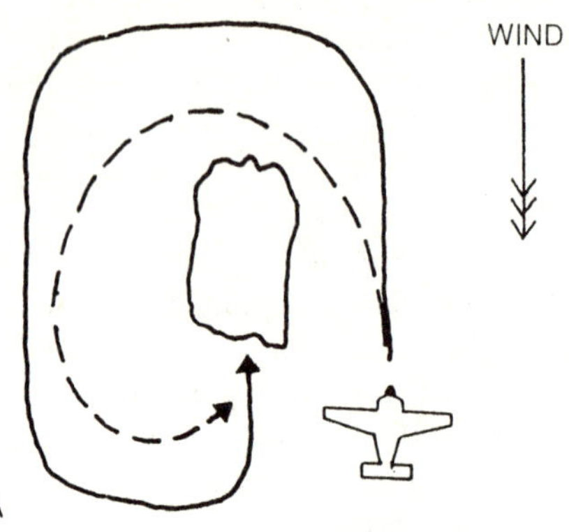

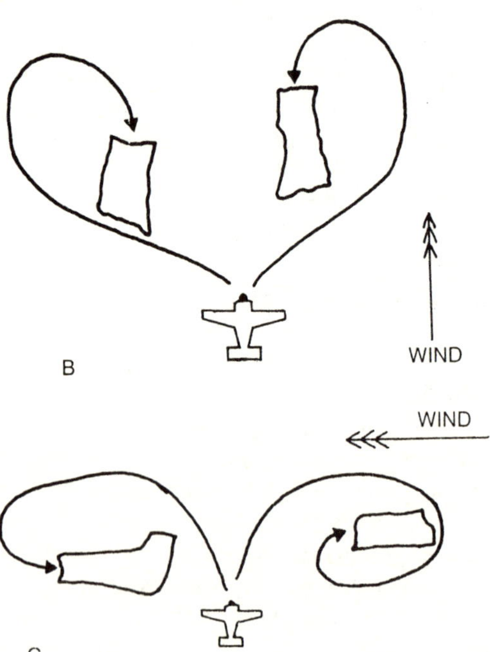

Fig. 139

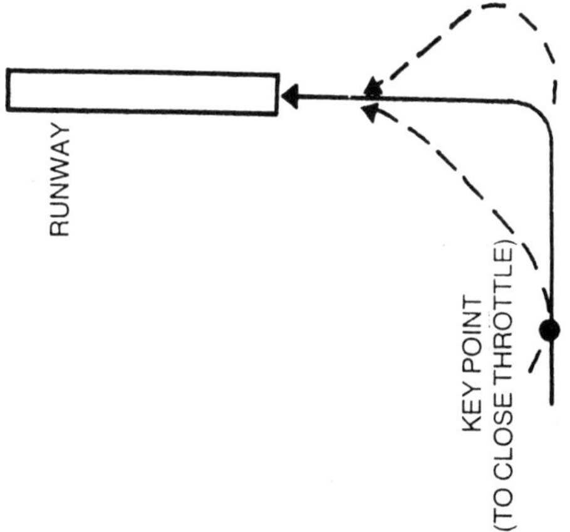

Fig. 140

various wind conditions before you can close the throttle and complete a safe glide approach and landing. The height at which the throttle is closed is often the circuit height, which is usually 1,000ft agl. You must use the same judgement to determine the key point (or 1,000ft point) for your forced field landing. From the key point the remainder of the forced landing will be just like a normal glide approach. Provided you assess your progress and time your actions accordingly, you will arrive in a safe position for a landing. You must remember, however, that the ROD during an actual engine failure is much higher than in a normal glide, so the key point should be closer than normal.

From the key point position you must aim to touchdown halfway into the field, although this should not be your actual intention. If you aim to touch down in the normal position you may end up undershooting the field if wind conditions are other than expected. Remember, you will have no power to adjust the descent path.

As you progress towards the field, when you are absolutely sure that the halfway point can be reached, aim to touch down one quarter of the way into the field (see Fig. 141) then increase the ROD by lowering one stage of flaps. Excessive height can easily be

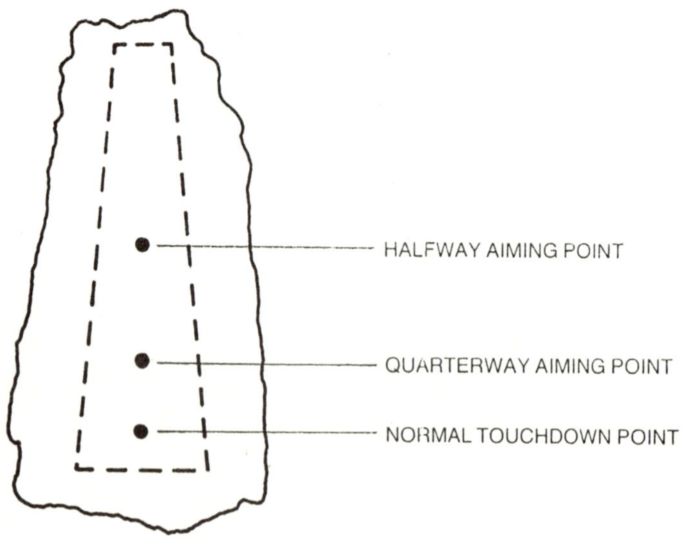

Fig. 141

lost by moderate sideslips or making S turns. On the final approach, when a landing in the desired field is inevitable, lower full flaps. The aeroplane should be landed firmly and brought to a stop. As the aircraft decelerates look out for holes, ditches and other obstructions and take avoiding action if necessary. Remember, fields are not normally prepared to accommodate aircraft.

Change of plans

At any stage, except when you are totally committed to a landing, be prepared to change plans and even choose another field. You may see cables across the approach path of your field, or other dangerous obstructions in the field that were not noticed at higher altitudes. In most cases, however, a slight modification to the original plan is more likely. You may notice another more suitable field within easier reach, or, because of your height, you may decide to land in a different direction on the same field, as Figure 142 illustrates.

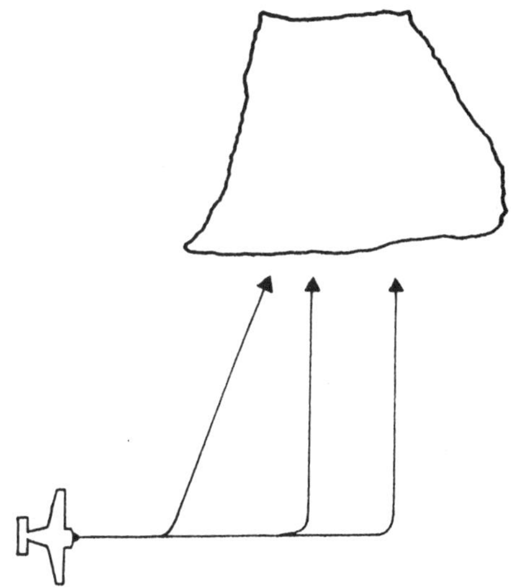

Fig. 142

The objective is to make a safe landing, so if you feel that your original plan has become dangerous, change it.

Observation of Speed

It is absolutely vital that you maintain the best gliding speed at all times when carrying out a forced landing, especially during turns. Keeping sight of your field is difficult and when visibility is also a problem the additional concentration required could make you neglect to monitor the airspeed. This can be fatal, turning an engine failure situation into a stall/spin accident. So watch the airspeed.

Maintaining the best gliding speed not only keeps the aeroplane controllable, but it ensures that aerodynamic efficiency is at its optimum. Glide range is at its maximum at this speed (in zero wind). Increasing or decreasing it will both reduce range. If you feel the aeroplane is undershooting at any stage, do not raise the nose to try and stretch the glide. Although the perspective of the field may change, you will not reach it. Additionally, airspeed will reduce and a wind shear encounter may result in a stall. In an undershoot situation you will have to consider a modification or complete change of plan. At worst, a controlled crash landing may have to be made.

Engine Restarts and Forced Landing Checks

After becoming established on the descent route to the field an attempt to discover the cause and possibly rectify the engine failure can be made. These checks will be contained in the checklist and must be memorized.

Usually the first item to check is the fuel situation. The tank selection should be changed and the electric fuel pump switched on. It could be that one fuel tank has run dry, or the mechanical fuel pump is defective. Then ensure that the mixture is fully rich and the fuel primer is locked securely. Next, check that the ignition system is on. You may have mistakenly turned it off earlier. Select each magneto in turn also. Finally, operate the carburettor heat system to clear any ice in the engine. In fact, since carburettor icing is a common cause for an engine failure it will be worth considering operating the heat system as early as possible. If this check is left too late, there may not be sufficient heat remaining to clear any ice, if this was the cause of the engine stoppage.

Should the engine fail to start after these checks you will be committed to a forced landing, so carry out the necessary landing checks that you should have memorized by now. Make the

Mayday call before turning off the master switch. Ensure the safety belts are secure and the door is unlatched.

Do not lose sight of the field while carrying out these checks.

Precautionary Landings (on or off an airfield)
When the engine fails, you will have no other option but to make an emergency landing. However, the precautionary landing, often called a forced landing with power, is a course of action that you will seriously have to consider taking if continued flight is possible but likely to be dangerous. The sort of reasons that may lead to such a decision are as follows:

1. Deteriorating weather.
2. Insufficient fuel reserves.
3. Impending nightfall (if you are not trained to fly at night or the aeroplane is not properly equipped).
4. A large oil or fuel leak that is clearly visible.
5. Low oil pressure combined with a high oil temperature. Low fuel pressure. Remember, gauges can be faulty so a second sign of the abnormality should be sought.
6. Partial power loss.
7. Serious engine or airframe vibrations.
8. Structural damage in flight (including serious bird strikes, broken windscreens and damage caused by hailstorms).
9. Possible pilot incapacitation due to illness or injury in flight.
10. Becoming totally lost when help is unavailable and fuel reserves are low.
11. Any other reason that may affect the safety of continued flight.

Now, it is not possible to give you a specific set of circumstances that will determine the decision to make a precautionary landing. Rapid weather deterioration, obvious fuel shortage, serious airframe damage or injury to yourself and any other extreme situation should give no doubt that emergency actions must be taken. It is when such situations appear less extreme and there seems to be some chance of reaching the destination, that the decision to make a precautionary landing becomes difficult. No pilot particularly likes to interrupt plans, or risk damage to the aircraft by landing in a field and then have to deal with the awkward situation afterwards. Nor does anyone like having to explain their actions to the authorities, especially if it transpires that the flight could have been continued safely. These types of thoughts may influence you to continue flying. Such a decision can be a dangerous gamble. You could end up in an engine failure predicament or completely lose control of the aeroplane in cloud. Having said this, however, this does not mean that every single time you have a slight doubt a precautionary landing will have to be made. You will have to weigh up your particular circumstances realistically and evaluate the risks involved, bearing in mind two things: the survival and safety of the aircraft occupants. If you are certain that the flight can be continued in safety, then carry on. If, however, you have any reasonable doubts about this, carry out a precautionary landing. Survivability odds are increased if you can maintain control of the aircraft and land with power.

It should be noted that many things that could give cause for a precautionary landing could be appreciated and given due consideration during the pre-flight preparations. There is an old saying in aviation – 'It is better to be down on the ground wishing you were up in the air than being up in the air wishing you were down on the ground.'

Making a Precautionary Landing

The advantage of a forced landing with power will be that you will have much more choice in terms of landing areas. Additionally, you will be able to have much more control during the approach and landing and have the ability to overshoot.

It may be that you are within reasonable reach of an airfield nearby, in which case you should proceed towards it. Establish radio contact with the airfield control service if possible. If the airfield appears to be a large, busy, international type, or military airport, it is not advisable to land without radio contact unless you are compelled to do so. If this is the case at any active airfield, in fact, exercise extreme caution and when you are on the final approach switch your landing lights on and off continuously as a sign that you are forced to land. After landing park the aeroplane in a suitable area and inform the airfield authorities.

Off-airfield landings

If an active airfield is not available, a precautionary landing can be made on a disused airfield, or, failing this, a normal field. Notify the radio service you are in contact with of your intentions. If this is not possible broadcast them on the emergency frequency 121.5.

If a landing has to be made in a field, choose the longest and flattest one available with as few obstructions as possible in both the approach and climbout paths (in case an overshoot becomes necessary). Aim to land as much into wind as possible. Then fly to one side of the field in the landing direction at about 500ft agl and at a slow, safe speed with flaps lowered, so that the field can be inspected closely (see Fig. 143 (a)). While this is being done note the landing direction so that headings for a circuit can be worked out. Alternatively, set the DI to 0°, as this will make heading calculations easier.

If the field is found to be reasonable, make another low level run over the middle of the field at about 200ft agl to inspect the nature of the ground surface, looking for holes, ditches, rocks and other obstructions (see Fig. 143 (b)).

Fig. 143

If you decide the field is suitable complete a low-level circuit, carry out the prelanding checks and land the aeroplane using the soft field technique.

In reducing visibility the second inspection run may not be advisable, so during the field selection stage and initial inspection run find suitable features around the field to help your orientation in the circuit. Timed legs may be necessary.

After landing, secure the aeroplane, inform the local police and obtain assistance.

These procedures should also be used if you intend to land on a disused airfield.

Forced Landings on Extreme Terrain

In mountainous or hilly terrain the available landing areas will be severely limited. Try to select the flattest area possible, an uphill slope is usually more advisable than a downhill one. A landing may be possible on a stretch of road, or even a riverbank. Consider a tree landing. You must take the course of action that appears to have the greatest chance of survival. Prepare for a crash landing.

Ditching

When flying over large expanses of water you are required to carry a lifejacket and a dingy. A forced landing on water has its own set of problems. You will have to determine the condition of the sea. In a calm sea a landing can be made into wind. In choppy or rough seas you will have to assess the direction of swells and waves as well as the wind (see Fig. 144).

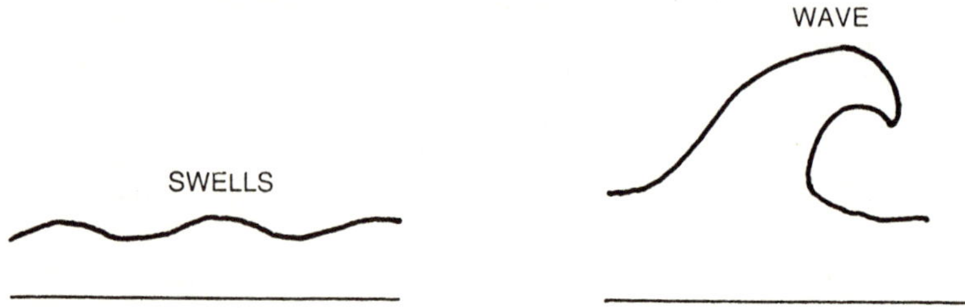

Fig. 144

The aim should be to land on the crest of a wave or swell, but never directly into the face of either. When landing into a river, land downstream unless strong winds dictate otherwise.

The landing on water should be made in a tail-down attitude, with the wings as level as possible. Depth perception is difficult over water, so be very careful. Stalling above water, or raising the nose too high so that the tail strikes the water, will both result in the aircraft nosing over into the water. This must be avoided as it will seriously reduce your ability to abandon the aeroplane. Similarly, try to prevent a wing entering the water first.

Aim to land near some shipping, but not too close to large ships as they require considerable distances to stop. The usual emergency checks apply, but ensure that headsets and microphones are removed and stowed away and the door is unlatched. The rate of deceleration will be rapid on entering the water. It is estimated that a light aircraft will sink in under 2 minutes, so abandon the aircraft as quickly and as orderly as possible. Do not inflate life jackets or the dinghy until the aircraft has been evacuated, otherwise you may not be able to get out of the door. Once in the water, swim clear of the sinking aircraft.

In this book it is only possible to give general advice for such extreme emergencies. A forced landing of any kind is clearly something you will want to avoid. Thorough pre-flight preparations, good-in-flight operating practices and sound decisions all round will reduce the chances of a forced landing having to be made. Regular simulations and practice will ensure you are able to cope with such situations.

AIRMANSHIP

During any forced landing keep a very good lookout for obstructions and other low flying aircraft. Make sure all the safety lights are switched on to draw attention to yourself, especially when landing unannounced at active airfields or ditching. Do not neglect Mayday calls during any emergency situation, and report your position as accurately as possible. Crash checks must always be carried out. Remember, secure seatbelts may save lives or at least minimize injury. Doors must be unlatched and wedged open if possible. A jammed door during a crash landing will prevent exit from the aircraft.

During practice forced landings, do not infringe the low flying rule, and do not scare farm animals. While practising forced landings without power open the throttle regularly to keep the engine at a reasonable operating temperature. All emergency checks should be simulated (touch checks), otherwise the situation may turn into a real emergency.

AIR LESSON

The air lesson will be spread over two flights. The first lesson will be simulated engine failures at cruising altitudes. The second flight will concentrate on the selection of suitable fields for a precautionary landing and the inspection runs. On neither occasion will actual landings be made.

The Forced Landing without Power

At first a suitable field will be chosen and the aircraft positioned above as required. The altitude chosen for the lesson will depend on local circumstances. A circuit, or partial circuit, will be planned and the 1,000ft key point established. Then the throttle will be closed to simulate an engine failure. Your instructor will be talking you through the procedures and checks and you will be able to observe how the aircraft's descent route is adjusted to reach the key point at the correct height and from there to the proper position for the approach. You will be observing the selection of aiming and touchdown points and how cautiously the decision to use flaps is made. When it is clear that a landing can be made, a climb is initiated. Care will be taken not to descend below 500ft agl. The aircraft will be climbed back to the original position and you will be given the opportunity to practise the procedure. When you have grasped the procedures and techniques involved your instructor will simulate more engine failures at various altitudes and times and you will have to complete the whole sequence, selecting your own fields.

If an engine failure occurs at cruising altitudes:

1. Lower the nose and trim for the best gliding speed.
2. Assess the wind and select a landing area.
3. Determine and initiate a descent plan.
4. Determine the 1,000ft point.
5. Keep the field in sight at all times and lookout for cables and other obstructions.
6. Attempt an engine restart (touch checks only). During practice sessions open the throttle every 500ft or so to keep the engine warm.
7. If a restart is not possible carry out the emergency landing checks, including a Mayday call (touch checks only during practice).
8. Aim to arrive at the key point at the correct height.
9. At the key point proceed as for a normal glide approach and landing, aiming at first to touchdown well into the field to ensure that you do not undershoot.
10. When you are absolutely sure of reaching the field, the ROD can be increased by lowering flaps in stages so that the touchdown can be made in the intended position.
11. Land firmly and take avoiding action if necessary.
12. After landing, stop and secure the aircraft.
13. Notify the police and base airfield. Do not attempt to take off again until you have done this and obtained assistance.

Precautionary Landings in a Field

If you decide a precautionary landing has to be made:

1. Notify ATC.
2. Select the most suitable field nearby. In bad visibility select features around the field to establish turning points for a circuit.
3. Descend to about 500ft agl and carefully fly at a slow speed to one side of it in the landing direction to inspect it. Set the DI to 0°.
4. Check for and note the obvious obstructions in the field and in the approach and climbout paths.
5. After flying the full length of the field climb away (if possible) and complete a circuit around the field.
6. Descend to about 200ft agl and fly over the field for a closer inspection.
7. Check for holes, ditches, rocks etc., so you know what to expect during the landing run if you decide that this field is the most suitable under the circumstances.
8. Climb away and complete another circuit, timed if necessary and this time with the intention of landing.
9. Complete the pre-landing checks and unlatch the doors if you envisage any landing problems.
10. Land using the soft field technique if possible, but do not hesitate to overshoot if you have any doubts.
11. On touchdown, shut down the engine immediately if there is a danger of collision or damage.
12. After landing, secure the aircraft and notify the police. Do not take-off again until you have done so and obtained assistance if required.

Instructor's Guide
Ex. 17

LESSON PLAN

Forced landings due to engine failure

Objectives
To teach the student to cope with an engine failure in cruising flight and to make an emergency forced landing.

Content
1 Preflight briefing
Revise gliding flight and the effects of wind, airspeed, flaps and turning manoeuvres on the rate and angle of descent; explain the actions to be taken in the event of an engine failure in cruising flight; discuss the choice of landing area, descent plans and changes of plan; and revise emergency landing procedures.

2 Flight lesson
Review:

(a) glide approaches
(b) sideslipping, then *simulate an engine failure at cruising altitudes and demonstrate the sequence of actions. Simulate more engine failures. Student practice.*

3 Postflight discussion and preview of the next lesson

Completion Standards
This lesson will have been successfully completed when the student displays sound judgement in relation to the aircraft's descent towards the selected landing area. The student must carry out all the emergency actions competently and demonstrate the ability to make prompt decisions when a change of plan becomes necessary.

LESSON PLAN

Forced landings with power (precautionary landings)

Objectives

To develop further the student's skill in the forced landing without power procedure and introduce the student to precautionary landings.

Content

1 Preflight briefing

Revise forced landings without power; discuss possible reasons for a precautionary landing on or off an airfield and the procedures involved in each case; discuss field selection, inspection runs and landing technique.

2 Flight lesson

Review:

(a) forced landings without power, then *demonstrate the selection of a field for a precautionary landing and the inspection runs. Student practice.*

(b) circuit rejoin.

3 Postflight discussion and preview of the next lesson

Completion Standards

This lesson will have been successfully completed when the student can competently handle an engine failure in cruising flight, appreciates the factors that may necessitate a precautionary landing and can competently carry out the field selection and inspection run procedures.

Exercise 18

PILOT NAVIGATION

Objectives

1. to learn the principles and techniques involved in basic pilot navigation
2. to learn to apply these to compile a navigation flight plan
3. to learn how to assess progress and make corrections in flight.

You will also be taught diversionary procedures and the actions to be taken if you become unsure of your position or lost during a flight.

Introduction

Navigation is the art of getting from one place to another. Almost everyone navigates in one way or another. During a drive to another town you would follow roads, observe road signs, street names, landmarks and perhaps stop and confirm your position on a map so you don't get lost. Basically, you will be establishing where you are, the direction you are travelling in and how long it will take to reach the destination. The same basic principles apply in aerial navigation, except the skills and application required are much more involved. Unlike other forms of transport, aircraft are constantly concerned with distance above the ground as well as horizontal distances. Unknown weather conditions or undetected weather changes can create serious problems for aircraft, so aerial navigation is also concerned with weather maps, radio weather reports and forecasts.

The scientific side of navigation is basic; it supplies the facts, tools and techniques. The art of navigation is the application of these instruments, charts and other aids in plotting a course and flying the aeroplane over it according to plan. Air navigation is more than checking position, speed and direction after take-off. Much of the work of navigation takes place on the ground (pre-flight planning). Navigation is essentially the setting up of a travel plan and then trying to stick to it. The planning must be thorough. Maps and charts must be studied with the fuel load, speed and other characteristics of the aeroplane in mind. Various publications on airfields, airspace, etc., must be consulted and special attention should be given to the weather.

With all this information, using a ruler, protractor and a navigation computer, a course is plotted and a flight plan compiled. Once the aeroplane is airborne the task is to follow the planned course, making adjustments for weather changes. If the basic plan is at fault it may not always be possible to make major corrections.

The navigation of an aircraft is necessarily a responsible job, which is why it is an essential part of your training. As airspace becomes more congested it is vital that pilots are able to navigate accurately.

Methods of Navigation

There are basically two systems of navigation that are commonly used by light aircraft pilots today – pilot navigation and radio navigation. The former method, which is navigation by visual contact with the ground, is covered in detail in this manual as this is the basic form of navigation that all pilots must understand. Radio navigation procedures can be used to assist pilot navigation but its main use is for flight under IFR (instrument flight rules) when it is a necessity. Radio navigation procedures are not covered in this manual as they do not form part of the PPL syllabus.

PRINCIPLES OF PILOT NAVIGATION

In visual flying conditions a pilot can navigate using just a map and the magnetic compass, or even only a map in very good weather. But for efficient pilot navigation seven basic items are required in total – a suitable map, a correctly functioning magnetic compass, clock, airspeed indicator and altimeter and reliable aircraft and weather data. With these relatively simple aids you must be able to apply the techniques you will soon learn to implement and maintain a flight plan.

Basically, during flight planning, with the aid of a navigation protractor the map is used to determine the direction from the departure to the destination point and the distance between them is measured using the appropriate scale. Then using weather information and aircraft data, headings are worked out as well as estimated times and fuel required. All these details are written down on a flight log sheet to be referred to in the air. In flight the calculated headings must be steered accurately using the compass and progress along the desired ground tracks monitored by reference to the map, using ground features to establish position. The desired cruise speeds must be maintained accurately and if the aircraft's ground speed appears to be faster or slower than expected the estimated arrival times must be revised. Similarly, if the aircraft appears to be drifting off track it must be returned to the original track and the heading readjusted to maintain it. Establishing position and monitoring progress using landmarks is the most basic and simplest way of navigating in an aircraft, but it is limited to visual meteorological conditions only. These are the basics of pilot navigation.

Maps

Maps are an essential part of a pilot's equipment. There are several types of aviation maps in use today and details of these can be found in the 'Map' section of the *Air Pilot*. The type you will be concerned with mainly at this stage will be the ICAO Aeronautical Chart 1:500,000 series (half million maps). You have already been introduced to maps and map reading, but it is now necessary to go into them in some detail as an understanding of maps and their construction will form the basis for understanding navigational principles.

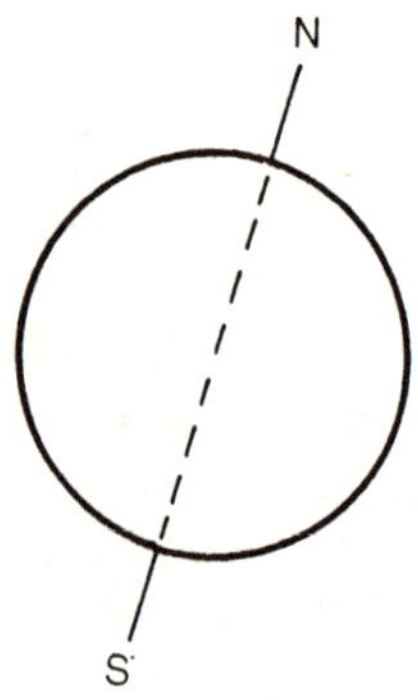

Fig. 145

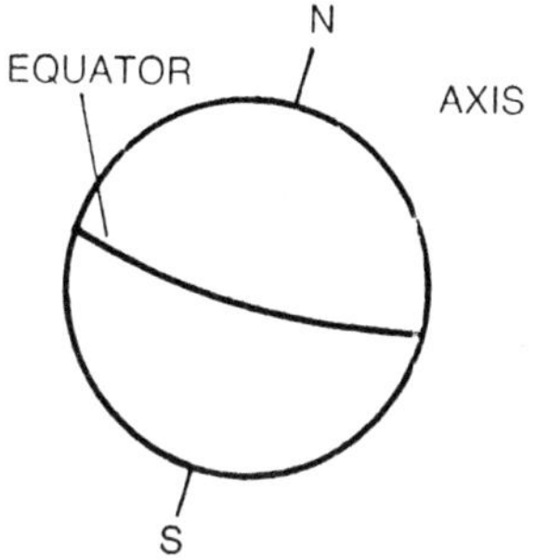

A

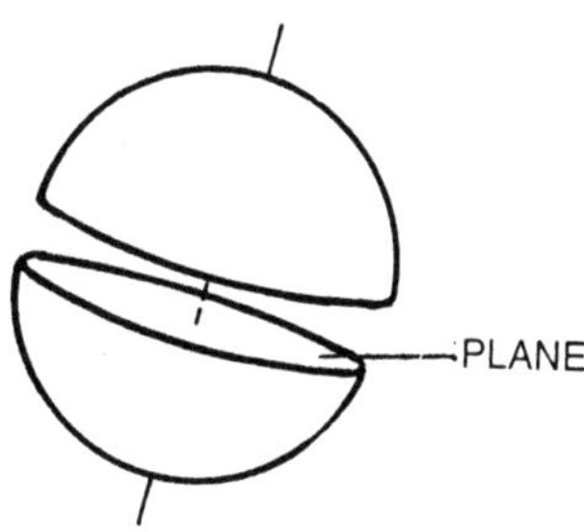

B

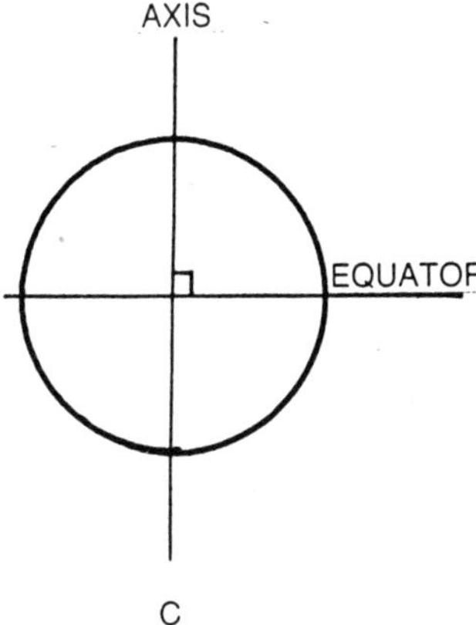

C

Fig. 146

EQUATOR
EARTH'S CENTRE
N
PARALLELS OF LATITUDE
N
EARTH'S CENTRE
EQUATOR
S
PARALLELS OF LATITUDE
N
EQUATOR

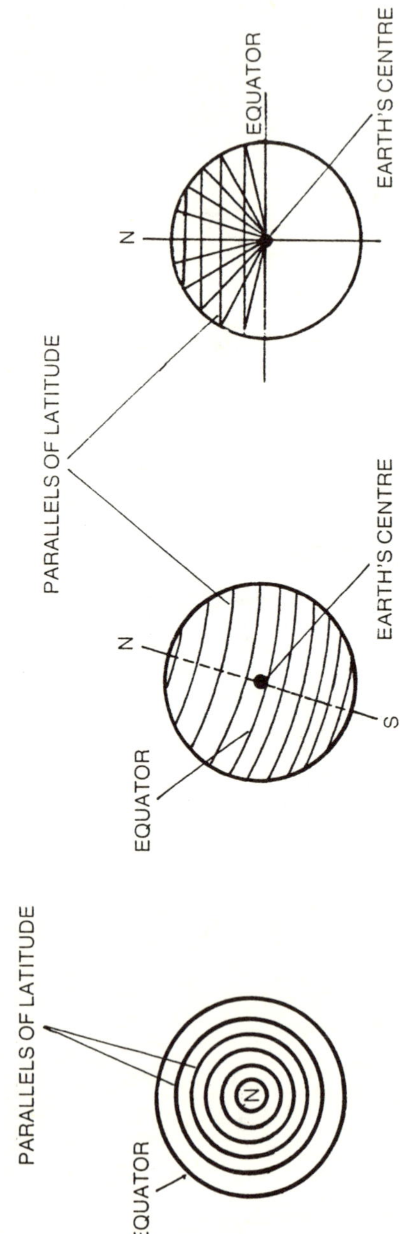

Fig. 147

Form of the Earth

The Earth, for all practical purposes, is a spinning sphere. Its shape and movements have made it possible for scientists to establish accurate lines of reference that can form the basis for measurements. First, there is the axis of the Earth, which is an imaginary line that extends from the North Pole to the South Pole (see Fig. 145).

The other imaginary lines (circles) are on the surface of the earth. These can be thought of as thin flat edges or planes going through the centre of the Earth. The Equator is a circle that is exactly halfway between the two poles (see Fig. 146 (a)). The plane of the Equator extending through the centre of the Earth would divide the Earth into two equal parts (see Fig. 146 (b)).

When any circle on the Earth does this, it is called a Great Circle.

Parallels of Latitude are circles whose planes are parallel to the Equator extending to the North and South Poles (see Fig. 147).

These circles have the axis of the Earth going through their centres, but only the Equator has the centre of the Earth as its centre. This means that all other parallels of Latitude are not great circles. Note that as the parallels of Latitude extend to the Poles

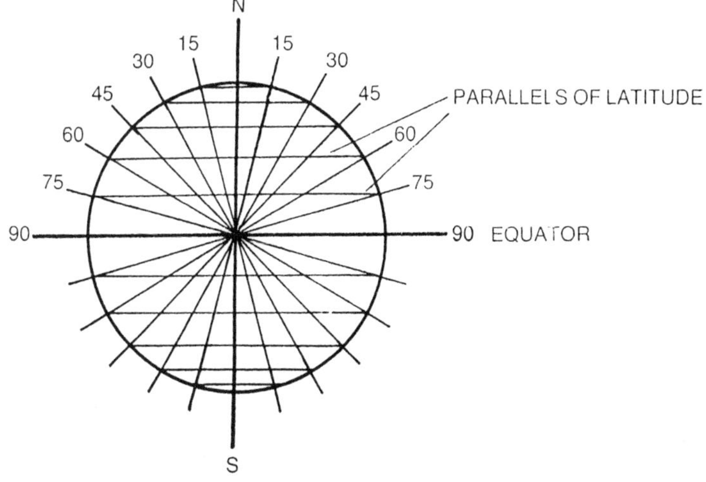

Fig. 148

they become smaller and smaller, so they are often called small circles.

Now, since the circumference of a circle is by convention divided into 360 equal parts (degrees), parallels of Latitude can be drawn north and south of the Equator at 1° intervals up to 90° (see Fig. 148).

These parallel-of-Latitude circles constitute North-South lines of reference and can be used to locate features on the Earth in terms of distance from the Equator.

The other set of reference lines on the Earth are the East-West circles called Meridians of Longitude (see Fig. 149).

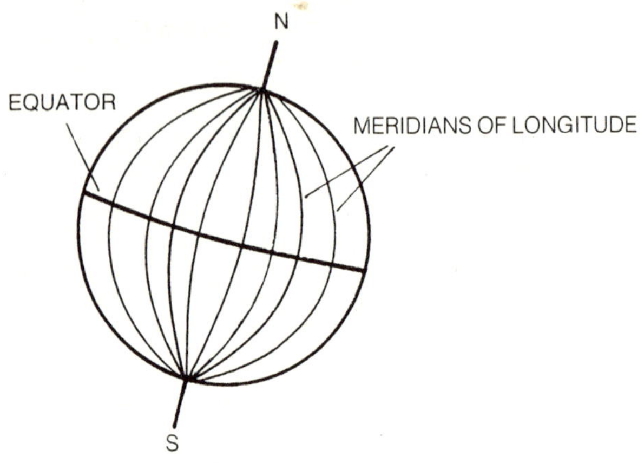

Fig. 149

Unlike parallels of Latitude, Meridians of Longitude are all of the same size. They meet and pass through both the North and South Poles and all are great circles (their planes divide the Earth in half). Only one parallel of Latitude, the Equator, is a great circle and parallels never meet. Therefore, it is impractical to measure Longitude in the same way as Latitude. Now, by convention the Meridian of Longitude that passes through the London suburb of Greenwich, called the 0° or Prime Meridian, is used as the datum for measuring Longitude. If the Equator is divided into 360 degrees, Longitude can be measured as East or West of the Prime Meridian in 1° intervals up to 180 degrees in either direction (see Fig. 150).

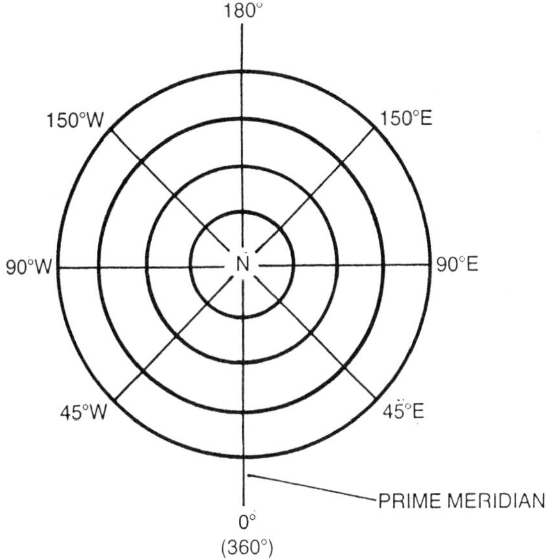

Fig. 150

Meridians of Longitude and parallels of Latitude divide the Earth into a spherical grid (graticule). Each division, however, is not the same size because the Meridians converge at the Poles. But with this system, features on the Earth can be located easily in a similar way that streets are located on a standard road map. For greater accuracy each degree of Latitude and Longitude is further divided into 60 minutes (′) and each minute into 60 seconds (″). These minutes and seconds are divisions of distance on a circle. They have the same names as the divisions of time and the degrees, minutes and seconds of Longitude can be converted into the units of time.

Each degree of Latitude, or a degree measured on any great circle, is about 69 miles. A minute of Latitude or great circle measure is 1nm (6080 ft) and one second is about 100ft. With this system any place on the Earth's surface can be located very accurately. On your map, at the edges and other suitable places, degrees and minutes of Latitude and Longitude are indicated. A feature pinpointed using these Latitude and Longitude references (called geographical co-ordinates) would be within an area that is approximately one square mile, so it can be easily located from the air.

Geographical co-ordinates given for locations on the Earth are shown in the following way:

Latitude: Degrees Minutes Longitude: Degrees Minutes

Example: 54 22 N. (I.at.) 3 42 W. (Long.)

To find a location given in this way first establish the Latitude, then the Longitude and where the two intersect will be the location of the feature. Figure 151 illustrates an example.

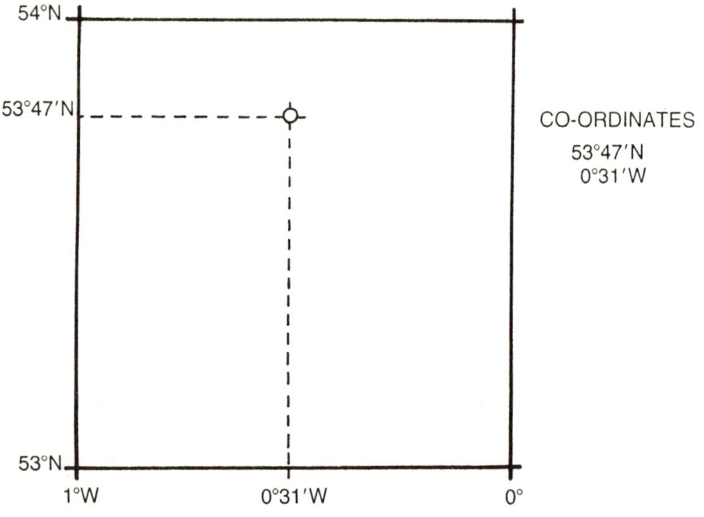

Fig. 151

It is important that you are able to find locations in this way and also to establish the co-ordinates of any location. For practice choose various airfields depicted on your map and try to work out their co-ordinates. You can check your results using the *Air Pilot*, which will contain the actual co-ordinates of airfields.

The centres of all great circles coincide with the centre of the Earth. It is possible to establish more great circles besides the Equator and Meridians. Great circles may be drawn at any angle and go in any direction as long as their planes divide the Earth in half (see Fig. 152).

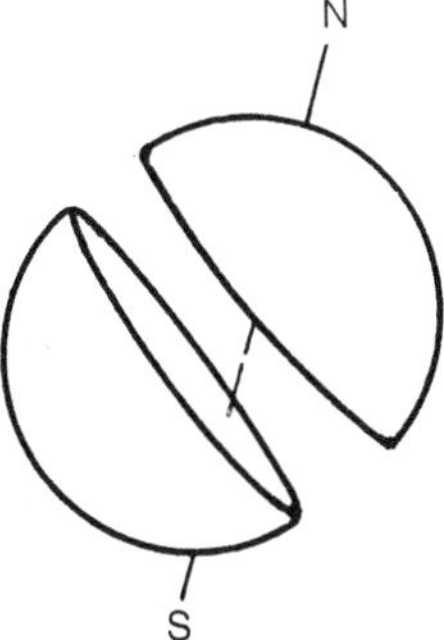

Fig. 152

The shortest distance between two points on a flat surface is a straight line. However, on a sphere the shortest distance between two points will be a great circle. If you stretch a length of thread tightly between any two points on a globe you will establish the shortest route between them and this route will be part of a great circle.

Despite surface irregularities and the fact that the diameter between North and South Poles is slightly smaller than the diameter of the Equator, the Earth is almost a perfect sphere. This means that every time you fly you will be above a sphere. Therefore, the route you make will almost always be part of some circle. If you can visualize this you may find that it will help you understand the intricacies of maps and their construction.

Map Construction

Because the Earth is a three-dimensional sphere it cannot be truly represented on a flat piece of paper. This means that every map is a compromise. You can demonstrate this for yourself by trying to wrap a piece of paper around a ball. This cannot be done without folding and creasing the paper, i.e. creating distortions. Maps are constructed by means of projections, and these are briefly and simply outlined below.

The Mercator Projection

This type of projection transfers the surface of the Earth on to a cylinder of paper, as shown in Figure 153.

MERCATOR PROJECTION

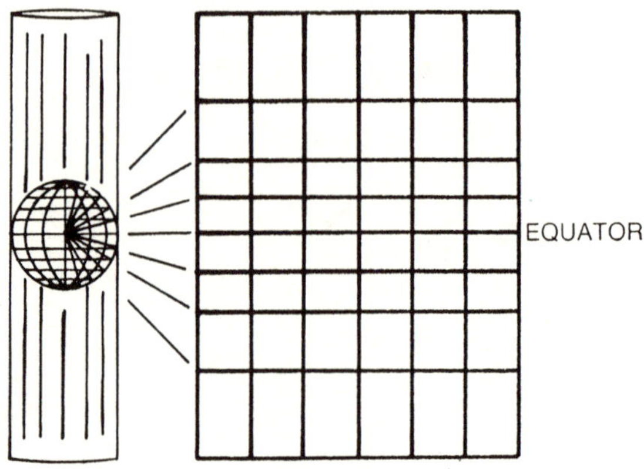

Fig. 153

However, the fact remains that the Earth is a sphere. Note that the distance (scale) between the parallels of Latitude increase away from the Equator. Meridians should converge but they are equally spaced on Mercator charts. A Mercator map is most accurate near the Equator and the distortion increases rapidly making shapes unduly large at the polar regions. So, briefly, Mercator charts do not give a true presentation of the Earth's surface. Therefore, they are not really suitable for pilot navigation purposes, except in equatorial regions. However, they are satisfactory for other uses as they have certain advantages. Angles can be measured accurately and since parallels and meridians are at right angles, when a certain type of course, called a rhumb line (described later) is plotted on a Mercator chart it will appear as a straight line.

The Lambert Conical Projection
This type of projection is similar to the Mercator method except that a cone of paper is placed on top of the globe instead of a cylinder, as shown in Figure 154.

Note that although the polar regions do not touch the cone a good part from the Equator to the Poles does. Lambert Projections are designed to be accurate within two parallels, called standard parallels. By using larger or smaller cones different

LAMBERT CONIC PROJECTION

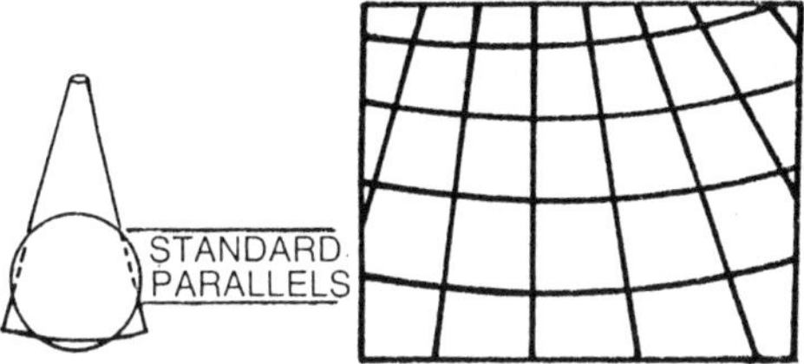

Fig. 154

regions (or standard parallels) can be projected. At points North and South of the standard parallels distortions appear, but these are very small. This is basically a simplification of the Lambert Projection.

On Lambert maps the Meridians are straight lines that converge at some point off the map. The parallels of Latitude are shown as concentric circles. Meridians cross the parallels at right angles as on Mercator maps, which helps in using the map. A distinct advantage of the Lambert Projection is that a straight line drawn on the map approximately represents part of a great circle. Therefore, a straight line on a Lambert map generally shows the shortest distance between two points. This is very different from a Mercator map, where a straight line is *not* the shortest distance between two points.

Scale of maps

The scale of a map is very important as it tells you the relationship between the size of the map and the Earth. A map is minutely smaller than the Earth, but how much smaller is the critical question. The scale on a Lambert map is practically constant so that one inch on the top of the map represents much the same distance that it does on any other part. On Mercator Projections scale increases away from the centre of the map. This distortion will make outer regions look disproportionally larger than they really are. The constant scale of Lambert maps is another advantage as distance and areas can be more readily compared.

The scales on maps are represented as a ratio, such as 1:500,000, and this can be converted into any unit of distance. There are also two other methods of presenting scale on maps. A statement in words, such as 1 inch equals 8 nm, is often used, and Graduated Scale Lines in statute miles, nautical miles and kilometres. These will be given at the bottom of your topographical chart.

A statute mile measures 5,280ft. A nautical mile (6,080ft) is the average length of one minute of latitude. Its use simplifies converting degree measure into distance when navigating. A kilometre is one 10,000th of the distance from the Equator to the Poles and it is equal to 3,280 ft. Units of distance can be converted on your navigation computer. Your navigation ruler is calibrated to measure distances on your Lambert map and also on a variation of the Mercator Projection called a Transverse Mercator Chart, where distances can also be considered as constant. On normal Mercator maps distances must be measured using the appropriate scales given for different latitudes.

Scales differ with the uses of maps. The map you will be using has a scale of 1:500,000. This means that one inch on the map equals half a million inches or about eight miles on the ground. These maps contain sufficient detail for contact flying. Smaller scale maps, such as ICAO World Aeronautical Chart Series (1:1,000,000), where one inch equals about 16 miles, depict much larger areas and so contain much less detail. They are used mainly for long-distance flight planning.

Your half million topographical map is a Lambert Projection. Angles and distances can be measured accurately and the shape of features are presented correctly. Now, although maps have a definite scale, not all the features on the map are shown true to scale. If this were so, important features such as high obstacles and railways would be too small to be seen. Significant features are presented larger than true scale to emphasize their importance.

Using Maps

Projection and scale are an introduction to a map. To be able to use a map you must be able to understand the information presented. There are basically four groups of features on a map – water, relief (terrain), culture (towns, railways and other man-made features) and aeronautical data. Each has its own colours and conventional symbols. The symbols used on maps are good commonsense markings for the things they represent. They are basically the alphabet of aeronautical charts and they must be learned before you can read and understand a map. In the air you see the Earth below unfolding like a huge map. Like the letters of the alphabet the map symbols have little meaning on their own, but you can put them together and make them tell you exactly what you wish to know. A map is a bit like a guide book, best read before and while you fly, so that you can recognize and understand the things you see.

Maps must be kept up to date, so they are constantly checked and corrected. Using outdated maps can be very dangerous. Check the validity of your map.

BASIC PLOTTING SKILLS

There are a few practical exercises that can help you understand maps while at the same time develop basic and useful navigation skills.

Estimating Direction

It is very important to be able to visually estimate direction on a map. You are already familiar with the compass rose and now it is time to really get to know it. Select any two prominent landmarks on the map. Start with your base airfield and another one some distance away. Then, without using a ruler, draw a line as straight as you can connecting the two points. Next, using your knowledge of the compass rose, try to visually estimate the direction from your base airfield to the other airfield, or vice versa. You can check your estimate by measuring the direction accurately using the protractor. This is done by setting the North-South line of the protractor on the meridian nearest to the halfway point of your line with the centre of the protractor over the point where the meridian intersects with your line, as Figure 155 illustrates. Directions can then be read off easily.

Choose more features and keep practising this until your ability to draw freehand straight lines improves and your direction estimates become accurate to, say, within 10°.

Estimating Distance

The ability to assess distance visually on a map is also very important. Look at the appropriate scale lines on your map and try to remember approximately how long they are and how many units of distance they represent. Next, in the same way as before,

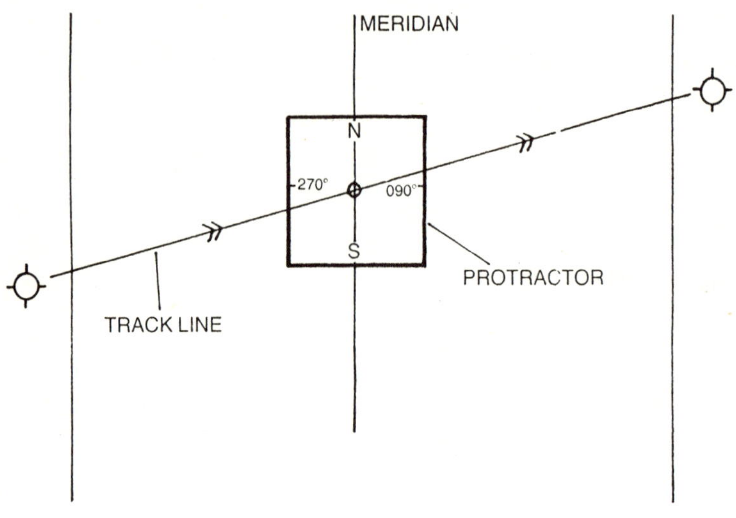

Fig. 155

draw freehand straight lines between various points and estimate the distances. Then, using the appropriate scale on your ruler, measure the distance to check your estimate. Practise this several times until your estimates become accurate to, say, within 2 nm.

Another useful and quite literal rule of thumb is to measure the digit of your thumb on a scale, as shown in Figure 156. If you can remember this length, your thumb can be used to measure distances quite accurately and quickly on the map. Measuring the span of your hand will also be useful.

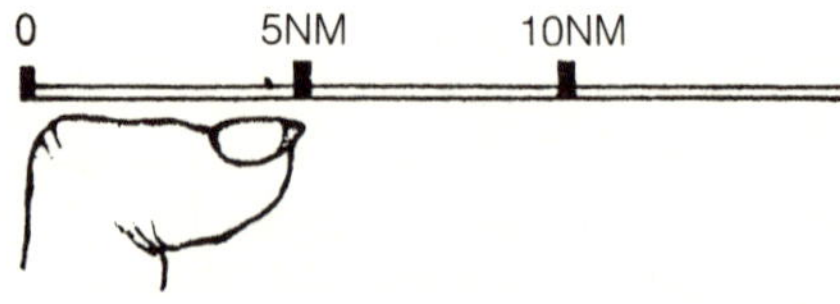

Fig. 156

Obviously, during pre-flight planning you must use rulers and protractors for greater accuracy. But these skills, which you should acquire, will be invaluable if an unplanned diversion has to be made in flight. In such situations rulers and protractors will be impractical. Also, these methods can be used as a means of cross-checking your pre-flight measurements. More rules of thumb will be introduced later in this chapter.

Direction and the Compass

The map and compass are the most basic of navigational tools and the compass is the most important navigational instrument in the cockpit.

In very good weather and with the availability of several ground features such as roads, railways, coastlines etc., it is possible to navigate using only a map. But this will be extremely limiting. Straightforward landmarks are not always present and in instrument flying conditions the aircraft is not likely to be in sight of the ground. So the pilot uses the magnetic compass as the primary means of reference as to the desired direction of travel.

The magnetic compass of an aircraft is basically a very sophisticated magnet system. The Earth itself is a huge magnet, having it own North and South poles. Now, magnetic North and South lie in different positions from the geographic North and South poles which exist at either end of the Earth's axis (or at the points where the meridians meet). Magnetic North lies in northern Canada and Magnetic South off the Antarctic Coast.

The magnetic fields of the Earth and the magnetic compass affect one another. In the northern hemisphere the north-seeking end of the compass is attracted to and swings toward the magnetic North pole, and in the southern hemisphere the south-seeking end is attracted to the South magnetic pole. The compass points to the magnetic pole wherever on the Earth it may be.

In the working of a compass two magnets are involved. One large and fixed (the Earth) and the other small and movable. Now, the total energy of the interaction of the magnetic field of the Earth and that of a small swinging magnet is very minute, so any resistance, motion and vibration, such as those produced by an aircraft, is likely to mask or nullify the magnetic attraction. This means the magnetic compass of an aircraft needs to be quite sophisticated if it is to be effectively used. The magnetic compass in your aircraft consists of a rotating card in a bowl full of liquid. Attached to this card are several magnetized needles and it is delicately balanced to respond freely to the movements of the aircraft. The liquid dampens oscillations and vibrations produced by the aeroplane and also helps support the magnet system. The card is divided and numbered every 30° (with the zero omitted), with further divisions of 10° and 5° marked by lines. On the glass front of the compass is a straight vertical line called the Lubber Line, which represents the direction the aircraft is travelling (see Fig. 157).

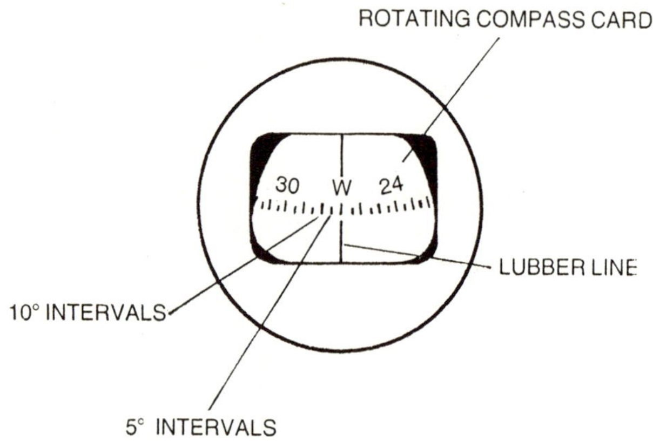

Fig. 157

Deviation

The compass cannot be used until every factor in the aircraft that may affect it is discovered. These factors will cause the compass to deviate from giving an accurate indication of magnetic direction. They may be caused by electrical circuits in the aircraft or iron components in the vicinity of the compass. Errors due to these causes are called deviation and will differ from aircraft to aircraft and also on varying directions. The compass is corrected for deviation by engineers, but only major corrections can be made and small errors of a few degrees may persist. These errors are given on a card placed near the compass showing the deviation of the compass from various magnetic directions. You will have to refer to this card when calculating headings for navigation (dealt with later).

Variation

The use of a compass involves much more detail than the compensation for installation errors. You will have to *learn* how to use a compass. You will have to pay as much attention to what a compass does do as to what it does not do. The compass does *not* show true North. It does not constantly point in the same direction and it does not accurately show a change in direction. You are already aware of its various turning and acceleration errors. But despite all these peculiarities the compass is still a very essential and useful instrument.

The first thing you must learn and constantly remember is that the magnetic compass will never point to true North except in certain parts of the world. It points generally towards magnetic North, but as far as true direction is concerned it may be pointing north, south, east or west of true North, depending on its location on the Earth. For example, in the UK when the compass shows North, it is actually pointing a few degrees to the west of true North. In the Western USA it will point to the east of true North. The actual amount of this variation will depend on exactly where you are on the Earth.

World-wide geological surveys have made it possible to establish lines of equal magnetic variation. These can be thought of as magnetic meridians emanating from the North and South magnetic poles, as Figure 158 illustrates.

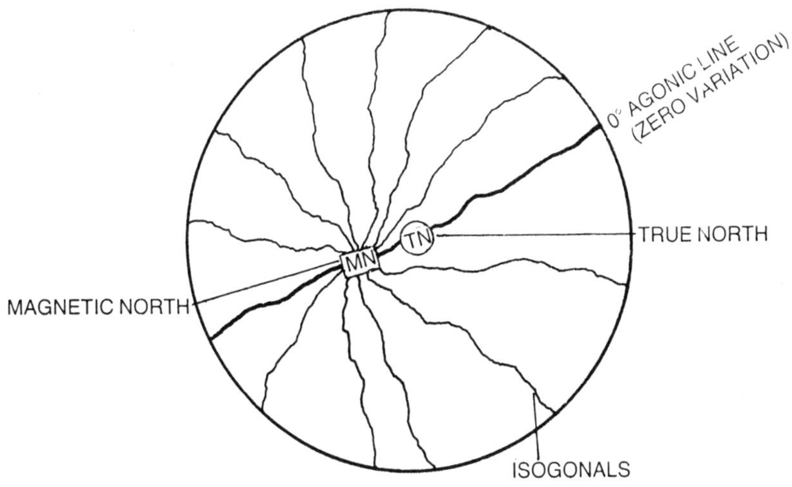

Fig. 158

These lines are irregular because magnetic variation is also influenced by localized deposits of magnetic minerals.

Magnetic meridians are called Isogonals and are depicted on your maps at 1° intervals. Just as the Prime Meridian is established as a datum for measuring Meridians of Longitude, a datum must be determined for isogonals. This is the Agonic Line (0° variation). An aircraft anywhere along this particular isogonal will point to true North as well as magnetic North. Positions either side of the agonic line will produce an angular difference called magnetic variation. East of this line the compass will point west of true North and west of this line it will point east of true North. Magnetic variation is very distinct from deviation. Whereas deviation is a result of local disturbances within the aircraft, variation is due to the fact that the magnetic poles of the Earth are not in the same place as the geographical poles. There is nothing that can be done about variation but accept it. In all calculations involving the compass it will be necessary to add or subtract the magnetic variation for the particular part of the country where the compass reading is being made. When plotting a course during pre-flight planning the direction measured by your protractor will indicate direction in relation to true North. These true directions must be converted to magnetic directions by applying variation and deviation in order to arrive at headings that may be steered directly on the magnetic compass.

Another fact about variation is that it is not constant but is continually changing. The changes are extremely small, but they are taken into consideration whenever maps are revised.

Despite being a very involved instrument the compass is a sound and basic guide to direction, provided you understand how to make the compensations (covered later). Many aircraft have more sophisticated types of compass but these are not covered in this manual. In flight you will normally be using the DI to maintain headings due to its greater stability. But you must remember that this instrument has no North-seeking properties and will be useless for navigation unless it is frequently synchronized with the magnetic compass.

THE NAVIGATION FLIGHT COMPUTER

The flight computer is used for a wide variety of navigational computations from conversions to swift calculations of headings and times and as such it is an essential part of a pilot's equipment.

However, due to differences between the types of computer currently on the market and the increasing availability of electronic varieties detailed coverage of the operations of flight computers has been omitted from this manual. You must study the handbook provided with the particular type of computer you decide to use.

Plotting the Course

Plotting a course is an essential procedure in navigation. You have already had some experience in this if you carried out the exercises given earlier. Plotting a course is not always necessary for short flights in very good weather. The familiar landmarks around an airfield and references to the map and compass may be sufficient. You have probably noticed that these were all your instructor used on your earlier training flights in the local area. However, when distances and time in the air increase, flying a plotted course is a necessity. It is good flying practice and a safeguard. You must have the route carefully worked out in advance so that all you have to do in the air is check position and perhaps modify the plan for weather changes or navigation errors. The preparation for course plotting requires simple arithmetic (addition and subtraction) and your present knowledge of maps.

In course plotting you will have to decide first where the destination is and then how to steer the aircraft to get there. If winds, variation and deviation did not exist navigation would be simple. All you would have to do is measure the direction required on the map and then fly this heading. But because of the facts that true North and magnetic North do not coincide, that the compass is imperfect and that weather varies, it is likely that you will have to point the nose in any direction but the one that was measured on the map in order to fly and maintain that direction and reach your destination.

Having located the destination the true course may be plotted. This brings us back to map projection. On your Lambert chart the meridians converge at an angle of about 0.78° when one degree apart. This means that direction will have to be measured on the meridian closest to the halfway point of the course. This will establish the average direction of the course. If the course is long, extending more than four degrees of longitude, it will have to be divided into sections and the direction measured midway between each section.

When a constant heading is steered on the compass the line or route followed will cross each meridian at the same angle. Such a course is called a Rhumb Line, and will produce a somewhat curved path over the ground in relation to the meridians (see Fig. 159).

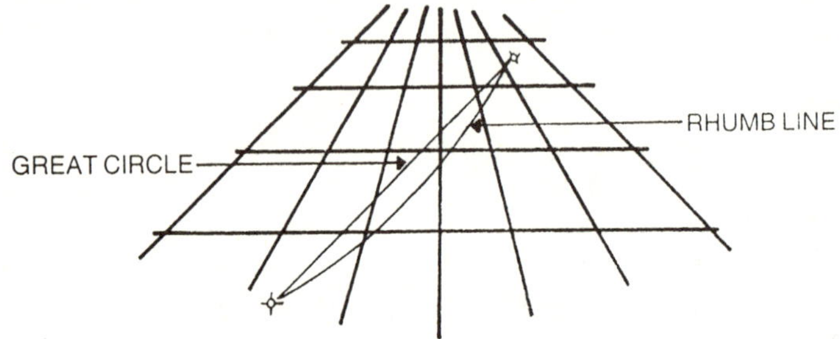

Fig. 159

It can be seen that a rhumb line course is slightly longer than a great circle course, but despite this it is much easier to navigate. To fly a great circle course the pilot will have to change direction continually. The Meridians of Longitude and the Equator are the only courses that are both rhumb lines and great circles.

Rhumb line courses and great circle bearings

Course is the direction of a rhumb line measured on the halfway meridian. A bearing is the direction of a great circle, measured through the meridian at the point where the measurement is made. As meridians converge on a Lambert Projection a bearing is constantly changing as the aircraft progresses along a great circle route. Since course is on a rhumb line that crosses each meridian at the same angle it may be followed without change although it is somewhat longer than the great circle route. For example, the rhumb line course from London to New York is about 140 miles longer than the great circle route. Over short distances the difference between rhumb lines and great circles are virtually insignificant.

True track, true heading, magnetic heading and compass heading

The course you plot on your map is called the true track. Direction is measured from true North. The true track must be transferred into a true heading and this heading turned into a magnetic heading and then, finally, into a compass heading to be steered in flight. This simply means that the true track must be corrected for wind, variation and deviation.

The true heading is the heading required to offset drift and is calculated by correcting for the effects of wind (covered later).

To arrive at the magnetic heading you must *add* westerly variation to the true heading and *subtract* easterly variation, as shown in the examples below:

True track	*Variation*	*Magnetic heading*
090°	6°W	096°
260°	4°E	256°
156°	8°W	164°
335°	10°E	325°

Obtaining the magnetic heading is an intermediate step. To arrive at the compass heading, deviation must be compensated for in the same way as for variation, by *adding* westerly deviation and *subtracting* easterly deviation, as shown below:

Magnetic heading	*Deviation*	*Compass heading*
096°	2°E	094°
256°	3°W	259°
164°	4°E	160°
325°	1°W	326°

This final calculation for deviation will provide the heading you steer in flight. Provided your calculations are correct and you maintain this heading accurately, you will proceed along the desired track to your destination. These calculations are very simple but you may easily end up steering the wrong heading if you have added when you should have subtracted, or vice versa. So be meticulous during pre-flight planning.

Wind

Calculation of true airspeed, true heading and ground speed

Wind has a most significant effect on a cross-country flight and it must be seriously considered if a flight plan is to work. It will determine the time taken to reach the destination at any given airspeed. You have already observed how wind affects an aircraft's path over the ground in terms of speed and drift. If you are flying in a tailwind ground speed increases and you will reach the destination quicker. The opposite happens in a headwind. If the wind is at an angle to your flight path you will experience a certain amount of drift as well as a headwind or tailwind component. Unlike for very short flights, or flights in the circuit, you will have to determine exactly how the wind affects your chosen flight path and exactly what corrections need to be made, if any.

An aircraft's actual track over the ground (track made good) will be the resultant of two velocities, the wind direction and speed and the aircraft's heading and true airspeed. Before every cross-country flight you must obtain the latest wind velocity and air temperature for the cruising altitude desired.

Calculating true airspeed

It was explained in an earlier chapter that the airspeed indicated by the ASI is not the true speed of the aircraft through the air. True airspeed must be determined before calculations for wind effects (true heading and ground speed) can be made. To work out TAS you must first decide the indicated cruising speed to be used. The indicated airspeed must then be corrected for errors that are the result of the position and installation of the pressure source of the ASI. These errors are small and can be found in the aircraft's flight manual. IAS corrected for these errors is called rectified airspeed (RAS) or calibrated airspeed (CAS). Having established the RAS true airspeed is determined by correcting this figure for air density (altitude) and temperature. This is done on your flight computer.

Calculating true heading and ground speed

With the TAS figure it will now be possible to work out the true heading and ground speed using the wind velocity and true track. Once again, you can calculate these figures very quickly using the flight computer.

The Triangle of Velocities

This is the basic method of calculating true heading and ground speed and is the basis of the method used on your computer. The triangle of velocities is a vector triangle with each side representing two variables, as shown below.

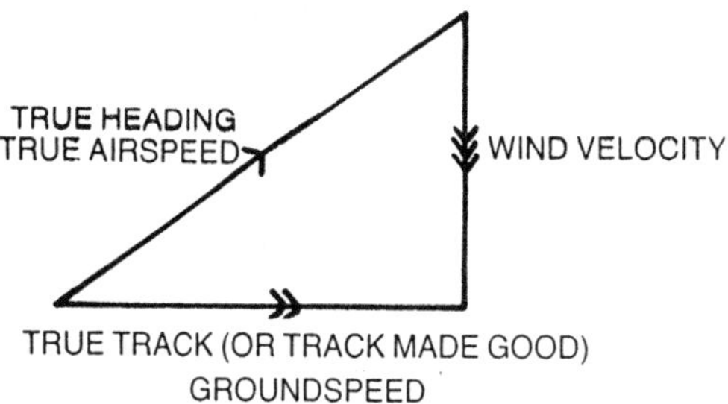

Fig. 160

To construct a vector triangle you will need a pair of dividers, a ruler, protractor and squared paper. With a knowledge of the wind velocity, true track and TAS, the true heading and ground speed can be worked out using the following steps, as shown in the example below.

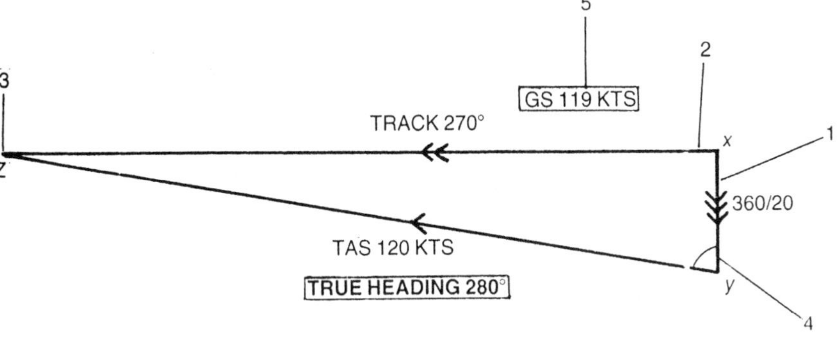

Fig. 161

Steps

1. Draw in the wind velocity.
2. Draw the true track line upwind of the w/v (point x).

3. Measure out the TAS on the dividers and with one point on position y, mark an arc on the track line to locate z.
4. Measure the angle xyz to obtain the true heading.
5. Measure the length of the track line to obtain the ground speed.

Calculating times

The time taken to cover the distance to the destination will depend on the ground speed. The distance divided by the ground speed will give you the time (D ÷ S = T). The circular slide rule side of your computer can be used to calculate times quickly.

It is usual for the track to be divided into one-quarter segments, or, for shorter trips, into halves, so that the estimated arrival times can be revised if the ground speed is other than expected.

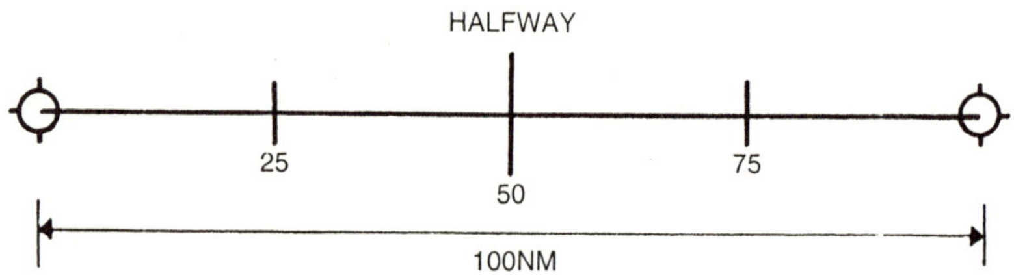

Fig. 162

The ability to estimate approximate times for various speeds and distances is another useful skill to acquire. Figure 163 is a table which can be used for this purpose and it is suggested that you make a copy of it or compile your own to carry with you on flights.

DISTANCE (NAUTICAL MILES)	SPEED (KNOTS)							
	60	70	80	90	100	110	120	130
2	2′.00″	1′.42″	1′.30″	1′.20″	1′.12″	1′.05″	1′.00″	0′.55″
5	5′.00″	4′.17″	3′.45″	3′.20″	3′.00″	2′.43″	2′.30″	2′.18″
10	10′.00″	8′.34″	7′.30″	6′.40″	6′.00″	5′.27″	5′.00″	4′.36″

Fig. 163

On your computer you can also calculate the distance that will be covered in a given time at a given speed (T × S = D) and also the ground speed, when a given distance is flown in a given time (S = D ÷ T).

Dead Reckoning

The term dead reckoning (DR) is short for deduced reckoning and originated from maritime navigation. It means 'reckoning or reasoning one's position relative to something stationary or dead in the water'. As far as air navigation is concerned DR is a method of predicting progress based on the estimated ground speeds since the last known position. In effect, the headings, ground speeds and times you will be calculating will be DR estimates. In flight, however, you will be monitoring your progress and making adjustments if weather conditions are not as forecasted. When

PILOT NAVIGATION

PLOTTING THE COURSE
DEAD RECKONING

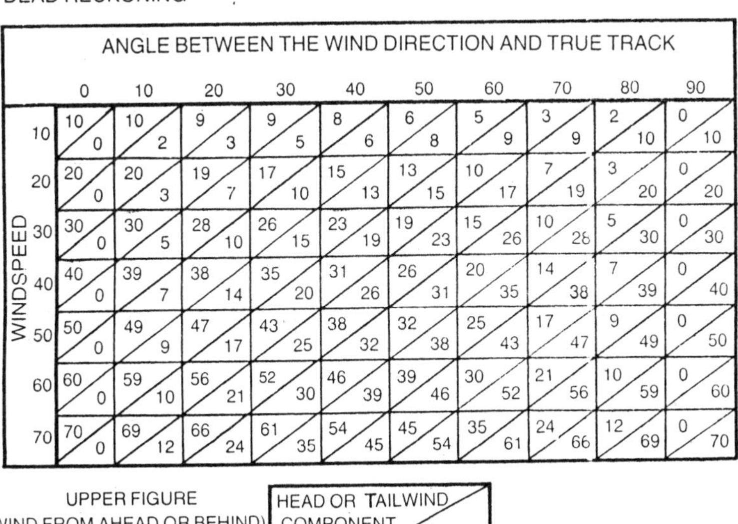

ANGLE BETWEEN THE WIND DIRECTION AND TRUE TRACK

WINDSPEED	0	10	20	30	40	50	60	70	80	90
10	10 / 0	10 / 2	9 / 3	9 / 5	8 / 6	6 / 8	5 / 9	3 / 9	2 / 10	0 / 10
20	20 / 0	20 / 3	19 / 7	17 / 10	15 / 13	13 / 15	10 / 17	7 / 19	3 / 20	0 / 20
30	30 / 0	30 / 5	28 / 10	26 / 15	23 / 19	19 / 23	15 / 26	10 / 28	5 / 30	0 / 30
40	40 / 0	39 / 7	38 / 14	35 / 20	31 / 26	26 / 31	20 / 35	14 / 38	7 / 39	0 / 40
50	50 / 0	49 / 9	47 / 17	43 / 25	38 / 32	32 / 38	25 / 43	17 / 47	9 / 49	0 / 50
60	60 / 0	59 / 10	56 / 21	52 / 30	46 / 39	39 / 46	30 / 52	21 / 56	10 / 59	0 / 60
70	70 / 0	69 / 12	66 / 24	61 / 35	54 / 45	45 / 54	35 / 61	24 / 66	12 / 69	0 / 70

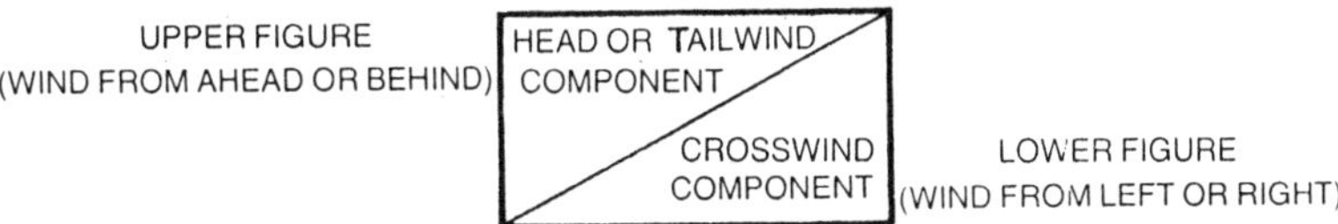

Fig. 164

	HEADING CORRECTION TRUE AIRSPEED					
		80	100	120	140	160
CROSSWIND COMPONENT	5	4°	3°	2°	2°	2°
	10	7°	6°	5°	4°	4°
	15	11°	9°	7°	6°	5°
	20	14°	12°	10°	8°	7°
	25	18°	14°	12°	10°	9°
	30	22°	17°	14°	12°	11°
	35	26°	20°	17°	14°	13°
	40	30°	24°	19°	17°	15°

Fig. 165

making unplanned diversions again you will be making DR estimates, computing headings and times to reach the alternate airfield. Below are two tables that can be used to work out true headings and ground speeds.

To use these tables the following steps must be taken:

1. Determine the wind angle (the angle between the desired true track and the wind direction).
2. Determine if the wind has a head or tailwind component and the direction of drift.
3. Using the wind angle and speed determine the head/tailwind component and the crosswind component using Fig. 164.
4. Add or subtract the head/tailwind component from your TAS to obtain the ground speed.
5. Using the crosswind component figure and the TAS determine your wind correction angle.
6. Add or subtract this figure from your true track to arrive at a true heading.

For example, say the wind velocity is 060°/30 kts, the TAS is 120 kts and the track required is 090° true. The steps to determine the groundspeed and true heading are:

1. Wind angle equals 30°.
2. The wind is from the left and ahead. Therefore, a headwind will be experienced and the drift will be to the right.
3. On Fig. 164 a 30° wind angle at a speed of 30 kts will produce a headwind component of 26 kts and a crosswind component of 15 kts.
4. The ground speed will be 94 kts (120-26).
5. The wind correction angle for a crosswind component of 15 kts at a TAS of 120 kts will be 7°.
6. The true heading will therefore be 083° (090-7).

These steps will become very quick and easy after a little practice, steps one and two being likely to be the most difficult at first. The results will be accurate to within a few degrees, or knots, which is good enough for DR purposes when unplanned diversions have to be made. You are advised to learn how to use these tables and a few true heading and ground speed problems are given below for you to practise.

Find the true heading and groundspeed when the w/v and TAS are:

1.	Track 270°	TAS 100 kts	W/V 285/20
2.	Track 150°	TAS 130 kts	W/V 300/15
3.	Track 235°	TAS 90 kts	W/V 180/10
4.	Track 020°	TAS 115 kts	W/V 070/25
5.	Track 315°	TAS 125 kts	W/V 200/30

You will have to interpolate in some cases. Compare your answers with those obtained on the computer. The tables are easy to use and the arithmetic is simple. You are advised to make a copy of these tables to carry with you on flights. Their simplicity will prove invaluable for unplanned diversions and may also be used to cross-check computer calculations.

The advantage of learning basic navigational skills and rules of thumb is similar to that of learning multiplication tables at school. They will be useful in the future although learning them may be a rather tiresome task.

STUDYING THE ROUTE

The study of your plotted routes is a very important procedure. Although it is more convenient to fly direct to the destination, this may not always be practical or safe. The presence of restricted airspace, controlled airspace, high terrain and large expanses of water may make it necessary for 'dog legs' to be made, as shown in Figure 166.

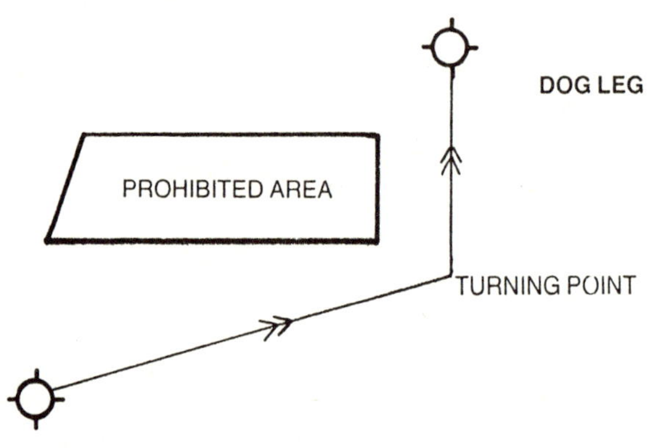

Fig. 166

Details of the restricted airspace affecting your route can be found in the 'RAC' section of the *Air Pilot*. If your route lies close to the edge of the map at any stage you must carry the adjoining map(s) in flight as well.

Selecting the Cruising Altitude and Minimum Safe Altitude

In light aircraft most cross-country flights take place between 2,000 – 4,000ft amsl (in visual conditions) although higher levels may be used. Cruising altitudes above 10,000ft amsl must not be used without the proper oxygen equipment.

Usually, however, the maximum altitude you can select will depend on the proximity of controlled airspace at upper levels and more often on the cloud ceilings.

The first step in deciding the altitude to fly will be to study the route and determine the minimum safe cruising altitude (MSA). This is usually done by reviewing the height of the ground and obstructions within 10 nm either side of the track and then adding 1,000ft to the highest obstruction on the ground. On very long flights the route should be divided into segments and MSAs worked out for each individual segment, as shown in Figure 167. The normal time section segments can be used.

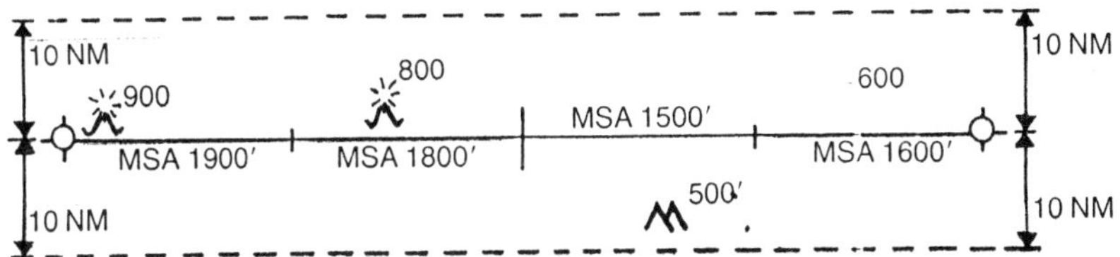

Fig. 167

Then ensure that these altitudes can be safely maintained without entering cloud (check weather forecasts) and controlled airspace. Remember, these are minimum safe altitudes. If cloud and controlled airspace permit, higher cruising altitudes can be chosen.

Selecting Alternate Airfields

This is another very important item in navigation planning. Study the area around the track and note airfields that may be used as alternates should the weather or any other situation make a diversion necessary. Ideally your alternate airfield should be close to your track and a direct route should be possible to reach it from anywhere along your route. This may not always be possible, of course.

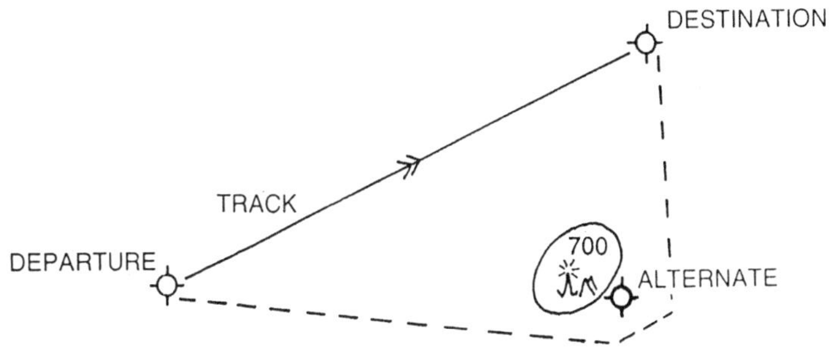

Fig. 168

Study the area approaching the alternate from your track. Note and circle any obstacles and high ground, as shown in Figure 168. Work out a minimum safe altitude.

Selecting Checkpoints

While studying the route, select and mark checkpoints (ground features), close to the halfway point and other positions, that can be used to establish the aircraft's position in flight. Look for features that will appear easily in your line of sight as you fly towards them. Usually more than one feature is required to establish position, unless the checkpoint is an unmistakable one such as a lake or a river bend.

Checkpoints are not used just to establish position, but also as a means of checking estimated times (ground speed) and progress along the desired track. For example, say you estimated arriving at a halfway point at 13.00 hours as shown below.

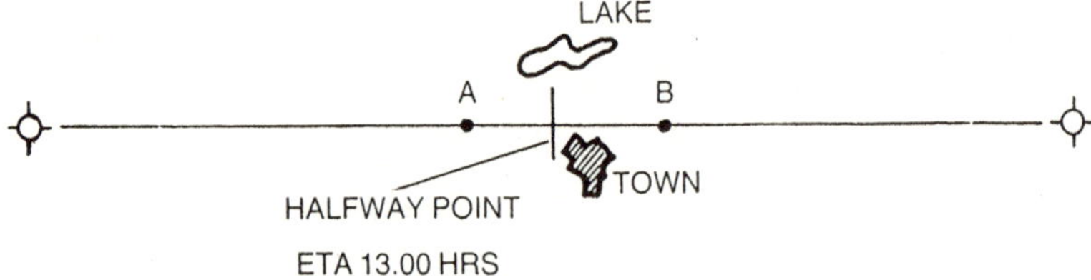

Fig. 169

If the time and position check agree, you are proceeding as planned. If, however, the checkpoints are still ahead of you at 13.00 hours as at point A, your ground speed is slower than expected, so your ETA for the destination will have to be amended. Similarly, if you pass the checkpoints before 13.00 hrs your ground speed is faster and you will reach the destination sooner.

Checkpoints anywhere along and around the track can be used also to check if your drift corrections are correct. If you find yourself too close or too far away from a checkpoint, as shown in Figure 170, you have drifted away from track and corrections will have to be made to regain it.

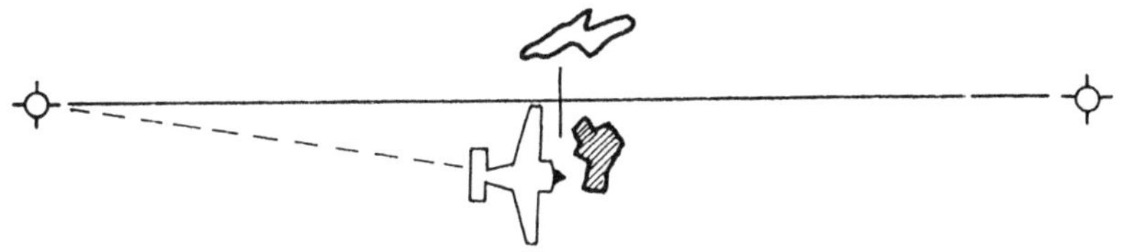

Fig. 170

To help assess how much drift is being experienced drift lines can be drawn on the chart during flight planning. These are drawn at 10° either side of track, as in Figure 171. Five degree lines may also be added.

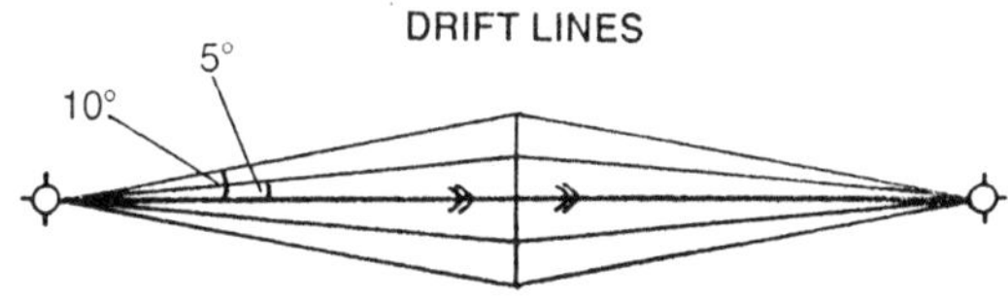

Fig. 171

These can be used to make calculations to regain the track in flight (covered later).

Make a note of suitable checkpoints near your destination and alternate airfields which may help you in their location from the air.

FUEL CALCULATIONS

These are very important calculations for a navigation flight. Using the fuel consumption figures in the Flight Manual you must work out how much fuel is required for the time estimated to reach the destination and add allowances for the fuel required during start-up, taxi-ing, climbout to the cruising altitude and the circuit and landing at the destination. In training aircraft these allowances should amount to a total of at least four gallons. In addition to this you must make another allowance for diversions or delays due to becoming lost or increased headwinds. This should amount to a minimum of one hour's fuel at the cruise consumption rate. If your aircraft happens to carry more fuel than you require (including all the allowances) note the exact figure and work out your total time available in the air (endurance) at the cruising speed. An example of typical fuel calculations are given below:

Consumption:	7 gph
Route time:	90 mins (fuel required 10.5 galls)
Start-up, taxi etc:	4 galls
Diversion:	1 hour (7 galls)
Total fuel required:	21.5 galls
Total carried:	28 galls
Endurance at 7 gph:	4 hours

These calculations can be made on your computer. Note that fuel consumption figures in the Flight Manual are based on proper leaning procedures. If you do not lean the mixture in flight your fuel consumption will increase up to 20 per cent.

PUBLICATIONS TO BE CONSULTED

For up-to-date information on airfields, airspace and procedures the *Air Pilot* must be consulted. You will be able to obtain details of the operating hours, length of runways, radio frequencies etc. for your departure, destination and alternate airfields.

Notams (Notices to Airmen) must also be consulted before a navigation flight. These will contain important information on temporary or permanent changes in the services affecting an aircraft, such as runway serviceability, changes in radio frequencies etc. They will also inform you of air displays, military training exercises, Royal Flights and other activities of a similar nature.

Finally, the Flight Manual must be used for weight and balance, performance and other operating information on your aircraft.

COMPILING A NAVIGATION FLIGHT LOG

A navigation flight log basically presents all the information relevant to the planned flight in an organized manner so that it can be quickly and easily referred to in the air. You compile the log as you go along, filling in wind velocities, true tracks, distances etc. as you obtain them. Some columns are filled in on entering the cockpit, and others in the air. Figure 172 illustrates a typical VFR flight log.

VFR FLIGHT LOG

PILOT ____________ DATE ________ CALL SIGN __________ PASS ______

FROM / TO	MSA	CRUISING ALTITUDE	TR° T	HDG° T	HDG M	HDG C	GS	DIST	TIME	ETA	ATA	REVISED HDG C	REVISED ETA	OBSERVATIONS
/														
/														
/														
/														
/														
/														
/														

DEPARTURE			
VDF		RWY	
ZONE		QFE	
APP		QNH	
TWR		W/V	
START		TAKE -OFF	

DESTINATION			
VDF		RWY	
ZONE		QFE	
APP		QNH	
TWR		W/V	
LAND		STOP	

ALTERNATE			
VDF		RWY	
ZONE		QFE	
APP		QNH	
TWR		W/V	
LAND		STOP	

FUEL		
GPH		
TOTAL REQUIRED		
TOTAL CARRIED		
ENDURANCE		

WINDS AND AIR TEMP	
IAS	
TAS	

RADIO FREQUENCIES	

Fig. 172

The following summarizes the procedure for planning a cross-country flight:

1. Obtain the latest weather information and forecasts and ensure that the weather is within your limitations.

2. Draw track lines to your destination ensuring that any intervening airspace or high ground do not pose a threat to safety or legality.
3. Study the route and determine MSAs and ensure that these can be maintained without entering cloud (refer to weather information).
4. Select cruising altitudes.
5. Select alternate airfields and study the area around them.
6. Measure true tracks and distances, dividing each route into half or quarter segments.
7. Note suitable features along and either side of your tracks to use as checkpoints.
8. Calculate TAS, true headings, ground speeds and magnetic headings.
9. Calculate the estimated times for each segment of the route and to reach the destination.
10. Calculate the fuel required, including the reserves.
11. Consult the *Air Pilot* and *Notams*.
12. Note down all relevant radio frequencies and other pertinent information.
13. Carry out weight and balance calculations.
14. Consider any other aspects relevant to the particular flight, such as take-off and landing performance, filing of flight plans, the need for life-jackets, dinghies, survival equipment etc.
15. Carry out normal pre-flight checks.

FLYING ACCORDING TO THE PLAN

Before Take-off

In the cockpit enter the compass headings in the navigation log referring to the deviation card. Also write down the altimeter settings given by ATC and the surface wind velocity. Fold the map neatly and in a way that will allow you to read the ground features around your track. Keep the cockpit neat and tidy and make sure you do not leave any items with metallic components near the compass.

Setting Heading

After take-off make a note of the time the aircraft became airborne. During training the usual procedure is to climb above the airfield to the selected cruising altitude before setting heading.

At large and busy airfields this may not be possible and you will normally have to climb out on to the required heading soon after take-off, or proceed according to instructions. Once established on the heading, immediately note the time and then enter the estimated arrival times in the appropriate columns.

The Gross Error Check

After setting heading and ensuring that the aircraft is flying level and trimmed properly, you must check that you have set course correctly. First of all synchronize the DI and magnetic compass. Then check that the heading you are steering agrees with the heading you planned. Headings can easily be misread. For example, you may easily find that you are steering 300° instead of 030°. Next, using the map, establish your position in relation to the airfield and the track line. It may be that you are on the right heading, but are flying parallel to the desired track for one reason or another, as Figure 173 shows.

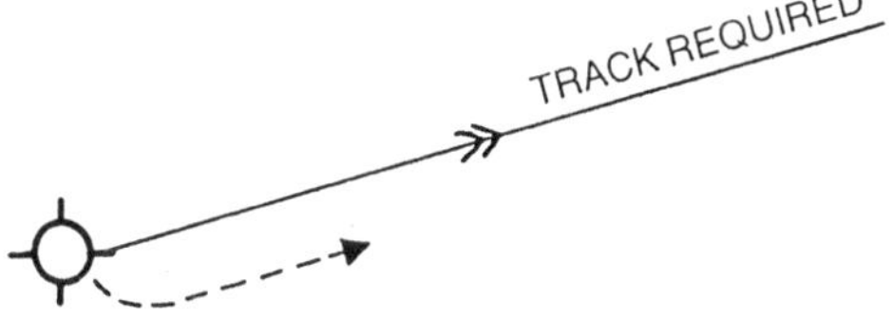

Fig. 173

If this is the case, you will have to intercept the track, as shown in Figure 174.

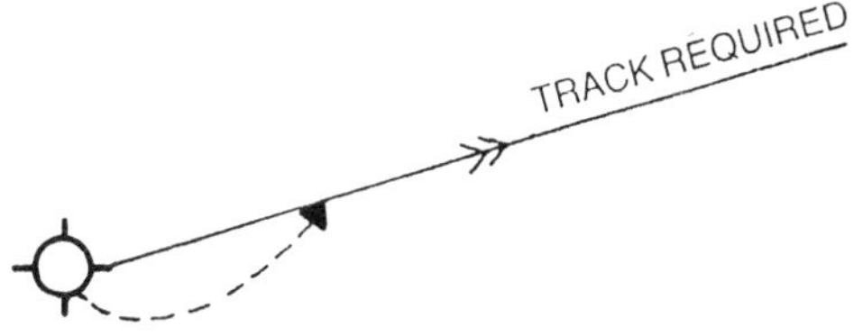

Fig. 174

If you don't carry out these checks you may soon start to wonder why the ground features do not agree with what you expect and why your checkpoints are not appearing. It is important that the Gross Error Checks are done as early as possible, as this is the first step in ensuring that you don't get lost or at least spoil the flight plan.

En Route Progress

During the en route phase you will be concentrating mainly on straight and level flight and map reading. The normal cruise checks should be carried out regularly, the main emphasis being on fuel management, including leaning procedures and compass synchronizations. If military zones, special rules areas, or other similar types of airspace have to be crossed make sure you establish radio contact with the ATSU before doing so.

While flying and map reading, look ahead of the aircraft and not directly below. Try and locate landmarks far ahead instead of waiting to come across them. This way you will be able to track towards your checkpoints and keep one step ahead of the situation at all times. Hold the map in a manner that will allow you to orientate yourself properly, i.e. with the track line aligned with the flight direction ('flying up the map'). This way features on the ground to the right and left of your flight path will appear to the right and left of your track line on the map. If you are flying long distances, or cross from one altimeter setting region into another, obtain a revised QNH.

Revisions to Estimated Times

As the ETA for your half- or quarter-way marks approaches start positively establishing your position using ground features. Usually more than one feature will be necessary to fix your position accurately, unless the landmark is unmistakable. Once you have established your position note the time. If you arrive earlier or later than the estimated time you will have to revise the ETA for the next checkpoint, or the destination. For example, if you arrive at the halfway mark 3 mins later than estimated you can expect to arrive at the destination 6 mins later than estimated. This method of revising times is accurate enough for pilot navigation. Be sure of entering revised times in the flight log.

Revisions to Headings

The forecast winds during a flight may change and this will require you to make adjustments to your headings. After the setting heading procedure you must steer the planned headings as accurately as possible and map read. After a few miles, if you find that the aircraft has drifted away from the required track (track error) you will have to regain the track and then steer another heading which will maintain it. Alternately, a heading can be worked out to reach the destination directly, as Figure 175 illustrates.

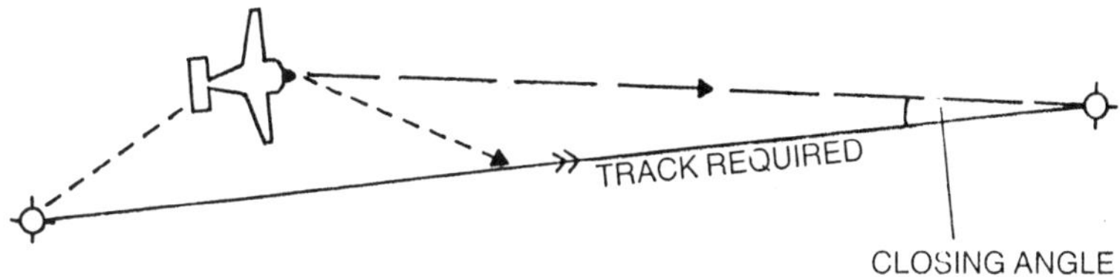

Fig. 175

But before doing anything you must synchronize the magnetic compass and DI as this could be the cause of the drift rather than changes in the wind. If you have drawn the drift lines described earlier you will have a useful means of establishing your track error. For example, in Figure 176 the aircraft is found to be about 5° off track.

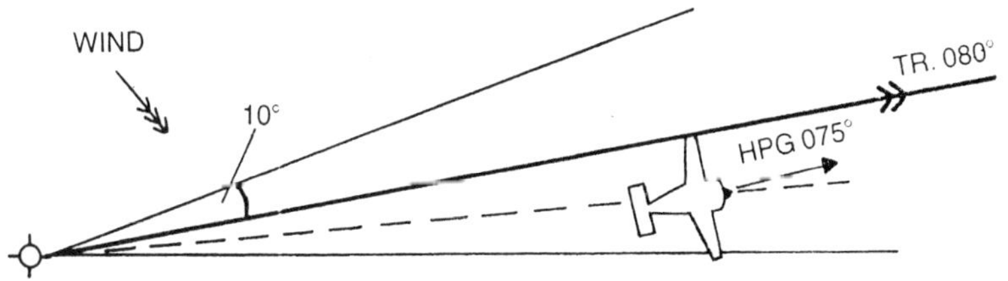

Fig. 176

To return to the original track the track error must be doubled and the heading altered accordingly towards the original track. In this example the track error of 5° must be doubled to 10° and the heading altered to 065°. This heading must be steered for the same length of time as the original heading was flown before the correction was made. For example, if 075° was steered for 10 mins you will have to steer 065° also for 10 mins. When using this method make sure you make a note of the relevant times before making any corrections. When the original track is intercepted (you will have to verify this using outside references as well as time checks), estimate a heading that will maintain the original track. Trial and error will be necessary in this case, but the new heading is likely to be only a few degrees either side of your calculated heading unless wind changes are large, or your pre-flight calculations have proved to be inaccurate.

Provided this method is used early on during a flight (before the halfway mark) the aircraft will intercept the track before the destination. If the correction is left until after the halfway point the aircraft will fly past the destination, as Figure 177 illustrates.

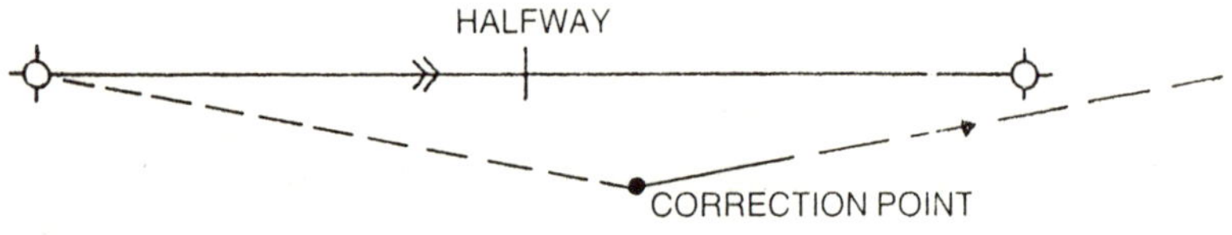

Fig. 177

The 1 in 60 rule

A more accurate method of determining track error will be to establish first how many miles the aircraft has drifted from track and the total distance flown, then applying the following formula:

$$\frac{60}{\text{Distance flown}} \times \text{Distance away from track} = \text{Track error}$$

For example, if the distance flown was 20 miles and the distance off track was 4 miles, the track error would be:

$$\frac{60}{20} \times 4 = 12°$$

This formulae is based on the fact that if an aircraft is one degree off track after a distance of 60 miles, it will be one mile to one side of the track.

After establishing the track error a heading can be worked out to reach the destination directly instead of regaining the original track. This is done by using a similar formula:

$$\frac{60}{\text{Distance remaining}} \times \text{Distance away from track} = \text{Closing angle}$$

This closing angle figure must be added to the track error and the heading alteration made towards the original track. So, if the track error is 12°, the distance off track 4 miles and the distance remaining to the destination is 30 miles, the heading alteration would be:

$$\frac{60}{30} \times 4 = 8\ (+\ 12^\circ \text{ track error} = 20^\circ \text{ heading alteration})$$

These alterations do not take into consideration the changing wind angle as heading is altered, so a further alteration of heading into wind may be necessary.

To summarize, therefore, if the aircraft has drifted off track either double the track error to regain the original track, or add the track error to the closing angle in order to arrive at a heading to steer directly to the destination. Make a note of all heading revisions in the flight log.

Procedure at Turning Points

If your route involves dog legs, carry out the cruise checks before you reach the turning point. As you arrive over the turning point note the time, turn on to the new heading and enter the ETA for the next checkpoint. After establishing the aircraft on the new course perform the gross error checks.

UNCERTAINTY OF POSITION

If at any time you become unsure of your position carry out the following actions:

1. Maintain heading.
2. Synchronize the MC and DI.
3. Check that the heading flown agrees with the log.
4. Check the heading against the track on the map.
5. Check previous checkpoints and log entries.

Whenever you navigate using pilot navigation techniques there will be times when you will become temporarily unable to fix your position accurately. This is nothing to worry about unduly as it is usually due to the lack of good ground features. Remember, position is established by time checks as well as the identification of landmarks. So, provided the heading flown agrees with the flight log and map and previous checkpoints have been identified satisfactorily, maintain heading until the next time checkpoint and continue to map read. Trust your calculations. Provided you are certain a gross error has not been made you will reach the next checkpoint, but do not overconcentrate on map reading as this may disorientate you more. Look for easily identifiable features. Do not get too worried if a checkpoint does not appear right on time, but if one is long overdue and you are unable to fix your position afterwards, you are lost. Procedures to follow in this situation are covered later.

ARRIVAL AT THE DESTINATION

About 10 mins before you arrive at your destination airfield establish radio contact with the control service (if any) to obtain landing instructions and other relevant airfield information (runway in use, QFE etc.). Aim to enter the airfield traffic zone at the circuit height, so begin the descent from your cruising altitude while still a few miles away from the airfield if possible.

The usual airfield approach checks must be carried out. Join the circuit as instructed. If the airfield has no control or advisory service you will have to carry out the standard circuit joining procedure. As you get close to your destination remember to increase your lookouts. After landing park the aircraft in a suitable area and then proceed to the reception office to book in. This procedure will be covered by your instructor. Landing fees may have to be paid and you may have to consider refuelling the aircraft and obtaining revised weather information if another flight is to be made.

DIVERSIONS

It has already been explained that for various reasons, particularly deteriorating weather, a precautionary landing at an alternate airfield may become necessary. Such diversions need not pose any great problems if you have considered the possibility during pre-flight preparations and have a basic procedure to follow in flight.

Pre-Flight Preparations

During pre-flight planning you must obtain all the necessary information on your chosen alternate airfield(s) in the same way as for the planned destination. Most flight log sheets have a section where you can fill in radio frequencies and other information for an alternate airfield. In flight any remaining navigation columns on the log sheet can be used to enter details of the diversion. If this information cannot be entered clearly on the main flight log, you can construct a mini flight log for the alternate on the reverse side of the log sheet. Figure 178 illustrates a simple layout and the type of information needed. Make sure there is sufficient room for any miscellaneous items that you may need to write down in flight.

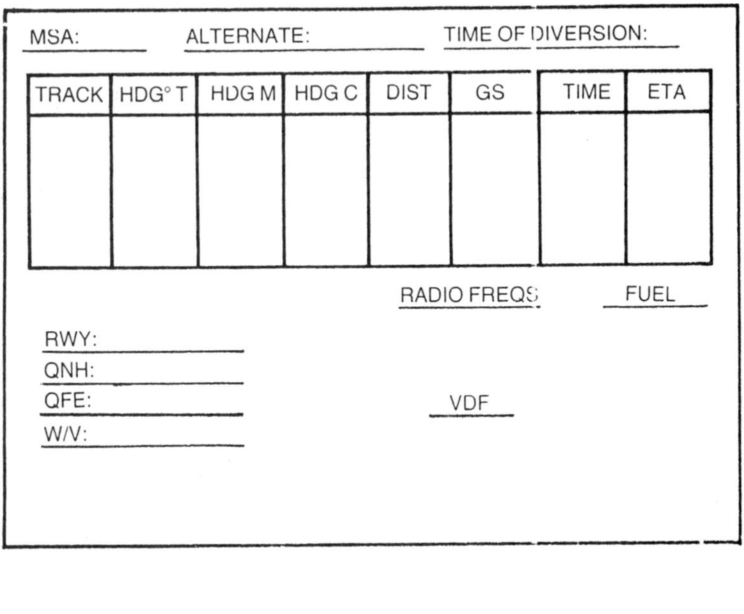

MSA: ALTERNATE: TIME OF DIVERSION:

TRACK	HDG° T	HDG M	HDG C	DIST	GS	TIME	ETA

RADIO FREQS FUEL

RWY:
QNH:
QFE: VDF
W/V:

Fig. 178

In-Flight Procedure

Once the decision to divert has been made carry out the following actions:

1. Operate the aircraft according to conditions, i.e. if weather is

deteriorating descend if necessary and perform cockpit checks (see 'Operation at Minimum Level' (p. 271)) and inform ATC of your intentions.

2. Establish your position on the map.
3. Draw a line from this position to the alternate airfield. Mark in the halfway point.
4. Estimate the direction and note this down on the log.
5. Estimate and note down the distance.
6. Determine the wind angle.
7. Work out a true heading and ground speed. Calculate an approximate estimated time of arrival and note all this down in the log.
8. Add variation and deviation and note down the compass heading.
9. Steer this heading and note the time of the diversion.
10. Make a gross error check soon after changing heading.
11. Map read to the alternate.
12. If the alternate airfield has a VDF facility be sure to use it if you can as this will make things much easier, especially in poor weather.

There is no doubt that the workload will increase during a diversion. You will have to fly the aeroplane as well as replan, but if you are proficient in the basic navigation plotting skills, you will arrive at reasonably accurate headings to steer within a short time. The actions given above should give you an idea of the things that must be considered during a diversion, but how you actually deal with such a situation will depend on your circumstances. It may be that you are able to maintain the original track for a time while planning for a diversion, aiming to alter heading at a specific point ahead. Or, circumstances may force you to estimate and steer a heading in a short space of time, leaving further calculations until later. Whatever the situation, it is far better to have a plan of action rather than to be aimlessly changing heading. Mental adjustment to a new situation is made easier with a plan to follow.

BECOMING LOST

The two most probable causes of becoming lost are misreading the headings in the flight log and incorrect synchronization of the magnetic compass and DI. Other reasons are diversions from track and deteriorating weather. Any of these combined with poor map reading and progress monitoring will result in you becoming more and more unsure of position and eventually lost.

All flight procedures are designed with safety in mind. As long as you play your part correctly nothing should go wrong with a flight. As far as navigation is concerned, this means thorough pre-flight planning and in the air you must conduct the flight in an organized and systematic manner, never neglecting gross error checks and other important navigation procedures. Provided you proceed sensibly there is no reason why you should become lost.

However, diversions from track combined with deteriorating weather and wind changes will increase the chances of becoming lost, so pilots must have a basic procedure to follow in such situations. So, to follow on from the uncertainty of position procedure given earlier, if you are unable to fix your position after about 20 mins carry out the following actions:

1. Write down the time in the flight log.
2. Check the fuel state and determine the amount of daylight hours remaining. Any or both of these may force you to make an off-airfield landing at some stage.
3. Work out how much time you have in the air and adopt a slow cruising speed with flaps lowered if necessary.
4. Maintain a constant height and heading, or orbit a ground feature while trying to establish position.
5. Double check calculations.
6. Inform ATC.

The keeping of a good flight log will prove to be very useful in establishing the approximate position of the aircraft. From the last known checkpoint you can estimate your position using the time elapsed since that checkpoint and the heading flown. For example, in Figure 179 the last known checkpoint was A.

Using time and ground speed information an approximate dead reckoning position can be established a given distance from point A in the direction flown. By drawing a circle with a radius of 10 per cent of the distance flown you will have established the area the aircraft is likely to be in. All that remains afterwards will be to look for features within this circle, reading from ground to map. Remember, look for easily identifiable features, i.e. those likely to be presented on your maps.

If you are still unable to fix your position, choose a line feature

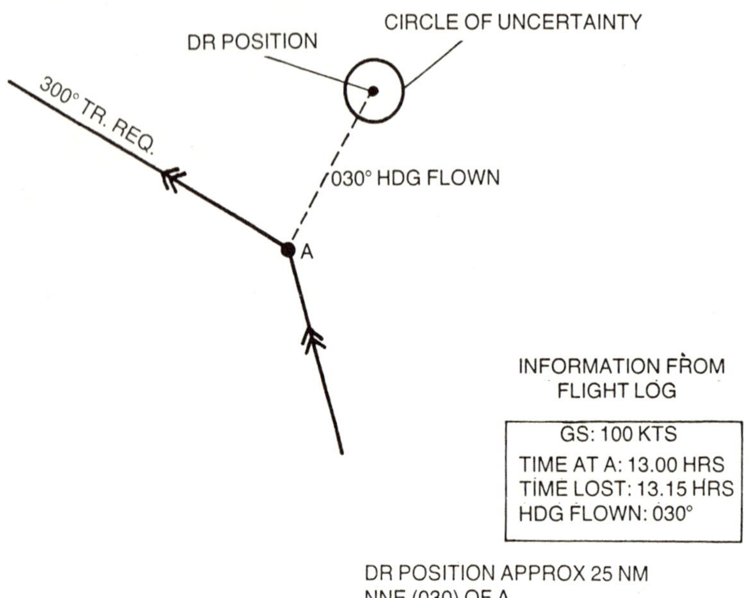

Fig. 179

such as a road, railway, or river and follow it. Line features always end up at a town or junction from where you will find it easier to establish your exact position. It is very important not to wander about aimlessly, changing heading all the time. Choose a ground feature for orientation and orbit around it if necessary while you sort out the situation and plan a course of action. You must be decisive in these types of situations. Try to determine first why you have become lost. This way you will have a better idea of where you might be. Now, you can really only be to the right or left of the track and a given distance away from it. If you maintain a constant heading or remain within a certain area, it will be easier to locate your position. Wandering about will only disorientate you even more.

Once you have positively identified your position you can work out a heading to return to the original track or to proceed to another airfield depending on the situation.

Any time you get lost do not hestitate to use the radio to obtain assistance, especially if fuel or daylight remaining is a problem, or there is a danger of straying into controlled airspace. If you are not already in contact with someone use the emergency frequency 121.5 mhz (see the 'COM' section of the *Air Pilot*). Air Traffic Control is equipped to deal with such situations and you will be given all the help possible to get you out of trouble.

Continually check the fuel state and daylight remaining. If you are unable to fix position, or obtain assistance from ATC, seriously consider a precautionary landing.

Summary of Actions to Avoid Becoming Lost

Meticulous pre-flight planning:

1. accurate measurements of tracks and bearings
2. accurate calculations of headings, times, speeds and fuel required
3. detailed study of routes (checkpoints, MSAs)
4. neat, clear and logical compilation of flight log
5. thorough check of weather forecasts.

In-flight procedures:

1. fly according to plan and monitor progress
2. keep one step ahead of the situation
3. note times accurately
4. note all heading, speed and time revisions
5. carry out gross error checks after take-off and at turning points
6. make frequent cruise checks, particularly compass and DI agreement
7. positively identify all checkpoints (by time and ground features).

LANDING ON UNFAMILIAR RUNWAYS

It is quite likely that most, if not all, the landings you have made so far have been only at the runway(s) at your training airfield. This means that your judgement of the approach path and of the flareout height will be based largely on the length and width of these runways. In other words, you have been conditioned to land on specific runways. This does not mean you will not be able to land on any other runway. It simply means that if a runway at an unfamilar airfield is of significantly different dimensions to the runway you are most accustomed to, the result of this conditioning will give misleading clues as to the height of the aircraft above the ground. For example, if you are used to landing on a short runway, when on the final approach to a longer runway you may get the impression that you are closer and lower than you really are. On the other hand, if you are more used to a longer runway when on the approach to a short runway you may given the impression that you are higher and further away than you really are. This latter illusion is potentially more hazardous as you may be tempted to adopt a dangerously low approach.

During the flareout phase you unconsciously use peripheral vision to assess height off the ground. You know when to commence the flareout because the perspective of the runway and surroundings appears correct. This is something you have learnt after practice and experience of landing regularly at a particular runway. When descending towards an unusually wide runway you may end up flaring out too early because the correct runway perspective, in terms of the runway you are most used to, will appear while the aircraft is still high off the ground. On the other hand, while descending towards a very narrow runway you may end up delaying the flareout. Both situations will result in a hard landing.

Different types of obstructions and surrounding terrain will also affect the landing at an unfamiliar airfield. All this means that you will have to be more alert and assess your height and progress according to conditions as they are, rather than what you expect them to be.

AIRMANSHIP

Lookouts, as usual, are of prime importance. Be more alert when passing by zones and airfields.

Do not enter any zone without getting in touch with the ATSU beforehand. It is usual procedure to write down all the frequencies of any zones, airfields, or other service that may affect your route.

AIR LESSON

This part of your course will consist of a number of dual and solo cross-country flights. The first few flights will usually return directly to the base airfield. Later navigation flights will involve landings at unfamiliar airfields.

THE NAVIGATION FLIGHT TEST

The following information is taken from the CAA publication CAP53.

1. The Navigation Flight Test (NFT) is intended to determine the applicant's ability to navigate safely by visual methods. It is a Pass/Fail Test and must, therefore, be completed in one flight and partial passes are not allowed.

2 Test Content
2.1 The test will consist of assessments of:

(a) Flight planning and self-briefing including assessment of weather suitability) for a triangular route of approximately 1.5 hours airborne duration.
(b) In flight recording of the progress of the flight.
(c) ATC liaison and compliance. Observance of Air Traffic Control Regulations and Rules of the Air.
(d) DR navigation (correction of track error, revision of ETAs, heading setting technique including synchronizing the Directional Gyro with the Magnetic Compass in flight).
(e) Map reading.
(f) Maintenance of heading/height/airspeed at normal cruising levels and at lower levels (but not below 500ft agl and without contravening Rule 5 of the Rules of the Air and Air Traffic Control Regulations) in conditions of simulated lowering cloud base.
(g) Re-establishment of position by visual methods following disruption of the original flight plan.
(h) Diversion following simulated adverse weather conditions en route.

2.2 Candidates will not be allowed to use either VHF radio or the radio navigation equipment fitted in the test aircraft to obtain position lines or ranges during the first two legs. However, should they wish to make use of radio navigation aids to assist in carrying out the diversion they may do so, and correct use of the radio navigation equipment and information will then be assessed.

2.3 A pictorial summary of the flight test is shown on the diagram at the end of this section. The first leg will include setting heading and DR navigation to a destination about 30 minutes away. On the second leg, lowering cloud conditions will be simulated requiring the candidate to demonstrate an ability to navigate at a lower level for not more than 10 minutes. Subsequently, having climbed back to normal cruising altitude, a situation will be engineered requiring the candidate to deviate sufficiently from the planned track to check ability to establish position and to regain track or steer to destination from a point off track. At some stage during the remainder of the second leg, the candidate will be told that the weather is deteriorating and to carry out a practise diversion. The test will end when the candidate has demonstrated ability to track towards the diversion aerodrome for not less than 10 minutes, has told the Examiner the location of the aircraft, and has given an acceptable ETA.

3 Navigation Flight Test for the PPL(A)

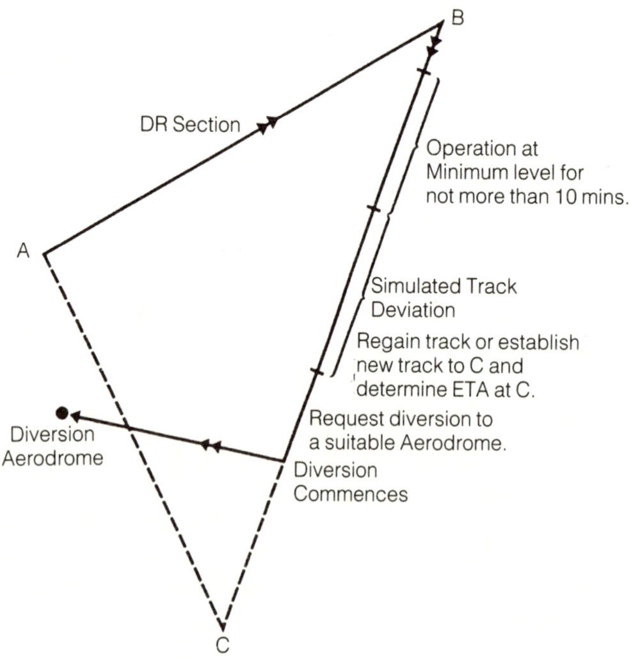

FLIGHT PLAN THE ROUTE A – B – C – A

CAA C(G)6 Carte DO Drg No 9065 4-8-86

Instructor's Guide
Ex. 18

LESSON PLAN

Pilot navigation

Objectives
To develop the student's ability to plan, plot and fly cross-country details; to develop the student's proficiency in navigating using pilot navigation and dead reckoning; and to develop the ability to cope with emergencies and new and unexpected flight situations.

Content
This period of training will involve a number of dual and solo flights. The main emphasis during these lessons should be as follows:

1. planning a flight (use of *Air Pilot, Notams* etc.)
2. obtaining and deciphering weather information
3. plotting the course, use of navigation computer
4. preparing the log
5. filing of flight plans
6. pilot navigation and dead reckoning techniques
7. departure, en route and arrival procedures and radio communications
8. updating the flight log
9. simulated diversions and lost procedures
10. unfamiliar airport procedures
11. emergencies, including VDF and radar procedures.

Completion Standards
Before being sent on solo cross-country flights the following standards must be attained:

1. The student must be able to plan, plot and fly the planned course without assistance.

2. Estimated times of arrival should be accurate to within an apparent error of not more than 10 minutes.
3. Off-course corrections must be accomplished accurately and promptly.
4. The student must be able to give an accurate position report at any time without hesitation.
5. The student must be able to initiate and follow appropriate lost and diversionary procedures during simulations.

Exercise 19

INSTRUMENT APPRECIATION

Objectives

1. To teach you the dangers of flight into conditions beyond your flying ability.
2. To teach you to maintain control of the aeroplane by reference to the flight instruments alone.

In previous lessons it has been emphasized that you must endeavour at all times to remain in visual flying conditions. Not only is it illegal to fly in adverse weather without the proper qualifications, it is also positively dangerous to do so without adequate training. The fact that once you have entered adverse weather you will not know where you are going is only part of the danger. The real danger is the likelihood of your losing control of the aeroplane completely due to the lack of outside visual references. To understand why this will occur you must understand how human beings achieve their sense of balance.

Sensory Balance

Humans are able to stand, walk, run, balance on one leg etc. because of three physical senses – vision, vestibular sense and muscular (kinesthetic) sense. In fact, even without vision, as in the case of a blind person, a sufficient degree of balance can be effectively obtained by the remaining senses. All three senses transmit information to the brain which then tells you if you are standing up, sitting down, walking, turning around etc.

Vision

Vision is the most important of the balance senses. You have learnt to fly using outside visual references and therefore you will be able to recognize instantly what the aircraft is doing by simply looking out of the cockpit.

Vestibular sense

This sense basically provides us with a sense of movement. The organ for sensing movement, called the vestibular apparatus, is located in the inner ear near the hearing centres of both ears. The vestibular apparatus has two components – the semi-circular canals and the otolith organ, as shown in Figure 180.

THE VESTIBULAR APPARATUS

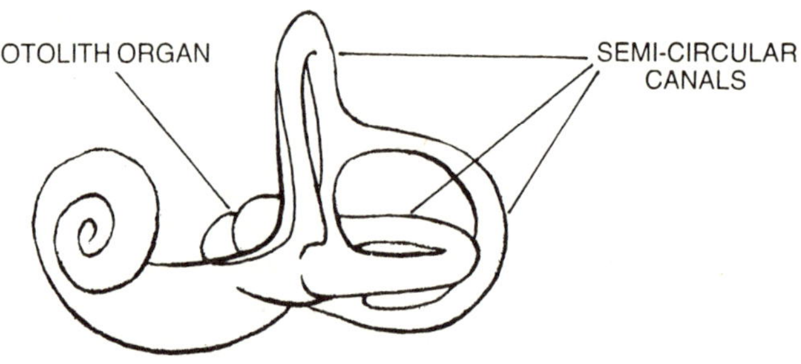

Fig. 180

The three semi-circular canals are each filled with a fluid. One of the canals is in the horizontal plane while the other two lie in the vertical plane. At the base of each canal are numerous tiny hairlike nerve endings. Whenever your head is moved the fluid in the canals resists movement due to inertia, thus applying pressure to the nerve endings. This stimulation of the nerve endings is sensed as movement. Together, all three canals can sense forward and backward movements and turning motions.

The otolith organ is located close to the semi-circular canals. Basically, it consists of tiny nerve endings which protrude into a gelatinous layer containing tiny deposits of calcium carbonate called otoliths. These otoliths respond to gravity or 'g' forces. When the head is moved, the otoliths react to the forces acting on the head and cause the nerve endings to produce a nervous impulse which is sensed as linear acceleration. In other words, the otolith organ senses speeding up, slowing down and sideways motions.

Muscular senses

The pressures, tensions and contractions of the muscles in your body are all transmitted to your brain and tell you what configuration you are in (lying down, standing, moving, raising an arm, etc.). This positioning, or postural sense, is often called the 'seat of the pants' sense.

So, all three senses combine to tell you what the position of your body is and what it is doing. If you stand up and begin to lean forward continuously you will eventually reach a point of unbalance and fall over. This will be sensed by your eyes because you will see that things are not normal. Your vestibular apparatus will also sense this and so will your muscles as you feel them become tense. Your instinctive reactions will be to straighten up, or place one foot forward for support.

This is basically how sensory balance works. Now, humans are land-based creatures and hence our vestibular and muscular senses have evolved to interpret and deal effectively only with forces we are likely to be exposed to during normal activities on the ground. Thus a blind person is able to walk around quite normally. But when we take to the air the forces and accelerations experienced are far greater and more varied than those on the ground and this is where the problem arises. In normal visual flying conditions your vestibular and muscular senses react to these forces and give you misleading information as to what is happening, but your vision overrides this. In fact, you rely on your eyes so completely to find out what the aircraft is doing that it is likely that you do not even acknowledge what your other senses are telling you.

When you enter cloud, however, all outside references disappear and you will suddenly become acutely aware of your other senses. This is instinctive – when one sense becomes unreliable the remaining ones take over, as in the case of blind people. In other words, you will try to fly the aeroplane according to what you feel it is doing. Your senses will be responding to the forces produced as the controls are operated and also to those created by any turbulence. Conflicting information will be fed to the brain and soon you will not know what is happening and the aircraft will be out of control. The general terms for describing the effects of sensory confusion are vertigo or spatial disorientation.

During the air lesson you will be asked to close your eyes and lower your head while the instructor manoeuvres the aircraft. Then you will be asked what you think the aeroplane is doing.

When you open your eyes again you will be quite surprised to see what it is actually doing.

The semi-circular canals are unable to detect turning motions less than rate one (5° per second). This means that a pilot untrained to fly on instruments can easily enter an unintentional turn. Such a turn will develop into a shallow spiral dive. The pilot will become aware of increasing altitude and increasing engine speed, but relying on vestibular and muscular sense only he is likely to think that the aircraft is in a wings level dive and start applying back pressure to try and arrest the descent. This will only tighten up the turn and an accelerated stall may result. It can be seen, therefore, that on entering cloud, or when flying in severely reduced visiblity, it would be extremely unwise to rely on the vestibular and muscular senses to maintain control of the aeroplane. It is interesting to note that even birds do not fly in cloud.

INSTRUMENT FLYING

It is, of course, possible to fly an aeroplane without outside visual references. The pilot will have to transfer his vision to those instruments in the cockpit that can provide attitude (pitch, roll and yaw) and performance information. But this is not quite so simple. The pilot will have to learn to ignore the other balance senses and learn to interpret the instruments correctly and maintain control of the aeroplane according to their indications. In normal visual flying conditions not only are you able to focus your eyes near and far, you also use your peripheral vision, although unconsciously. When flying on instruments you have to focus your eyes on dials not much more than a foot or so from your face and this is hard work and very tiring as you will discover. On the PPL course a few hours will be spent teaching you to maintain control of the aeroplane on instruments and also the basic manoeuvres. It must be emphasized that this training does *not* entitle you to enter cloud or fly in severely reduced visibility. To be able to fly competently on instruments requires many hours of training (including instrument navigation procedures) and frequent practice. Even an instrument-trained pilot can suffer from the effects of vertigo. The purpose of introducing you to instrument flying is firstly to make you appreciate the dangers of continued flight into weather conditions beyond your flying ability and, secondly, as a safeguard so that if you do have to enter cloud you will be able to maintain sufficient control of the aeroplane and return to visual conditions.

The Flight Panel

Most modern light training aircraft are equipped with a standard flight instrument layout, known as the T Panel, which you are probably quite familiar with by now.

'T' FLIGHT PANEL

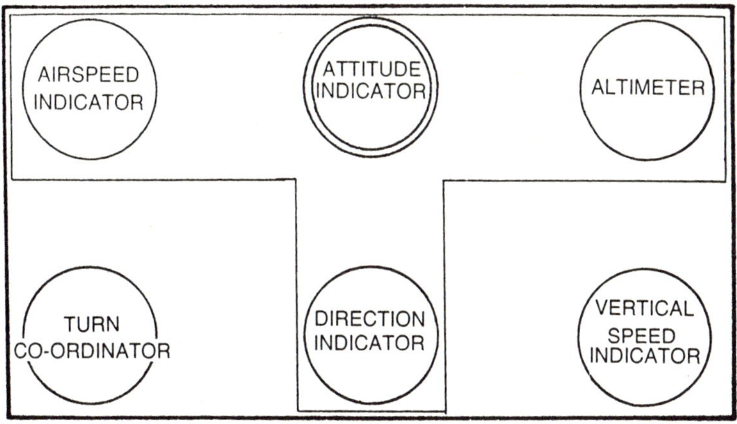

Fig. 181

This arrangement permits an organized technique of instrument scanning when flying on instruments.

Controlling the Aircraft's Attitude

In visual flying conditions you controlled the attitude of the aeroplane using the natural horizon. When flying on instruments you must use the miniature aircraft and the artificial horizon on the attitude indicator as the reference for controlling pitch and bank.

The attitude indicator is a gyroscopic instrument and is the only instrument that will give you accurate and instantaneous indications of the aircraft's attitude in relation to the natural horizon. Provided the instrument is serviceable you can rely on it completely in flight when controlling pitch and bank.

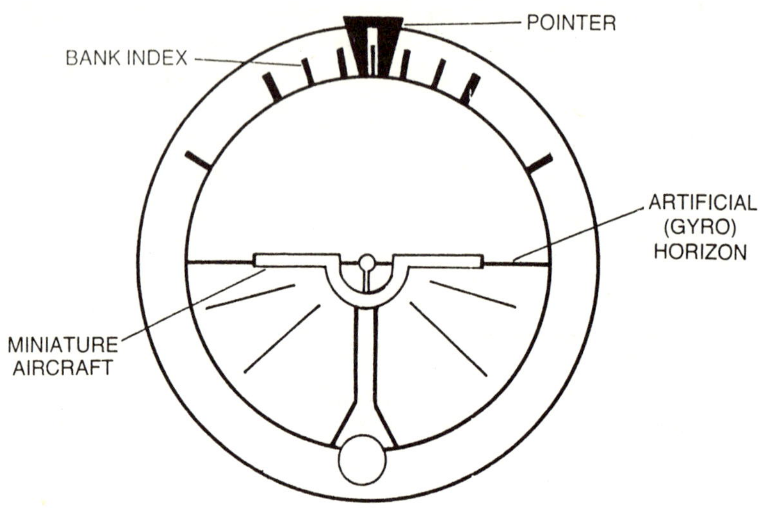

Fig. 182

Pitch and bank control

When adjusting the aircraft's pitch attitude pressure is applied to the control column in the normal way and the miniature aircraft is raised or lowered in precise amounts, known as bar widths. A bar width is simply the width of the wings of the miniature aircraft. For example, the attitude would be raised one bar up, or half a bar down and so on as required. Adjustments to the bank angle are made by reference to the pointer and bank indexes of the instrument. In the air lesson you will be practising changing the aircraft's attitude using the attitude indicator and you will be able to compare the attitude of the aircraft in relation to the natural horizon to that of the miniature aircraft and the artificial horizon.

Scan Technique

When flying on instruments the attitude indicator is considered the Master Instrument and therefore it must be given the maximum attention at all times. You fly the aeroplane (controlling pitch and bank) looking at the attitude indicator in the same way as you would look out of the cockpit at the natural horizon. For performance information glance quickly at the required instrument and return your attention to the attitude indicator immediately afterwards. In other words, your scan must radiate to and from the attitude indicator.

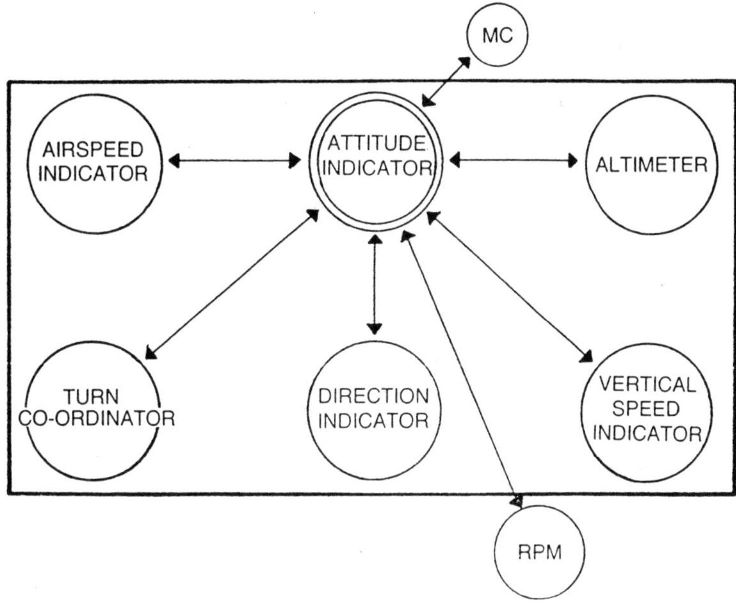

Fig. 183

Of course, you do not have to scan all the instruments all of the time. You must select those instruments most relevant to the particular manoeuvre being performed. For example, in straight and level flight you will be concerned mainly with maintaining height and heading, so you will be radiating your scan from the attitude indicator to the DI and altimeter more frequently than to the other instruments. While flying on instruments other aspects of aircraft management (such as cockpit checks) must not be neglected.

Basic Manoeuvres

Essentially, the only difference between flying on instruments and flying in visual conditions is that visual references are transferred from outside the cockpit to those inside the cockpit. The techniques for operating the controls and the pressures used are still the same and the formula Power + Attitude = Performance still applies. You already know how to control the aeroplane and perform various manoeuvres. Pitch and power control is very important. You will learn the correct pitch attitudes (in bar widths) for straight and level, climbing, descending and other modes of flight during the air lesson. You should already know the power settings required for different speeds, rates of descent and so on. The next few pages contain instrument scan diagrams for basic manoeuvres. It is not necessary to memorize the different scans. For any manoeuvre it is really a question of knowing what the objectives of the manoeuvre are. For example, during a straight climb the objective is mainly to maintain airspeed, balance and direction.

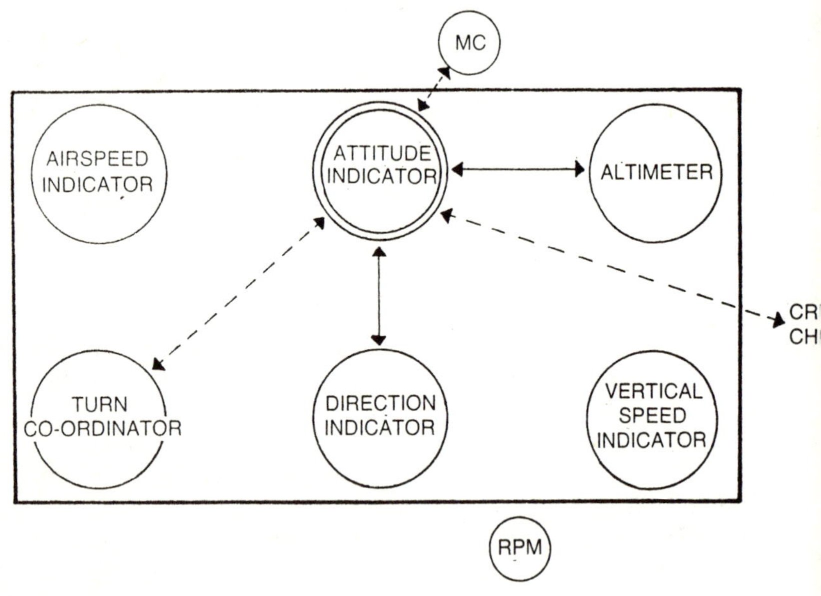

Fig. 184

Straight and Level

Objectives

To maintain height, heading and balance.

To attain straight and level:

1. Select cruise power.
2. Select the straight and level attitude.
3. Trim.

To maintain straight and level:

1. Keep the wings level and the ball central.
2. Ensure that the correct RPM is set and that the pitch attitude is held constant.

Accurate trimming is very important in all instrument flying manoeuvres.

Climbing

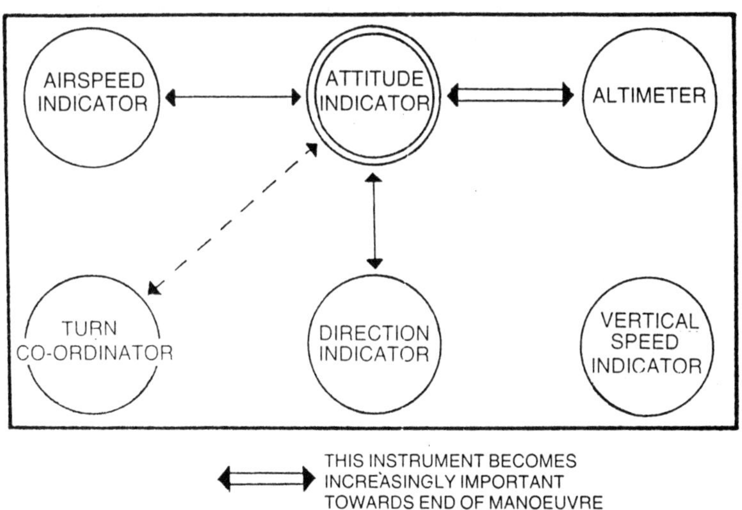

Fig. 185

Objectives during a climb: to maintain airspeed, heading and balance.

Enter and maintain a climb in the normal way (Power, Attitude, Trim) and when levelling off (Attitude, Power, Trim) gradually transfer the climbing scan to the straight and level scan.

DESCENDING

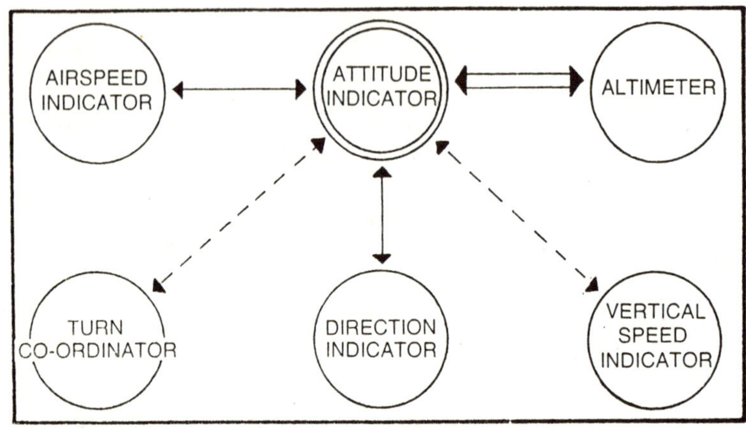

Fig. 186

Descending

Objectives during a descent: to maintain a constant airspeed, heading, balance and rate of descent.

Enter and maintain a descent in the normal way, but in IMC conditions powered descents only must be used. As the desired altitude is reached, gradually return to the straight and level scan. Aim not to descend below the reference altitude during all descents. Use a lead factor of 100 ft.

Level Turns

Objectives during a turn: to maintain height, balance and rate of turn.

Enter and maintain a level turn in the normal way, but limit all turns to rate one only during instrument flying. When rolling out use a 10° lead factor and gradually transfer to the straight and level scan.

Climbing Turns

Objectives during manoeuvre: to maintain a constant airspeed, balance and rate of turn.

LEVEL TURNS

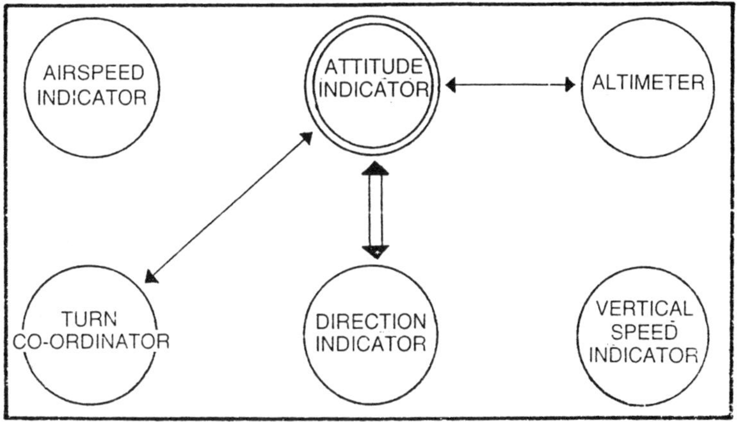

Fig. 187

Enter as normal but limit bank angles to a maximum of 15-20°. Return to the straight and level scan as the desired heading and altitude are reached.

CLIMBING TURNS

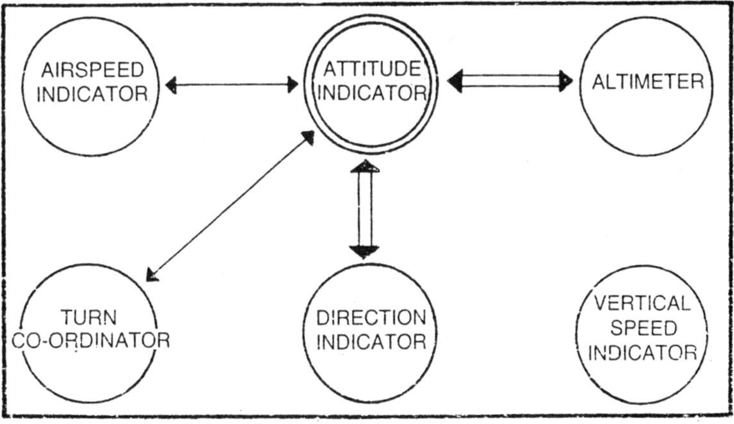

DESCENDING TURNS

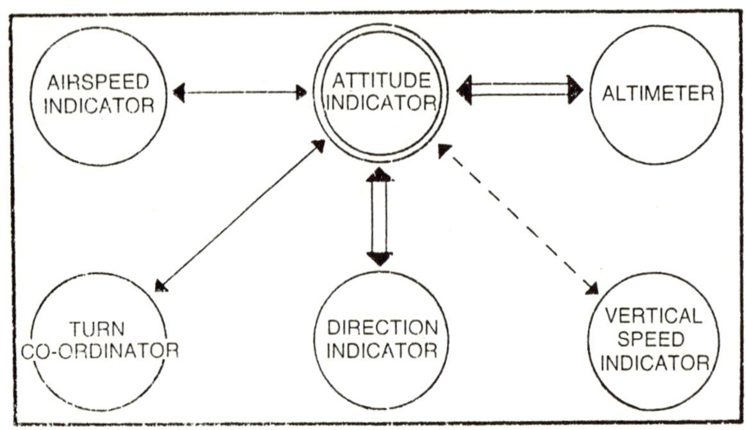

Fig. 189

Descending Turns

Objectives during manoeuvre: to maintain airspeed, balance, rate of turn and rate of descent.

Enter as normal (powered descents only) and limit turns to rate one. During the level-off return to the straight and level scan.

The scanning techniques covered in this book are only an introduction to instrument flying. A pilot is considered to be proficient in instrument flying only when his responses become automatic and this can only come after hours of dedicated practice. Once you become a licensed pilot and obtain more experience of flying you can go on to more advanced flight training for higher ratings.

ACTION ON ENTERING CLOUD

Avoid flying in cloud or in adverse visibility conditions and at night until you are suitably qualified. However, if you are forced into such a situation carry out the following actions:

1. Maintain control of the aircraft by reference to the instruments. This is your first priority. Concentrate on keeping

the wings level and maintaining a constant pitch attitude.
2. Check that the power setting is correct.
3. Trim the aircraft. This is important as it will make instrument flying much easier.
4. Turn on the pitot heater. This is vital, especially in cloud.
5. Check the engine and fuel condition and check for carburettor ice. Carry out each action one at a time returning your attention to the attitude indicator immediately.
6. Ensure seat belts and doors are secure.
7. Check your MSA and, if necessary, enter a climb.
8. Check the ammeter and suction gauges.
9. If you are unable to return to visual conditions inform ATC as soon as possible and proceed according to instructions. Be sure to give details of your flying ability.

Remember, fly the aeroplane at all times.

AIRMANSHIP

Obviously, if you fly in cloud it will not be possible to keep a lookout for other aircraft. Therefore, it is important to get in contact with ATC as soon as the aircraft is under control and the main actions carried out.

Instructor's Guide
Ex. 19

LESSON PLAN

Introduction to instrument flying

Objectives
To instil in the student the dangers of continued flight into adverse weather conditions without adequate training; to introduce the student to attitude instrument flying; to train the student to maintain control of the aeroplane by reference to instruments.

Content
1 Preflight briefing
Revise previous lessons; discuss the objectives and airmanship considerations of this lesson; explain the dangers of continued flight into bad weather (spatial disorientation); discuss the concept of instrument flying, the basic manoeuvres in relation to the flight instruments, and the actions on entering cloud.

2 Flight lesson
Demonstrate how the senses can be confused in the absence of visual data. Demonstrate the basic manoeuvres on instruments. Student practice.

Completion Standards
This lesson will have been successfully completed when the student fully appreciates the dangers of flight into adverse weather; displays an understanding of attitude instrument flying and can maintain control of the aeroplane to a reasonable standard by sole reference to the flight instruments.

Care of Passengers

When you obtain your PPL you will be licensed to carry passengers. This is a very big responsibility. Some if not most of the people you take up flying in an aeroplane will not have the slightest idea of what is really involved in the operation of an aircraft and they will be placing all their trust in you. You must honour this trust. Remember, a fare-paying passenger on a commercial flight has a guarantee that there are highly trained and responsible individuals in charge of the aircraft. The friends you take flying have no such guarantee. So, be safe, responsible and professional in your attitude whenever you fly and your passengers will have confidence in you. The following information is taken from a publication by the Safety Data and Analysis Unit of the CAA entitled *General Aviation Safety Sense – Care of Passengers*.

Introduction

The pilot of an aircraft is responsible for the safety and well-being of his passengers. Article 33 of the Air Navigation Order states that, before a public transport flight, the commander of the aircraft shall

> before the aircraft takes off, take all reasonable steps to ensure that all passengers are made familiar with the position and method of use of emergency exits, safety belts or harnesses, oxygen equipment and lifejackets and all other devices required by and under this Order and intended for use by passengers individually in case of an emergency occurring to the aircraft and, in an emergency, take all reasonable steps to ensure that all passengers are instructed in the emergency action which they should take ...

This requirement for the commander to brief public transport passengers is equally relevant and sensible for all passengers, irrespective of the type of operation. Although the guidance given here is comprehensive and too long to be used on every flight, it is up to you to decide what is appropriate on each occasion. You should use simple language, as some words (e.g. leading edge, trailing edge, port and starboard) may not be familiar to all passengers. It would help passengers new to flying in light aircraft to have a pre-flight discussion about the differences from larger aircraft they may have experienced.

Before Boarding

1. Advise passengers to beware of other aircraft (and their propellers) when going to and from the aircraft.
   - Propellers and helicopter rotors are extremely hazardous and should be avoided at all times, even when stationary.
   - Rotating propellers and rotors (particularly tail rotors) may be very hard to see, especially from the side.
   - The hazard can be masked if other nearby aircraft have engines running.
   - Propeller-driven aeroplanes must always be approached and left from behind the wing. The only exceptions are a small number of types with pusher propellers or entry doors forward of the wing. With these aeroplanes the engine(s) must always be stopped when passengers are boarding or leaving. Passengers must *never* step forward off the wing leading edge towards a propeller, and must avoid entering or leaving an aircraft when the engine is running.

2. Someone must be in charge of children, particularly small ones, both in flight and when going to and from the aircraft.

3. Beware of the hazards under the wings of high-winged aeroplanes, such as struts and pitot tubes.

4. Passengers should be instructed on the use of any steps or hand-holds. If there are wing walkways, make sure that passengers know where they must *not* step because of the risk of holed fabric or dented skin.

5. Passengers should know how to operate external door catches and locks. A door suddenly opening, helped by the wind, can cause injury to passengers and crew, or damage to the door hinges.

6. Luggage must not be overweight, must be properly stowed and should not contain hazardous items, such as:
   (a) flammable liquids and solids, e.g. firelighters, paint

(b) explosives, e.g. fireworks, toy gun caps
(c) compressed gases, e.g. camping gas, aqualung cylinders
(d) magnetic materials, e.g. loudspeakers
(e) corrosives, e.g. acids, alkalis, wet cell car batteries.

7. Advise passengers if there is any restriction on smoking in or near the aircraft.

8. Passengers should wear sensible clothing as bare limbs or thin nylon are hazardous if there is a fire. In winter warm clothing should be available for use in any diversion or forced landing: a Scottish hillside in winter would be no fun in shirtsleeves.

9. Advise on the effects of flying when ill, or when recovering from illness or a cold.

10. Make sure your passengers *know* that they must *not* fly when they are drunk.

11. Tell passengers that they must not distract you at critical times, e.g. by asking questions in the middle of the Vital Actions, or by interrupting your navigation or monitoring of the flight by excessive conversation.

When on Board
Make sure your passengers:

1. Are familiar with how to fasten, adjust and release seat belts or harnesses. Suggest they keep them fastened throughout the flight in case of turbulence.

2. Know about the closing, locking and opening of doors or canopy. Locks and handles should be left alone once the doors are closed.

3. Do not obstruct the controls with objects such as cameras, handbags, knees or feet. Do not put metallic or magnetic objects near the compass and do not interfere with the controls in flight.

4. Can use the intercom, if fitted, and know how to communicate if there is no intercom.

EMERGENCIES

Forced Landing and Ditching:
Before flight, instruct passengers that they should brace themselves if impact or ditching appears likely. There are two prime reasons for this:

1. to reduce secondary impact that may cause injury.
2. to reduce flailing of the body.

Secondary impact can be reduced by placing the body, particularly the head, against the surface it would be likely to strike during the impact. Flailing can be reduced by flexing, bending or leaning the body forward over the legs.

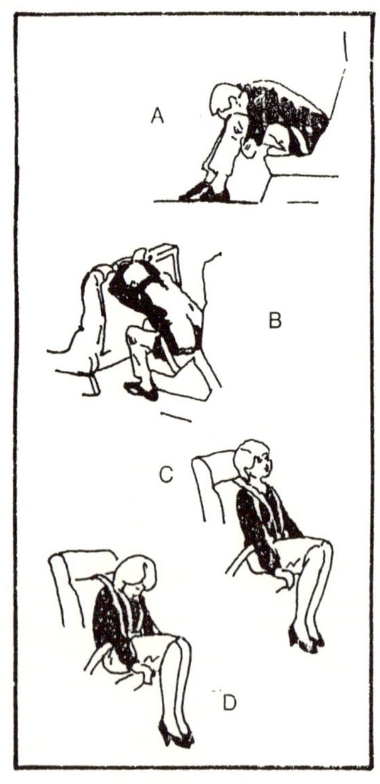

Fig. 190

Where there is room, passengers should adopt position A, resting their heads and chests against their legs. Flailing is reduced by grasping the legs or ankles, or by wrapping the arms under the legs. If there is no room for position A, passengers should put their heads and arms against the seat or bulkhead in front of them, as in position B. In aft-facing seats, adopt position C. Front seat passengers with upper torso restraint should use position D, with their chins resting on their sternum, but if an inertial reel system is fitted position C is better. (Incidentally, much of this advice is equally applicable to car passengers).

Decide the order in which the aircraft should be abandoned.

Harnesses and belts should be tight and headsets removed and stowed.

Brief passengers to unlock the cabin doors just before landing or ditching, but not to unfasten doors before impact.

Keep seat belts fastened until the aircraft has stopped, undo belts, open the doors and get out fast.

Make sure that passengers know how to operate the front seat-back release (which releases rear-seat passengers in some aircraft) and door locks. If the pilot is unconscious it is too late to ask.

Tell passengers to kick or force out a window if the doors or canopy cannot be opened, or if the aircraft has overturned.

Extra precautions when ditching:

Lifejackets

Before flying over water in a single-engined aircraft, make sure that passengers are wearing lifejackets, know how to inflate them, and how to use any ancillary items such as lights, whistle etc. If the aircraft is twin-engined point out the location of lifejackets and how to put them on. If one engine stops, get the passengers to put on their lifejackets – it is now a single-engined aircraft.

Impress on your passengers that lifejackets should *not* be inflated until outside the aircraft.

Liferafts

Decide which passenger is responsible for getting the liferaft out – it's too late when the aircraft has sunk with it still in the aircraft. The liferaft should not be left unsecured on top of the baggage where it can strike people's heads during deceleration. Passengers should know how to inflate the liferaft and what emergency equipment it contains, e.g. fluourescent dye, flares etc.

Tell passengers to swim away from the aircraft before inflating the liferaft so that there is no danger of its being holed. When inflated, make sure it does not blow away leaving some or all the passengers still in the water.

Above all, impress on your passengers not to panic. There will be a lot of water flying around, perhaps through a broken windscreen, but there is usually about one or two minutes to get out.

Passengers New to Flying in Light Aircraft

Those who haven't flown before, or who are more used to package holiday jets, may find a light aircraft a very different experience. No one wants an early return with a sick or frightened passenger. Chat to them beforehand about:

(a) The higher noise level – cotton wool in the ears may help.
(b) Turbulence – the light aircraft will be more affected. Don't fight it. Relax and go with the motion.
(c) Pressure changes and the ears – most light aircraft are unpressurized and climb quite slowly and the ears automatically compensate. During fast descents holding the nose and blowing it with the mouth closed will work, or follow the practice of some airlines and have a few sweets handy.
(d) Mention the stall and other warning horns. A sudden unexpected blast on landing will not help passengers' nerves.
(e) Lookout – discuss the usefulness of another pair of eyes when joining the circuit and for the blind spots which can be covered from the passenger's seat, noting that high-flying airways jets can be ignored.
(f) What to do if feeling unwell, but do not mention the word 'sick'. (Make sure there are sick bags on board.)
(g) The lack of toilet, even in some larger twin-engined aircraft.

Index